Willem J. Ouweneel

FOREVER

with the

LORD

The Bible and the Hereafter

Willem J. Ouweneel

FOREVER
with the
LORD

The Bible and the Hereafter

Edited by
Nelson D. Kloosterman

PAIDEIA
PRESS

PAIDEIA
PRESS

www.paideiapress.ca
www.reformationaldl.org

Published by Paideia Press
P.O. Box 1000
Jordan Station, Ontario, Canada L0R 1S0

ISBN: 978-0-88815-300-5

Unless otherwise indicated, Scripture quotations referenced by chapter and verse are from the ESV® Bible (The Holy Bible, English Standard Version®) copyright © 2001 by Crossway, a publishing ministry of Good News Publishers. Used by permission. All rights reserved.

Scripture quotations marked NASB are from the New American Standard Bible, copyright © 1960, 1962, 1963, 1968, 1971, 1972, 1973, 1975, 1977, 1988, 1995 by the Lockman Foundation. Used by permission.

Scripture quotations marked RSV are from the Revised Standard Version of the Bible, copyright © 1946, 1952, and 1971 by the Division of Christian Education of the National Council of the Churches of Christ in the United States of America. Used by permission. All rights reserved.

Scripture quotations marked NKJV are from the New King James Version®. Copyright © 1952 by Thomas Nelson. Used by permission. All rights reserved.

Book Design: Steven R. Martins, Project Manager, Paideia Press

Printed in the United States of America

CONTENTS

CONTENTS EXPANDED

For this we say to you by the word of the Lord,
that we who are alive,
who remain behind until the coming of the Lord,
will by no means precede those who have fallen asleep,
because the Lord himself will descend from heaven
with a cry of command,
with the voice of an archangel,
and with the trumpet of God,
and the dead in Christ will rise first.
Then we who are alive, who remain behind,
will be caught up in the clouds together with them
to meet the Lord in the air.
And so we will be forever with the Lord.

1 Thessalonians 4:15–17 (MOUNCE)

Und nach dem Tod da werd ich sein
Bei Christo meinem Herren.

And after death, I will be
with Christ, my Lord.

Der Herr ist mein getreuer Hirt
[The Lord Is My Faithful Shepherd]
Bach cantata BWV 112

FOREWORD

As a theologian, I am very interested in the various schools of Christian eschatology. As a philosopher, I am very interested in the phenomenon of theological paradigms, how they come about, and how they perniciously survive, even after some of their vital elements have been refuted. Paradigms, which are comprehensive thought systems, exercise enormous power, more than many theologians seem to realize. One reason for this power is that they bring together a large number of biblical subjects in a (seemingly) logical and coherent framework. When an opponent attacks a certain part of a paradigm, its adherents shift attention to other parts of that paradigm that they believe to be adequately solid. Consciously or unconsciously, they realize that, if their opponent is right, their entire paradigm risks collapse. This would be unbearable for a number of (partly psychological) reasons. Therefore, their logic decrees that either their opponent simply must be wrong, or if that opponent is right, then the rest of their paradigm will be strong enough to survive the attack.

One such paradigm is called amillennialism. It maintains that the second coming (Parousia) of Christ is followed immediately by the new heavens and the new earth, not by some millennial kingdom; the millennial kingdom exists *now*. In this book, the millennial kingdom is merely a collateral subject. My main point is that because the event of the Parousia was relocated already in the fourth century to the end of times—which by definition is far away—the Christian hope came to focus increasingly on what was much clos-

1

er: a person's physical death, and the heavenly bliss that followed. In this book, I will speak of the "going-to-heaven-when-you-die" theology (with its counterpart: the wicked go to hell when they die; I will speak of these together as interim theology). In a practical sense, the Lord's (supposedly) short-term and individual promises, wrapped up in the notion of "heaven," became far more important than his long-term and cosmic promises connected with his Parousia: the restoration of his creation.

Another thought system, more dubious than amillennialism, involves the Greek scholastic dualism of the soul substance and the body substance. This dualism is not at all biblical; it is thoroughly Greek, partially (Neo-)Platonic, partially Aristotelian. Moreover, it easily gives rise to the ideas that the soul is far more important than the body, and that physical death is a kind of liberation of the soul. Such unbiblical ideas encourage focusing on one's physical death: it sets the soul free, so that it can now reach its highest goal, to be forever with the Lord "in heaven." The Parousia and the resurrection remain part of orthodox belief, but eventually in practical spirituality they come to play scarcely any role. The believer's "sweet death" and the heavenly bliss that is to follow are sufficient to satisfy Christian expectations.

Amillennialism and the Greek body-soul dualism together form an almost unbreakable bond. It was defended by Augustine, by the Reformers, by the great Protestant creeds and catechisms, by many British Puritans, by many German Pietists (as illustrated by the texts of Bach's cantatas), and by many Dutch theologians of the Second Reformation. In this book, it is specifically this interim theology that I will be carefully investigating. But we do well to remember that this theology belongs to a much larger totality. Even if my critics remain unable to answer the objections presented in this book, they will likely maintain their interim theology because it belongs to that much broader, entrenched theology of amillennialism and Greek body-soul dualism.

Nonetheless, I want to make the attempt. One day, believers will be "forever with the Lord." The intermediate state—between death and resurrection—is only a foretaste of this. The ultimate denouement is the Parousia and the resurrection, and after that, the new heavens and the new earth. It is my prayer that the focus of Christians will once again be that of the apostles: we are waiting eagerly, not for the redemption *from* our bodies, but the redemption *of* our bodies (Rom. 8:23). We are waiting for the revealing of our Lord Jesus Christ (1 Cor. 1:7; cf. 1 Thess. 1:10; Titus 2:13; 2 Pet. 3:12–14). "Amen. Come, Lord Jesus!" (Rev. 22:20).

Bible quotations in this book are usually from the English Standard Version. When other translations are used, this is indicated. Quotations from deuterocanonical books are usually from the Common English Bible.

I thank Dr. Nelson D. Kloosterman again very warmly for his expert editorial work on the manuscript of this book. And I am again deeply thankful to my publisher, John Hultink, for his initiatives and constant encouragement in this entire project.

Loerik (near Houten, the Netherlands), Spring 2020
Willem J. Ouweneel

ABBREVIATIONS

Bible Versions

AMP	Amplified Bible
AMPC	Amplified Bible, Classic Edition
ASV	American Standard Version
CEB	Common English Bible
CEV	Contemporary English Version
CJB	Complete Jewish Bible
DARBY	Darby Translation
DRA	Douay-Rheims 1899 American Edition
ERV	Easy-to-Read Version
ESV	English Standard Version
EXB	Expanded Bible
GNT	Good News Translation
GNV	1599 Geneva Bible
GW	God's Word Translation
HCSB	Holman Christian Standard Bible
ISV	International Standard Version
KJV	King James Version
LXX	Septuagint
MOUNCE	Mounce Reverse-Interlinear New Testament
MSG	The Message
NABRE	New American Bible (Revised Edition)
NASB	New American Standard Bible
NCV	New Century Version
NETS	*New English Translation of the Septuagint, A.* 2014 (repr. 2009). Including corrections and emendations made in the second printing (2009) and corrections and emendations made in June

	2014. Oxford: Oxford University Press. Available at http://ccat.sas.upenn.edu/nets/ edition/.
NIV	New International Version
NKJV	New King James Version
NMB	New Matthew Bible
NOG	Names of God Bible
RSV	Revised Standard Version
TLB	Living Bible
TLV	Tree of Life Version
VOICE	The Voice
YLT	Young's Literal Translation

Other Sources

CD   Barth, K. 1956. *Church Dogmatics*. Translated by T. H. L. Parker et al. Vols. 1/1–4/4. Louisville, KY: Westminster John Knox.

COT   Commentaar op het Oude Testament

CNT   Commentaar op het Nieuwe Testament

CR   *Corpus Reformatorum*. 1st series and 2nd series. Vols. 1–87. Brunswick: Schwetschke, 1834–1900.

CW   Darby, J. N. n.d. *The Collected Writings of J. N. Darby*. Kingston-on-Thames: Stow Hill Bible and Tract Depot.

DD   Kuyper, A. 1910. *Dictaten Dogmatiek*. Kampen: Kok.

DNTT Brown, C., ed. 1992. *The New International Dictionary of New Testament Theology*. 4 vols. Carlisle: Paternoster.

DOTT Van Gemeren, W. A., ed. 1996. *The New International Dictionary of Old Testament Theology and Exegesis*. 4 vols. Carlisle: Paternoster.

EBC   The Expositor's Bible Commentary

EDR   Evangelische Dogmatische Reeks

EGT   Expositor's Greek Testament

KDC   Keil, C. F. and F. Delitzsch. 1976–1977. *Commentary on the Old Testament* 10 vols. Grand Rapids, MI: Eerdmans.

KV   Korte Verklaring der Heilige Schrift

NICNT   New International Commentary on the New Testament

NICOT   New International Commentary on the Old Testament

RC   Dennison, J. T., Jr., ed. 2008–2014. *Reformed Confessions of the 16th and 17th Centuries in English Translation.* 4 vols. Grand Rapids, MI: Reformation Heritage Books.

RD   Bavinck, H. 2002–2008. *Reformed Dogmatics.* Edited by J. Bolt. Translated by J. Vriend. 4 vols. Grand Rapids, MI: Baker Academic.

SBB   The Soncino Books of the Bible

ST   Chafer, L. S. 1983. *Systematic Theology.* 15th ed. 8 vols. Dallas, TX: Dallas Seminary Press.

SYN   Darby, J. N. n.d. *Synopsis of the Books of the Bible* (https://www.sacred-texts.com/bib/cmt/darby/).

TDNT Kittel, G. et al., eds. 1964–1976. *Theological Dictionary of the New Testament.* Translated by G. W. Bromiley. 10 vols. Grand Rapids, MI: Eerdmans.

TNTC Tyndale New Testament Commentaries

TWOT Harris, R. L., G. L. Archer, and B. K. Waltke. 1980. *Theological Wordbook of the Old Testament.* 2 vols. Chicago: Moody Press.

1

WHAT "HEREAFTER" ARE YOU EXPECTING?

After this I looked, and, behold,
a door was opened in heaven:
and the first voice which I heard was as it were of a trum-
pet talking with me;
which said, "Come up hither,
and I will shew thee things which must be hereafter."

Revelation 4:1 (KJV; emphasis added)

Wohlan, mit Jesu tröste dich
Und glaube festiglich:
Denjenigen, die hier mit Christo leiden,
Will er das Himmelreich bescheiden.

Well then, comfort yourself with Jesus
and believe firmly:
whoever suffers here with Christ
will be given by him a share in the
kingdom of heaven.

Schau, lieber Gott, wie meine Feind
[*Behold, dear God, how my enemies*]
Bach cantata BWV 153, Unknown poet[1]

_____

1. Here and at other places in this book, the person identified as an unknown
poet may have been Bach himself. In his views of the hereafter, Bach

1.1   Deathbeds
1.1.1   My Grandfather

As the eldest grandchild of my maternal grandfather, I was the last person to visit him as he lay dying (in 1978), before he went to be with the Lord. Only the two of us were together. These were memorable moments that we enjoyed together. My grandfather, who had always been full of jokes, whose spiritual life could not be easily fathomed, was now almost in ecstasy because he was soon going to be "with the Lord." With delighted eyes, he looked at the ceiling while singing one hymn after another. It reminded me of the four yours he had spent in my parents' home after my grandmother had passed away, and before he remarried. This was between the thirteenth and sixteenth years of my life. Many times I had played the organ, and Grandfather had sung the old hymns. He had a good voice; in his younger years he had been the lead singer in our congregation. Now, in his final moments, I could no longer accompany him. Now, my grandfather spoke and sang alone, he sang of the bliss that awaited him, and he sang with ebbing strength. And I sat there, loving my grandfather more than ever before.

One of the hymns he quoted was his favorite, which he had sung several times as I accompanied him. It was in German; my grandfather had lived a number of years in Germany when he was young (until his thirtieth year), and he knew quite a few German hymns by heart. This particular hymn had been written by a lady named Adeline Birke-Schöneborn, about whom I know nothing except that she lived from 1832 to 1869. So she died young, which makes the hymn all the more remarkable. Here are the first, second

---

was influenced by orthodox Lutheran theologians, but also by Pietists like Philipp Jakob Spener, Johann Jakob Rambach. and, to some extent, Salomon Franck. My quotations from the Bach cantatas do *not* reflect my own views, but rather help to expose the orthodox Protestant views of the time, as the footnotes will show. The English translation of the German original is available at http://www.bach-cantatas.com/Texts/BWV153-Eng3P.htm.

and final stanzas of the hymn, first in German, then in English:

Himmelsheimat, über Sternen droben,
Ziel der Sehnsucht, hier in Mesechs Land,
Ruhplatz derer, die bald aufgehoben,
Himmelsstadt, dem Glauben wohl bekannt.

O Jerusalem! zu deinen Toren
Ziehen bald im Siegsgepränge ein
Müde Pilger, die aus Gott geboren,
Um sich deiner Ruhe zu erfreun.[. . . .]

O mein Jesus! stille bald das Sehnen
Deiner Heil'gen, noch im Pilgerkleid,
Trockne bald des Heimwehs heiße Tränen,
Hol' sie heim in Deine Herrlichkeit.

Heavenly fatherland, beyond the stars,
Goal of longing, here from Meshech's land,[2]
Place of rest for those who will soon be lifted up there,
Celestial city, well-known to faith.

O Jerusalem, with victorious pomp
Into your gates soon will enter
Tired pilgrims, born of God
In order to look forward to your rest [. . . .]

O my Jesus! Soon fulfill the longing
Of your saints, who are now still in their pilgrims' garments,
Soon dry the hot tears of nostalgia,
Take them to you into your glory.

Please look carefully at this hymn! I am sure that many readers will inadvertently think that this is a song about "going to heaven when you die." This would be all the more understandable because my grandfather *was* dying. There are hundreds of such hymns about

---

2. The term comes from Psalm 120:5: "Woe to me, that I sojourn in Meshech," the foreign land, where I am a stranger far from home.

"going to heaven when you die." But this hymn is not one of those. Look again! The hymn does not speak of the individual dying believer, but about those—plural!— who will soon be lifted up, who will be taken to Jesus, *by* Jesus in person, into his glory.

This is what Jesus himself had promised: "In my Father's house are many rooms . . . . And if I go and prepare a place for you, I will come again and will take you to myself, that where I am you may be also" (John 14:2–3). There can be no reasonable doubt that Jesus was speaking here of his Parousia,[3] as many expositors have emphasized (see §6.4). Yet, it is amazing how many expositors (also) wish to find here a reference to the death of believers, to their "going to heaven."[4] It is as if, at the death of each individual believer, Jesus comes down in person to fetch that believer (or even worse, the soul of that believer) to heaven. This book seeks to refute these errors. Jesus' words are directly related to what the Apostle Paul wrote twenty years later:

> [W]e who are alive, who are left until the coming of the Lord, will not precede those who have fallen asleep. For *the Lord himself will descend from heaven* with a cry of command, with the voice of an archangel, and with the sound of the trumpet of God. And the dead in Christ will rise first. Then we who are alive, who are left, will be caught up together with them in the clouds to meet the Lord in the air, and so we will always be with the Lord (1 Thess. 4:15–17; italics added).

1.1.2 My Parents and I

On my parents' gravestone (the first passed away in 2001, the second in 2009), the words just quoted are engraved: "Always with the Lord" (MOUNCE: "Forever with the Lord"). I am not denying that

---

3. I will consistently refer to the second coming of Christ as the *Parousia*, a Greek word used sixteen times in the New Testament for the return of the Lord (Matt. 24:3, 27, 37, 39; 1 Cor. 15:23; 1 Thess. 2:19; 3:13; 4:15; 5:23; 2 Thess. 2:1, 8, 9; James 5:7, 8; 2 Pet. 1:16; 3:4; 1 John 2:28).
4. Several examples can be found at https://biblehub.com/commentaries/john/14-3.htm.

my parents are "with the Lord" now, in the sense of Philippians 1:23, "My desire is to depart and be *with Christ*, for that is far better [than staying down here]" (italics added). But that is not what the Apostle was thinking of—nor were my parents. Death is a transitional and transitory stage; they were looking forward to the day of resurrection, that is, to the Lord "descending from heaven," when the risen and transformed believers (cf. 1 Cor. 15:51–55) will all be "caught up together"—and *then*, says the Apostle, we will always be with the Lord. This is what my grandfather was looking for: not "going to heaven when he died," but the Parousia. This is what my parents were looking for: the day when the Lord would descend, they would rise from their grave, and, with millions of other believers, be "caught up," and *thus* always be with the Lord. In the last period of his life, my father confessed to me that he had firmly expected the return of the Lord during his lifetime, but now he had to reckon with the possibility that he would have to "go" first.

On his deathbed, an elderly brother in one of our congregations was visited by a few friends who came to comfort and encourage him. They told him that he would soon pass away to be with the Lord. With what little strength remained, the elderly brother lifted his finger, and said, "He can still come"—that is, before I die. He was not waiting for "going to heaven when he died"—even in these last moments on earth he was still waiting for the Parousia.

In his sermons, my father often told a story about the Dutch theology professor Johannes Hermanus Gunning Jr. (1829–1905). When this Professor Gunning was advanced in years, he attended the funeral of an acquaintance. On the way back from the cemetery, a friend of his made the remark that the elderly Gunning might be the next one to pass away. Gunning straightened his back—so my father told the story—and solemnly said, "Gentlemen, I do not pay any honor to Death by waiting for *him*; I am rather waiting for my King in glory."

If the Lord does not come again before my own passing away,

I may ask my children to have the people attending my funeral sing a song by the Dutch poet Hermanus Cornelis Voorhoeve (1837–1901):

Daarboven in de hemel,
Ver van het aards gewemel,
Is Jezus, onze Heer.

> *Up there, in heaven,*
> *Far beyond all earthly tumult,*
> *Is Jesus, our Lord.*

Those attending my funeral may well be thinking, "Ah, this is because Willem is now in heaven." No, this is not the intention of the hymn at all. The stanza continues:

Zijn hand zal ons geleiden,
Hij ging ons plaats bereiden,
En komt dra tot ons weer.

> *His hand will guide us,*
> *he went to prepare a place for us,*
> *and will soon come back to us.*

Maar boven al ons denken
zal Hij ons eenmaal schenken,
als we eeuwig bij Hem zijn.

> *But beyond all our thinking*
> *he will grant us one day,*
> *when we will be eternally with him.*

Haast zal Hij aan de zijnen
in heerlijkheid verschijnen;
ja, Hij komt spoedig weer.

> *Soon he will appear*
> *to his own in glory;*
> *yes, he will return soon.*

At my funeral, I wish to have the people sing not about my intermediate state (Lat. *status intermedius*, the interim between death and resurrection), or about whatever notions they may have regarding that, but about the Parousia which is soon to take place.

1.2 Christian Eschatology

1.2.1 Expecting the Future

The word "eschatology" refers to the doctrine of the last things. (The Greek adjective *eschatos* means "last," and the cognate noun *eschaton* means "end.") The Bible speaks of the "latter times,"[5] of the "last days,"[6] and even of the "last hour" (1 John 2:18). Eschatology is concerned with Christian expectations of the future of the world in general, and of the righteous in particular. The passages mentioned in the footnotes show that the phrases "last times," "last days," and "last hour" sometimes refer to the past (Heb. 1:2; 1 Pet. 1:20) or the present (1 John 2:18, "it *is* the last hour"). Usually, however, they point to the future; more specifically, to the future that involves the Parousia, and the wonderful restoration of God's creation. Listen to the beautiful words of the Apostle Peter: "Repent therefore, and turn back, that your sins may be blotted out, that times of refreshing may come from the presence of the Lord, and that he may send the Christ appointed for you, Jesus, whom heaven must receive until *the time for restoring all the things* about which God spoke by the mouth of his holy prophets long ago" (Acts 3:19–21; italics added).

This Parousia and the restoration of all things belonged to the expectation of the early Christians. They rarely thought about the time between their death and their resurrection, the so-called "intermediate state" or the "interim"; the few instances when they apparently did will be considered extensively below. Their real expectation involved the Parousia. They were not waiting for the

---

5.   1 Tim. 4:1; also 1 Pet. 1:20, "last times," literally "the last of times."

6.   Acts 2:17; 2 Tim. 3:1; Heb. 1:2; James 5:3; 2 Pet. 3:3; "latter days" in many Old Testament passages.

presumed blessings into which they would enter at death; rather, they were waiting for the Parousia, for the resurrection, and for the kingdom of Christ established in power and majesty in this world. Recall Simeon and the elderly Anna who were "waiting for the consolation of Israel" and "for the redemption of Jerusalem" (Luke 2:25, 38). In one of the parables, men "are waiting for their master to come home from the wedding feast" (Luke 12:36).

The Apostle Paul said that believers "wait eagerly for adoption as sons, the redemption of our bodies." This is not the redemption *from* the body—a thought that is more Greek than biblical, as we will see—but the redemption *of* the body, namely, when the "body of our humiliation" (the literal phrase in Phil. 3:21) will be conformed to the body of Christ's glory, that is, at the resurrection (Rom. 8:23). Believers are waiting, not for their death but for the Lord: "[Y]ou wait for the revealing of our Lord Jesus Christ" (1 Cor. 1:7). Remember "how you turned to God from idols to serve the living and true God, and to wait for his Son from heaven, whom he raised from the dead, Jesus who delivers us from the wrath to come" (1 Thess. 1:9–10); believers are ". . . waiting for our blessed hope, the appearing of the glory of our great God and Savior Jesus Christ" (Titus 2:13).

Believers "are eagerly waiting for him" (Heb. 9:28), the One who "sat down at the right hand of God, waiting from that time until his enemies should be made a footstool for his feet" (Heb. 10:12–13). So Jesus himself, in heaven, is waiting for, which implies that he is longing for, the moment when he will obtain the ultimate victory over his enemies. This will occur at the time of his Parousia and the establishment of his kingdom in glory and power. As an American friend of mine put it, "We are not waiting for the undertaker but for the up-taker" (cf. again 1 Thess. 4:17). (My friend said this during a sermon preached in the Netherlands that I had to translate, which was very difficult because the wordplay does not come through in Dutch.)

The Apostle Peter wrote:

Since all these things are thus to be dissolved, what sort of people ought you to be in lives of holiness and godliness, *waiting for* and hastening the coming of the day of God, because of which the heavens will be set on fire and dissolved, and the heavenly bodies will melt as they burn! But according to his promise we are *waiting for* new heavens and a new earth in which righteousness dwells. Therefore, beloved, since you are *waiting for* these, be diligent to be found by him without spot or blemish, and at peace (2 Pet. 3:11–14; italics added).

Such was the eschatology of the early church. Such was also the eschatology of its early creeds. About Jesus and the future, the Nicene Creed says that he

. . . ascended into heaven and sits at the right hand of the
Father.
and he will come again with glory to judge the living and the
dead;
whose kingdom shall have no end. . . .
[A]nd we look forward to the resurrection of the dead,
and the life of the world [or, age] to come.

(Lat. . . . *ascendit in caelum, sedet ad dexteram Patris.*
Et iterum venturus est cum gloria, iudicare vivos et mortuos,
cuius regni non erit finis. . . .
Et exspecto resurrectionem mortuorum,
et vitam venturi saeculi.)

The Apostles' Creed says the same thing more briefly. This is our briefest possible formulation: Christians look forward, not so much to what happens at death, but to what happens after the resurrection: *the world [or, age] to come.*

The Greek term *aiōn* can mean either "world" or "age";[7] per-

---

7.   Matt. 12:32; Mark 10:30 par.; Eph. 1:21; Heb. 6:5; cf. "this age" or "the present age," Matt. 12:32; Gal. 1:4; Eph. 1:21; 1 Tim. 6:17; 2 Tim. 4:10; Titus 2:12.

sonally I usually prefer the latter meaning. This ambiguity is also present in the Latin term *saeculum*, although here too I prefer the temporal interpretation ("age" or "eternity," as in the expression *in saecula saeculorum*, "in the ages of ages," that is, "in all eternity"). The Hebrew term *olam* shares this ambiguity: in the Old Testament, the temporal interpretation ("age") is preferable, but in modern Hebrew, *olam* means only "world."

My point here is that the ancient creeds always refer to life after resurrection, *not* to "life" (whatever this may be taken to mean) after death. Strictly speaking, there is no question of "life" between death and resurrection. The expression "resurrection of life" (John 5:29; MOUNCE: "unto life") implies that, between their deceasing and rising, believers are "dead"; the Apostle Paul speaks of the "dead in Christ" (1 Thess. 4:16). Regarding the resurrection, the Bible speaks of a "coming to life," also in regard to dead believers (Rev. 20:4–5). At the same time, *for God* deceased believers do "live" in some way: "[T]o him they are all alive," as many translations render Luke 20:38. As Jesus told Martha, "I am the resurrection and the life. Whoever believes in me, though he die, yet shall he live, and everyone who lives and believes in me shall never die" (John 11:25–26). Here, we have it both ways: the believer "dies," and yet "shall live," but Jesus also says that the believer "shall never die." Both sayings are true in a certain sense. The believing Dorcas "died" (Acts 9:37), yet Jesus says of the daughter of Jairus, "[T]he girl is not dead but sleeping." We will return to this point later (see §5.5).

1.2.2 "The Great Shift"

Between the ancient creeds and later creeds, confessions, and catechisms, we see a remarkable shift of focus, which I am calling "The Great Shift." It is the shift of attention, beginning in the fourth century of church history, from the Parousia to the believer's death. The focus has come to lie more on the (supposed) blessings following a person's death than on the (biblical) blessings following that person's resurrection. Later we will examine the manner of and reasons for this Great Shift.

For instance, in the *Westminster Larger Catechism* (1647), Q&A 82, we read:

> Q. *What is the communion in glory which the members of the invisible church have with Christ?*
>
> A. The communion in glory which the members of the invisible church have with Christ, is in this life (2 Cor. 3:18), immediately after death (Luke 23:43), and at last perfected at the resurrection and day of judgment (1 Thess. 4:17).[8]

This expression, "immediately after death," is explained further in Q&A 86:

> Q. *What is the communion in glory with Christ, which the members of the invisible church enjoy immediately after death?*
>
> A. The communion in glory with Christ, which the members of the invisible church enjoy immediately after death is, in that their souls are then made perfect in holiness (Heb. 12:23), and received into the highest heavens (2 Cor. 5:1, 6, 8; Phil. 1:23; Acts 3:21; Eph. 4:10), where they behold the face of God in light and glory (1 John 3:2; 1 Cor. 13:12), waiting for the full redemption of their bodies (Rom. 8:23; Ps. 16:9), which even in death continue united to Christ (1 Thess. 4:14), and rest in their graves as in their beds (Isa. 57:2), till at the last day they be again united to their souls (Job 19:26–27). . . .[9]

It is amazing how few of the assertions presented here can be found in the Bible. "Communion in glory," "made perfect in holiness" (this formulation is simply *wrong*, as we will see in §1.3.3), "received into the highest heavens, where they behold the face of God in light and glory"—such assertions are never made about the

8. *RC*, 4:316.
9. *Ibid.*, 4:317.

intermediate state. In the New Testament, these blessings are *consistently linked to the resurrection and glorification* of the saints rather than to the intermediate state. Even Luke 16:19–31, a passage we will discuss much more extensively (see §5.1), says nothing of the kind.

Another feature here disturbs me deeply: the Greek scholastic[10] body-soul dualism underlying the claim that the soul goes to the highest heavens, whereas the body dies and at the resurrection is reunited to the soul. The Bible *never* speaks of a person's body and soul being separated at death and reunited at the resurrection. It is pure speculative imagination, inspired by pagans.[11] What we do read, for instance, is that the rich man died, he was buried, *and* "he lifted up his eyes" in Hades (Luke 16:23), not that his body was buried in the ground and his soul went to Hades. *Jesus* was buried (John 19:42), not just his body (v. 40); and "at the same time" *he* was in paradise (Luke 23:43), not just his soul. The same is true of the resurrection: the *person* rises, not a part of him or her, namely the body, in contrast to another part, namely the soul or the spirit. All of this will be discussed much more extensively in later chapters.

1.2.3 Other Reformed Confessions

We encounter the emphasis on individual eschatology also in the Heidelberg Catechism. On the one hand, we find in Q&A 52 the cosmic eschatological perspective, linked to the Parousia and the establishment of the Messianic kingdom. On the other hand, we also encounter several times the individual perspective, as in Q&A 42: "Our death is . . . only a dying to sin and an entering into eternal life (John 5:24; Phil. 1:23; Rom. 7:24–25)."[12] These words are remark-

---

10. Scholasticism was the prevalent Christian (theological and philosophical) mode of thinking during the Middle Ages (especially after 800), which was heavily influenced by Greek, especially Aristotelian, ideas. Soon after the Reformation, scholasticism conquered early Protestantism as well.

11. Later, we will see that Luke 23:46 ("Father, into your hands I commit my spirit!") and Acts 7:59 ("Lord Jesus, receive my spirit") have nothing to do with such a body-soul dualism.

12. Dennison, *RC*, 2:779.

able because the Bible never speaks like this. The Catechism refers to three proof texts: John 5:24 (but this verse speaks about coming to faith, not about our dying), Philippians 1:21–23, and 1 Thessalonians 5:9–10 (but these verses do not speak of "eternal life").

In the Bible, dying is *never* identified as entering into eternal life, for eternal life is either a present possession (the divine life in us; see, e.g., John 5:24; 17:3; 1 John 5:11–12, 20), or it is connected to the resurrection (Dan. 12:2) and the Messianic kingdom (Matt. 25:46; Mark 10:30)—but never with the intermediate state (see more extensively in chapter 9 below). Perhaps, in the perspective of John, we might say that eternal life is life in the Father's house (John 14:2); however, believers enter the Father's house not when they die but when Christ returns (v. 3; see §5.5). In this respect, the Nicene Creed speaks in a more biblical way than does the Heidelberg Catechism: it is the "life of the age to come" that we must think of, not the "life" (whatever this may be) of the intermediate state.

In the Heidelberg Catechism, Lord's Day 22, Q&A 57 and 58, we read:

Q. *What comfort do you receive from the "resurrection of the body"?*
A. That not only *my soul* after this life shall be *immediately* taken up to Christ its Head (Luke 23:43; Phil. 1:21–23), but also that this my body, raised by the power of Christ, shall be reunited with my soul, and made the glorious body of Christ (1 Cor. 15:53–54; Job 19:25–27; 1 John 3:2).

Q. *What comfort do you receive from the article "life everlasting"?*
A. That, inasmuch as I now feel in my heart the beginning of eternal joy (2 Cor. 5:2–3), I shall *after this life* possess *complete blessedness*, such as eye has not seen, nor ear heard, neither has entered into the heart of man (1 Cor. 2:9), therein to praise God forever (John 17:3) (italics added in the answers).

This enjoyment apparently begins in the intermediate state.

Unfortunately, here again we encounter the unfortunate body-soul dualism. For the rest, the Catechism teaches several very biblical insights: 1 John 3:2 is properly linked here with the resurrection, not with the intermediate state, and the believer is "immediately after this life" "with Christ." However, it goes too far to suggest that this implies "complete" blessedness. G. C. Berkouwer rightly wrote:

> What is the connection between this already perfect blessedness and the promises of a future yet to come? The vision of the Parousia threatens to dissolve in the face of the seemingly all-absorbing importance of this perfect blessedness. What does one do, then, with the message of Paul about the ultimate future: "When Christ, who is our life, appears, then you also will appear with him in glory" (Col. 3:4)?[13]

This ostensible completeness is mentioned also in Heidelberg Catechism, Q&A 115: ". . . that we be renewed more and more after the image of God, until we attain the goal of *perfection after this life* (1 Cor. 9:24–25; Phil. 3:12–14)" (italics added).[14] This must be a reference to the intermediate state as well. This is quite remarkable because the perfect image of God in believers will be manifested only at the resurrection; I refer here again to Philippians 3:20–21 and 1 John 3:2.

It must be appreciated that the Belgic Confession strongly emphasizes the cosmic perspective. The believer's individual redemptive expectation is barely mentioned, except perhaps in Article 15, referring to believers "desiring to be delivered from this body of death."[15] This is a reference to Romans 7:24: "O wretched man that I am! who shall deliver me from the body of this death?" (KJV). However, in my view this reference does not involve physical death at all. As modern expositors emphasize, the Greek word *sōma* re-

---

13. Berkouwer (1972), 37.
14. *RC*, 2:796.
15. *Ibid.*, 2:433.

fers not to the physical body but to "mode of existence," as in 6:6 ("the body of sin"); hence, the rendering of the AMP: "this corrupt, mortal existence"; or the NLT: "this life that is dominated by sin and death": or Phillips: "the clutches of my sinful nature."

Finally, in the Canons of Dordt 2.8 we read: ". . . and having faithfully preserved them even to the end, should at last bring them, free from every spot and blemish, to the enjoyment of glory in His own presence forever."[16] Here, the individual redemptive expectation (linked to physical death) and the universal redemptive expectation (linked to the Parousia) seem to merge. The expression "even to the end" refers to the end of this earthly life, whereas the words "should at last bring them, free from every spot and blemish, to the enjoyment of glory in His own presence forever" (cf. Eph. 5:27) refer to the resurrection and glorification of the believers. In the Canons of Dordt 5.2 we find a similar blending: ". . . and to press forward to the goal of perfection, until at length, delivered from this body of death, they shall reign with the Lamb of God in heaven."[17] First, perfection is not reached at the believer's death but at their resurrection. Second, we find here again the mistaken reference to Romans 7:24. Third, believers are *not* reigning with Christ during the intermediate state; such rule is linked to the resurrection (Rev. 20:4–6).

1.3 Various Authors
1.3.1 Hillenius

What change occurred within Christian understanding such that, throughout the centuries, their expectations were altered so drastically? In what we are calling "The Great Shift," the main emphasis was placed no longer on the Parousia but on "going to heaven when you die"; in my terminology, Parousia theology gave way to Interim Theology.

---

16. *Ibid.*, 4:131.
17. *Ibid.*, 4:144.

Let me give a striking example from an early Reformational pamphlet written by the Flemish pastor Cornelis van Hille (1540–1600, also called Cornelius Hillenius) who served the congregation of Dutch refugees in Norwich, England. In 1571 he wrote *Ziekentroost* ("Consolation of the Sick"), which remarkably makes no mention that the sick person being addressed could possibly be healed![18] The document presumes that the sick person is gravely ill and must prepare for imminent death.[19] The pamphlet became so popular that Bibles of stricter Reformed Christians in the Netherlands included a copy of it, a practice that continues to this day. The pamphlet presents the gospel in a brief form: you cannot be saved if you do not believe in Jesus Christ as your Lord and Savior. Subsequently, Hillenius addresses true believers, and says:

> *We should long for death. We must move out of this body* [Dutch: uit dit lichaam verhuizen; italics original] *before coming to the Lord* [2 Cor. 5:8]. Knowing for certain that through Christ we have been reconciled to God, therefore we should (according to God's word) have a perfect desire to be released from this mortal body, in order to come to the glorious inheritance of all God's children [Eph. 1:18], which is prepared for us in heaven. . . . Furthermore, [Paul] says: "For we know that if the tent that is our earthly home is destroyed, we have a building from God, a house not made with hands, eternal in the heavens. For in this tent we groan, longing to put on our heavenly dwelling. . . . We are always of good courage. We know that while we are at home in the body we are away from the Lord. . . . Yes . . . we would rather be away from the body and at home with the Lord" [2 Cor. 5:1–2, 6, 8]. Once again, Paul says: "For we know that the whole creation has been groaning together. . . . And not only the creation, but we ourselves, who have the firstfruits of the Spirit, groan

---

18. Van Hille (1913), 97.
19. We find a similar presumption among Roman Catholics: what was originally the Sacrament of the Sick eventually became the Sacrament of the Dying—but through Vatican II it again became the Sacrament of the Sick.

inwardly as we wait eagerly for adoption as sons, the redemption of our bodies" [Rom. 8:22–23]. And since we are "strangers and exiles on the earth" (Heb. 11:13), who would not desire to be home in his homeland (Heb. 11:14–16)? For here "we walk by faith, not by sight" [2 Cor. 5:7]. "For now we see in a mirror dimly, but then face to face" [1 Cor. 13:12]; "we shall see him as he is" [1 John 3:2]. Who would not long for this vision, seeing that the holy men of God longed for it?

. . . This is the glorious mansion of which Christ says in the Gospel of John: "In my Father's house are many rooms. If it were not so, would I have told you that I go to prepare a place for you? And if I go and prepare a place for you, I will come again and will take you to my-self, that where I am you may be also" [John 14:2–3)]. That is, in that New Jerusalem that "has no need of sun or moon to shine on it, for the glory of God gives it light, and its lamp is the Lamb" [Rev. 21:23]. There "God will wipe away every tear from their eyes, and death shall be no more" [Rev. 21:4]. . . . There the Lord has prepared a glorious wedding feast, where we will recline with Abraham, Isaac, and Jacob at the table of the Lord [cf. Matt. 8:11]. And blessed are those who are invited to the marriage supper of the Lamb [cf. Rev. 19:9].

. . . *Now we can come to this supper only through death.* Therefore, Paul says: "For to me to live is Christ, and to die is gain" [Phil. 1:21] (italics added).[20]

Look carefully at what is occurring here. Hillenius quotes a number of Bible passages that, to my mind, all refer to the time *after the Parousia and the resurrection of the dead.* But Hillenius understands them to refer to the time *after the believer's death, but before the resurrection.* Only at the end does he mention the resurrection of believers. But his main point is this: don't worry about your sickness; you may die soon, but if you are a believer you will enter into all the promised glories and blessings of heaven.

---

20. Van Hille (1913), 97.

This is what I call "The Great Shift." Christians are no longer focused on the restoration of God's creation, on the coming kingdom of Christ, and on the resurrection of believers. This will comprise a cosmic and collective restoration. Instead, these Christians are taught to focus on their imminent death and the blessings which they will then enjoy. This is a highly individual matter. Thus, there is a double aspect to this "Great Shift": (a) the collective, cosmic restoration has been turned into individualized restoration, and (b) the expectation of the Parousia has been replaced by the expectation of what will happen at the believer's death (Parousia theology has been replaced by Interim Theology).

Hillenius was only one early Reformational example; let us now look at three men who are far better known than he is, who represent both the Roman Catholic and the Protestant eschatological traditions. We will see that these two traditions have much in common; they both underwent "The Great Shift" in their eschatological thinking. It is one of many examples of teaching in which traditional Protestants did not and do not differ from Roman Catholic thinking at all, but unthinkingly continued to propagate the old ideas.

1.3.2 Dante and Thomas à Kempis

Many examples illustrate "The Great Shift" whereby Parousia eschatology was replaced by Interim eschatology. In my recent book, *The Eden Story*,[21] I referred to Dante Alighieri (d. 1321), author of *The Divine Comedy* (Italian *La Divina Commedia*), to Thomas à Kempis (d. 1471), author of *The Imitation of Christ* (Lat. *De imitatione Christi*), and to John Bunyan (d. 1688), author of *The Pilgrim's Progress* (see the next section). These three works have exerted an enormous influence among Christians. They belong to the best-sold Christian works of all time, appearing in numerous translations.

---

21. Ouweneel (2020).

These three principal and thoroughly Christian works have in common that each of them ignores the Parousia almost entirely. Instead, they all present an eschatology in which at death the believer "goes to heaven" (that is to say, according to Dante, through the middle station of purgatory; see §6.3), and the unbeliever goes to hell. Dante has described hell (Italian *l'inferno*) most extensively. At death, people take one of two journeys: through the fire of purgatory to heaven, or to the fire of hell. Given this picture, one wonders about the place and function of the Parousia and of human resurrection; why are they still necessary at all?

Thomas à Kempis went so far as to describe the death of a believer using Bible verses that in reality point to the Parousia, such as Luke 12:40 ("You also must be ready, for the Son of Man is coming at an hour you do not expect"). He argued that the believer must be prepared for his death for "here we have no lasting city" (Heb. 13:14)—a verse that refers to the Messianic kingdom. It seems that, in his thinking, the believer's death and the Parousia merge completely.

Here we must mention the enormous influence of what is called "replacement theology" (also called supersessionism: A has superseded B),[22] which has spiritualized:

(a) Israel (ethnic Israel has been replaced by the church, which is ninety-nine percent non-Jewish);

(b) the Messianic kingdom (a kingdom here on earth, beginning at the Parousia) into the "kingdom of heaven," that is, a kingdom *in* heaven, which the believer enters at death. (The intermediate state has superseded the Messianic kingdom; see further in §1.4.1.); and

(c) the "throne of David" in Jerusalem (Luke 1:32; cf. Isa. 9:7) into the heavenly throne of God (despite the clear distinction made in Rev. 3:21 between "my throne" and my Father's throne).

One of the consequences of supersessionism has been that biblical descriptions of the *earthly* post-Parousia Messianic kingdom

---

22. See extensively, Ouweneel (2011; 2012; 2017; 2019).

are transferred to *heaven* during the intermediate state. This is both an error of time and an error of place. Thomas à Kempis and many other authors are clear examples of the supersessionist way of thinking.

With Thomas' reference to the "city" we encounter a set of complex biblical city metaphors, varying from "the city that has foundations" (Heb. 11:10; cf. v. 16), and the "city of the living God, the heavenly Jerusalem" (12:22), to the "city of my God, the new Jerusalem, which comes down from my God out of heaven" (Rev. 3:12), and the "holy city, new Jerusalem, coming down out of heaven from God" (21:2; cf. v. 10; 22:19). Many supersessionists—Catholic, Eastern Orthodox, and Protestant—do *not* link these metaphors to the Messianic kingdom, or to the new heavens and the new earth, but to "heaven" in the sense of the "hereafter," that is, the intermediate state between death and resurrection. This erroneous approach belonged to an ancient Catholic tradition, which, unfortunately, was readily adopted by many Protestant theologians. This is "The Great Shift": post-death "heaven" has superseded the Parousia, the resurrection, and the great restoration of the entire creation.

1.3.3 John Bunyan

John Bunyan expanded the city metaphor in his great work, in which he described the life of Christian who, as a pilgrim, is on his way—not to the Messianic kingdom and the new creation, which will follow upon the Parousia, but—to the "celestial city," which is the "hereafter," the interim, the intermediate state. Again, post-death hopes have superseded post-resurrection hopes. Bunyan supplied us with a marvelous description of "heaven," but this description had no room for the resurrection and the Parousia. As a good Christian he would certainly have *believed* these things, but they did not function in his description of Christian's final destiny. Just as with Thomas à Kempis, Bunyan merged death and the Parousia: at the moment Christian enters the celestial city he is "transfigured" (cf. 1 Cor. 15:51, "transformed"). Bunyan also tells us that when Christian enters "heaven," he is immediately invited to the marriage supper of the Lamb (Rev. 19:6–9).

The celestial city is described in terms derived from the New Jerusalem (streets of gold) and many other metaphors in Revelation, none of which refers to the intermediate state. Rather, the Bible tells us that, in fact, the New Jerusalem is identical to the glorious *post-resurrection* state of the bride of the Lamb (Rev. 21:9–10). It is not the place where believers go when they die, but the city in which they will participate when the Bridegroom has returned, and when the new heavens and the new earth will finally be established.

Let me supply some representative quotations from *The Pilgrim's Progress*, Part I, the Tenth Stage, where Christian and Hopeful reach the Celestial city.[23] I do this in the form of nine quotes, to which I add some comments. According to Bunyan, the description of "heaven" includes the following:

(a) It is Mount Zion, with the "spirits of just men made perfect" (Heb. 12:22–24). But in Hebrews it is clear that believers who have died but have not yet been raised did *not* reach "perfection" yet (read, the resurrection). Hebrews tells us that the deceased Old Testament saints had to wait for the New Testament saints, so that all would reach this "perfection" of the resurrection *at the same time* (carefully examine Heb. 11:40).

(b) It is the "paradise of God" with the "tree of life." Regarding "paradise" see my study *The Eden Story*.[24] I will be developing this further in the current volume.

(c) "There you shall not see again such things as you saw when you were in the lower region upon earth; to wit, sorrow, sickness, affliction, and death; 'For the former things are passed away.' Rev.

---

23. See Bunyan (1853).
24. Ouweneel (2020).

21:4." In the book of Revelation, these things are not linked to the intermediate state at all, but rather to the new heavens and the new earth. Again, post-resurrection existence is confused with post-death existence.

(d) "You must there receive the comfort of all your toil, and have joy for all your sorrow; you must reap what you have sown, even the fruit of all your prayers, and tears, and sufferings for the King by the way. Gal. 6:7, 8." Galatians 6 speaks of reaping "eternal life," which is *never* linked to the intermediate state but rather with the Messianic kingdom: "inheriting" the kingdom (Matt. 25:34; 1 Cor. 6:9–10; 15:50; Gal. 5:21; Eph. 5:5) is apparently equivalent to "inheriting" eternal life in its ancient Old Testament sense (Dan. 12:2; Matt. 19:29; Mark 10:17; Luke 10:25; 18:18), which, in accordance with Jewish expectations, was the coming Messianic kingdom (see extensively, chapter 9).

(e) "In that place you must wear crowns of gold, and enjoy the perpetual sight and vision of the Holy One; for 'there you shall see him as he is.' 1 John 3:2." But 1 John 3:2 clearly shows that this "seeing" is linked not to the believer's death, but to the appearance of Christ, that is, the Parousia.

(f) "There you shall enjoy your friends again that are gone thither before you; and there you shall with joy receive even every one that follows into the holy place after you." This is one of the clearest proofs that Bunyan is thinking not of the Parousia,[25] when all the saints will enter glory at the same time, but of the believers' deaths, that is, people who enter the "holy place" one by one by dying one by one.

(g) "Then the heavenly host gave a great shout, saying, 'Blessed are they that are called to the marriage-supper of the Lamb.' Rev. 19:9." This supper can be held only after the (entire) bride of the Lamb has entered glory.

25. Although he briefly refers to it; see *ibid.*, 24 and 89.

(h) "And now were these two men [Christian and Hopeful], as it were, in heaven, before they came to it, being swallowed up with the sight of angels, and with hearing of their melodious notes." This is one of the few times that Bunyan actually uses the word "heaven" for the place that Christian and Hopeful had entered.

(i) "Now I saw in my dream, that these two men went in at the gate; and lo, as they entered, they were transfigured; and they had raiment put on that shone like gold. There were also that met them with harps and crowns, and gave them to them; the harps to praise withal, and the crowns in token of honor." From 1 Corinthians 15:51–55 (cf. John 14:1–3; 1 Thess. 4:13–17), it is very clear that this "transfiguration" or "transformation" will occur, not at the moment of the believer's death but at the moment of the Parousia. The Apostle Paul spoke clearly and especially of those believers who will *not* be deceased at the moment of the Parousia, and therefore shall be "transformed": Paul said elsewhere that at his coming, their lowly bodies will be transformed to be like Christ's own glorious body (Phil. 3:20–21).

1.3.4   Other Authors

Some of the authors who in our day have most strongly advocated interim theology are C. S. Lewis with his book *The Great Divorce*, Randy Alcorn with his book *Heaven*, and Elyse Fitzpatrick with her book *Home*.[26] The great difference between these three and Dante, Thomas, and Bunyan is that especially Alcorn and Fitzpatrick did pay significant attention to the return of Christ and to the future of believers following this event. The great similarity is that like Dante, Thomas, and Bunyan, these three describe the place where believers go when they die as "heaven"—as thousands have done before them. Lewis, Alcorn, and Fitzpatrick sold many copies of their respective books, but that does not mean their views about the hereafter are any better than those of Dante, Thomas, and Bunyan.

---

26. Lewis (2002); Alcorn (2004); Fitzpatrick (2016).

They all fell into the same age-old error: focusing on Interim The-ology. This involves "The Great Shift" in Christian eschatological thinking: post-death "heaven" has superseded post-resurrection glories.

I could also mention here a number of authors who, in the spirit of supersessionism, have taken out of context passages that clearly refer to the Messianic kingdom, and applied them to the intermedi-ate state. Consider Psalm 16:11: "You make known to me the path of life; in your presence there is fullness of joy; at your right hand are pleasures forevermore." The Annotations to the Dutch States Translation explain this quite correctly: the "path of life" means, "Leading and conducting me in this life, and afterward raising me up from the dead, and bringing me into the glory of life everlast-ing,"[27] which is the Messianic kingdom (cf. Ps. 133:3; Dan. 12:2). However, Reformed theologian William Hendriksen applied this verse to the intermediate state, as he did with New Testament pas-sages such as Matthew 8:11 ("kingdom of heaven"), Romans 8:18 ("the glory that is to be revealed to us"), Hebrews 12:23 ("the spirits of the righteous made perfect"), Revelation 5:9 ("they sang a new song"), 7:15 ("they are before the throne of God, and serve him day and night in his temple"), 14:3 ("they were singing a new song before the throne"), and 20:4 ("the souls of those who had been beheaded for the testimony of Jesus and for the word of God").[28] I am convinced that *none* of these passages refers to the intermediate state. All of them refer to the resurrection state.

In order not to praise the Dutch Annotations too quickly, let me briefly quote what they said about Hebrews 12:23 ("the spirits of the righteous made perfect"): "That is, the souls of those who possess the perfect holiness and salvation in heaven (see 1 Cor. 13:10), although they expect yet another these expect still another

---

27. Haak (1918), *ad loc.*
28. Hendriksen (1959), 55–56, 58, 66–67.

perfection with their bodies at the last day (2 Tim. 4:8)."[29] The first phrase is mistaken: there is no "perfection" yet in the intermediate state (see §§1.2.2 and 1.2.3). But at least the Annotations wisely added the last phrase: the ultimate fulfillment is in the resurrection state.

1.4   A Revolutionary Eschatology

1.4.1   The Kingdom of Heaven

From the Middle Ages onward, this has been the eschatology of many Christians, Roman Catholic and Protestant: when they die, they go to heaven, and that will be glorious. There is not much more to their eschatology. They can write it on a small postcard. You can ask them about the personal significance of the resurrection and the Parousia, but they often have no clear answer. Of course, they believe in these future events, if only because they are part of every great Christian creed, confession, and catechism. To be sure, one day Christ will come again and the dead will rise from death. But when is this day? It is the "last day,"[30] which is the last day of world history, and therefore necessarily still far away. At least these matters are irrelevant to one's personal life here and now. These are highly *theoretical* matters, stuff for theologians. There is one very *practical* and very important matter: "[I]t is appointed unto men once to die" (Heb. 9:27 KJV); "the putting off of my body will be *soon*" (2 Pet. 1:14). *This* is what Christians must reckon with, not certain events that will take place on the very *last* day of world history. Jesus may say, "Behold, I am coming *soon*" (Rev. 22:7, 12, 20), but he said this two thousand years ago. The "soon" of our dying is far more realistic than the "soon" of the Parousia.

I remember my radio discussion about eschatology, many years ago, with a well-known Reformed theologian. At a certain moment, he said, "Every day a Christian must think of his death." I burst out: "Every day a Christian must think of the second coming of

---

29. Haak (1918), *ad loc.*
30. John 6:39–40, 44, 54; 11:24; 12:48.

Christ." The Christian hope of believers is focused not upon entering the intermediate state, but upon entering the resurrection state.

"The Great Shift" in eschatology is illustrated, for instance, in the way many Christians understand the term "kingdom of heaven," namely, as the place where a believer goes when they die; in short: "heaven." When Martin Luther made his German translation of the New Testament, he used the word *Himmelreich* ("kingdom of heaven") thirty times in his rendering of Matthew's Gospel. The German word *Himmelreich* can be easily understood as "realm of heaven," that is, "heaven" as such. This was exactly the way Luther used the term in his writings: the *Himmelreich* is the heavenly hereafter. For instance, in Matthew 6:9 he translated the opening words of the Lord's Prayer thus: "Our Father who is in *heaven*"; but in a well-known hymn that he wrote he said, *Vater unser im Himmelreich*, "Our Father in the realm of heaven." To Luther, this was the same thing.

Luther was not the first to interpret the "kingdom of heaven" this way; it was common in the Middle Ages. I refer again to Thomas à Kempis (mentioned in §1.3.2), who said, "That is the highest wisdom, to cast the world behind us, and to reach forward to the heavenly kingdom [or, kingdom of heaven]."[31] He also wrote about "Thy Saints, O Lord, who now rejoice with Thee in the kingdom of heaven, waited for the coming of Thy glory whilst they lived here."[32] In Calvin's *Catechism of the Church of Geneva* (1545), Q&A 300, Calvin speaks of "[God's] holy Word, which is, as it were, an entry into His heavenly Kingdom."[33] Numerous other examples could be mentioned.

Since Luther, many Lutheran poets have written about the *Himmelreich* in this same celestial sense. Recently, a beloved pastor in the

---

31. *The Imitation of Christ* 1.1.3 (http://www.gutenberg.org/cache/epub/1653/pg1653.txt).
32. *Ibid.*, 4.11.3.
33. Dennison, *RC*, 1:509.

Netherlands, who was terminally ill, wrote while on his deathbed that he was looking forward to entering the "kingdom of heaven" soon. Who would criticize him in the hour of death? Not I. Yet, theologians have the duty to establish from Scripture what *is* the kingdom of heaven.

The multitude of jokes about "Saint Peter at the pearly gates" relies on the same misunderstanding. Jesus gave to this disciple the keys of the "kingdom of heaven" (Matt. 16:19), and because this kingdom was thought to be "heaven" as the abode of the deceased, Peter was thought to stand at the gate of heaven, and to give access to it. Faith is not enough: you must get past Peter if you want to "go to heaven when you die."

I am convinced that the "kingdom of heaven"—an expression found only in Matthew's Gospel—is identical with what the other Gospels, together with the Epistles, call the "kingdom of God." It is used in a twofold sense: a *present* sense, in which the kingdom of heaven, here *on earth*, includes all the followers of Christ on earth,[34] and a *future* sense, in which the kingdom is established by Christ in glory and majesty *on earth*, when he returns, and "heaven" will rule over the earth (cf. Daniel's word to king Nebuchadnezzar: ". . . that you may know that Heaven rules," Dan. 4:26). In both cases, it is a kingdom *on earth*, never in "heaven" (in any sense).

Please note, among other things, the following:

(a) John the Baptist and Jesus told their listeners that the kingdom of heaven was "at hand" or "had come near" (Matt. 3:2; 4:17); that is, it was coming to *them on earth*; this is not about believers on their way *to heaven*.

(b) This "coming near" *here on earth* is also illustrated in Matthew 11:12, "the kingdom of heaven has suffered violence" (ESV), or, "has been forcefully advancing" (EHV), namely, in the world of that day. In heaven, there is no kingdom that can suffer violence, or can be thought to advance forcefully.

---

34. See extensively, Ouweneel (2011; 2017).

(c) The kingdom of heaven is compared to a mixture of good and bad seed (Matt. 13:24–25) and to a net full of good and bad fish (vv. 47–48). This refers to the spiritual condition of Christianity *on earth*; how could it ever refer to conditions in heaven? See especially verses 38–41:

> The field is the world, and the good seed is the sons of the kingdom. The weeds are the sons of the evil one, and the enemy who sowed them is the devil. The harvest is the end of the age, and the reapers are angels. Just as the weeds are gathered and burned with fire, so will it be at the end of the age. The Son of Man will send his angels, and they will gather out of his kingdom all causes of sin and all law-breakers.

How could it be expressed more clearly that the kingdom of heaven is a kingdom *on earth*? How could it ever be said that bad things are gathered out of *heaven*?

1.4.2 Lutheran Hymns

I am a great lover of the works of Johann Sebastian Bach, not least his cantatas. I discussed all these cantatas in comments broadcasted to a Dutch radio audience throughout more than ten consecutive years. I could always agree with Bach's music, but not always with the Lutheran texts he used. Let me give three examples. The first is from cantata BWV 41, *Jesu, nun sei gepreiset* ("Jesu, now be praised"). This cantata is based upon a hymn by Johannes Hermann (d. 1593), in which the poet says, "Teach us patience in suffering, / . . . until we happily depart / into the eternal heavenly kingdom [Ger. *Himmelreich*, kingdom/realm of heaven], ..." That is, at death the believer goes to heaven.

Cantata BWV 56, *Ich will den Kreuzstab gerne tragen* ("I will gladly carry the Cross"), contains a text written by an unknown poet (some have presumed that it was Bach himself), in which we read: "My pilgrimage in the world / is like a sea voyage [passing through much havoc]: . . . / And when the raging torrents / are come to an end, / then I will step off the ship into my city, / which is the kingdom of heaven [Ger. *Himmelreich*], / where with the righteous / I will emerge out of many troubles."

Cantata BWV 153, *Schau, lieber Gott, wie meine Feind* ("See, dear God, how my enemies, . . ."), also contains a text written by an unknown poet (again, some have presumed that it was Bach himself), in which we read: "Well then, comfort yourself with Jesus / and believe firmly: / those same who suffer here with Christ / will share the kingdom of heaven [Ger. *Himmelreich*] with Him."

The general thought in these texts, and in hundreds of other Protestant texts, is clear: the Christian's earthly walk is full of misery, persecution, and tribulation. But it is as Paul and Barnabas told the believers at Antioch, ". . . encouraging them to continue in the faith, and saying that through many tribulations we must enter the kingdom of God" (Acts 14:22). Here, again, is the crux: What were the apostles saying? Were they telling believers that, after many sufferings, they would "go to heaven," *or* that, after many sufferings, the Lord would come again and establish his kingdom? Were they referring to the believer's "blessed death," *or* to the coming King?

The Apostle Paul gives an indirect answer in his letter to Timothy: "I charge you in the presence of God and of Christ Jesus, who is to judge the living and the dead, and by *his appearing and his kingdom*: preach the word,..." (2 Tim. 4:1–2; italics added). In the same epistle, Paul wrote, "If we have died with him, we will also live with him; if we endure, we will also reign with him" (2:11–12). This is not "in heaven," during the intermediate state, but after the Parousia. As Paul wrote elsewhere, ". . . provided we suffer with him in order that we may also be glorified with him" (Rom. 8:17); again, this is not during the intermediate state but at the moment of resurrection (cf. Phil. 3:21). As the Apostle Peter wrote: "[R]ejoice insofar as you share Christ's sufferings, that you may also rejoice and be glad when his glory is revealed" (1 Pet. 4:13).

The Apostle John wrote, in connection with the victory over Satan, "Now the salvation and the power and the kingdom of our God and the authority of his Christ have come, for the accuser of our brothers has been thrown down, who accuses them day and night before our God" (Rev. 12:10). Regardless of one's understanding of these eschatological events in the book of Revelation, the direction-ality of events is clear: *a kingdom will come down here*, it is not *we who are going up into heaven*. Believers pray, "Your kingdom come" (Matt. 6:10), not: "Let us come into your kingdom," that is, heaven. As I said, insofar as there is a kingdom which believers enter, it may be the kingdom in its *present* form on earth, encompassing all the followers of Jesus (cf. Matt. 5:20; 7:21; 18:3; 19:23–24; 23:13). Or it may be the kingdom in its *future* form on earth, arriving at the Parousia: "I tell you, many will come from east and west and recline at table with Abraham, Isaac, and Jacob in the kingdom of heaven" (Matt. 8:11); compare the parallel text in Luke 13:28, "In that place [i.e., hell] there will be weeping and gnashing of teeth, when you see Abraham and Isaac and Jacob and all the prophets in the kingdom of God but you yourselves cast out." The kingdom in this latter meaning is of a heav-enly origin and of a heavenly nature; but for the rest it is *just as much here on earth* as is the kingdom in its former meaning.

Here, then, are the crucial questions with which we are confront-ed in our Christian eschatology:

(a) Are we looking forward to "heaven," or to the new creation?
(b) Are we looking forward to our death, or to the Parousia and Christ's kingdom?
(c) Are we looking forward to our own, individual blessings, or to the blessings of God's new world?

What is the biblical approach: Parousia theology or Interim The-ology? We will have to address these questions in the coming chap-ters. However, we can deal with them properly only if we consider them in the broader context of what people have called "the after-life," that is, every mode of existence after physical death. This is what we must discuss first.

2

THE AFTERLIFE:
NEW INTERESTS

Do not marvel at this, for an hour is coming
when all who are in the tombs
will hear his voice and come out,
those who have done good to the resurrection of life,
and those who have done evil to the resurrection of
judgment.

John 5:28–29

Auch bei dem himmlischen Verlangen
Hält unser Leib den Geist gefangen; . . .

Even in heavenly longing
our bodies hold our spirits prisoner; . . . .[1]
Wachet! betet! betet! wachet! [*Watch! Pray! Pray! Watch!*]

Bach cantata BWV 70
Unknown poet[2]

2.1   Life after Death

2.1.1   New and Old Interest

We are living after a period when materialism was strongly advocated. This view insisted that human beings are mere dust; when

---

1. This is a typical example of Greek scholastic thinking: the body is the "prison" of the soul (see extensively chapter 8).
2. See chapter 1, note 1.

death comes, it is all over. Many theologians believed scarcely anything about any hereafter. One example was Norman Pittenger, who could not accept any version of the afterlife except a kind of "being in God's hands."[3] Many people, including supposedly enlightened theologians, believed that surviving one's physical death in any form was impossible. When the brains die, everything that we may call "soul" or "spirit" dies as well, because the functions of our soul or spirit are nothing but particular brain functions. Nothing survives.[4]

In more recent times, however, an entirely new and deepened interest in a possible afterlife has arisen. This interest was closely related to the great popularity of Eastern religions and the psychic experiences linked to them. Furthermore, many publications as well as the media drew attention to the near death experiences (NDE) of people who, under extreme circumstances, had reportedly stepped out of their bodies (astral projection), and in this way had even visited the hereafter, the meaning of which remains unclear.[5] The Apostle Paul was quoted as one who hinted about this type of experience: "I know a man in Christ who fourteen years ago was caught up to the third heaven—whether in the body or out of the body I do not know, God knows. And I know that this man was caught up into paradise—whether in the body or out of the body I do not know, God knows" (2 Cor. 12:2–3; see §5.3).

Somewhat older is the interest in extra-sensory perception (ESP), which again may involve people who ostensibly had some experience of the hereafter. In addition, we hear of the reincarnation experiences of people who, especially through hypnosis, had supposedly been led back to previous lives. Whether or not there are reliable elements in these experiences (see §7.1) and their interpretation, it is a fact that enormous new interest in the supernatural

---

3. You will find something similar with Berkhof (1986), 530–31.
4. Cf. the neurobiologist Swaab (2014).
5. See, e.g., Van Lommel (2011).

world has arisen, especially in the world that people are supposed to enter, or are said to experience, after physical death. Scientists became interested in phenomena like materializations, which some people supposedly encounter in spiritism—referring to ostensible material, and therefore tangible, appearances of dead people (see §7.3).[6]

In the past, all religions, and also many philosophical schools took great interest in a possible afterlife. Such views were often referred to as a belief in the "immortality" of the soul. Where pagan philosophers did this, this is understandable (see chapter 8). It is less understandable that Christians adopted this , as happened, for instance, at the Fifth Lateran Council (1513). Also John Calvin's anthropology is, unfortunately, in many respects far more Greek than biblical.[7] Repeatedly, he speaks of the "prison" or "fetters" of the body, in which the soul is imprisoned, this soul being "freed" from this prison at death.[8] Consider this phrase in particular: "If to be freed from the body is to gain full possession of freedom, what is the body but a prison?"[9]

The unknown poet of Bach's cantata BWV 82 (*Ich habe genug*, "I have enough") says, "Ah! if only the Lord might rescue me / from the chains of my body; . . . ." In cantata BWV 70 (*Wachet! Betet! Betet! Wachet!*, "Watch! Pray! Pray! Watch!"), the poet (Bach himself?) says, "Even in heavenly longing / our bodies hold our spirits prisoner; . . ."

Note carefully that this is something totally different from the believer's wish to be freed from a life of miseries and sufferings (e.g., 2 Cor. 5:2–4; Phil. 1:21–24), or from a body affected by sin and death (if one wishes to understand Rom. 7:24 in this way; cf.

---

6. E.g., Defares (2009); also see Moody (2001); Fontana (2005); Shushan (2009); D'Souza (2009). Much earlier, Hans Küng (1984) analyzed the medical, philosophical, and theological evidence for an afterlife.
7. https://www.ccel.org/ccel/c/calvin/institutes/cache/institutes.pdf.
8. *Institutes* 1.15.2, 2.7.13, 3.3.14, 20; 3.6.5.
9. *Institutes* 3.9.4.

§1.2.3). Calvin does not refer here to a life of misery, but to the body *as such* as a prison, in which the soul dwells until it is set free. This is an erroneous view, even though J. van Genderen sought to smooth it over by claiming that Calvin is stating this in a context different than that of Plato's dualism.[10] Other Reformed theologians, such as Herman Bavinck, Louis Berkhof, Paul Badham, Anthony Hoekema, as well as Gordon R. Lewis and Bruce Demarest, carelessly adopted the Greek philosophical expression "immortal soul," and accepted it[11] (see further below and in chapter 8).

2.1.2 The Immortal Soul?

The Bible knows nothing of an immortal soul that human beings might possess. The Bible does not even say that human beings are immortal. Van Doornik et al. wrote: "Scripture, properly speaking, does not teach the immortality of the soul, but lays great emphasis on the immortality of the whole man. Man continues to exist for ever as he is."[12] The first point is well taken; but the second point identifies continued existence with immortality. This is inaccurate.

Strictly speaking, only God has immortality (cf. 1 Tim. 6:16), and with respect to human beings, the Bible says that only at the Parousia of Christ must "this mortal body . . . put on immortality" (1 Cor. 15:53–54; cf. 2 Tim. 1:10). Moreover, the Bible does not apply this designation to unbelievers; even if one believes in the everlasting existence of the wicked, it is the "second death" in which they dwell (Rev. 2:11; 20:6, 14; 21:8)—something quite different from immortality. The notion of an immortal soul that continues to exist after physical death—where death pertains only to the body—is saturated with the Greek scholastic body-soul dualism. This dualism teaches that human beings possess, in addition to

---

10. Van Genderen and Velema (2008), 827.
11. *RD*, 4:593–98; Berkhof (1981), 746–49; Badham (1976), chapter 9; Hoekema (1979), chapter 8; Lewis and Demarest (1996), 446–47; more critically, e.g., Hoek (2004), 136–38; P. J. van Leeuwen (1955).
12. Van Doornik et al. (1956), 447.

their mortal bodies, an immortal constitutive part: the soul and/or the spirit—sometimes distinguished, sometimes conflated—which constitutes what is proper to and essential in human beings (see extensively, chapter 8).

If this were true, this would imply a denial of the mortality of *human beings*. In this case, only the "outer shells" would be mortal, whereas humans themselves, as such, would be immortal. This would contradict the testimony of Scripture. The Bible says, "The *soul* who sins shall die"[13]—in which statement the "soul" is not a constitutive part of a person but refers to their entire being: the *person* dies, not a part of them.[14]

To be sure, what theologians like Herman Bavinck mean by the immortality of the soul is clear. They wished simply to express the undeniably biblical truth that, at death, human existence does not end, but human beings continue somehow to exist after physical death. These theologians are expressing this truth in a Greek scholastic, clumsy manner, but this does not deny the core of the matter: human beings continue to exist after death, forever. Moreover, the fear of substantialist dualism should not drive us to the opposite extreme, so that we close our eyes to certain metaphors in the Bible itself, metaphors belonging to everyday (*experiential*) language, and not to theological (*theoretical*) parlance. Examples include "the putting off of my body" (2 Pet. 1:14), there is a "body" that can be killed, and a "soul" that cannot be killed (Matt. 10:28), there is an existence of being disembodied that is called "naked" (2 Cor. 5:3), and there is a body that "apart from the spirit is dead" (James 2:26). Such expressions in no way derive their power from Platonism.[15]

Following death, there is indeed an "afterward": "[I]t is ap-

---

13. Ezek. 18:4; cf. Num. 23:21; Judg. 16:30; Job 36:14; Ps. 78:50; of course, the term "soul" has many meanings (see Ouweneel [2008], 114–16), so that it is equally valid to assert that people cannot kill a person's "soul" (Matt. 10:28).

14. Something that Bavinck, *RD*, 4:616–18, knew very well.

15. *Contra* Ridderbos (1975), 503, including note 47.

pointed for man to die once, and *after that* comes judgment" (Heb. 9:27). One of the main intentions of this book is to shed some light on the meaning of this phrase "after that." The Bible says about the king of Babylon after his death: "Sheol [or, Hades] beneath is stirred up to meet you when you come; it rouses the shades to greet you, all who were leaders of the earth; it raises from their thrones all who were kings of the nations" (Isa. 14:9). What exactly is being depicted here? What exactly did the dead king experience? Similarly, Jesus said, "The poor man died and was carried by the angels to Abraham's side. The rich man also died and was buried, and in Hades, being in torment, he lifted up his eyes and saw Abraham far off and Lazarus at his side" (Luke 16:22–23). Again, what exactly is being depicted here? What exactly did Lazarus and the rich man experience?

One thing is certain: the Bible does not say that their *bodies* went into the ground, whereas their *souls* entered Hades. There is no mention in these passages of an immortal soul. If we ask *who* was in Hades, the only possible answer is: The king of Babylon, the rich man, and Lazarus, respectively. What continue to exist in the hereafter are *persons*, not just their souls.

2.2   Resurrection in the Old and New Testaments
2.2.1   In the Old Testament

If our eschatological expectation is directed toward what happens at death—"when I die, I go to heaven, and that's it" (an idea derived from Interim Theology)—then belief in the future resurrection becomes far less relevant to life here and now. If, however, we focus instead on the coming Parousia and our concomitant resurrection, belief in the revival of the deceased is far more relevant to that living. In the former case, the future resurrection is a collateral blessing; in the latter case it is a primary blessing. Let us therefore consider first the biblical importance of belief in the future resurrection.

It is remarkable that the New Testament speaks of the future resurrection frequently, but the Old Testament does so only rarely. Five passages come to mind, two of which appear in the book of Isaiah:(1) God "will swallow up death forever; and the Lord GOD will wipe away tears from all faces" (Isa. 25:8).

(2) "Your dead shall live; their bodies shall rise. You who dwell in the dust, awake and sing for joy! For your dew is a dew of light, and the earth will give birth to the dead" (Isa. 26:19; cf. the contrast with v. 14: "They are dead, they will not live; they are shades, they will not arise").

(3) "Then he said to me, 'Prophesy to the breath;[16] prophesy, son of man, and say to the breath, "Thus says the Lord GOD: 'Come from the four winds,[17] O breath, and breathe on these slain, that they may live.'"' So I prophesied as he commanded me, and the breath came into them, and they lived and stood on their feet, an exceedingly great army. . . . 'Behold, I will open your graves and raise you from your graves, O my people. And I will bring you into the land of Israel'" (Ezek. 37:9–12).

(4) "[M]any of those who sleep in the dust of the earth shall awake, some to everlasting life, and some to shame and everlasting contempt" (Dan. 12:2).

(5) "After two days he [i.e., God] will revive us; on the third day he will raise us up, that we may live before him" (Hos. 6:2).

It is not altogether clear that every one of these passages is talking about physically dead people coming to life again;[18] in Hosea 6:1–2 this is almost certainly not the case. Perhaps Isaiah 26:19 is the only Old Testament passage that speaks clearly about the coming physical resurrection of the dead, though this is doubted by some.[19] Rather, *doubt* about the future resurrection seems to prevail in the Old Testament: "If a man dies, shall he live again? All the

16. Heb. *ruach*, "breath, wind, spirit"; cf. other translations.
17. Heb. *ruchot*, the very same word (here in the plural) as in the previous note.
18. Cf. Berkouwer (1972), 177–79.
19. E.g., this is doubted by Küng (1984), 84, and by Oswalt (1986), 485–86, though not by the rabbis—see Slotki and Rosenberg (1983), 121.

days of my service I would wait, till my renewal should come" (Job 14:13). "[T]he living know that they will die, but the dead know nothing, and they have no more reward, for the memory of them is forgotten" (Eccl. 9:5).[20]

One verse worth mentioning here is Hosea 13:14: "I shall ransom them from the power of Sheol [or, Hades]; I shall redeem them from Death. O Death, where are your plagues? O Sheol, where is your sting?" The Apostle Paul quotes this verse in 1 Corinthians 15:55 to support belief in the future resurrection. But is Paul not changing a prophecy of mischief into a prophecy of bliss? To understand this question, one need only compare some of the modern translations of Hosea 13:14, like the CJB: "Should I ransom them from the power of Sh'ol? Should I redeem them from death? Where are your plagues, death; where is your destruction, Sh'ol? My eyes are closed to compassion." However, if we view this verse as a positive prophecy,[21] it constitutes a striking proclamation of the end of the power of Death and Hades (Rev. 20:13–14).

The Old Testament describes three instances when people who had died came back to life: the son of the widow at Zarephath was raised by the prophet Elijah (1 Kings 17:17–22), the son of the Shunammite woman was raised by the prophet Elisha (2 Kings 4:18–37), and an unknown dead person came to life through contact with the bones of Elisha (2 Kings 13:20–21). In addition, two other Old Testament events—Enoch being taken away by God (cf. Gen. 5:24), and Elijah going up by a whirlwind "into heaven," that is, "to the sky," such that neither of these men saw death (cf. Heb. 11:5)—bear witness about a life that surpasses death.

Perhaps we may mention Job 19:26, as well: "[A]fter my skin has been thus destroyed, yet in my flesh I shall see God." Though the verse is not very clear, some, especially older expositors, have

---

20. Küng (1984), 84–86, viewed only Dan. 12:2 (which he dated in the second century BC) as evidence of a growing belief in the resurrection.
21. As do, e.g., De Bondt (1938) 87–90, and Wood (1985), 221–22; Van Gelderen and Gispen (1953), 416, are less convinced.

understood this to refer to the resurrection. The link to verse 25 is important: when "at last" "my Redeemer" "will stand upon the earth," I shall see "God," that is, my Redeemer, "in my [restored] flesh."

In the apocryphal 2 Maccabees 7, several of the seven martyred brothers express their hope of resurrection (GNT): "You butcher! You may kill us, but the King of the universe will raise us from the dead and give us eternal life, because we have obeyed his laws" (v. 9). "God gave these [i.e., my tongue and my hands] to me. But his laws mean more to me than my hands, and I know God will give them back to me again [i.e., in the resurrection]" (v. 11). "I am glad to die at your hands, because we have the assurance that God will raise us from death. But there will be no resurrection to life for you,[22] Antiochus!" To the youngest son, the mother says, "So I urge you, my child, to look at the sky and the earth. Consider everything you see there, and realize that God made it all from nothing, just as he made the human race. Don't be afraid of this butcher. Give up your life willingly and prove yourself worthy of your brothers, so that by God's mercy I may receive you back with them at the resurrection" (v. 29).

2.2.2 In the New Testament

In Jesus' day, the doctrine of the future resurrection was not yet completely formed, for the religious party of the Sadducees adamantly opposed it (Matt. 22:23 par.). One of their main arguments was that the Pentateuch contained no hint of the future resurrection. Therefore, when Jesus answered them, he appealed to that very Pentateuch: "[A]s for the resurrection of the dead, have you not read what was said to you by God: 'I am the God of Abraham, and the God of Isaac, and the God of Jacob'? He is not God of the dead, but of the living" (Matt. 22:31–32). In other words, if God

---

22. This means that this son either denied the resurrection of the wicked, or meant to say that that resurrection is not "unto life" (cf. John 5:29; Rev. 20:12–14).

is God of the living, and he is the God of the fathers, then the fathers, though they have died, still exist in his presence, in a way that will culminate one day in their resurrection.

By contrast, the religious party of the Pharisees, and the ordinary Jewish people (cf. Luke 9:8, 19) did believe in the resurrection: "For the Sadducees say that there is no resurrection, nor angel, nor spirit, but the Pharisees acknowledge them all" (Acts 23:8).

The sparseness of Old Testament data concerning the future resurrection is in stark contrast to the many references to the subject in the New Testament, from Matthew 9:25 (raising Jairus's daughter) to Revelation 20:12–13 (raising the wicked). As surely as there is continued existence after death, so surely will there be a resurrection of the dead: the dead will return to life in renewed bodies. In this connection, there is a significant and fundamental difference between, on the one hand, the raising of the daughter of Jairus, the raising of the young man at Nain (Luke 7:14–15), and the raising Lazarus (John 1:43–44) and, on the other hand, the resurrection of Jesus and the future resurrection of the dead. The former returned to their mortal bodily mode of existence, and therefore after some time they died again (though this is nowhere stated). But Jesus, and all those who are still dead, arose and will rise with an immortal resurrection body, which will never again undergo physical death.[23]

Remarkably, in a time when belief in the future resurrection was still being vigorously questioned, Jesus raised the dead. Compare the very general statement in Matthew 11:5, "the dead are raised up," which suggests that there were (many) more cases than just the daughter of Jairus, the young man at Nain, and Lazarus. Jesus commanded the disciples to do the same: "[R]aise the dead" (Matt. 10:8), although no examples of this are recorded in the Gospels. Yes, with calmness and certainty he announced his own resurrection from the dead.[24]

---

23. Strangely enough, Pinchas Lapide (2002), who was both a New Testament scholar and an Orthodox Jew, never understood this vital difference.
24. Matt. 26:32; Mark 7:31; 9:9–10, 31; 10:34; Luke 24:6; John 2:19–22.

Belief in the future resurrection requires that we distinguish three stages: (a) life on earth in the mortal body; (b) continued existence in a disembodied state between death and resurrection; and (c) new life in the immortal resurrection body. As far as (b) is concerned, we know of no human case where death was followed immediately by reaching an eternal destiny; on the contrary, one day *all* people will rise.[25] Physical death leads to what has traditionally been called the intermediate state (Lat. *status intermedius*), the temporary, provisional stage between death and resurrection. The *only* people who do not pass through this intermediate state are believers who will be alive on earth at the moment of the Parousia ("we who are alive," 1 Thess. 4:15), who will be transformed, and will receive their glorified bodies without having died (1 Cor. 15:52–54).

The Apostle Paul seems to be referring to this in Philippians 3:10–11, ". . . that I may know him and the power of his resurrection, and may share his sufferings, becoming like him in his death, that by any means possible I may attain the resurrection from the dead." Notice the expression "by any means." Basically, there are two means: one is that Paul might have lived until the Parousia (as he says, "*we* who are alive," 1 Thess. 4:15), and then he would have received the resurrection body without having died. The other means is that he might first have died like Christ ("becoming like him in his death"), and thus, through death, reached the resurrection from the dead. By either of these means, he would have reached the same goal: the resurrection state. The advantage of the former manner is that the believer is saved from having to die. The advantage of the latter manner is that the believer will resemble Christ by reaching the resurrection through death.

Please notice that the Bible contains no (balanced and detailed) doctrine of the intermediate state. Nowhere in the Bible does this matter become a topic of teaching. The Bible nowhere explicitly states that the intermediate state—*our* phrase, not the Bible's—is

25. John 5:28–29; Acts 24:15; 1 Cor. 15:22; Rev. 20:1–6, 11–15.

49

only temporary, and that, through the future resurrection, a person passes from the intermediate state to a new mode of existence (although the future resurrection will result in a new mode of existence). When the believer dies, they are described as being "with Jesus" (Luke 23:43), "with Christ" (Phil. 1:23), "with the Lord" (2 Cor. 5:8), in a way that cannot be distinguished from being "always with the Lord" in 1 Thessalonians 4:17, where the Parousia is involved. However, if we connect these expressions too narrowly to the intermediate state as such, then it is not surprising that the expectations of many believers—those "wishing to be with Jesus"—gradually became focused less on the Parousia and the future resurrection, and more on physical death and what supposedly followed immediately thereafter. This point must now be considered a bit more fully. Key passages involved in this matter will be discussed separately in chapter 5.

2.2.3   A Lost Hope

It is vitally important to see that the Bible is nowhere preoccupied with a purely *individual* eschatological hope, but always with *cosmic* salvation. (This is not to deny the eternal perdition of the wicked, but to underscore the ultimate restoration of "all things," as Peter called it in Acts 3:21.) What matters most is not my private individual redemption, but rather the kingdom of God, which will one day encompass the entire creation. This also implies that what matters most is not primarily what happens at the death of individual people but rather what happens at the Parousia. Eschatology is entirely about the expectation of the kingdom, the rule of God in Christ in power and glory. G. K. Beale speaks of the "eschatological concept" of New Testament theology: it is not the hereafter but the new creation which is the center of New Testament thinking.[26]

H. Berkhof said, "As a reaction against an individualistic eschatology, we are today in danger of forgetting that the core of all

---

26. G. K. Beale in Brower and Elliott (1997), 11–44.

expectation and the climax of God's covenantal saving work is the perfection of *persons*."[27] This is true, to be sure, but this consummation will occur in the cosmic and collective framework of the future manifestation of God's kingdom in splendor and majesty, and ultimately in the new heavens and the new earth.

The moment we see this, we begin to discover the evidence for it everywhere in the New Testament. John the Baptist preached the *kingdom* of heaven (Matt. 3:1–2)—which is not "heaven," as we have seen (§1.4.1). The first thing that Jesus preached was the kingdom of God (Mark 1:14–15). And the last thing that he preached was [also] the kingdom of God (Acts 1:3). The first thing that Paul preached was that Jesus is the Son of God and the anointed King (Acts 9:20, 22). Later, he notes that he had "gone about proclaiming the kingdom" (20:25). The last thing we are told about his preaching is that he was "testifying to the kingdom of God" (28:23) and "proclaiming the kingdom of God" (v. 31). Almost the last written words of his which have been handed down to us are about the Lord's "heavenly kingdom" (2 Tim. 4:18) (which is, remember, a heavenly kingdom *on earth*). Jesus, John the Baptist, and the Apostles Paul and Peter were all filled with the message of the kingdom of God—not some kingdom "in heaven" but a heavenly kingdom within God's physical creation.

None of the New Testament preachers ever proclaimed what thousands of their successors have preached, namely that whoever believes in Jesus will go to heaven when they die (Interim Theology). Sermons in the New Testament simply were not about this at all. Their point was not what will happen to *you* when you *die* but with what will happen *to the cosmos* at the *Parousia*. Salvation *is* indeed linked to the forgiveness of sins (Acts 3:19), that is, of individuals, but, more than that, with the "times of refreshing" that will "come from the presence of the Lord," and with sending "the Christ appointed for you, Jesus, whom heaven must receive until the time for

---

27. Berkhof (1986), 489; cf. 529–37.

restoring all the things about which God spoke by the mouth of his holy prophets long ago" (vv. 20–21).

Consider this small detail. For centuries, the following words have been uttered during the (Latin) Roman Catholic mass: "Lamb of God, who takes away the *sins* of the world"(Lat. *Agnus Dei, qui tollis peccata mundi*).[28] However, John 1:29 speaks of Jesus taking away "the *sin* of the world." This difference is enormously significant. It means that, one day, Christ as the Lamb of God will remove sin from the cosmos as an evil power. His primary purpose is not to propitiate God the Father for the *sins* of (individual) people, but to defeat *sin* as a power that dominates the cosmos in order to attain a renewed, pure world. The primary focus is not my redemption, but the redemption of the cosmos.

The consequence of this is that when they die, believers have not yet reached the goal of their hope; on the contrary—to put it crassly—they simply have the misfortune of dying before the promised restoration of all things has occurred. They have entered the intermediate state, an expression pointing simply to a temporary, transitory stage, one that was never the goal for which believers on earth should be longing. We will see that, in certain respects, this state is better for believers than sojourning on this earth, because sin, sickness, and suffering will no longer affect them. This state involves being "with Christ," which is "far better" than what they had before (Phil. 1:23). However, at the same time, we must remember that in a very real sense, in the intermediate state, believers are worse off, for they are disembodied; their bodies lie in the grave (cf. Matt. 27:52, 58–59; Acts 9:40), and this is most unnatural.

Therefore, it is a basic mistake to call the intermediate state a state of perfection (see §§1.2.2 and 1.2.3). It is said of Old Testament believers that "apart from us they should *not* be made perfect"

---

28. Interestingly, both the old Vulgate and the new Vulgate read in John 1:29: *Agnus Dei, qui tollit peccatum* [sin] *mundi,* which is the correct version. The words of John the Baptist start with "Ecce" (Behold).

(Heb. 11:40), that is, apart from the New Testament believers they will not arrive at the Parousia and the Messianic kingdom and the resurrection connected with it. Or, to put it more positively, at the Parousia *both* Old and New Testament believers, at the very same time, will attain perfection, namely, in the resurrection, in their glorified bodies. No perfection without resurrection.

We encounter here the astonishing fact that, throughout the centuries of church history, the focus of the Christian hope has gradually but steadily shifted from (resurrection) life to death; this is what I have called "The Great Shift" (§1.2). Of course, for the believer dying means entering rest (Rev. 14:13).[29] But nowhere does the Bible call this "heaven," and surely this is never identified as the ultimate and final goal of our eschatological expectations. At this moment, Jesus himself is *waiting*, namely, for the time when his enemies will be made "a footstool for his feet" (Heb. 10:13; cf. Ps. 110:1). In a sense, even believers existing in the intermediate state can be said to be "waiting" (no matter how consciously or unconsciously), namely—just like us—for the arrival of the kingdom of God in glory and majesty.

As long as the kingdom has not yet arrived in its manifest, glorious form, all believers, whether deceased or alive, are waiting for this event, which also means that they are longing for it. In our state this is called "waiting," in the intermediate state it is called "resting and waiting."[30] Two New Testament examples may illustrate this. The Apostle Paul desired "to depart and be with Christ, for that is far better" (Phil. 1:23). But this was not exactly what he was *waiting for*; rather, he says, "[W]e *await* a Savior, the Lord Jesus Christ, who will transform our lowly body to be like his glorious body" (3:20–21)—this is not physical death but physical resurrection. Similarly, the Apostle Peter knew that the "putting off" of his body, that is,

---

29. This "rest" is not to be confused with the "rest" spoken about in Heb. 4:9, which refers to the sabbatical rest of the Messianic kingdom (see §§10.3.3 and 12.2.3)!

30. Van Genderen and Velema (2008), 837.

his physical death, would occur soon (2 Pet. 1:14). Yet, he includes himself when he says, "[A]ccording to his promise *we* [!] are waiting for new heavens and a new earth in which righteousness dwells" (3:13). Keeping this in mind will prevent both the confusion of and the competition between individual eschatology and universal eschatology.[31] Paul and Peter knew that the end of their earthly life would soon be reached. But they were not waiting for *this*; rather, they were waiting for the Parousia and the resurrection, and even the new creation.

2.3 Death
2.3.1 Natural or Unnatural?

On the one hand, death is "the last page of our book of life,"[32] and on the other hand, it is "the first of the 'last things.'"[33] If the Parousia does not occur before we die, death is the first "eschatological experience" on the agenda. It is also the only experience about which believers and unbelievers agree: death is inescapable. "What man can live and never see death?" (Ps. 89:49). "[W]hat happens to the children of man and what happens to the beasts is the same; as one dies, so dies the other. They all have the same breath, and man has no advantage over the beasts, for all is vanity. All go to one place. All are from the dust, and to dust all return" (Eccl. 3:19–20). "[D]eath spread to all humans" (Rom. 5:12). "[I]n Adam all die" (1 Cor. 15:22). "Human beings have to die once" (Heb. 9:27 CJB). This is so certain that one can understand the assertion that "death belongs to life." According to our present biological knowledge, this may be the case, but is it also theologically true that "death belongs to life"?

H. Bavinck emphasized that "in antiquity it was also realized by all peoples that death is a punishment, that it is something unnatural, something inimical to the essence and destiny of human

---

31. Berkouwer (1972), 36.
32. C. Hartshorne, quoted in Pittenger (1980), 4.
33. Helm (1989), 55.

beings."[34] Modern people view this very differently. Especially as a consequence of evolutionism, they began viewing death as something natural, that is, as something that is given with the nature of humanity. Death belongs to life just as much as birth does, it is claimed. According to the Christian view, however, a person's death is an *un*natural thing, and according to 1 Corinthians 15:26 death is an enemy; it is an enemy because of the fall of the first humans.[35] Nowadays, however, many progressive Christians advocate the modern view.

We cannot think about the afterlife or the hereafter without considering whether physical death is a natural or an unnatural matter. It goes without saying that the answers to this question lead to quite different eschatologies. We are facing either a future in which, through human effort, the world is en route to great political and social renewal, perhaps something like a paradise on earth, which is then called the "kingdom of God," but in which human death remains an inevitable necessity. Or we are heading toward a future in which one day the kingdom of God will break into this cosmos so radically that that physical death will be abolished.

Orthodox Christians believe the latter. As the Bible says, God "will swallow up death forever" (Isa. 25:8). Jesus Christ "must reign until he has put all his enemies under his feet. The last enemy to be destroyed is death" (1 Cor. 15:25–26). "And the sea gave up the dead who were in it, Death and Hades gave up the dead who were in them, and they were judged, each one of them, according to what they had done. Then Death and Hades were thrown into the lake of fire. This is the second death, the lake of fire" (Rev. 20:13–14).[36] God "will wipe away every tear from their eyes, and

---

34. *RD*, 4:600; cf. Jager (1984); Hoek (2004), 129–32; for a modern standpoint, see Pannenberg (1992), 3:556–63.

35. See passages such as Gen. 2:17; John 8:44; Rom. 5:12–14; 6:23; James 1:15; see extensively, Ouweneel (2008), 190.

36. Please notice the difference: physical death will be destroyed, whereas the "second death," eternal perdition, will remain.

death shall be no more, neither shall there be mourning, nor crying, nor pain anymore, for the former things have passed away" (Rev. 21:4; italics added).

Death entered the world for the first time at the Fall (Gen. 3; Rom. 5:12), which implies that if human history began with human beings for whom death was not an inevitable necessity, then death cannot be natural (although we may view it as natural *since* the Fall). Similarly, the way death will be abolished from the world (cf. also 2 Tim. 1:9–10; Heb. 2:14–15) shows that death is something unnatural.[37] For the newly created humans, death was a *possibility* (hence the warning in Gen. 2:17), but it was not an *inevitable necessity*; the tree of life formed the guarantee for this (Gen. 3:22). Since the Fall, humanity is not only mortal but each human being actually dies (see already in Gen. 5 the constantly repeated "and he died"). At the coming resurrection, the believer will be invested with immortality for the first time (1 Cor. 15:53–54).

Death is something "foreign and hostile."[38] Believers look forward to a world *without* sin and death; as Wolfhart Pannenberg put it, "Christian hope expects a life without death (1 Cor. 15:52–55)."[39] Already the apocryphal book of Wisdom (1:13a) says, "God didn't make death" (CEB). At the same time, it becomes evident that death is an "essential consequence of sin rather than a punishment that God has arbitrarily set and imposed."[40] That is, since the Fall, sin and death are organically correlative.

Believers know that if the Parousia does not occur before this, they will have to die. But Scripture shows that for the believer, physical death has lost its threat and power. Jesus said, "I am the resurrection and the life. Whoever believes in me, though he die, yet

---

37. Regarding this matter see extensively, Berkouwer (1962), chapter 7; cf. Noordegraaf (1990), 89–92.
38. Erickson (1998), 1177.
39. Pannenberg (1992), 2:271; cf. Vogel (1949/50), 124, *contra* Barth, *CD* 3/2:587–640.
40. Pannenberg (1992), 2:274.

shall he live, and everyone who lives and believes in me shall never die" (John 11:25–26). The latter phrase—"shall not die"—is strong language. It does not mean that, after Jesus' resurrection, the words "to die" (Gk. *apothnēskō*) and "death" (Gk. *thanatos*) are no longer used to indicate the end of a Christian's earthly life:[41] Dorcas "became ill and died" (Acts 9:37); Paul wrote, "to me to live is Christ, and to die is gain" (Phil. 1:21). "Indeed he [i.e., Epaphroditus, a friend of Paul's] was ill, near to death. . . . he nearly died for the work of Christ" (2:27, 30). "If anyone sees his brother committing a sin not leading to death . . . ." (1 John 5:16). "Be faithful unto death, and I will give you the crown of life" (Rev. 2:10).

2.3.2 Reckoning with Death

The Apostle Paul wrote optimistically about "we who are alive," that is, at the Parousia (1 Thess. 4:17). But when a believer faces imminent death, they know they must reckon with the possibility that they will die before the Parousia. Thus, Jesus himself said, just before he died, "Father, into your hands I commit my spirit!" (Luke 23:46). And as he was being stoned, Stephen said, "Lord Jesus, receive my spirit" (Acts 7:59).[42] The Apostle Paul says, "[I]n this tent [i.e., the body] we groan, longing to put on our heavenly dwelling, if indeed by putting it on we may not be found naked. For while we are still in this tent, we groan, being burdened—not that we would be unclothed, but that we would be further clothed, so that what is mortal may be swallowed up by life" (2 Cor. 5:4–5). I understand this difficult passage to mean that Paul would love to receive the glorified body, and does not wish to be unclothed first, that is, to relinquish his mortal body first; yet he reckons with the possibility that this may happen—as indeed it did (see more extensively, §5.4).

To Timothy the Apostle wrote: "I am already being poured out as a drink offering, and the time of my departure [Gk. *analysis*, lit-

---

41. Thus Hough (2000), 57–58.
42. Later we will see that this has nothing to do with the Platonic "immortal soul" being separated from the mortal body.

erally "unloosing" the bonds with the present life] has come. I have fought the good fight, I have finished the race, I have kept the faith" (2 Tim. 4:6–7). Notice carefully, however, that he was not looking forward to what awaited him in the hereafter, but to what the Lord would give to him when, *after the Parousia*, he, Paul, would stand before the judgment seat of the Lord: "Henceforth there is laid up for me the crown of righteousness, which the Lord, the righteous judge, will award to me on that day, and not only to me but also to all who have loved his appearing" (v. 8). Even though Paul saw his earthly end approaching, his hope was focused not on the intermediate state, but on the Parousia. He spoke of a crown to be given to "all who have loved his *appearing*" (which refers to the Parousia)—not all who have loved their going-to-heaven-when-they-die.

In 2 Peter 1:13–15, we read that the Apostle Peter also knew, this time through divine revelation, that his departure was imminent:

> I think it right, as long as I am in this body, to stir you up by way of reminder, since I know that the putting off of my body will be soon, as our Lord Jesus Christ made clear to me. And I will make every effort so that after my departure you may be able at any time to recall these things.

However, Peter too was not preoccupied with what awaited him after his passing, but with the Parousia:

> For we did not follow cleverly devised myths when we made known to you the power and coming of our Lord Jesus Christ, but we were eyewitnesses of his majesty. . . . And we have the prophetic word more fully confirmed, to which you will do well to pay attention as to a lamp shining in a dark place, until the day dawns and the morning star rises in your hearts" (2 Pet. 1:16, 19).

We may conclude that in such passages, the Apostles differed from hundreds of Christians who have written about their longing for "sweet death" (cf. §7.4).

2.4 Which Death?

2.4.1 Four Forms of Death

How a person dies, spiritually speaking, depends on *how they lived* before this moment. By nature every human is spiritually dead in their "trespasses and sins" (Eph. 2:1; Col. 2:13); therefore, Jesus could say, "Leave the dead to bury their own dead" (Luke 9:60), that is, leave the spiritually dead to bury their own physically dead. Such spiritually dead people not only undergo physical death, but after their resurrection they are still viewed as "the dead" (Rev. 20:12). In their case, spiritual death ultimately passes through physical death into "second death," that is, eternal death, which is the "lake of fire."[43] In summary, death is always an event involving separation.

(1) Spiritual death involves the human personality being separated from God and his wholesome workings.

(2) Physical death involves the human personality being separated from their bodily mode of existence.

(3) Eternal death involves the human personality being eternally separated from God.[44]

It is not always easy to distinguish which of these three forms of death is intended in a particular Bible passage, as some examples may show.

(a) Genesis 2:17 ("the tree of the knowledge of good and evil you shall not eat, for in the day that you eat of it you shall surely die") apparently refers not (only) to physical death (see 3:19) but (also) to spiritual death. At any rate, it is not a reference to eternal death, for the first human beings could repent of their sin, and thus be saved from eternal death.

---

43. Rev. 2:11; 20:6, 14; 21:8; cf. Matt. 5:22 and 18:9 ("hell of fire"); 25:42 ("eternal fire") and 46 ("eternal punishment" in contrast with "eternal life").
44. Erickson (1998), 1175.

(b) A similar distinction between the physical and the eternal arises in a passage like this: "You shall therefore keep my statutes and my rules; if a person does them, he shall live by them" (Lev. 18:5; cf. Ezek. 20:11, 13). Within the scope of the Old Testament, this means primarily: ". . . that it may go well with you and that you may live long in the land [or, on the earth]" (Eph. 6:3; cf. Exod. 20:12; Deut. 5:16). But within the scope of the New Testament this seems to be extended to eternal life (Luke 10:27–28; Rom. 10:5; Gal. 3:12).

(c) Jesus said to the church in Sardis, "You have the reputation of being alive, but you are dead" (Rev. 3:1). This shows that believers, too, in a certain sense can exist in a deadly condition; hence, Paul's admonition: "Awake, O sleeper, and arise from the dead, and Christ will shine on you" (Eph. 5:14). These passages hint at a fourth meaning of the term "death": that of a "death sleep" that carnal Christians experience. The entire notion of a revival happening among believers (literally, a "coming to life again"; cf. Ps. 85:6; Isa. 57:15; Hos. 6:2) presupposes such a death sleep.

(d) A passage like James 5:19–20 ("My brothers, if anyone among you wanders from the truth and someone brings him back, let him know that whoever brings back a sinner from his wandering will save his soul from death and will cover a multitude of sins") seems to refer to eternal death rather than to physical death.

(e) So too opinions differ widely about whether the term "death" in 1 John 5:16–17 ("If anyone sees his brother committing a sin not leading to death, he shall ask, and God will give him life—to those who commit sins that do not lead to death. There is sin that leads to death; I do not say that one should pray for that. All wrongdoing is sin, but there is sin that does not lead to death") refers to physical death or to eternal death.

In order to be and remain spiritually dead, a person need do nothing, since every human being is by nature spiritually dead from birth, and remains so in eternity—unless they repent and come to faith. If a person believes in Christ, she passes from (spiritual) death to (spiritual) life (John 5:24). This is such a radical transition that even physical death cannot affect it: "[I]f anyone keeps my word, he will never see death" (8:51); "everyone who lives and believes in me shall never die" (11:26). We might put it this way: if a wicked person dies, he passes, as a spiritually dead person, to a more intense form of death, and at the coming resurrection he attains the most profound form of death. But if a righteous person dies, he passes, as a spiritually living person, to a more intense form of living, and at the resurrection he attains the most profound form of life.

2.4.2 Why Then Must We Die?

A last question that we wish to consider in this context is why believers must still die at all. Is it not too facile to assert that believers, too, in death, "which awaits us all," "pay the final installment on 'the wages of sin' (Romans 6:23)"?[45] Does not the phrase "the wages of sin" in this verse stand in contrast to the phrase "the free gift of God," that is, "eternal life"?[46] In the words of Anthony Hoekema, "Death is for us who are in Christ not a satisfaction for sin: It was that for Christ, but not for us. . . . For Christ death was part of the curse; for us death is a source of blessing."[47] Death remains our "last enemy" (1 Cor. 15:26) but a *defeated* enemy (Heb. 2:14), to be sure. Thus, our death has become "gain" with respect to our physical life on earth, as Paul puts it (Phil. 1:21).

This does not alter the fact that the death of believers, too, belongs to the consequences of the Fall. We see this especially where dying was a form of discipline, as in the cases of Ananias and Sapphira (Acts 5), of the immoral person in the church of Corinth (1 Cor. 5:5), and of "quite a few" who had died as a consequence of bad conditions in that same church (1 Cor. 11:30 CEB; cf. 1 John

---

45. Cf. Spykman (1992, 550).
46. Because of this contrast, the text was referring to eternal rather than physical death; see Erickson (1998), 1176.
47. Hoekema (1979), 84; see chapter 7 in its entirety.

5:16–17). But Jesus also said that for believers, death is no longer a dying in the actual sense, since it is a transition to true life (John 8:51; 11:25–26). Here, physical death is made subservient to life; it is the means through which believers move from one state of spiritual life—ultimately in the future resurrection—to an even higher level of life.

Through a very different cause, the believer is still constantly confronted with death, namely, through oppression and persecution, which can end in the martyr's death: ". . . always carrying in the body the death [Gk. *nekrōsis*; literally, the killing] of Jesus, so that the life of Jesus may also be manifested in our bodies. For we who live are always being given over to death for Jesus' sake, so that the life of Jesus also may be manifested in our mortal flesh. So death is at work in us, but life in you" (2 Cor. 4:10–12). Here, death is the consequence, not of one's own sinfulness, but of the sinfulness of the world in its totality.

Of course, believers might desire to be taken from this earth without having to die, just as Enoch and Elijah were (see §4.1.1). Eventually, this will occur, namely, at what has been called the "rapture" (not a secret rapture!) of the church.[48] But only believers who are alive at that time will be "caught up" without having died first:

> [T]he Lord himself will descend from heaven with a cry of command, with the voice of an archangel, and with the sound of the trumpet of God. And the dead in Christ will rise first. Then we who are alive, who are left, will be caught up together with them in the clouds to meet the Lord in the air, and so we will always be with the Lord (1 Thess. 4:16–17).

Then, the bodies of these living believers will be invested immediately with immortality, with "the imperishable," and with glory

---

48. This is not the place to discuss whether this will occur before, after or during the Great Tribulation, or whether such a tribulation will even occur; regarding this, see Ouweneel (2012a), chapter 10.

(1 Cor. 15:43, 51–54; Phil. 3:20–21). This privilege is unavailable for the great majority of believers: they have passed away, and will pass away, before the Parousia.

Louis Berkhof claimed that even for these living believers, physical death would somehow still be necessary in order that believers would be able to identify with the Lord, who also attained glory through death.[49] Death would be part of their spiritual education and perfection. M. J. Erickson argued that this is a rather forced explanation.[50] He claimed—in my view rightly—that as long as they are still in the present body, believers will deal with certain consequences of the Fall; these include not only physical death but also diseases and illnesses:

> Although the eternal consequences of our own individual sins are nullified when we are forgiven, the temporal consequences, or at least some of them, may linger on. . . . We will not experience the second death. Nonetheless, we must experience physical death simply because it has become one of the conditions of human experience. It is now a part of life, as much so as birth, growth, and suffering, which also ultimately takes its origin from sin. One day every consequence of sin will be removed, but that day is not yet.[51]

2.4.3 Through Death to Heaven?

Many Christians would argue something like this: physical death is still an enemy, a harsh reality, also for believers, but at least it brings us to heaven. However, the argument of this book is that, to be sure, deceased believers are "with Jesus" (Luke 23:42–43), "with Christ" (Phil. 1:23), and "with the Lord" (2 Cor. 5:7), and this is *far better* than anything they have enjoyed on earth. But at the same time, this disembodied state is *far less* than what believers will enjoy in the resurrection state.

---

49. Berkhof (1981), 742.
50. Erickson (1998), 117.
51. *Ibid.*

In fact, the *only* descriptions that we have of believers in the intermediate state are found in Luke 16:19–31 (the rich man and Lazarus; see §5.1) and Luke 23:43: ". . . today you will be with me in Paradise" (see §5.2). But are they really descriptions of the intermediate state as such? At this early point in our discussion, I ask rhetorically how the *disembodied* condition of any person could ever be described as eternal blessedness, or could be understood as the believer's final destiny. Only people who adhere to a Greek body-soul dualism, in which the soul is more than the body, and death is deliverance from the body—an ancient Greek heresy (see chapter 8)— could think that dying leads to the highest and final Christian destiny.

The deepest truth is that many Christians actually believe the pagan idea of transmigration of the soul at physical death: at this moment, the immortal soul (or spirit) leaves—or is liberated from—the body, and moves to the hereafter. From that moment on, every human being exists, as it were, in two places at the same time: one part rests in the grave, and the other part dwells in the hereafter. People who argue this way do not know how to think about and how to understand the resurrection of the body. The best they can come up with is that, at the future resurrection, both parts will be coming from different directions, as it were: the body rises from the grave in a renewed condition, and the soul/spirit comes from the hereafter, in order to be reunited to form one complete human being.

These stages leading to and including the reuniting of body and soul are taught in various orthodox confessions and catechisms, as we have seen in chapter 1,[52] but *nowhere in the Bible*. The idea of a person being split into two parts, which are later reunited, belongs to Greek scholastic thinking, not to biblical thinking. The fact that this idea has been repeated in creeds and catechisms, and learned

---

52. Cf. Heidelberg Catechism Q&A 57: at the resurrection, my body will be "reunited with my soul" (Dennison [2008], 2:782).

treatises does not make it biblical.

The Apostle Paul knew better; he did not speak about any redemption (of the soul or spirit) *from* the body, but about the ultimate redemption *of* the body, and called *this* our true sonship: the believers with their glorified bodies (Rom. 8:23). He was never preoccupied with the supposed blessedness of the intermediate state. Instead, he looked forward to the resurrection state, when his person would dwell in a renewed, redeemed, glorified body. I repeat: being with Christ is far better than living our present lives. At the same time, existence in the disembodied state is far inferior to existence in the resurrection state.

What Christians *look forward to*, or *should* be looking forward to, is not a "heavenly hereafter," in which they will be divested of the body, but they are "waiting for and hastening the coming of the day of God, because of which the heavens will be set on fire and dissolved, and the heavenly bodies will melt as they burn! But according to his promise we are waiting for new heavens and a new earth in which righteousness dwells" (2 Pet. 3:12–14).

What Jesus placed before his disciples was never the supposed blessings of the intermediate state, but rather this: "[A]n hour is coming when all who are in the tombs will hear his voice and come out, those who have done good to the resurrection of life, and those who have done evil to the resurrection of judgment" (John 5:28–29). And this: "[I]f I go and prepare a place for you, I will come again and will take you to myself, that where I am you may be also" (14:3; see §6.4). The latter verse also explains the following one, from the Son's prayer to the Father: "Father, I desire that they also, whom you have given me, may be with me where I am, to see my glory that you have given me because you loved me before the foundation of the world" (John 17:24).

Similarly, Paul's hope was the "resurrection of both the just and the unjust," in accordance with Jewish expectation (Acts 24:15). "[O]ur citizenship is in heaven, and from it we await a Savior, the

Lord Jesus Christ, who will transform our lowly body to be like his glorious body, by the power that enables him even to subject all things to himself" (Phil. 3:20–21). The future blessing to which we must look forward is not the intermediate state but the resurrection state. This was the hope of Jesus, the apostles, and the early church. And this should be our hope as well, despite so many centuries of Interim Theology.

3

THE AFTERLIFE: IMMEDIATELY AND LATER

> We do not look at the things which are seen,
>> but at the things which are not seen.
> For the things which are seen are temporary;
>> but the things which are not seen are eternal.
>> 2 Corinthians 4:18 (NKJV)

Ich bin gewiß
Und habe das Vertrauen,
Daß mich des Grabes Finsternis
Zur Himmelsherrlichkeit erhebt.
Mein Jesus lebt,
Ich habe nun genug,
Mein Herz und Sinn
Will heute noch zum Himmel hin,
Selbst den Erlöser anzuschauen.

I am certain
and have assurance,
that the darkness of the grave
will raise me up to heavenly glory;[1]
my Jesus lives,

---

1. The idea is that at death, the body goes to the grave, but the soul is lifted up to the glory of heaven.

now I have enough.
My heart and mind
will be in heaven even today,
to behold the Redeemer Himself.

Ich lebe, mein Herze, zu deinem Ergötzen
[*I Live, My Heart, for Your Pleasure*]
Bach cantata BWV 145
Christian Friedrich Henrici (Picander)

3.1 The Intermediate State and Time

3.1.1 "Depart in Peace"

One of the most intriguing and beautiful works that the great Russian composer Sergei Rachmaninoff wrote was entitled *All-Night Vigil*, better known as *Vespers*, a title that is not entirely correct. It is a spiritual *a cappella* work consisting of fifteen parts. The first six parts are settings from the Russian Orthodox vespers (the evening service), and numbers seven through fourteen are settings from the Russian Orthodox matins (the morning service). Rachmaninoff himself loved this work very much; he requested the fifth part to be sung at his funeral (1943). This part, called *Nïne otpushchayeshi*, is a setting of the Song of Simeon in Luke 2:29–32: "Lord, now you are letting your servant depart in peace, according to your word; for my eyes have seen your salvation, ..."

We read of Simeon that "it had been revealed to him by the Holy Spirit that he would not see death before he had seen the Lord's Christ [or, Messiah]" (Luke 2:26). After he had indeed seen the Christ child, and had even held him in his arms, we can understand that he exclaimed: "Lord, now you are letting your servant depart in peace." That is, he was now ready to "see death." No wonder that this Song has become the farewell Song of many Christians, who, at the end of their earthly lives, are left with this single desire: Let me now go, Lord, in peace. It was written on tombstones of Christians who had passed away, to indicate what their longings at the end of their earthly lives had been. I hope that Rachmaninoff was such a believing man that Simeon's Song indeed expressed his own longings: to depart in order to be with Christ.

In the Lutheran liturgy, the hymn was sung to commemorate the Purification of Mary (Ger. *Mariae Reinigung*; see Luke 2:22), every year on February 2 (forty days after Christmas; Lev. 12:1–4). Johann Sebastian Bach (cf. §1.4.2) wrote several wonderful cantatas for this festival, such as *Ich habe genug* ("I have enough," BWV 82) and *Mit Fried und Freud ich fahr dahin* ("With peace and joy I depart," BWV 125), in which the believer is looking forward to "heaven" with the words of Simeon. Many other composers have set the text to music. In the Anglican liturgy, in the so-called Common Worship, Simeon's Song belongs to the "Canticles for Use at Funeral and Memorial Services," for obvious reasons. A setting of the *Nunc dimittis* (the Latin version of the Song of Simeon) by Charles Villiers Stanford was sung at the funeral of the former British prime minister, Margaret Thatcher in 2013. "Lord, now lettest thou thy servant depart in peace" (KJV)—what song could be more appropriate at the funeral of a Christian, one might think?

But the question is this: Is this hymn, as many have thought, really a hymn about "going to heaven"? There is no doubt, given the connection between Luke 2:26 and 29, that Simeon was referring to his physical death. But was he also referring to "going to heaven when he died"? Was he occupied with the wonderful bliss and blessings he was going to enjoy on the other side of the threshold of death? Not in the least. Rather, he was looking *beyond the intermediate state* to the wonderful work the Messiah was going to accomplish among Israel and the nations: "Lord, now you are letting your servant depart in peace, according to your word; *for* my eyes have seen your *salvation* that you have prepared in the presence of *all peoples, a light for revelation to the Gentiles, and for glory to your people Israel.*" Entirely in line with the Old Testament (see the next chapter), and with his own expectation ("waiting for the consolation of Israel," v. 25; cf.

v. 38), he was looking forward to the Messianic age, in which the Messiah would rule the world, and in which the nations would be blessed, particularly Israel. How many Christians, wishing Simeon's Song to be sung at their funeral, were and are aware of this? How many of them were and are focused, not so much on the supposed blessing of the intermediate state, but on the resurrection state, and on the Parousia and the Messianic kingdom connected with it?

3.1.2 Now and Soon

In chapter 1.2.2 and 1.2.3, we found two important expressions in Protestant confessions, namely "immediately (after death)" (i.e., the intermediate state) and "at (the) last (day)" (i.e., the resurrection state). In the Westminster Larger Catechism we read in Answer 82: "The communion in glory which the members of the invisible church have with Christ, is in this life (2 Cor. 3:18), *immediately* after death (Luke 23:43), and *at last* perfected at the resurrection and day of judgment (1 Thess. 4:17)" (italics added).[2] And in Answer 86 we read:

> The communion in glory with Christ, which the members of the invisible church enjoy *immediately after death*, is, in that their souls are then made perfect in holiness (Heb. 12:23), and received into the highest heavens (2 Cor. 5:1, 6, 8; Phil. 1:23; Acts 3:21; Eph. 4:10), where they behold the face of God in light and glory (1 John 3:2; 1 Cor. 13:12), waiting for the full redemption of their bodies (Rom. 8:23; Ps. 16:9), which even in death continue united to Christ (1 Thess. 4:14), and rest in their graves as in their beds (Isa. 57:2), till *at the last day* they be again united to their souls (Job 19:26–27). . . .[3]

In the Heidelberg Catechism, we find in Answer 57 (see §1.2.3): "That not only my soul after this life shall be *immediately* taken up to Christ its Head (Luke 23:43; Phil. 1:21–23), but [*later*] also that this my body, raised by the power of Christ, shall be reunited with my

---

2.   Dennison, *RC*, 4:316.

3.   *Ibid.*, 4:317.

soul, and made like the glorious body of Christ (1 Cor. 15:53–54; Job 19:25–27; 1 John 3:2)" (italics added).[4] On the one hand, the two catechisms speak of an event occurring "immediately after death (or, after our present life)," and on the other hand of things that will occur (much) later, namely, in the resurrection ("at last," "at the last day").

The difficulty with this presentation of things is that the "now" and the "later" are being confused. That is, things that belong to the "immediately," that is, the intermediate state, are derived partially from things that belong exclusively to what comes "later," at the resurrection. Take, for instance, what we found in the Heidelberg Catechism in Answer 58 (see §1.2.3): ". . . I shall *after this life* possess *complete blessedness*, such as eye has not seen, nor ear heard, neither has entered into the heart of man (1 Cor. 2:9), therein to praise God forever (John 17:3)" (italics added).[5] But, as we have seen several times already, "completeness" does not belong to the intermediate state at all, but rather to the resurrection state.

Indeed, how could completeness belong to a state in which the person *themselves* are still very imperfect, namely, disembodied, having "put off" their body (2 Pet. 1:14)? People can believe such a thing only if and when they conceive such disembodiment to be irrelevant to them. This is unmistakably a consequence of Greek scholastic thinking, in which the soul is valued much more highly than the body, or is viewed as primary (see more extensively, chapter 8). The body is of secondary importance to such an extent that its absence is apparently not viewed as a hindrance to complete blessedness. Such people may put forward supposedly biblical evidence. such as the body being *only* "dust" (Gen. 2:7; 3:19), or *only* a "tent" (Gk. *skēnos* or *skēnōma*, 2 Cor. 5:1; 2 Pet. 1:13–14). Such people forget the enormous importance that the Bible, especially the New Testament, attaches to the resurrection of this very body.

---

4. *Ibid.*, 2:782.
5. *Ibid.*

When the Apostle Paul spoke to the Greeks in Athens about the resurrection of the body, they began to mock him as well as his teaching (Acts 17:31–32). To them, it was the most ridiculous idea that the soul, *set free* from the body, would one day return to the body. Plato had taught in his *Phaedo* that the body is a grave for the soul (Gk. *sōma sēma*) and that at physical death the soul is liberated from this grave. The more that Christians began to adopt such ideas (see Calvin, mentioned in §3.3.1), the less relevant the body became: without the body, believers can enjoy perfect joy, perfect bliss.[6] In reality, the reverse is true: a person is never so *im*perfect as when their body is taken away from them. This imperfection is different from the one caused through the Fall, but it is an imperfection all the same. Complete bliss is reserved for the resurrection state.

This is an important point. It helps us to understand some New Testament references to the intermediate state that contain expressions to be complete fulfilled only in the resurrection state. In chapter 5 we will investigate some of these passages more closely. But here I ask the reader to look at Philippians 1:23, where the Apostle Paul wrote, "My desire is to depart and be with Christ, for that is far better." No doubt this is primarily a reference to the intermediate state. However, Paul's actual *expectation* was not at all the intermediate state as such. In the same letter, he tells us what he was really *waiting* for: "[O]ur citizenship is in heaven, and from it we *await* a Savior, the Lord Jesus Christ, who will transform our lowly body to be like his glorious body" (3:20–21). That is, his actual hope was not for the intermediate state as such, but for the resurrection state.

Let me put it this way: it is "far better" to be with Christ in the intermediate state than to endure the miseries of earthly life—but it is "far better" *still* to be with Christ in the resurrection state than to

---

6. David Van Biema quoted N. T. Wright, who said, "I've often heard people say, 'I'm going to heaven soon, and I won't need this stupid body there, thank goodness'" (http://content.time.com/time/world/article/0,8599,1710844,00.html); see also Wright (2016).

be with him in the intermediate state. Being with Christ is certainly a reality for believers in the intermediate state; but this is a mere shadow of that to which they are really *looking forward*. What this entails is found in 1 Thessalonians 4:17, which teaches that we "will be caught up together with them [i.e., the risen saints] in the clouds to meet the Lord in the air, and so we will always be *with the Lord*." Being "with the Lord" in the fullest sense will be realized only in the resurrection state, when believers will possess their glorified bodies. In other words, Philippians 1:23 is mainly *anticipation*, at best a foretaste of what awaits believers after they have received back their bodies, and this in a glorified state.

3.2   More Biblical Examples
3.2.1   The "Shades"

Another example of this is 2 Corinthians 5:1: "[W]e know that if the tent that is our earthly home is destroyed, we have a building from God, a house not made with hands, eternal in the heavens." As I will demonstrate later (§5.4), this verse does not say that believers have a "heavenly home" during the intermediate state. This is then taken to mean more or less the same as "heaven." Thus, some claim this verse as evidence for the belief that the righteous "go to heaven when they die." But Paul is not looking forward to this kind of "being in heaven" between his death and his resurrection, but rather to the "building," the "house" made by God and granted to him in the resurrection. The contrast is between the "tent" in which Paul dwelt at the time he was writing, and the "heavenly dwelling" that he would "put on" one day, with which he would be "clothed."

Thus, in this passage we begin with a "tent," then move to a "building" or a "heavenly dwelling"; if the tent is our present mortal body, the "building" or "dwelling" from God can hardly be taken in any other sense than as the resurrection body. Paul does not say that we move from "our earthly home" (our present body) to "heaven" when we die, but rather that, at some point after death, we will receive the resurrection body, which is called an "eternal house in the heavens." Paul's description moves immediately from death to the resurrection body, without devoting any words to the intermediate state (but see later in vv. 6–8).

In the words of G. C. Berkouwer: "Since there is no division in the *one* expectation, we cannot find the intermediate state as an independent theme in Paul. . . . [Paul taught] a single expectation of the future."[7] In other words, New Testament believers are aware that those existing in the intermediate state are "with Christ" (Phil. 1:23), or "with the Lord" (2 Cor. 5:6–8), and in a sense they look forward to that, but that is not their actual *expectation*, their proper Christian *hope*, which is rather the Parousia and the resurrection connected with it.

It is like a monetary allowance that a person receives from a testator, which this person receives as long as the testator is still alive, but which cannot be compared with the full inheritance, which the person will receive after the testator's death. It is like the swimming exercises practiced in one's exercise room, which may be pleasant but cannot be compared with those done in the swimming pool. It is like enjoying reading a cookbook, which may be pleasant, but cannot be compared with the real dinner. It is like tuning the instruments before the concert begins, which may heighten the tension of the listeners, but cannot be compared with the actual concert.

The prophet Isaiah speaks about the "shades" in Sheol (or Hades) (Isa. 14:9; cf. 26:14, 19). If the dead, whose bodies are in the grave, are likened to "shades," how can they be compared with the saints in their glorified bodies? The Hebrew word for "shades" is *r'pha'im*, a word that appears elsewhere, and is usually rendered "the dead" (cf. §4.4.1).[8] It is thought to be derived from *r-ph-h*, "to be feeble (slack, weak)." The Scripture verses just mentioned certainly do not indicate that only unbelievers are meant. It is a general description of the dead: what are they without their bodies? Feeble

---

7. Berkouwer (1972), 57.
8. Job 26:5; Ps. 88:10; Prov. 2:18; 9:18; 21:16.

shades. Naked people sitting in the waiting room, waiting for their clothes (cf. 2 Cor. 5:2–4).

For this simple reason, believers in both the Old Testament and the New Testament are never said to look forward to the intermediate state. After they have passed away, New Testament believers knew that they would be "with Christ"—but what is being "with Christ" in their disembodied state compared to their being "with Christ" in their glorified state? The former is just the foretaste, the latter is perfect bliss. The former is the anticipation, the latter is the realization. The former is the dusk; the latter is the full splendor of the dawn. It is like stepping from the shadows into the full light. It is like the old black-and-white drawings as compared to modern four-color photography.

3.2.2 Two Churches?

Believers have often spoken as though they were looking forward to being redeemed *from* their bodies. This is understandable when their bodies are very sick, emaciated, suffering from unbearable pain, or when the believer is facing a martyr's death. But this is not the ordinary Christian expectation; on the contrary, this expectation is far more Platonic than Pauline. The Christian's true hope is the redemption, not *from* the body but *of* the body (Rom. 8:23). That is, the body is *itself* redeemed by being transformed to be like the "body of his [Christ's] glory" (Phil. 3:21 NASB).

It is all the more amazing that Joseph Benson understood the latter passage (Phil. 3:20–21), which begins with the phrase, "our citizenship is in heaven," as referring primarily to "our spirits, at the dissolution of this earthly tabernacle."[9] In a sermon by Jacobus Nyloe (1707), I found this comment on the same Bible passage:

> It is with the heavenly Jerusalem as with the earthly one, which was one city, although it was divided into two. It is the same with the church: one part of this city is above, the other part is down here, in

9. https://biblehub.com/commentaries/philippians/3-20.htm.

which believers, though still walking in the body, are fellow citizens with all the saints and blessed in heaven.

A commentator who praised this quotation identified this as the distinction between the church militant and the church triumphant.[10]

The latter distinction involves a doctrine that has really "slain its ten thousands." It is the traditional notion (both Roman Catholic and Protestant) of the church militant (Lat. *ecclesia militans*),[11] which is the church on earth (or that part of the church that is still on earth), as distinct from the church triumphant (Lat. *ecclesia triumphans*), which consists of the saints who are already "in heaven," that is, *existing in the intermediate state*. It is amazing how strong this idea remains, not only among Roman Catholics but also among, for instance, Anglicans, Lutherans, Reformed,[12] and Methodists. If the common view of the intermediate state is mistaken, then, naturally, so too is this bi- or tripartition of the church. There will indeed be a *triumphant church*—but not before the Parousia and the resurrection, that is, at the very moment when there will no longer be any *militant church* on earth.

Part of this erroneous presentation of things is the idea that the saints "in heaven" are already "reigning" with Christ (Rev. 20:4–6; cf. 1 Cor. 6:2; 2 Tim. 2:12). But there can be no "reigning" before the Parousia and the resurrection (see more extensively, chapter 12).

We could almost say that, wherever in the New Testament we find the word "heaven," or related terms, many expositors link those passages with the intermediate state. Take "heaven" in Philippians 2:10, where the "knees [bowing] in heaven" are thought to refer to

---

10. Both the citation and the commentary are available at https://vroegekerk.nl/content.php?id=117.
11. Catholics add to this the suffering church (Lat. *ecclesia dolens*), which supposedly consists of believers in Purgatory (see §6.3).
12. Wilhelmus à Brakel, in his *The Christian's Reasonable Service*, is just one example of many. A more recent example is L. Berkhof (1981), 625.

the "souls of men departed."[13] This tendency is especially true for the phrase "my Father's house" (John 14:2–3; see §1.1.1, and extensively §6.4). Despite the absence throughout the New Testament of descriptions of the blessings and glories of the intermediate state, John 14:2–3 is simply one of those passages that many believe must and shall constitute such a description. This interpretation is advocated despite the obvious fact that Jesus was telling us explicitly that he would "come again" in person to gather his people, and take them to this glorious place.

Another well-known example, already mentioned in §1.4, is the "kingdom of heaven" (sometimes one word: German *Himmelreich*; Dutch *hemelrijk*), which traditionally has been identified repeatedly with the intermediate state.

Or take the references to "heaven" in the book of Revelation, such as 11:12 ("went up to heaven") and 13:6 ("his tabernacle, and them that dwell in heaven"), which have often been connected with the intermediate state (see more extensively, §10.1.1). Or take the New Testament references to the inheritance of believers, which is invariably associated with "heaven," including the intermediate state (see extensively, §12.2). One could mention many more examples of such Interim Theology, as I am calling it.

3.2.3 With Jesus in Paradise

Another example of focusing on the intermediate state is provided by the most famous verse for all those who wish to locate all their heavenly blessings in the intermediate state. At the crucifixion of Jesus, one of the criminals on the cross said, "'Jesus, remember me when you come into your kingdom.' And he said to him, 'Truly, I say to you, today you will be with me in paradise'" (Luke 23:42–43). What better proof could there be for the bliss and the glories of the intermediate state? It is called "paradise," which by definition is a "garden" of pleasure and delight!

---

13. John Gill (also cf. Barnes and Poole,
    https://biblehub.com/commentaries/philippians/2-10.htm.

I will discuss this passage more extensively in §5.2, but here I would like to pose a counter-question: How can all the blessings that we attach to the term "paradise" be applied to the intermediate state, given the fact that believers exist there in an *imperfect*, and especially a *disembodied* condition? Like the people who are there, the intermediate state itself is just a "shade," not yet the splendorous light of a glorious summer day. In the New Testament sense, the future paradise is entirely connected with the Messianic kingdom, and with the new heavens and the new earth (see especially Rev. 22:1–2 about the "river of the water of life" and the "tree of life," *the* characteristic tree of the Garden of Eden, Gen. 2:9; 3:22, 24; also see Rev. 2:7).[14] It would be quite amazing if we were required to accept that Jesus suddenly, and exceptionally, was here describing the intermediate state as "paradise."

The righteous do not "go to paradise" when they die, because the state of paradise exists after the resurrection. But the righteous who have passed away are somehow "with Christ" already now, and this very fact is a *foretaste* of paradise; it is "paradisal" in nature. It is paradisal in anticipation, not yet in full realization; it is the foretaste of the dinner, not the dinner itself; it is the prelude to the play, not the play itself, it is the overture to the concert, not the symphony. Such a foretaste is really a *taste*; it is good and pleasant. You taste the food, you see the wonderful dishes, you smell the delicious aromas. The marriage supper of the Lamb, however, is not for naked shades, but for a Bride clothed "with fine linen, bright and pure" (Rev. 19:6–9).

3.3 Beatitude and Expectation

3.3.1 Calvin

The interesting comments of John Calvin in this context deserve our attention:

---

14. Cf. Isa. 51:3: "For the LORD comforts Zion; he comforts all her waste places and makes her wilderness like Eden, her desert like the garden of the LORD; joy and gladness will be found in her, thanksgiving and the voice of song."

Now it is neither lawful nor expedient to inquire too curiously concerning our souls' intermediate state. Many torment themselves overmuch with disputing as to what place the souls occupy and whether or not they already enjoy heavenly glory. Yet it is foolish and rash to inquire concerning unknown matters more deeply than God permits us to know. . . . What teacher or master will reveal to us that which God has concealed? Concerning the place, it is no less foolish and futile to inquire, since we know that the soul does not have the same dimension as the body. The fact that the blessed gathering of saintly spirits is called "Abraham's bosom" [Luke 16:22] is enough to assure us of being received after this pilgrimage by the common Father of the faithful, that he may share the fruit of his faith with us. Meanwhile, since *Scripture everywhere bids us wait in expectation for Christ's coming*, and defers until then the crown of glory [1 Pet 5:4], let us be content with the limits divinely set for us: namely, that the souls of the pious, having ended the toil of their warfare, enter into blessed rest, where in glad expectation they await the enjoyment of promised glory, and so *all things are held in suspense until Christ the Redeemer appear* (italics added).[15]

Notice the following important points:

(a) We should not "inquire too curiously" into the matter of the intermediate state because we easily fall into all kinds of unwarranted speculations, such as "whether or not they already enjoy heavenly glory." Calvin does not wish to express himself on this point, because he considers it to be speculation that is "neither lawful nor expedient." I agree with this entirely.

(b) I will demur from Calvin's own speculations—for it is difficult, when we speak of such mysterious things, to avoid speculative talk ourselves—on the dimensions of the soul, and the abode of the blessed spirits.

(c) I find this particular point highly important: Calvin insisted

---

15. *Institutes* 3.25.6; see also his *Commentary on First Corinthians* on 1 Cor. 15:18–19, and his work *Psychopannychia.*

that we should look forward to the Parousia rather than speculate about the intermediate state. The saints who have passed away do obtain "blessed rest" (Rev. 14:13), but apart from this, they *wait for* the fruition of promised glory. Thus, the final result is *suspended* till Christ the Redeemer appears. In other words, during the intermediate state, they do *not* yet possess the promised glory, nor the final results of Christ's redemptive work; in order to receive these things, the saints must wait for the resurrection state. One would wish that the followers of Calvin had paid more attention to these warnings.

(d) The "crown of glory" (cf. 1 Pet. 5:4, where this reward seems to be given in particular to the shepherds in the churches) is *not* given to (certain) saints at the moment of their falling asleep, but only at the Parousia.

3.3.2   Anticipation and Realization

The intermediate state consists of the merging of beatitude and expectation.[16] There is room for the term "beatitude" (Latin *beatitudo*, equivalent to Gk. *makarismos*), for we read, "'Blessed [Gk. *makarioi*, beatified] are the dead who die in the Lord from now on.' 'Blessed indeed,' says the Spirit, 'that they may rest from their labors, for their deeds follow them!'" (Rev. 14:13). But this beatitude exists as a foretaste, an advance, a prelude, an overture. Therefore, there is the second element, the *expectation*, which is focusing upon the *full* taste, the *full* payment, the *full* diner, the *full* concert. There is no need to speak here, with Heinrich Quistorp, of a "double and almost contradictory aspect,"[17] just as there is no contradiction between foretaste and full taste, advance and full payment, anticipation and realization.

In his work *Psychopannychia* ("The Sleeping of the Soul"; cf. §7.2 below), Calvin characterized this difference between waiting on earth and waiting in the intermediate state as follows (in the words of G. C. Berkouwer): "On earth the believer hopes but does not

---

16. Berkouwer (1972), 49.
17. Quistorp (1941), 80–81.

see, whereas in death, the believer witnesses what he has long expected." This might be a little speculative, but the underlying notion is quite valuable: beatitude and expectation do not constitute a contradiction. That is, "[r]est and salvation are not qualities in isolation, but are indissolubly connected to the resurrection. . . . [T]he bliss is made visible in the expectation of the return of Christ."[18]

In summary:

(a) In our present state, we are expecting God's bliss, but do not yet "see" what we are expecting.

(b) In the intermediate state, we will *still be expecting*, but we will also "see" (to some extent) what we are expecting (this is what I have described as foretaste, advance, allowance, anticipation, prelude, overture).

(c) In the resurrection state, we not only see but *receive* what we have expected.

3.3.3   Ongoing Debate

Throughout history, theologians have wrestled with the problem of time: the relationship between the "immediate" of the intermediate state and the "afterward" of the resurrection state. Herman Bavinck wrote that later Lutherans no longer discerned any difference between the two to the extent that they ascribed to believers a "full and essential beatitude" already in the intermediate state, thus neglecting the difference with the resurrection state.[19] Underlying this is "The Great Shift" about which I wrote in chapter 1: all the blessings and glories of the resurrection state have been transposed to the intermediate state. Christians no longer look forward to the Parousia, but to "sweet death," when they will "enter glory."

Let me refer here to Bach's cantatas again, where the resurrection state is certainly not overlooked but death is indeed a "sweet death," leading to immediate bliss. Take, for instance, Cantata BWV

---

18. Berkouwer (1972), 50.
19. *RD*, 4:611.

161 (*Komm, du süße Todesstunde*), which begins as follows: "Come, O sweet hour of death, / when my spirit / laps honey / out of the lion's mouth [cf. Judg. 14:8]; . . . / Make my departure sweet, / do not delay, / last light, / so that I may kiss my Savior" (see more extensively, §7.4.1).

Some Reformed theologians have maintained the proper distinction in beatitude between the intermediate state and the resurrection state. Louis Cappel (or Ludwig Cappellus) believed that the intermediate state was more beatified than the pre-death state, yet that it differs markedly from the beatitude beginning with the resurrection. The arguments are obvious; for instance, Paul implicitly stated that the intermediate state is "far better" than the pre-death state (Phil. 1:23), and John quoted the voice from heaven stating that the believers who have passed away are "blessed" (or rather, "beatified"; Rev. 14:13). However, it is equally clear that all the great New Testament passages about the blessings and the glories of believers in the future refer, directly or indirectly, to the Parousia and the resurrection state. As Cappel put it, the intermediate state consists entirely "in the hope and expectation of a future [!] glory, not indeed in the enjoyment of that glory."[20]

Here we see both continuity and discontinuity, similar to the differences between foretaste and full taste, advance and full payment, anticipation and realization, prelude and symphony, and so on. On the one hand, deceased believers are "with Christ" (*syn Christōi*, Phil. 1:23); on the other hand, in the resurrection state, believers will be "with the Lord" (*syn kyriōi*, 1 Thess. 4:17). Unless people wish to make a subtle distinction here between "with Christ" and "with the Lord," we must conclude that "being with Christ" is the tremendous foretaste of "being with the Lord." This is the continuity. On the other hand, there is a clear discontinuity between the picture of the lamenting "souls" of the deceased (disembodied) martyrs "under the altar" (Rev. 16:9) and this other picture from the same

---

20. Cited by Bavinck, *RD*, 4:612).

book: "I saw what appeared to be a sea of glass mingled with fire—and also those who had conquered the beast and its image and the number of its name, standing beside the sea of glass with harps of God in their hands. And they sing the song of Moses, the servant of God, and the song of the Lamb" (Rev. 15:2–3). The former is the intermediate state, the latter is the resurrection state (also cf. 20:4, 6) (see further in chapter 5 below).

3.4 Time and Eternity
3.4.1 Two Dualisms

J. Verkuyl made the striking remark that after death (and resurrection), believers will not be "eternalized," which apparently means: placed outside the framework of time: "We [will then] live in a new history. God's children will experience in an entirely new way the progress of time, and [after this] the eternal progress of time, consisting in this that repeatedly there will be a beginning, a surprising beginning."[21] This claim contains a speculative element, of course, but the importance of the remark is that we should not say that, one day, "time will cease," or that we will pass from time to eternity, which thus necessarily implies timelessness.

Wolfhart Pannenberg called the "relationship between time and eternity" "the key problem of eschatology." But to my mind, he made no valuable contribution to this discussion with expressions like "the kingdom of God as the end of history" and "the coming of eternity into time."[22] Nor did Chris Fahner help with his formulation: "View of the end of time."[23] There is no biblical evidence at all for this way of speaking. The Bible does not speculate about the phenomenon of time; Scripture is uninterested in philosophical puzzles in general. Only philosophers cherish such interests, and this is unobjectionable as long as they do not read the results of their thinking back into the Bible.

---

21. Verkuyl (1992), 450; cf. Berkhof (1986), 529–30; Erickson (1998), 1240–41.
22. Pannenberg (1992), 3:586, 595.
23. Fahner (1997), This is the title of his article.

As I try to show in this book, there are two Greek scholastic dualisms that for many centuries have played a role in our discussions concerning the afterlife. On the one hand, there is the body-soul dualism, which has burdened so many traditional views of the afterlife (see chapter 8). However, those who rightly *reject* this dualism have sometimes moved to the other extreme by rejecting every form of intermediate state (see §7.2). The former expositors *overemphasize* the intermediate state, due to their body-soul dualism. The latter expositors *downplay* the intermediate state, due to their time-eternity dualism. Although these two groups emphasize opposite conclusions, both are, or were, influenced by (different parts of) the same Greek scholastic thinking.

Some of those who reject every form of intermediate state adhere to another form of Greek scholastic thinking, namely, the time-eternity dualism.[24] The dead are supposedly beyond time, and therefore no conscious existence would be possible in the hereafter because such an existence supposedly presupposes time. Here, Greek scholastic ideas about time are being read into biblical thinking. Ostensibly, the person who dies leaves temporal existence behind, and in the resurrection enters into an atemporal mode of existence, which supposedly belongs to the new creation, which will be a timeless creation. In the interim, there is nothing, no intermediate state, because such a state would presuppose an earlier and a later.

However, some who believe in an intermediate state have claimed that eternity implies timelessness, or else they are confused about the matter. Bach's cantatas again supply us with an excellent example, namely, cantata BWV 20 (*O Ewigkeit, du Donnerwort*, "O eternity, you word of thunder"). The cantata is based on a chorale by Johann Rist (1642), which begins as follows: "O eternity, you

---

24. See Cullmann (1962), Berkhof (1966), and Berkouwer (1972), 40–46, who combat this view.

word of thunder, / O sword, that bores through the soul, / O beginning without end! / O eternity, timeless time, ..." At the same time, the poet speaks of the "thousand million years" that the "damned" will spend in torment, and it will still not be over for them. So which is it? A timeless eternity, or an eternity without end? Will time cease one day, or will it go on forever?

In earlier centuries, people found one argument for the idea of timelessness in Revelation 10:6, ". . . that there should be time no longer" (KJV), or ". . . that there would be no more time" (NTE). The Annotations to the Dutch States Translation tell us that some understand the word "time" in this verse as "the time which by the course of heaven is measured out in days, months, and years; which time will end with the end of the world."[25] The Annotations do mention other views as well, though. The idea is that, when the present world ends, the sun and the moon will end too, so that time can no longer be measured. Today, we realize that even were the sun and the moon to disappear, our timepieces would continue to indicate the movement of time just as before. Our reckoning of time no longer depends on the movement of the sun and the moon. Nonetheless, this view that time will one day cease was defended by Abraham Kuyper,[26] and later by Karl Barth.[27]

However, Matthew Henry understood that, in Revelation 10:6, the Greek word *chronos* has the sense of "delay,"[28] and this is how many modern translations render the text, or they render the word "time" in such a way that clearly entails "delay"; see, for instance, the AMPC ("[He swore] that no more time would intervene"), the CEB ("The time is up"), and the HCSB ("There will no longer be an interval of time"). The Bible does not teach that, before creation there was no time and that after the present creation, time will

---

25. Haak (1918), *ad loc.*
26. Kuyper, *DD*, 3:102–103.
27. *CD*, 1/2:50; 3/2:624–25.
28. www.biblestudytools.com/commentaries/matthew-henry-complete/revelation/10.html.

cease; actually, it is uninterested in such philosophical speculations. It does not contain such expressions as "exchanging the temporal for the eternal," where "the eternal" would imply a timeless eternity.

The only verse that seems to come close to this view is 2 Corinthians 4:18, "[W]e look not to the things that are seen but to the things that are unseen. For the things that are seen are transient (Gk. *proskaira*), but the things that are unseen are eternal (Gk. *aiōnia*)." However, in this verse, the temporal is definitely not being placed opposite the atemporal, but what is of limited duration is being placed opposite what is everlasting (what is of infinite duration).[29] If we read the verse this way, the eternal is not timeless, but rather refers to that state in which time goes on forever.

3.4.2   A Different Time Scale?

The Bible does not teach that the person who dies will be redeemed from the temporal, and will enter timelessness. H. Bavinck said, "[S]ouls [of the dead] . . . must be somewhere and pass through a succession of moments in time,"[30] and "[T]he dead remain finite and limited and can exist in no way other than in space and time"; they are "not elevated above all structured time, that is, above all succession of moments, inasmuch as they have a past they remember, a present in which they live, and a future toward which they are moving."[31]

At the conclusion of several arguments, G. C. Berkouwer insisted:

> From all this it is obvious that any criticism of the doctrine of the intermediate state that presupposes an antithesis between time and eternity must be rejected. Even though these critics may dispute the rebuttal that their way of thinking tends toward pantheism and a notion of participation in the eternity of God, they can no longer speak

---

29. Cf. the KJV and others, which have "temporal," whereas the NKJV and others have "temporary" or "transient."
30. *RD*, 4:629.
31. *Ibid.*, 4:641–42.

of life and death in a meaningful biblical way.[32]

Other Reformed theologians have spoken in a similar way. For instance, Geerhardus Vos wrote:

> Paul nowhere affirms that to the life of man, after the close of this aeon, no more duration, no more divisibility in time-units shall exist. Life so conceived is plainly the prerogative by nature of the Creator: to eternalize the inhabitants of the coming aeon in this sense would be equivalent to deifying them, a thought whose place is in a pagan type of speculation but not within the range of biblical religion.[33]

This is an important point: the idea of a timeless eternity is thoroughly pagan, and by no means biblical.

Of course, the reverse occurs as well, namely, the idea that time as we know it will continue in the hereafter exactly as it did before, here on earth. H. Berkhof spoke of the "conviction that life on the other side of the death line proceeds similarly within time as it does here," and said of this:

> Existence on the other side is thus entirely conceived of as a continued existence in time. We who live on this side have no other conceptual categories. We should realize, however, that we are ignorant of what "time" means beyond the leap. Thus it makes no sense either to say that beyond the two boundaries [i.e., death and resurrection] we come into (the one) "eternity." For eternity as God's sphere is not intended for us. Time is an integral aspect of the good creation, and thus also of human existence.[34]

John Stafford Wright has suggested, too, that a time scale functions in the intermediate state that is different than in earthly life, even though we cannot imagine how this will be;[35] Geerhardus Vos

---

32. Berkouwer, (1972), 45.
33. Vos (1979), 290.
34. Berkhof (1986), 530; cf. 543–44.
35. See extensively, Stafford Wright (2007).

and William Hendriksen [have] agreed with this.[36] In my view, however, we are entering a domain here that confronts us with the peril of falling into speculations that we cannot justify biblically.

3.4.3 A Possible *Aevum?*

In scholasticism, Thomas Aquinas, in line with Boethius and Siger of Brabant, tried to develop the idea of a kind of "intermedium" (not to be confused with the intermediate state in the rest of this book!). This would be an intermedium between, on the one hand, the "eternity" of God as the "measure of permanent being" (Lat. *mensura esse permanentis*), in which there is no future but only an "eternal now" (Lat. *nunc aeternum*), and, on the other hand, "time" as the "measure of changeable being" (Lat. *mensura esse transmutabilis*), which is proper to creation, including human existence, and in which there is past and future.[37] Between these two, Thomas postulated "created eternity" (Lat. *aevum*, or *aeternitas creata*), as the measure of the *aeviterna*, which according to Thomas are both celestial bodies [!] and angels. These are the subjects whose natural being (Lat. *esse natural*) is not perishable (as in empirical creation), but they possess an "added transmutation" (Lat. *transmutatio adjuncta*), and according to the latter are measured by time. This *aevum* has in itself no future], which can, however, be connected with it.

In his early writing, H. Dooyweerd proposed something that Thomas had not considered. He attributed this *aevum* also to the human Ego, the human personality, as long as the latter is not viewed as a hypostasized rational-moral function complex, but rather as the transcendent, supra-functional Ego. This is what the Bible refers to as the heart, and sometimes as the spirit or the soul, in the emphatic meaning of these words[38] (see more extensively in chapter 8, espe-

---

36. Hendriksen (1959), 72–74.
37. See Ouweneel (1986), 277.
38. For references, see *ibid.*; cf. also Ouweneel (2008), 117–21.

cially for the distinction between the Ego and the modal functions).

It is this Ego that, in some way or another, continues to exist after physical death during the intermediate state. Thus, the proposal is that the immanent creation is characterized by time in the ordinary sense of the word, and that the intermediate state is characterized by the *aevum*, a distinct form of "time." In later years, Dooyeweerd no longer used the term *aevum*, in order to avoid scholastic associations that the term might evoke. However, he did maintain the underlying notion of a "created eternity," which he now hinted at with the term "supra-temporality." The disadvantage of this term is that it is also applicable to the "uncreated eternity." God is supra-temporal, too, yet in a way different from the way the human heart is supra-temporal. We may put it like this (avoiding any reference to time): God is uncreational-transcendent, whereas the human heart is creational-transcendent.

In summary, Dooyeweerd postulated three "spheres," one marked by ordinary time (the empirical world), one marked by the creational-supra-temporal, and one marked by the uncreational-supra-temporal. These three spheres are separated by sharp boundary lines. First, the *law* is the boundary line between God and creation, the latter containing both the empirical cosmos and the human heart, say, the *aevum*. Second, *time* is the boundary line between the transcendent (including the human heart) and the immanent (the empirical cosmos, including the human modal-functional corporeal mode of existence). As Dooyeweerd put it:

> Thus, in this life, the aevum state is always bound to time. A speculation on the aevum state during the separation of body and soul, or in the case of the angels, is philosophically unfruitful, a *meteorica et vacua speculatio*, as it may be put in Calvin's language, because we have to do here with "mysteries" that have not yet been revealed to us. In this life, all our pictures, concepts and ideas are bound within time, and also our self-consciousness remains oriented toward the time hori-

zon, even though it transcends time in the aevum.[39]

In the light of the second sentence in this quotation, the first sentence must not be taken to mean that in the intermediate state, the *aevum* state and the human Ego would no longer be bound to time, or would no longer actualize within time, as if between death and resurrection, or after the resurrection, human beings would no longer be "within time." At a later stage, Dooyeweerd said that the human Ego is not destroyed by *temporal* death but continues to exist after having put off the immanent-functional mode of existence.

If the heart (the Ego, the personality) is called supra-temporal, this definitely does not mean extra-temporal or a-temporal. If we say that, in the eternal state, humanity will transcend time as we know it in the present creation, this does not mean the same as humanity passing over to non-temporality. In order to avoid this misunderstanding, I have proposed to replace the term "supra-temporal" in the case of the human heart with the term "pleni-temporal" (from Lat. *plenus*, "full"). In contrast to the multiplicity and diversity of our temporal reality, we find the unity and fullness of the future eternal reality. At present, it is only the human Ego that shares pleni-temporality (transcendence); but one day humanity will share it with spirit, soul, and body.[40]

In summary, if this model has any usefulness, we may say with some prudence and caution:

(a) In the pre-death state, the human modal-functional corporeal mode of existence (in simple language, the body) is temporal, and the human heart, or Ego, or personality (not to be confused with the Platonic "soul," as we will see in chapter 8), is pleni-temporal.

(b) In the intermediate state, the "tent" of the body has been put off, and the Ego continues to exist as pleni-temporal.

(c) In the resurrection state, not only the Ego but also the resurrection body will share this pleni-temporal condition.

39. Dooyeweerd (1939), 5.
40. See Ouweneel (2008), 117–21.

In chapter 8, we will see that such a model must not be confused with Platonic, Aristotelian or Thomistic views of body and soul.

3.5 The Meanings of "Heaven"

3.5.1 Terminology

The usual Hebrew word for "heaven" is *shamayyim*, presumably related to a Semitic word for "rain" (cf. §3.5.2, point [3]). According to its form, the word seems to be neither a plural, nor a singular, but a dual, implying "two-ness." In *shamayyim* this notion is lost, but it does give rise to Bible translations that render the word as a plural: "heavens." Everyone can see this by comparing the various translations of Genesis 1:1: "heaven" or "heavens." The most obvious reason to use the plural is in the Hebrew expression *shamayyim hashammayyim* "heaven of heavens" (Deut. 10:14; 1 Kings 8:27; 2 Chron. 2:6; 6:18; Neh. 9:6; Ps. 148:4), although this expression contains the same word *shamayyim* twice. The construction is that of a common Semitic superlative, just as in "a servant of servants" (Heb. *ᶜebed ᶜabadim*, Gen. 9:25), which means "lowest servants" (as many translate the phrase). Or take the expression "holy of holies" (Heb. *qodesh haqqod'shim*, Exod. 26:34 NASB), which is usually rendered as "Most Holy Place." Similarly, *shamayyim hashammayyim* can best be rendered as "the highest heaven" (ESV).

In reference to Old Testament matters, the Greek New Testament sometimes adopts this remarkable construction; for instance, the Greek of Hebrews 9:3 has *Hagia Hagiōn*, literally "Holy of holies," that is, the Most Holy Place. We speak here of a Hebraism in the Greek text, adopted from the Septuagint. The latter often adopts the same Greek construction, for instance *ho ouranos tou ouranou*, "the heaven of heaven [not heavens]" (Deut. 10:14; 1 Kings 8:27; 2 Chron. 2:6; 6:18; Neh. 9:6), or the plural, *hoi ouranoi tōn ouranōn*, "the heavens of heavens" (Ps. 148:4). This is called a Hebraism because it is not a typical Greek mode of expression. The English translator must decide whether to adopt this Hebraistic way of speaking or choose an English mode of expression: the "Most Holy Place" (as the literal KJV renders it) or "highest heaven" (as it is in the ESV).

The usual Greek word for "heaven," *ouranos*, is also the name of the Greek god of the sky, *Ouranos*. Moreover, the name was [also] given to the planet Uranus.

Another way to express the notion of the "high" heavens is Greek *en [tois] hupsistois*, "in the highest [heavens]" (Matt. 21:9; Luke 2:14; 19:38; cf. Gk. *eis hupsos*, ascended "on high," i.e., to heaven, Eph. 4:8, a reference to Ps. 68:19).

3.5.2 Natural Aspects

One can distinguish at least sixteen biblical aspects of the term "heaven," including seven natural aspects (this section) and nine spiritual aspects (next section).

(1) The expression "heaven and earth" (or, "the heavens and the earth") is a description of the entire (empirical) created world (frequently, from Gen. 1:1; 2:1; 14:19, 22 to Rev. 14:7; 21:1). God is "the LORD, the God of heaven and God of the earth" (Gen. 24:3).

(2) Nearest to the earth are the "birds of the heavens" (Gen. 1:28; Ps. 8:8; Matt. 6:25; 8:20; 13:32), that is, the birds in the air, the birds at the sky (as various translations render the phrase).

(3) The cloudy sky (Gen. 49:25; Deut. 11:11; 28:23; Job 38:29), specifically: "*your* heaven," that is, Israel's heaven, the sky above the Promised Land, viewed as the source of fertility (Lev. 26:19; cf. Acts 14:17; James 5:18). Compare the "windows of heaven" in connection with rainfall (Gen. 7:11); also the "door of heaven" for manna (Ps. 78:23–24). When the clouds are absent, there is the blue sky (Exod. 24:10). Sometimes, "*your* heaven" is *God's* heaven (Lam. 3:66), that is again, the sky. Notice also the expression "the clouds of heaven" (Dan. 7:13; Matt. 24:30; 26:64).

(4) The starry sky (Gen. 15:5); compare the "expanse of the heavens" (Gen. 1:14); the "stars of heaven" (22:17; Isa. 13:10; Heb. 11:12; Rev. 12:4). In connection with the stars, note also the expres-

sion "the interpreters of the heavens, the observers of the stars" (Isa. 47:13 DARBY). Note as well the connection between heaven and the daily course of the sun (Josh. 10:13; Ps. 19:4–6). "Under (the) heaven" usually means "under the sky" (Job 28:24; 37:3; 41:11; Eccl. 1:13; 2:3; 3:1), or "(belonging to) the entire world" (Acts 2:5; 4:12; Col. 1:23).

(5) The part of the world "between earth and heaven" is "in the air" (2 Sam. 18:9; 1 Chron. 21:16; Ezek. 8:3; Zech. 5:9; cf. Eph. 2:2 with 6:12; the latter two passages have more to do with the spiritual aspects of heaven; see next section).

(6) The expression "to heaven" means primarily, upward, toward the sky (Exod. 9:8, 23; 1 Sam. 5:12; 1 Kings 8:54; 2 Kings 2:11; Job 2:12). But sometimes it means toward the dwelling place of God (perhaps Gen. 28:12; Matt. 14:19; Luke 18:13; John 17:1; Acts 7:55) (see next section).

(7) The "heaven of heavens" is the highest sphere of everything that is "above us" (Deut. 10:14; 1 Kings 8:27 [KJV]; Ps. 148:4 [KJV]), perhaps comparable with the "third heaven" (2 Cor. 12:2).

3.5.3 Spiritual Aspects

(1) Heaven as the dwelling place of God (1 Kings 8:30, 37, 43; Ps. 2:4; 11:4; 20:6; 115:3; 139:8; Isa. 14:13; Matt. 5:16, 45; 6:1, 9; 7:11, 21 etc.; cf. John 12:28; Rev. 4–5) (but also: God is greater than the highest heaven, 1 Kings 8:27); also compare the expression "the God of heaven" (many times, especially in the post-exilic books, and Rev. 11:13; 16:11).

(2) "The heavens" sometimes means the inhabitants of heaven, that is, the angels (Job 15:15; Ps. 89:5; cf. Matt. 18:10; 24:36; Luke 22:43; John 1:51; Gal. 1:8; Rev. 10:1; cf. 12:7–8); compare the "heavenly host" in Luke 2:13, 25 (the "host of heaven" in 1 Kings 22:19, an expression that usually refers to the celestial bodies). The "joy in heaven" is apparently that of the angels (Luke 15:17).

(3) The "kingdom of heaven" (many times in Matthew) is the kingdom of God, which descends from heaven (i.e., from God) on

earth, the Messianic kingdom in which "heaven" will rule (also cf. "heavenly kingdom" in 2 Tim. 4:18) (see extensively §1.4.1).

(4) Sometimes, "heaven" means "God," presumably often as a euphemism (Dan. 4:26; Mark 11:30; Luke 15:18, 21; John 3:27; cf. Matt. 5:34; James 5:12).

(5) Heaven is the place from which Jesus Christ came (John 3:13, 31; 6:38; 1 Cor. 15:47–49), and where he sat down at the right hand of God after his ascension (Mark 16:19; Eph. 1:20 [cf. 4:10 *above* all the heavens"]; Heb. 8:1; 1 Pet. 3:22; cf. Luke 24:51; Acts 1:11; 3:21; 7:56; Heb. 4:14 ["passed through the heavens"]; 7:26; 9:24). Because Christ is there, the Christian hope (Col. 1:5) and the Christian's inheritance (1 Pet. 1:4) are linked to heaven (cf. §12.2.2).

(6) On the Day of Pentecost, the Holy Spirit descended "from heaven" (1 Pet. 1:12; cf. Matt. 3:16; John 1:32).

(7) Christians have become citizens of "heaven," which will be fully enjoyed after their resurrection and transformation (Phil. 3:20–21). Believers share in "a heavenly calling" (Heb. 3:1); they are "enrolled in heaven" (12:23).

(8) It is from "heaven" that Christians await the Parousia (1 Thess. 1:10; 4:16; 2 Thess. 1:7; Rev. 19:11).

(9) Ultimately, there will be a new heaven and a new earth (Isa. 65:17; 66:22; 2 Pet. 3:13; Rev. 21:1).

Please notice that by necessity *none* of these nine aspects has anything to do with the intermediate state, although in the Christian tradition most of them have been linked to it. This book seeks to refute this linkage.

4

OLD TESTAMENT REFERENCES TO THE HEREAFTER

Man is going to his eternal home,
 and the mourners go about the streets—
before the silver cord is snapped,
 or the golden bowl is broken,
or the pitcher is shattered at the fountain,
 or the wheel broken at the cistern,
and the dust returns to the earth as it was,
 and the spirit returns to God who gave it.
Ecclesiastes 12:5–7

Laß dein' Engel mit mir fahren
Auf Elias Wagen rot
Und mein Seele wohl bewahren,
Wie Lazrum nach seinem Tod.
Laß sie ruhn in deinem Schoß,
Erfüll sie mit Freud und Trost,
Bis der Leib kommt aus der Erde
Und mit ihr vereinigt werde.

 Let your angels travel with me
 on Elijah's [fire-]red chariot
 and guard my soul well

like Lazarus after his death.
Let it [i.e. my soul] rest in your bosom,
fill it with joy and comfort,
until the body rises out of the ground
and is reunited with it.[1]

Es erhub sich ein Streit
[*There Arose a Great Strife*]
Bach cantata BWV 19
Unknown poet

4.1   Old Testament Hints
4.1.1   The Historical Books

As we saw, many Christians put much more emphasis on what will happen to them after they die than on what will happen at the Parousia and the resurrection. No wonder, then, that when one begins to believe in a blessed hereafter, one will soon imagine that this notion is present in passages that do not speak of it at all. This process begins with the Old Testament, which in reality has almost nothing to tell us about the intermediate state.

Let me give seven well-known examples in this and the next section.[2]

(1) The first one is *Genesis 5:24* about Enoch, "God took him." The AMP renders it this way: "God took him [away to be home with Him]." However, the text says only that "God took him" (Heb. *l-q-ch*),[3] from which no possible conclusions about the hereafter can

---

1. Notice the interesting coupling of ideas: when the believers die, the angels take their souls, as they did with Lazarus (whose "soul" is not mentioned at all in Luke 16!), and they do so on Elijah's red (fiery) chariot (a mistaken juxtaposition, because Elijah did not die at all). The body goes to the grave, and in the resurrection, body and soul are reunited.

2. Bavinck, *RD*, 4:602, mentioned also Job 14:13–15, 16:16–21, 19:25–27 (resurrection!), Ps. 16:9–11, and 139:18, but I think these are less convincing than the passages discussed in the text.

3. *Contra* Van Genderen and Velema (2008), 31, who refer to this text and 2 Kings 2:9, "which deal with the *taking up* of Enoch and Elijah" (italics

be drawn. The AMP and many other translations have read the traditional view into the Bible text. Hebrews 11:5 also says "took him"
(NKJV; Gk. *metatithēmi* (literally, "to take to somewhere else"), but
the KJV quite misleadingly rendered the phrase as "translated him."[4]
Here, erroneous prejudices governed the rendering of the text. In
any case, Enoch's case is special because the latter verse tells us that
he did not die;[5] so it is hard to see the relevance of his story for
Christians who do die. There is no question here of an "ascending
to heaven," as in the case of Elijah (2 Kings 2:11, Heb. *wayyaʿal*
[. . .] *hasshamayyim*).

(2) Indeed, *2 Kings 2:1–11* does not help us either, for Elijah
also was taken away without dying. Thus, the text does not help
us understand what happens to deceased believers. However, it is
clear that the relevance of this text surpasses that of the text about
Enoch in two respects. First, we do not find the verb "to take away"
here, but "to take *up*" (Heb. *ʿ-l-h*). Second, the text uses the expression "to heaven." It is easy to understand here that Elijah went to
heaven in the sense of some blessed abode for the departed. However, going up "to heaven" ordinarily means nothing more than going up toward the sky, as is the case so often in the Old Testament.[6]
See, for instance, Joshua 8:20, "the smoke of the city went up [same
Heb. verb] to heaven" (cf. Judges 20:40).

In the Old Testament, "heaven" is *never* the abode of believers
who have passed away. Rather, as in Genesis 1:1 and 8, "heaven,"
together with the earth, is the totality of all empirical creation.[7]
"Heaven" can also be God's abode,[8] and for Old Testament believers there was presumably little difference between the two mean-

---

added).

4. These are examples of *eisegesis*: reading into the text things foreign to Scripture, which are found only in certain traditions.

5. *Contra* the rabbis; see Cohen (1983), 24.

6. Cf. Gen. 1:1, 8; 28:12; Exod. 9:22–23; 10:21–22; Deut. 4:19; and 32:40.

7. Cf. extensively, Schilder (1935), 114–16.

8. See, e.g., 1 Kings 8:30; Job 22:12; Ps. 115:3, 16; 123:1; and Dan. 2:28.

ings (although Solomon said, "Behold, heaven and the heaven of heavens cannot contain You." [1 Kings 8:27 NKJV]). But apart from all this, Elijah's being taken away without dying sheds very little light on what happens to believers when they undergo physical death.

(3) In *Genesis 49:18*, Jacob says, "I wait for your salvation, O LORD." In an older Dutch translation, the text was even more suggestive: "I wait for your *bliss.*" People concluded from this that the elderly Jacob is here speaking on his deathbed of the heavenly "salvation" or "bliss." Matthew Henry saw this "salvation" as referring first to the coming of Christ, the promised seed (cf. Shiloh in v. 10 in many translations), and second:

> He declared plainly that he sought heaven, the better country, Heb 11:13-14. Now he is going to enjoy the salvation, he comforts himself that he had waited for the salvation. Christ, as our way to heaven, is to be waited on; and heaven, as our rest in Christ, is to be waited for. It is the comfort of a dying saint thus to have waited for the salvation of the Lord; for then he shall have what he has been waiting for.[9]

In modern times, this interpretation resurfaces in that of V. P. Hamilton: Jacob expects "that he shall one day be delivered by his God and experience eternal salvation."[10]

Yet, from the context it is clear what Jacob meant in saying that he is looking forward to "salvation" by the Lord. G. C. Aalders understood this to refer to the "expectation that Jacob cherishes regarding God's help in the future troubles of Dan," and more broadly, of all his sons.[11] Indeed, verses 16–17 say: "Dan shall judge his people as one of the tribes of Israel. Dan shall be a serpent in the way, a viper by the path, that bites the horse's heels so that his

---

9. www.ccel.org/ccel/henry/mhc1.Gen.l.html. John Wesley strongly endorses these words (wes.biblecommenter.com/genesis/49.htm).
10. Hamilton (1995), 671.
11. Aalders (1936), 214. Rashi and Nachmanides thought specifically of the distress of Samson the Danite (Cohen [1983], 307).

rider falls backward." We can imagine how Jacob, while thinking of this future, prayed that his descendants might be rescued from all such perils. This is also the sense given by the Geneva Study Bible: "Seeing the miseries that his posterity would fall into, he [i.e. Jacob] bursts out in prayer to God to remedy it."[12] According to John Sailhamer, Jacob's words indicate that "[i]n the individual and future destiny of the sons is embodied the hope of all Israel."[13] Regardless of our final decision here, Jacob's words have nothing to do with his supposed expectation of "going to heaven."

(4) In *Numbers 23:10*, Balaam says, "Let me die the death of the upright, and let my end be like his!" (cf. ERV: ". . . Let my life end as happy as theirs!"). Some argue that Balaam must have had some idea of the happy ending of the lives of the righteous.[14] Yet, the verse gives little basis for such an interpretation; one could just as well suppose that Balaam desires his own offspring to be a people of righteous ones as well.[15] A. Noordtzij made the emphatic comment that verse 10b "does not, as was assumed in the past, reflect Israel's belief in a life beyond the grave, surrounded by divine blessing."[16]

4.1.2 The Poetic Books

(5) *Psalm 17:15:* "I shall behold your face in righteousness; when I awake, I shall be satisfied with your likeness." Several writers have linked this with 1 Corinthians 15:49, and therefore interpret the verse as referring to the resurrection.[17] L. Berkhof thought here of the intermediate state as well,[18] even though it is not clear in what sense he meant this. It seems, however, that Psalm 17 is an ordinary

---

12. https://biblehub.com/commentaries/genesis/49-18.htm.
13. Sailhamer (1990), 278.
14. See, e.g., Nachmanides in Cohen (1983), 922; Berkhof (1981), 757; Allen (1990), 898.
15. See Ashley (1993), 472.
16. Noordtzij (1983), 218.
17. Noordtzij (1934), 60; Dahood (1966), 1:93, 99; Van Gemeren (1991), 167.
18. Berkhof (1981), 757.

evening psalm, and that David speaks of a natural awakening in the morning. This was the understanding of J. Ridderbos, who defended a deeper meaning as well: David "longs in effect for nothing less than eternal salvation in the fellowship with his God."[19] But even on this understanding, one should think of the resurrection rather than of the intermediate state, the latter being a kind of sleep and the former a kind of awakening from sleep (cf. §5.5). The deeper sense could also be the mystical awareness of, or watchfulness regarding, the Divine Presence (cf. Num. 12:6–8).[20]

(6) *Psalm 49:15:* "But God will ransom my soul from the power of Sheol, for he will receive me." Again, this has often been interpreted as someone being received into "heaven."[21] Compare other renderings: "he will take me to himself" (EHV). The VOICE has: "He will fetch me *and take me into His eternal house.*" Others think of an earthly deliverance from the peril of death; [so thus the GNT ("he will save me from the power of death") and the NLT ("He will snatch me from the power of the grave")]. The destiny of the wicked is Sheol (vv. 11, 14, 19), which means basically the grave, but the righteous are confident that they will be kept from it.[22] Nowhere in Psalm 49 is there any explicit reference to a hereafter.

(7) *Proverbs 14:32:* "The wicked is overthrown through his evildoing, but the righteous finds refuge in his death." A. Ross believed this, though the book of Proverbs nowhere expresses a hope for an afterlife,[23] yet this verse is a "shadowy forerunner" of this truth.[24] The great Jewish rabbi Shlomo Yitzchaki ("Rashi") said about this verse, "When he [i.e., the righteous one] will die, he is confident that he will come to the Garden of Eden," that is, to paradise (see

---

19. Ridderbos (1955), 141.
20. Cohen (1985), 42.
21. Thus Rashi; see Cohen (1985), 154; see references in Ridderbos (1958), 71–72; also see Van Genderen and Velema (2008), 831.
22. So Cohen (1985), 154.
23. However, see Gispen (1952), 258.
24. Ross (1991), 991.

§4.4.4).[25] However, Abraham Ibn Ezra and other Jewish expositors have a simpler explanation: the righteous trust God so strongly that they do not give up hope, even when their misery is so great that they believe they are on the precipice of death.[26]

4.2   Special Proof Texts

4.2.1   Ecclesiastes 12:5–7

Ecclesiastes 12:5–7 says, "[M]an is going to his eternal home . . . . [T]he dust [of his body] returns to the earth as it was, and the spirit [Heb. *ruach*] returns to God who gave it." G. C. Aalders believed that especially because of verse 7, the "eternal house" referred not to "the grave or the Sheol but the eternal destiny of man *after* death."[27] However, verse 7 says nothing more than that the "life-breath" goes back to God who gave it (CEB, GW, GNT; cf. Gen. 2:7, where God breathes his own "breath" (Heb. *ruach*) into Adam's body). Here we must make an all-important comparison with Ecclesiastes 3, where the writer underscores that humans and animals have the same breath (Heb. *ruach*): "[W]hat happens to the children of man and what happens to the beasts is the same; as one dies, so dies the other. They all have the same breath [Heb. *ruach*], and man has no advantage over the beasts, for all is vanity. All go to one place. All are from the dust, and to dust all return" (vv. 19–20).

This comparison suggests, as several translations have it, that we must read the term "grave" in chapter 12:5: "The mourners will gather in the streets as they carry your body to the grave" (ERV; cf. NIRV, NLT). This is also the view of J. S. Wright: the "eternal home" is the inevitable end, the long-lasting house of Sheol, dedicated by the laments of the professional mourners.[28] This is also the view of T. Longman; after the description of old age in 12:1–5b, verse

---

25. Quoted in Waltke (2004), 608.
26. Cohen and Rosenberg (1985), 93.
27. Aalders (1948), 248.
28. Wright (1991), 1194.

5c forms the climax of the passage by speaking of death.[29] In the end, every person goes to their "eternal home," that is, the grave. It is "eternal" because either in Ecclesiastes the resurrection is not in view, or it simply means "very long." This was the view of K. J. Popma as well: "For the person goes to his eternal house, that is, the realm of the dead [Hades], where he must remain many days, cf. the many days of darkness in 11:8."[30] As F. van Deursen observes: "Every person is en route to the grave, that 'eternal house,' in which we will possibly have to dwell for a long time (in Scripture, eternal often means very long)."[31]

Ecclesiastes 3:19–20 and 12:5–7 clearly show that the Platonic notion of an immortal soul, returning to dwell with the Creator after the time of death, is far from the writer's mind. The "eternal home" is nothing more than Sheol, a term which is sometimes rendered in the Old Testament as Hades (the "realm of the dead," or "of death"[32]), but can be rendered almost always as "grave" (see §4.4.2 for possible exceptions). The reason why the resurrection lies outside the writer's (self-chosen) scope is that, for most of the book, he has chosen to look no further than at what is "under the sun," that is, what belongs to his empirical world.

Aalders unfortunately viewed the entire passage (Eccl. 12:5–7) from the viewpoint of two erroneous Greek scholastic models: the body-soul dichotomy and the notion of the immortality of the soul (see more extensively in chapter 8):

> Qohelet [i.e., Ecclesiastes] ties in with Gen. 2:7; it depicts the human being as consisting of two constitutive parts [!]: *afar* ["dust"], taken

---

29. Longman (1998), 272.
30. Popma (1961), 223.
31. Van Deursen (1988), 162.
32. Certainly not "hell," as the KJV and others render it. The word "hell" ought to be the rendering only of the Greek word *gehenna*, a word that does not appear in the Septuagint.

from *ha-ērets* ["the earth"[33]], and *ruach* ["spirit"], given by God. In death, these two constitutive parts are separated, and each now has its own destiny: the material part, the body, returns to the earth from which it has been taken, and the spiritual part goes to God who has given it. . . . One sees how one must wriggle and squirm to deny to Qohelet belief in the immortality of the soul. . . . At any rate, what is meant is that there is an immaterial constitutive part [!] of the human being that does not return to the earth but, apart from and independent of the dust, continues to exist in the hand of God.[34]

This is, unfortunately, the traditional view. The Greek scholastic notion of the immortal soul has captivated the mind of many theologians so strongly that they read it into the Bible at many places in many passages, and cannot understand why others cannot see it. These others are the ones "twisting and turning to deny to Qohelet the faith in the immortality of the soul." In reality, these others, after having utterly rejected the notion of the immortal soul, find no mention of immortality in Ecclesiastes: for the writer, who has chosen to look no further than at what is "under the sun," death is the end.

J. S. Wright correctly pointed out, though, that near the end of the book, there is also this statement: "Walk in the ways of your heart and the sight of your eyes. But know that for all these things God will bring you into judgment" (11:9).[35] Here, Solomon seems to be finally giving up his self-chosen narrow focus of attention: he is beginning to look beyond death, and sees that there is such a thing as God's judgment. However, this occurs not in the intermediate state but in the resurrection state (cf. Rev. 20:11–15), although Solomon himself does not tell us explicitly what he means by God's judgment.

4.2.2 Psalm 73:24

Psalm 73:24 says, "You guide me with your counsel, and after-

---

33. This is a small mistake; Aalders meant *ha'adamah*, "the ground."
34. Aalders (1948), 250–51.
35. Wright (1991), 1194.

ward you will receive me to glory." When we translate the text this way, it is no wonder that thousands of people have thought of the heavenly glory. This is how the text was read by, for instance, by A. Noordtzij ("a life of eternal fellowship"), W. Van Gemeren, W. Hendriksen, and J. van Genderen.[36] Gerhard von Rad wrote: "One could say that here the Old Testament faith in the hereafter finds its purest form."[37] Compare the TLB: ". . . afterwards receive me into the glories of heaven!" (cf. NIRV).

The Annotations to the Dutch States Translation referred here to 1 Timothy 3:16, which states that Christ was "taken up in glory"—but this was after his resurrection, not after his death. The Annotations referred also to 1 Thessalonians 4:17, "caught up together with them in the clouds to meet the Lord in the air," which is a reference to the Parousia (vv. 15–16). The writers of the Annotations apparently were not thinking only of death; here again, death and resurrection seem to merge. The same occurred with Matthew Henry:

> All who commit themselves to God . . . shall be received to his glory in another world; the believing hopes and prospects of which will reconcile us to all dark providences. . . . Heaven itself could not make us happy without the presence and love of our God. . . . Blessed Lord, who hast so graciously promised to become our portion in the next world, prevent us from choosing any other in this.[38]

Joseph Benson wrote along similar lines:

> As all those who commit themselves to God's conduct shall be guided by his counsel, so all those who are so guided in this world shall be received to his glory in another world. If . . . his glory [is] the end of all our actions, he will afterward, when our state of trial and preparation

---

36. Noordtzij (1935), 17; Hendriksen (1959), 50–51; Van Gemeren (1991), 482; Van Genderen and Velema (2008), 831.

37. *TDNT* 2:848.

38. www.ccel.org/ccel/henry/mhc3.Ps.lxxiv.html.

is over, receive us to his kingdom and glory.[39]

The key issue here involves what is meant by Henry's "next world" and Benson's "kingdom." It seems to me that both include at least the resurrection state.

The same merging of death and resurrection, whereby the believer appears to enter the Messianic kingdom immediately on dying, seems to occur here and there in the New Testament as well: "For in this way there will be richly provided for you an entrance into the eternal kingdom of our Lord and Savior Jesus Christ" (2 Pet. 1:11). After the earthly life (cf. vv. 5–10), there is an entering into the "eternal kingdom"—which nonetheless arrives only at the Parousia. This led John Gill to say:

> . . . [received] into a glorious place, a house not made with hands, a city whose builder and maker is God, into a kingdom and glory, or a glorious kingdom; and into glorious company, the company of Father, Son, and Spirit, angels and glorified saints, where glorious things will be seen, and a glory enjoyed both in body and soul to all eternity.[40]

Soul *and* body—so Gill was apparently thinking instead of the resurrection state.

Gill hinted at another, more literal translation of Psalm 73:24b; put in my own words, "after [the] glory [Heb. *achar kavod*] you will receive me." Gill, as well as the Targum he referred to, took this to mean: "[A]fter all the glory and honour thou hast bestowed upon me here, thou wilt take me to thyself in heaven," namely, either in heaven or in the Messianic kingdom. The idea that the verse refers to the glory that is granted to the believer in this life is found in some renderings: "with glory thou tookest me up" (WYC); "after honour dost receive me" (YLT). Similarly, J. Ridderbos correctly wondered whether the Hebrew word *kavod* "can be a straightfor-

---

39. *Ibid.*
40. *Ibid.*

ward reference to the heavenly glory,"[41] that is, the supposed "glory" of the intermediate state.

Others understand the expression "after the glory" to refer to the Parousia and the establishment of the Messianic kingdom: "after the glory you will receive," namely, in this kingdom. The text thus taken in this way could be parallel to Zechariah 2:8 (DRA), "After the glory [Heb. *achar kavod*] he hath sent me to the nations that have robbed you."[42] But this seems rather far-fetched; a rendering like "After he has honored me" (EXB; NCV) seems preferable.

At any rate, Psalm 73:24 does *not* say, "take me *up*" (*contra* CSB, HCSB), but rather "take away" (through death; cf. Isa. 53:8) *or* "receive," namely, in the glory of the coming Messianic kingdom (cf. 1 Pet. 5:10, "God . . . has called you to his eternal glory in Christ"). Ridderbos presumed that ". . . even though we do not read of 'taking up' or 'taking to himself,' the poet may still have thought that if God takes him away, he is in safe hands.; . . . ."[43] This we may conclude from the text with certainty. But everything beyond this, such as a "taking up into heaven," goes beyond the text.

4.2.3 "With His Fathers"

We conclude, then, that no passage indicates with certainty that Old Testament believers were aware of a "heavenly" bliss between death and resurrection, or more broadly, were aware of conscious existence in the intermediate state. Some Old Testament passages that have been put forward to prove the opposite will be dealt with in the remainder of this chapter.

One such argument that people employ entails the Old Testament description of the death of some believers as being "gathered to their fathers,"[44] or "sleeping with their fathers."[45] Of Abraham

---

41. Ridderbos (1958), 247; Cohen (1985), 235, calls this "improbable."
42. *SYN, ad loc.*
43. Ridderbos (1958), 248.
44. Gen. 49:20; Judg. 2:10; 2 Kings 22:20; 2 Chron. 34:28.
45. 1 Kings 1:21; 2:10; 11:21, 43; many times in the books of Kings and Chronicles

we read, "Abraham breathed his last and died in a good old age, an old man and full of years, and was gathered to his people" (Gen. 25:8; cf. Isaac in 35:29, and Moses in Deut. 32:50). The word rendered "people" is literally "peoples" or "nations" (Heb. ʿammim), here in the sense of "members of the same nation" or "family members (who had already passed away)." Sometimes the singular is used (Heb. ʿam), in the sense of the totality of the ancestors. Thus, Jacob tells his sons: "I am to be gathered to my people [Heb. ʿam]; bury me with my fathers in the cave that is in the field of Ephron the Hittite" (Gen. 49:29).

What exactly is meant here? The second part of Genesis 49:29 suggests that Jacob was not necessarily thinking of a hereafter where he would meet his forefathers. He seems to be thinking instead of the cave of Machpelah, where his grandparents (Abraham and Sarah) and parents (Isaac and Rebekah) lay buried.[46] Therefore, he says in Genesis 47:30, "[L]et me lie with my fathers. Carry me [therefore] out of Egypt and bury me in their burying place." Notice that here we find no idea of "heaven," nor any form of dualism: *I* wish to be with my fathers, *I* wish to be buried, not "my soul" or "spirit."

To King Josiah God sent this message: "Therefore, behold, I will gather you to your fathers, and you shall be gathered to your grave[47] in peace, and your eyes shall not see all the disaster that I will bring upon this place" (2 Kings 22:20; 2 Chron. 34:28). This may be compared with what God said to Moses: "Behold, you are about to lie down with your fathers" (Deut. 31:16), and to David: "When your days are fulfilled and you lie down with your fathers. . . ."[48] Of many kings after David it was said (in 1 and 2 Kings and in 2 Chronicles) that they "slept with their fathers." This does not necessarily imply that the persons involved met their fathers in the

---

46. Gen. 23:9, 17, 19; 25:9; cf. 50:13.
47. Here, the word "grave" renders the Heb. *q'borah*, not *sh'ol* (Sheol; see §4.3).
48. Cf. 1 Kings 1:21; 2:10; 11:21.

hereafter. The bodies of these kings were laid to rest in the places where their fathers had also been buried.

Patterson and Austel presumed that the expression "being gathered to one's fathers" contains a hidden clue of an Old Testament hope for an afterlife.[49] To this end, they used as evidence the well-known series of Old Testament passages that have been discussed. I think R. Youngblood was closer to the truth in thinking of multiple burials in large family graves.[50]

Notice how King Hezekiah responded to the message that he was going to die. To him, this did not mean going to heaven to see the LORD, but the very opposite: he would go to the land of the dead, where it is not even possible to see the Lord, even for a believer: "I said, I shall *not* see the LORD, the LORD in the land of the living" (Isa. 38:11). That is, if he had died, he would not have expected to see the LORD; on the contrary, now that he was healed, he was able again to see the LORD, not in the land of death but in the land of living! Consider how contrary this is to what traditional Christians read into the Old Testament; the Bible teaches us that believers see the Lord in the "land of living," *not* in the land of the dead. This will become even clearer in the next sections.

4.3   Sheol and Hades

4.3.1   Grave or Realm of the Dead?

For any investigation of the intermediate state, a study of the Hebrew word Sheol (*sh'ōl*) is indispensable.[51] The difficulty of such an examination surfaces immediately in the various Bible translations. The KJV renders the word either as "hell" (e.g., 2 Sam. 22:6; Ps. 16:10), "grave" (e.g., Gen. 37:35; Job 7:9), or "pit" (e.g., Num. 16:30, 33). Modern translations usually provide renderings like "nether world," the "world of the dead," the "place of death," or simply

---

49. Patterson and Austel (1988), 284.
50. Youngblood (1992), 828, 890.
51. See *TDNT* 1:146–49; *DNTT* 2:205–210; *TWOT* 2:892–93; *DOTT* 4:6–7; see also extensively, Salmond (2006).

the "grave." The Septuagint usually chose the Greek word *Hades* ("realm of the dead," "nether world"), which is also the word found in the New Testament quotation of Psalm 16:10 in Acts 2:27.

The error of translating *Sheol* or *Hades* as "hell" comes to light in Revelation 20:14, where the KJV says, "And death and hell were cast into the lake of fire"—whereas "hell and "lake of fire" are the very same thing (see §11.3.2). Therefore, Joachim Jeremias correctly argued for making a "sharp distinction between *hades* and *gehenna*": the realm of the dead (one word in Dutch: *dodenrijk*; cf. German: *Totenreich*) is the place where the disembodied wicked exist between death and resurrection, whereas hell is the place where the wicked will dwell forever *after* being raised, that is, *with* their bodies (Matt. 10:28).[52]

In the Old Testament presentation, *Sheol* or *Hades* is a dark place (Job 10:21–22), a closed place with barred gates,[53] where all people go at their death (Job 30:23; Ps. 89:48). People "go down" into it,[54] and those leaving this place "come up" from it.[55] Sometimes the text even speaks of the "depths of Sheol" (Deut. 32:22; Ps. 86:13). Of course, we should not assign any topographical significance to this; the words "above" and "below" here have "only an ethical meaning,"[56] or perhaps better stated, only a metaphorical meaning.

4.3.2 Multidimensionality?

Herman Bavinck insisted that "[a]ll fixation of the place of punishment for the dead—in the earth, under the earth, in the sea, in the sun, in the air, or on one of the planets—is mere conjecture."[57] One might better argue that such positionings are simply wrong.[58] Although it is equally speculative, I prefer the suggestion that the

---

52. *TDNT* 1:148; *contra* Greijdanus (1941), 86.
53. Job 17:16; Isa. 38:10; Matt. 16:18; cf. Job 38:17; Ps. 9:13; 107:18.
54. Gen. 37:35; Num. 16:30; Ps. 55:15.
55. Ps. 30:3; cf. 1 Sam. 28:14.
56. *RD*, 4:629.
57. *Ibid.*
58. *Contra* Duffield and Van Cleave (1996), 552, who suggested that Hades is in the heart of the earth.

deceased dwell in a fourth or even higher dimension.[59] That multi-dimensional world is as close to our world as the third dimension is to a two-dimensional flatlander, but inaccessible, unless one is allowed by God to peer into it. This is the miracle experienced by Elisha's servant, when God, at Elisha's intercession, "opened the eyes of the young man, and he saw, and behold, the mountain was full of horses and chariots of fire all around Elisha" (2 Kings 6:17). For some prophets, it was apparently quite common to peer into this other-dimensional world; they were called "seers."[60]

Perhaps this was similar to the Apostle Paul's experience when he ("whether in the body or out of the body I do not know, God knows") "was caught up to the third heaven" and "into paradise," and "heard things that cannot be told, which man may not utter" (2 Cor. 12:2–4; see §5.3). This being "caught up" is not in a purely cosmographical sense, for in that case, even if he moved with the speed of light, he would not have reached the edge of the universe even by today. Rather, I understand this as a being "caught up" from the three-dimensional world to a multidimensional one, which in these higher dimensions is very nearby, yet unattainable for us. In the same sense, we understand how David can say to God: "You hem me in, behind and before," such that, whether he ascended to heaven, or went down into Sheol, he would find God everywhere (Ps. 139:1–12). And of course, the disciples saw Jesus being "carried up into heaven" in the same way (Luke 24:51), "and a cloud took him out of their sight" (Acts 1:9).

We can imagine how, at death, a person passes the boundary of their three-dimensional world. We may also deduce from this that the resurrection body is not confined to our three dimensions, but exists in more dimensions. This is why, after his resurrection, Christ could appear in the midst of his disciples, although all the doors were closed (John 20:19). It does not say that the risen Jesus

---

59. See extensively, Ouweneel (1978), 101–109.
60. 1 Sam. 9:9, 11, 18–19; 2 Sam. 24:11; 2 Kings 17:13.

in some way penetrated through the doors or the walls. If his new body existed in more dimensions, such penetration would not have been necessary, for he could have entered the room from a higher dimension. Compare how a person can step from the third dimension into a (two-dimensional) square, without having to penetrate the lines that encompass this square. Given this perspective, the hereafter is also very nearby, and yet, for humans in their present bodies, unattainable because they are limited to their three-dimensional world.

In the light of Acts 8:39–40, where Philip is suddenly moved to another place, and 2 Corinthians 12:1–4, where Paul is caught up to another world, we might suggest that, also in cases of near-death experiences and astral projection—insofar as these phenomena are genuine—we are dealing with a temporary movement beyond the boundary of three-dimensionality.

4.3.3   One Place for the Wicked and the Righteous?

In later Jewish literature, the idea was developed that only the wicked are in Sheol/Hades. This is also the way Jesus spoke of it: poor Lazarus went to "Abraham's bosom," whereas the rich man went to Hades (Luke 16:22–23; cf. v. 26), which is a "place of torment" (v. 28). Thus, there seems to be a certain ambiguity in the use of the term Sheol/Hades. On the one hand, in the Old Testament, Sheol in the sense of "grave" is where *all* dead people go, without any distinction. Therefore, it can be said of Jesus that God did not leave him in Sheol/Hades, that is, in the grave (Acts 2:27). On the other hand, Sheol/Hades in the sense of the "hereafter" is where only wicked people are found, and this only until the day of the resurrection (Rev. 20:13).[61] Actually, this ambiguity largely disappears if we assume that, at least in the Old Testament, Sheol means little more than "grave."[62] When people die, they *all* without distinction enter

---

61. *Contra* Bavinck, *RD*, 4:604, who thought that in the New Testament, deceased believers are also in Hades.
62. So *TWOT* 2:892–93; cf. Berkhof (1981), 759–60.

the grave (leaving aside those who have been burned or devoured, where there is nothing to be buried).

In only a few Old Testament passages does Sheol mean more than "grave." Here, Sheol, just like Hades in the New Testament, is the place where the wicked continue to exist after death; it is the "prison" in 1 Peter 3:19 ("the spirits in prison"; see §6.1.2). See, for instance, Psalm 9:18, "The wicked shall return to Sheol"; 55:15, "Let death steal over them [i.e., the wicked]; let them go down to Sheol alive"; Proverbs 15:24, "The path of life leads upward for the prudent, that he may turn away from Sheol beneath" (see the next section for more examples).

Herman Bavinck believed that Sheol does not always mean "grave" because dead persons who have not been buried are also said to be in Sheol.[63] The only passage he mentioned that might be taken this way is Genesis 37:33 and 35, where Jacob believes that his son Joseph was devoured by a beast, and yet he believed that Joseph was in Sheol. Less convincing is the other passage referred to by Bavinck concerning Korah and his men (Num. 16:32–33): "[T]he earth opened its mouth and swallowed them up, with their households and all the people who belonged to Korah and all their goods. So they and all that belonged to them went down alive into Sheol, and the earth closed over them." But does this prove that Sheol cannot be a "grave" here? What was the crack in the earth other than a grave?

It is important to notice how often in biblical poetry Sheol is parallel to "pit" or "corruption" (or "destruction," or "Abaddon"[64]).[65] The meaning of "grave" is obvious especially where people are said to descend to Sheol with their "gray hairs,"[66] or where

---

63. *RD*, 4:599.
64. Abaddon is both a place of destruction, the equivalent of Hades, and the angelic prince of this place (Rev. 9:11).
65. Job 26:6; Ps. 16:10; 30:4; Prov. 1:12; 15:11; 27:20; Isa. 14:15; 38:18; Ezek. 31:16; cf. Hos. 13:14.
66. Gen. 42:38; 44:29, 31; 1 Kings 2:6, 9.

we hear of worms and maggots in Sheol (Isa. 14:11). Isaiah 66:24 speaks of "the dead bodies of the men who have rebelled against me. For their worm shall not die, their fire shall not be quenched, and they shall be an abhorrence to all flesh." Actually, there is a certain ambiguity in this verse: the worm refers to the corruption of the body, but the fire presumably to the torments of the spirit, as in Deuteronomy 32:11, "For a fire is kindled by my anger, and it burns to the depths of Sheol."

Other passages point to the corruption of the body in Sheol:

> If I hope for Sheol as my house, if I make my bed in darkness, if I say to the pit, "You are my father," and to the worm, "My mother," or "My sister," where then is my hope? Who will see my hope? Will it go down to the bars of Sheol? Shall we descend together into the dust? (Job 17:13–16).

Thus, Sheol is "in the dust," the earth; here again, the notion of the grave is prominent. Even where Hades is located in the deep (Matt. 11:23), or in the heart of the earth (12:40), it is primarily the grave to which a text is referring (cf. "descended into the lower parts of the earth," Eph. 4:9 [ESV note], which very probably also refers to the grave, here the grave of Christ). Psalm 49:14 says that the (physical) form of the wicked shall be consumed in Sheol, that is, by worms in the grave. Psalm 141:7 speaks of "bones scattered at the mouth of Sheol."

4.4 Special Aspects
4.4.1 Consciousness in Sheol?

In light of the previous section, if Sheol is primarily the grave, we should expect no Old Testament evidence for consciousness in Sheol. Think of two fathers in the Bible speaking of their deceased sons. Jacob says, "I shall go down to Sheol to my son, mourning" (Gen. 37:35). And David says, "I shall go to him, but he will not return to me" (2 Sam. 12:23). Such statements need not mean anything more than that these fathers expect that they themselves one day will descend to the realm of the dead, and thus be united with their sons in death. It does not prove at all that Jacob and David expected to commune with their sons in Sheol. Such an idea was unknown in the Old Testament.

The only Old Testament indication of a certain form of consciousness in Sheol is found in Isaiah 14 and Ezekiel 31–32. In the former passage it was said of the dead king of Babylon:

> Sheol beneath is stirred up to meet you when you come; it rouses the shades to greet you, all who were leaders of the earth; it raises from their thrones all who were kings of the nations. All of them will answer and say to you: "You too have become as weak as we! You have become like us! Your pomp is brought down to Sheol, the sound of your harps; maggots are laid as a bed beneath you, and worms are your covers. . . . [Y]ou are brought down to Sheol, to the far reaches of the pit" (vv. 9–11, 15).

Here, Sheol is depicted as populated with "shades" (see §3.2.1), shadowlike figures, ghosts, vague reflections of people that were once alive.[67] They are sitting on thrones, and rise in order to mockingly greet the "shade" of the king of Babylon who is entering their place and joining them. However, even here the meaning of "grave" is not far removed: notice the worms, the maggots, and the pit.

Something similar is found with regard to the Pharaoh of Egypt (according to some, the king of Assyria was meant here): "I cast it [i.e., the cedar, which is Egypt/Assyria] down to Sheol with those who go down to the pit [Heb. *bôr*]. And all the trees of Eden [i.e., the other sovereigns of those days] . . . were comforted in the world below [Heb. *ērets tachtit*, literally, the "land down there"[68]]." This passage is even vaguer than Isaiah 14; only the word "comforted" suggests something more than just lying in a grave.

---

67. Oswalt (1986), 318.
68. See also Ezek. 31:14, 18; 32:18, 24 (plur.).

In Ezekiel 32:18–21 we find something similar to Isaiah 14: let the "multitude of Egypt" go down "to the world below, to those who have gone down to the pit. . . . The mighty chiefs shall speak of them [i.e., the leadership of Egypt] with their helpers, out of the midst of Sheol: 'They have come down, they lie still, the uncircumcised, slain by the sword.'" Here again, a wicked king, entering Sheol as a dead person, seemed to be mocked by those who already dwell there. Again, the central theme is this mocking, which was due to the miserable destiny of these kings who were once so powerful but now share the destiny of all the dead.

As far as I am aware, these rather vague hints in Isaiah 14 and Ezekiel 31–32, which are still close to the meaning of "grave," are all we have. For the rest, we do not find in the Old Testament *any* evidence for a conscious existence between death and resurrection. Actually, such an afterlife was not at all the expectation of Old Testament believers. Their hopes were focused on the appearance of the Messiah, and the coming of the Messianic kingdom, at which moment they expected to rise from their graves. In fact, we find the very same situation in the New Testament, even though there we hear a bit more about the intermediate state (see the next chapter).

4.4.2   What Ghost?

The great exception in the Old Testament seems to be 1 Samuel 28:11–20, the passage about the appearance of the prophet Samuel to King Saul:

> Then the woman [i.e., a spiritistic medium] said, "Whom shall I bring up for you?" He [i.e., Saul] said, "Bring up Samuel for me." When the woman saw Samuel, she cried out with a loud voice. . . . And the woman said to Saul, "I see a god[69] coming up out of the earth. . . . An old man is coming up, and he is wrapped in a robe." And Saul knew that it was Samuel, and he bowed with his face to the ground and paid

---

69. Heb. *elohim*, here equivalent to a "supernatural being"; cf. AMP, "a divine [superhuman] being."

homage (vv. 11–14).

My strong impression is that this was a genuine appearance of Samuel.[70] The psychic began her common preparations and expected to go into a trance as usual in order to be used by the fortunetelling demon that was in her. However, these actions were suddenly interrupted by the actual, totally unexpected appearance of Samuel himself. The psychic stiffened and screamed out of fear, for she understood that God was really involved here, and that the appearance of Samuel could mean nothing else than that this was King Saul himself (incognito) who was visiting her.[71] This intense, frightened reaction suggests that she did not really expect Samuel; she did not work with the spirits of dead people at all, but with demons, and she herself knew that.

All these things underscore that this was a real appearance of Samuel, and that it had not been brought about by the actions of the woman, but by God for this exceptional occasion. Further evidence that it was indeed Samuel himself is that the sacred text itself referred to him as being "Samuel" (four times in vv. 14–20), and Saul knew it too (v. 14). Moreover, Samuel accurately predicted what would happen to Saul and his sons, admonished Saul, and used the divine name YHWH seven times.[72] Compare here the apocryphal book Sirach 46:20 (CEB), "Samuel prophesied after he had fallen asleep, and he showed the king what his end would be. He made his voice heard from the ground in prophecy to wipe out the people's lawless behavior."

By way of counterargument it is sometimes claimed that in verse 19 the ghost said: "[T]omorrow you and your sons shall be

---

70. See Ouweneel (1978), 124–25.
71. Beuken (1978), 8, believed that there could be no doubt that this was really Samuel.
72. See Bavinck, *RD*, 4:623–24, and the extensive discussion by Goslinga (1968), 458–62, who thought this was a hypnotic and spiritistic phenomenon; however, Youngblood (1992), 780–83, and Tsumura (2007), 622–28, carefully thought this was an appearance of the real Samuel.

with me." Since Samuel was with God, and Saul was to be lost, the real Samuel could never have said that the next day Saul would be "with him." This counterargument is based on a misunderstanding. As we have seen, the Old Testament did not identify two different places where the dead go, not even "heaven" and "hell"; it identifies only Sheol. The next day Saul and his sons would be with Samuel in the grave, in the nether world, the realm of the dead (cf. 2 Sam. 12:23).[73] When Jacob and David said that, one day, they would be with their sons in Sheol, they did not have to wonder first whether these sons were believers (Jacob was sure regarding Joseph, but what about David's young child?). Samuel was saying nothing more than that Saul and his sons would be dead the next day, just as Samuel himself was. Remarkably enough, the Septuagint says in 1 Samuel 28:19: "Tomorrow you and your sons will fall with you"— perhaps because the translator also had some trouble with the idea that after death Saul and Samuel would be in the same place.[74]

No matter how much we may resist the notion that a dead person can appear to people after their death (see also §7.3 on spiritism), at least we have an absolutely clear example of this phenomenon in the Bible, namely, the appearance of Moses "in glory" on the mount of transfiguration, together with Jesus and the prophet Elijah (Luke 9:30–31). I do not refer to Elijah as an example here because he had not died when he was taken up (2 Kings 2:1, 11). But although Moses's death and burial were unique, we are clearly told that he *died* (Deut. 34:5–6). All the more spectacular—and also unique—was his appearing on the Mount of Transfiguration. This is not an argument for spiritism; here we find no psychic summoning of a spirit, nor any mention of the spirit of Moses, but simply of Moses (just as no *spirit* of Samuel was mentioned in 1 Sam. 28). Moreover, Moses was not sleeping here in any sense of the term, but wide awake. If we have any proof that God is a God of the

---

73. Youngblood (1992), 783.
74. McCarter (1980), 419.

living and not of the dead (Luke 20:38), it is here.[75]

For the rest, I attach only limited value to this example, for the appearance of Moses with Elijah was so unique that no general conclusions can be drawn from it for any doctrine about the intermediate state that one would wish to defend.[76]

4.5 Post-Old Testament Literature

4.5.1 Intertestamentary Literature

After the Old Testament had been almost completely silent about the intermediate state, we see in the intertestamentary Jewish literature a growing awareness that the righteous and the wicked go to different destinies at death. The first evidence for this is found in 1 Enoch 1:22, where the angel Raphael spoke of "hollow places" where "the spirits of the souls of the dead should assemble therein, yea that all the souls of the children of men should assemble here. And these places have been made to receive them till the day of their judgement and till their appointed period [i.e., till the period appointed for them], till the great judgement (comes) upon them."[77] In one space, where there is a bright spring of water (reminding us of Eden), are the "spirits of the righteous." In another space are the "sinners," whose "spirits shall be set apart in this great pain till the great day of judgement and punishment and torment of those who curse forever and retribution for their spirits."

Also in 4 Ezra (or 2 Esdras) 7:48–56 we find such a separation between the various groups of the dead: on the one hand, there are "dwellings of health and safety," and a "paradise, whose fruit endures forever, wherein is security and medicine," where the faces of the righteous "shall shine above the stars" (cf. Dan. 12:3; Matt. 13:43).[78] On the other hand, there are those who will "suffer" for their sins "after death," apparently in some place of torment.

---

75. Pawson (2007, 55).
76. Cf. Duffield and Van Cleave (1996), 555.
77. www.ancienttexts.org/library/ethiopian/enoch/1watchers/watchers.htm.
78. www.earlyjewishwritings.com/text/2esdras.html.

According to the ancient Jewish historiographer Flavius Josephus, this notion of the separation among the dead in the hereafter was also the view of the Pharisees: they

> believe that souls have an immortal rigor in them, and that under the earth there will be rewards or punishments, according as they have lived virtuously or viciously in this life; and the latter are to be detained in an everlasting prison, but that the former shall have power to revive and live again.[79]

Josephus suggests here that the Pharisees believed in a resurrection only for the righteous, which seems at odds with Acts 23:8. He stated that the righteous who die are also in Hades,[80] whereas the wicked are in the "darkest place in Hades."[81]

The deuterocanonical books may not be inspired, but we may assume that they go back to very old Jewish traditions. These books also speak of a different destiny for the righteous and the wicked, such as the apocryphal book Wisdom of Solomon (1:7–9 CEB):

> The Lord's Spirit fills the whole world. It holds everything together and knows what everyone says. Therefore, those who utter unjust words don't escape notice. Justice will expose them and not pass them by. A proper inquiry will be made into the plots of ungodly people. News of their words will reach the Lord and make their lawless deeds known.

> The souls of those [i.e., the deceased] who do what is right are in God's hand. They won't feel the pain of torment. To those who don't know any better, it seems as if they have died. Their departure from this life was considered their misfortune. Their leaving us seemed to be their destruction, but in reality they are at peace. It may look to others as if they have been punished, but they have the hope of living

---

79. *Jewish Antiquities* 18.1.3 (reluctant-messenger.com/josephusA18.htm).
80. *The Wars of the Jews* 2.8.14 (reluctant-messenger.com/josephusW02.htm).
81. *Ibid.*, 3.8.5 (reluctant-messenger.com/josephusW03.htm).

forever. They were disciplined a little, but they will be rewarded with abundant good things, because God tested them and found that they deserve to be with him. He tested them like gold in the furnace; he accepted them like an entirely burned offering. Then, when the time comes for judgment [i.e., in the resurrection], the godly will burst forth and run about like fiery sparks among dry straw. The godly will judge nations [cf. 1 Cor. 6:2] and hold power over peoples, even as the Lord will rule over them forever. Those who trust in the Lord will know the truth. Those who are faithful will always be with him in love. Favor and mercy belong to the holy ones. God watches over God's chosen ones. The ungodly[, however,] will get what their evil thinking deserves. They had no regard for the one who did what was right, and instead, they rose up against the Lord (3:1–10).

"Things will go well at the end for those who fear the Lord. They will be blessed at the time of death" (Sirach 1:13). "Humble your whole being as much as possible, because fire and worms are the punishment of the ungodly" (7:17). "Be mindful of his wrath in times of death and in times of vengeance when he turns his face away" (18:24).

4.5.2   The Rabbis[82]

Traditional Christian expectation is that when believers die, they go to "heaven," and when unbelievers die, they go to "hell." I have little doubt that this Christian view also influenced the views of the medieval rabbis regarding the hereafter. I mention this here because they were the first and foremost interpreters of the Old Testament; therefore, their views of the hereafter are of interest to us.

The ancient rabbis believed that when they die, godly Jews go to the Garden of Eden (Heb. *Gan Eden*), that is, the heavenly paradise, the celestial counterpart of the earthly Eden of Genesis 2–3. Sometimes we encounter here the same phenomenon as among Christians who confuse paradise (the hereafter) with the Messianic

---

82. See Ouweneel (2020).

kingdom. That is to say, the rabbis sometimes referred to *Gan Eden* as the "world to come" (Heb. *Olam habbah*) (cf. Heb. 2:5), which in fact is the Messianic kingdom. The great Jewish expositor Nachmanides referred to *Gan Eden* as the *Olam haN'shamot*, "the world of the souls," namely, the departed souls of the righteous.[83] In this, we do not hear the language of the Old Testament but rather we encounter the Platonic doctrine of the immortal soul (see chapter 8). Either through Christians, or independently of them, the rabbis were influenced by Hellenistic thinking.

Rabbinic literature connects an incredible number of legends with *Gan Eden*. One of these is about Rabbi Joshua ben Levi (third century), who reportedly often met with Elijah (who had never died!) before the gates of paradise, where he also saw the Messiah sitting.[84] Rabbi Joshua obtained permission from the angel of death to visit paradise before he died, in order to inspect the place that had been assigned to him. The rabbis did not hesitate to supply their followers with extensive reports about, for instance, the various chambers of paradise, destined for various groups of righteous or penitent people. The third chamber is the best of all; here stands the tree of life, five hundred "years" high.

Let me quote here one of the many smaller *midrashim*, the *Midrash Konen*:

> The tree of life is like a ladder on which the souls of the righteous may ascend and descend. In a conclave above are seated the patriarchs,[85] the ten martyrs,[86] and those who sacrificed their lives for the cause of his Sacred Name. These souls descend daily to the Gan 'Eden, to join their families and tribes, where they lounge on soft

---

83. For references see the *Jewish Encyclopedia* s.v. "Paradise" (http://jewishencyclopedia.com/articles/11900-paradise).

84. Talmud: Sanhedrin 98a.

85. Abraham, Isaac, and Jacob, and his twelve sons.

86. Ten rabbis who were martyred by the Romans, Rabbi Akiva being the best known among them.

seats studded with jewels. Everyone, according to his excellence, is received in audience to praise and thank the Ever-living God; and all enjoy the brilliant light of the Shekinah [the pillar of the cloud, i.e., the glorious presence of the Lord]. The flaming sword, changing from intense heat to icy cold and from ice to glowing coals, guards the entrance against living mortals [cf. Gen. 3:24]. The size of the sword is ten years. The souls on entering paradise are bathed in the 248[87] rivulets of balsam and attar.[88]

Most amazing is the description of the fifth chamber:

The fifth chamber is built of precious stones, gold, and silver, surrounded by myrrh and aloes. In front of the chamber runs the river Gihon [cf. Gen. 2:13], on whose banks are planted shrubs affording-perfume and aromatic incense. There are couches of gold and silver and fine drapery. This chamber is inhabited by the *Messiah of David,* Elijah, and the *Messiah of Ephraim.*[89] In the center are a canopy made of the cedars of Lebanon, in the style of the tabernacle, with posts and vessels of silver; and a settee of Lebanon wood with pillars of silver and a seat of gold, the covering thereof of purple. Within rests the *Messiah, son of David,* "a man of sorrows and acquainted with grief" (Isa. 53:3), suffering, and waiting to release Israel from the Exile. Elijah comforts and encourages him to be patient. Every Monday and Thursday, and Sabbath and on holy days the Patriarchs, Moses, Aaron, and others, call on the Messiah and condole with him, in the hope of the fast-approaching end (italics added).[90]

Notice that in this Jewish writing, especially the reference to

---

87. This number refers to the 248 mandatory commandments in the Torah; together with the 365 prohibitive commandments, they form the 613 commandments of the Sinaitic Torah.
88. *Jewish Encyclopedia* s.v. "Paradise."
89. Jewish tradition distinguishes between Messiah ben Joseph and Messiah ben David, the former being the suffering Messiah, and the latter the victorious Messiah, Elijah being their forerunner and herald (Mal. 4:5–6).
90. *Jewish Encyclopedia* s.v. "Paradise."

Isaiah 53 is highly remarkable, because it shows that in certain Jewish traditions the awareness that this chapter refers to the suffering Messiah had definitely been preserved. This is important because, today, Jewish expositors prefer to see the suffering Servant of YHWH as a reference to Israel.

5

NEW TESTAMENT REFERENCES
TO THE HEREAFTER

The poor man died
and was carried by the angels to Abraham's side.
The rich man also died and was buried,
and in Hades, being in torment, he lifted up his eyes
and saw Abraham far off and Lazarus at his side.
And he called out, "Father Abraham, have mercy on me,
and send Lazarus to dip the end of his finger in water and
cool my tongue,
for I am in anguish in this flame."
But Abraham said, "Child, remember that you in your life-
time received your good things,
and Lazarus in like manner bad things;
but now he is comforted here, and you are in anguish."

Luke 16:22–25

"Heute wirst du mit mir im Paradies sein."
Mit Fried und Freud ich fahr dahin
In Gottes Willen, . . .
Wie Gott mir verheißen hat:
Der Tod ist mein Schlaf geworden.

> "Today, you will be with Me in paradise."
> With peace and joy I depart,

in God's will, . . .

As God has promised me:

death has become my sleep.[1]

> *Gottes Zeit ist die allerbeste Zeit*
> [*God's Time Is the Best of All Times*]
> Martin Luther (1524)
> Bach cantata BWV 106

5.1   Dives and Lazarus
5.1.1   Two Destinies

In the previous chapter, we saw that during the intertestamentary period, there was a growing awareness that, in the intermediate state, the condition of the righteous is different from that of the wicked. In the New Testament, Jesus himself shed some light on the matter. He did so, first, by his remark in the parable of the dishonest manager: "[M]ake friends for yourselves by means of un-righteous wealth [or, Mammon], so that when it fails they may receive you into the eternal dwellings" (Luke 16:9). The latter "they" can be viewed in an indeterminate sense ("people may receive you . . ."), or the phrase may be understood as a passive (as in many renderings: "you may be received"), but it may also refer to the "friends" mentioned earlier, who welcome the generous manager at his death into the "eternal dwellings."[2]

This is developed further in the subsequent story about the rich man (who, following the Vulgate, is often called Dives, "rich") and the poor Lazarus (Luke 16:19–31). This story explains more elab-orately how important it is to make friends for oneself with the unrighteous "Mammon"[3] (thus the KJV and others in v. 9), friends

---

1. Apparently, the "death sleep" of the believer does *not* imply a kind of coma; on the contrary, beyond death the delights of heaven await them (at least according to Luther's Interim Theology).
2. Greijdanus (1941), 77; Liefeld (1984), 989.
3. The term *Mammon* is an Aramaic word for "riches, money," presented here as a person.

who will welcome you to the "eternal dwellings (tabernacles, habitations)." It also shows what happens to those who do *not* handle their wealth properly. In Hades, Dives is not welcomed by Lazarus, for he did not treat him well, but he does see Lazarus from afar in a state of bliss—a fact that only worsens Dives's own torments. The "true riches" could not be "entrusted" to him, as they could be to Lazarus (cf. v. 11).[4]

Various expositors have hesitated to identify the story as a parable for three reasons. First, the story is nowhere called a parable. Second, the story tells us about a person who is given a name of his own, Lazarus. No other parable in the New Testament does this. Third, the story speaks of a person who has really lived, Abraham, and who is presented here in a speaking role.[5] Actually, whether this is a parable scarcely affects anything in the interpretation.[6] Notice that this is a different Lazarus than the one of John 11, despite the fact that both stories speak of death and resurrection, and in both cases there is a resurrection that does not convince unbelievers (Luke 16:31; John 12:10–11).[7]

Many writers have argued that the point of the story is not to supply us with detailed information about the hereafter, but to explain the destiny of the selfish Dives, who did not make for himself friends with Mammon. Therefore, we must be reluctant to build an eschatology on this story.[8] This may be true; nevertheless, we cannot avoid drawing a few theological conclusions: there are different destinies for the righteous and the wicked, that is, bliss for the former, disaster for the latter, and thus there is also a certain conscious experience after death.[9] This must be maintained, no

4. Greijdanus (1941), 83.
5. So, e.g., Summers (1972), 195; Prince (2006, [1995]), 459; cf. Pawson (2004), 190–91; this view is rejected by Zahn (1913), *ad loc.*; Geldenhuys (1983), 428.
6. Greijdanus (1941), 83.
7. Marshall (1978), 635.
8. Zahn (1913), *ad loc.*; Geldenhuys (1983), 429; Liefeld (1984), 991.
9. Greijdanus (1941), 86.

matter how metaphorical ("eyes," "bosom," "flame," "chasm") the language may be. As M. J. Erickson said, that whereas it was not Jesus' primary intention to teach us concerning the nature of the intermediate state, it is unlikely that he would mislead us concerning this subject.[10]

Lazarus was not only poor, but also ill, for he had sores (v. 20). According to tradition, he was a leper; hence the word "lazaret" originally referred to a hospital for contagious diseases. For the claim that Lazarus was a godly man despite his miserable condition there is no evidence in the story at all, except in his name, which functions, so to speak, as the key to his person and his life story.[11] The name is a Greek form of the Hebrew *El'azar* (which was also the name of Aaron's son; Num. 20:25–28), meaning "God helps," or "God has helped." In opposition to this, we find Dives, who is unnamed in the story. He was sufficiently characterized by his lifestyle: expensive clothing, constant partying, and no care for the poor and the ill. The latter detail especially characterized him as wicked, *not* the fact that he was rich.[12] Although, remarkably enough, he happened to know Lazarus by name (v. 24), he had never taken any interest in his misery. Dives was rich, but he was not "rich toward God" (12:21), as Lazarus was, according to his "code name."

The Bible does not condemn those who are rich simply *because* they are rich, as long as the rich do well with their riches:

> As for the rich in this present age, charge them not to be haughty, nor to set their hopes on the uncertainty of riches, but on God, who richly provides us with everything to enjoy. They are to do good, to be rich in good works, to be generous and ready to share, thus storing up treasure for themselves as a good foundation for the future, so that they may take hold of that which is truly life (1 Tim. 6:17–19).

---

10. Erickson (1998), 1182–83; cf. Pawson (2004), 191.
11. Greijdanus (1941), 83; Geldenhuys (1983), 428; *contra* Bruce (1979), 588.
12. See Ouweneel (2008), §§12.3 and 12.5.1.

This portrait is the very opposite of that of Dives.

After his death, the pious Lazarus found rest, relief, and peace, whereas the wicked Dives found a "place of torment" (v. 28). Lazarus was carried to his blissful place by angels. It is important to consider here the difference with the Parousia, and thus also between the intermediate state and the resurrection state. That difference is this: at death, the angels bring the individual believer to their rest, but at the Parousia, Jesus in person brings all his own to his Father's house, all of them at the same time (John 14:13; cf. §6.4). Thus, the story of Luke 16 was not primarily about the resurrection state, but about the intermediate state. At the same time, David Pawson was right in underscoring the fact that what was described here can indeed *eventually* be only the eternal state: eternal bliss for the righteous in their glorified bodies, and eternal torment of the wicked in the lake of fire.[13] This is the same as what we found in §3.1.1 for Philippians 1:23; that is, ultimately such passages find their fulfillment, never in the intermediate state but in the resurrection state.[14] The fact that the ultimate fulfillment of our story occurs in the eternal state is strongly underscored by the expression "*eternal* dwellings" in Luke 16:9. The term "eternal" is obviously associated with the resurrection state, but not with the intermediate state.

5.1.2 The Bosom of Abraham

The place where Lazarus was taken is described as the "bosom of Abraham" (Luke 16:22–23). No doubt, this is the metaphor of a meal[15] as an expression of fellowship and bliss, just as in 13:28–29:

> [In the place of eternal torment] there will be weeping and gnashing of teeth, when you see Abraham and Isaac and Jacob and all the

---

13. Pawson (2004), 195.
14. Rom. 8:11; 1 Cor. 15:51–55; Phil. 3:20–21; 1 Thess. 4:13–17; Rev. 20:4–6.
15. Greijdanus (1941), 85; Liefeld (1984), 992; Green (1997), 607; *contra* Geldenhuys (1983), 428, in reference to Strack and Billerbeck (1922), *ad loc.*, who thought of a child in her mother's lap.

prophets in the kingdom of God but you yourselves cast out. And people will come from east and west, and from north and south, and recline at table in the kingdom of God.

The contrast is remarkable: notice that in Luke 16:21, Dives was at table, while Lazarus received nothing but misery; in verses 22–23, Lazarus was at table, while Dives received nothing but misery.

In the pseudepigraphic Testament of Abraham 20 we read: "Take therefore my friend[16] Abraham into paradise, where are the tabernacles [dwelling places, cf. Luke 16:9] of my righteous ones, and the abodes of my saints Isaac and Jacob in his bosom [!], where there is no trouble, nor grief, nor sighing, but peace and rejoicing and life unending."[17] The same metaphor is probably present in John 1:18, where it is the Son who is reclining at a metaphorical table, lying in the bosom of the Father, in a supper of bliss and fellowship. Luke 12:37 says of the future state of the righteous: "Blessed are those servants whom the master finds awake when he comes. Truly, I say to you, he will dress himself for service and have them recline at table, and he will come and serve them." In John 13:23 we find a literal parallel with 1:18 and Luke 16:22–23, where one of the disciples, John, was reclining at table in the bosom of Jesus.

Of course, we should wonder whether, after the resurrection and ascension of Jesus, the "bosom of Abraham" is still the highest ideal for a believer to anticipate. If the story of Lazarus had been told after the ascension of Jesus, it might have spoken instead of the "bosom of Jesus" as the destiny for believers like Lazarus; think again of John 13:23. For the godly Jew of the Old Testament who was wondering about the hereafter, the bosom of Abraham was the highest place of blessing that one might have anticipated. It is a place where the believer is "comforted" (Luke 16:25; cf. Rev. 7:17;

---

16. See 2 Chron. 20:7; Isa. 41:8; James 2:23; cf. Gen. 18:17.
17. www.newadvent.org/fathers/1007.htm.

21:4; cf. Isa. 25:8), and it is a condition that can be left behind in one way only: through resurrection (v. 31), which leads to the real and final destiny of the godly.

Although the intermediate state involves disembodied persons, yet these are described as possessing certain body parts: eyes, a bosom, a finger, a tongue (Luke 16:23–24). Similarly, the deceased Samuel wore a robe (1 Sam. 28:14), and the "souls under the altar" receive a "white robe," although they have not yet attained the resurrection (Rev. 6:9–11; see §6.1).[18] The pagan kings in Sheol are sitting on thrones, and come forward to meet the dead king of Babylon (Isa. 14:9). These are not contradictory as long as we do not adhere to a substantialistic body-soul dichotomy (see more extensively, chapter 8).

Nonetheless, A. Plummer presupposed such a dualism when arguing that in the story of Dives and Lazarus, bodily features are attributed to "souls."[19] He used this assertion to argue his claim that the story does not give us any information about the unseen world. In a similar way, N. Geldenhuys asserted that the story did not really happen because Abraham exists in the hereafter only as a ghost, and therefore does not have a bosom.[20] This is a mistake, for three reasons. First, the story never even speaks of "souls" or "spirits": *Dives* was taken to Hades, not just his "soul," and *Lazarus* was carried to the bosom of Abraham, not just his "soul." By introducing a pagan body-soul dualism into the text, our vision is obscured *a priori* and we can never arrive at a proper exegesis.

Second, we should not forget that stories about things that really occurred can definitely be described in metaphorical language without such language necessarily detracting from their reality. Sometimes, the things that lie beyond our common everyday experience

---

18. I think Bavinck, *RD*, 4:618–19, and Heyns (1988), 397, are mistaken in viewing the persons mentioned in Rev. 7:9 and 20:4 as believers who have not yet risen.
19. Plummer (1922), *ad loc.*
20. Geldenhuys (1983), 428.

can hardly be described in any other terms than metaphorical ones.

Third, it is explicitly said that God is "spirit" (John 4:24), yet many "body" parts of his are mentioned in the Bible: his eyes and ears (e.g., 2 Kings 19:16), even his nostrils (e.g., Exod. 15:8), his hands (e.g., Ps. 28:5), his bowels (e.g., Jer. 31:20), even his heart (2 Chron. 7:16), and so on. We are not allowed to argue away the reality of such "body" parts by stressing that this is "only" metaphorical language: "He who planted the ear, does he not hear? He who formed the eye, does he not see?" (Ps. 94:9).

5.1.3 More Details

It is remarkable that Dives addressed Abraham as "father" (Luke 16:24).[21] Just like Lazarus, he was a Jew, conscious of his Abrahamic descent. Abraham acknowledged this by calling him "child" (v. 25). However, during his earthly life Dives did not behave like a true child of Abraham. On this subject, John the Baptist had said to the unrighteous Jews: "Bear fruits in keeping with repentance. And do not begin to say to yourselves, 'We have Abraham as our father.' For I tell you, God is able from these stones to raise up children for Abraham" (3:9). At another time, a careful distinction was made between those who are Abraham's physical descendants but not necessarily his spiritual children, and those who are his spiritual children, even if they are not necessarily physical descendants of Abraham (see John 8:33, 37, 39–40; Rom. 4:11–12).

The agonies of Hades are increased by the awareness that the wicked have of the blessings of the godly (v. 23), and of the impossibility of going to them (v. 26). In this way, the wicked know what they could have received if they had lived and believed as the righteous did. These agonies are described as "anguish" and "torment" (vv. 24–25, 28). The tormented ones also feel remorse for the misery which they experience (vv. 27–28, 30; see further in chapter 11).

Walter Liefeld believed that the story cannot be taken literally

---

21. Green (1997), 608.

because it would lead to an anachronism, namely, that Dives would already be undergoing agonies, whereas the judgment before the great white throne and being sent to hell had not yet occurred (Rev. 20:11–15).[22] There is some truth in this, for as we have seen, in this story, too, there is much anticipation of the eternal state. Yet, there is no reason why the "detention center," the place of the prisoner before the verdict, could not be a torment for the defendant to such an extent that it approximates the torments of prison after the verdict. But indeed, the prison is worse than the detention center. As J. Heyns put it: "[A]s the heavenly bliss will be enjoyed to the full only after the resurrection, thus also the fullness of the horror of hell will break out only then."[23] Again, Luke 16 does not dwell on the distinctions between the intermediate state and the resurrection state; the story anticipates the ultimate destiny of the righteous and the wicked.

With God, the punishment of the wicked is an established fact already at the moment of death (cf. Heb. 9:27), even if this punishment is officially pronounced only at the resurrection (Rev. 20:12–13), exactly as those who are suspected to have committed serious crimes are imprisoned already before their verdict. Therefore, S. Greijdanus remarked that Luke 16 "does not sharply distinguish between what is before the day of resurrection, and what will be after that day. . . . [The description lacks any] sharp delineation between the hellish suffering before and after the Day of Judgment at the end of the world, because they may differ in degree or measure, but not in essence."[24]

It may be pointed out here that the story of the rich man and Lazarus is not about the unbeliever versus the believer, but about the wicked versus the righteous. This is an important distinction. The same is found in Revelation 2:7, where it is not simply the

---

22. Liefeld (1984), 991, 993.
23. Heyns (1988), 399.
24. Greijdanus (1955), 2:85.

"believer" but the "conqueror" (or "overcomer") who will receive a share in paradise. This is not the same: in all the letters of Revelation 2–3 the "conquerors" are those church members who are not just Christians but who overcome the specific perils that threaten each church separately. Compare these words of Paul:

> [God] will render to each one *according to his works*: to those who by patience in well-doing seek for glory and honor and immortality, he will give eternal life; but for those who are self-seeking and do not obey the truth, but obey unrighteousness, there will be wrath and fury. There will be tribulation and distress for every human being who does evil, the Jew first and also the Greek, but glory and honor and peace for everyone who does good, the Jew first and also the Greek (Rom. 2:6–10; italics added).

"For we must all appear before the judgment seat of Christ, so that each one may receive what is due for *what he has done in the body*, whether good or evil" (2 Cor. 5:10 [italics added]; cf. Rom. 14:10).

And John wrote,

> I saw the dead, great and small, standing before the throne, and books were opened. . . . And the dead were judged by what was written in the books, according to what they had done. And the sea gave up the dead who were in it, Death and Hades gave up the dead who were in them, and they were judged, each one of them, *according to what they had done* (Rev. 20:12–13; italics added).

Of course, faith plays an essential role, but this is a faith "working through love" (Gal. 5:6). As a Jew, Dives was perhaps very religious, but his religion lacked love (cf. the Pharisee in the parable of Luke 18:9–14). He should have listened to the Apostle James, had he known him: "Religion that is pure and undefiled before God the Father is this: *to visit orphans and widows* [and all other people in misery] *in their affliction*, and to keep oneself unstained from the world" (1:27; italics added). "For judgment is without mercy to *one who has*

134

shown no mercy. Mercy triumphs over judgment. What good is it, my brothers, if someone says he has faith but does not have works? Can that faith save him?" And then we find, so to speak, the clearest portrait of Dives: "If a brother or sister is poorly clothed and lacking in daily food, and one of you says to them, 'Go in peace, be warmed and filled,' without giving them the things needed for the body, what good is that? So also faith by itself, if it does not have works, is dead. . . . You see that a person is justified by works and not by faith alone" (James 2:13–17, 24; italics added). Dives was perhaps religious, but not godly; Lazarus was poor but godly, as his name indicates.

5.2   "With Me in Paradise"
5.2.1   "Today"

As to the general meaning of "paradise," see my recent book *The Eden Story*, a work describing the various stages of the Garden of Eden, from the beginning of world history until the end of it.[25] The word "paradise" (Gk. *paradeisos*) occurs three times in the New Testament: (a) in Luke 23:42–43, in Jesus' answer to the criminal on the cross ("today you will be with me in paradise"; see below); (b) 2 Corinthians 12:3–4 ("this man was caught up into paradise"; see §5.3); and (c) Revelation 2:7 ("To the one who conquers I will grant to eat of the tree of life, which is in the paradise of God"). In other words, the word is used once each in the writings of Luke, Paul, and John. We will discuss here the first and second statements.

Many Christians have seen in Luke 23:43 the clearest possible reference to the intermediate state (between death and resurrection) for the believer. Yet, I venture to say that the passage has often been so misunderstood that this conclusion can hardly be warranted. Misunderstanding begins immediately with the prayer of the crucified criminal: "Jesus, remember me when you come into your kingdom [other manuscripts, in your kingly glory]." What does this

---

25. Ouweneel (2020).

mean? Is the criminal speaking of Jesus entering into the "kingdom of heaven" understood in the sense of "heaven" (cf. §1.4.1)? Not at all. This is the first misunderstanding. The criminal's question corresponded entirely with the Old Testament expectation of the Messianic kingdom, which was going to arrive at the coming of the Messiah.[26] The Old Testament Jews were not preoccupied with an intermediate state at all; they looked forward to the coming of the Messianic kingdom of righteousness and peace. The miracle experienced by the criminal on the cross was that the Holy Spirit had opened his eyes to the fact that *Jesus* was this Messiah. He understood that Jesus would pass *through* death, and would one day reappear:[27] "Remember me when you come as King" (CJB, GNT), or "when you begin ruling as king" (ERV)—not in heaven, but here on earth.

This is the prayer of the criminal: "Jesus, when you return and begin ruling as King on this earth, do not forget me. Let me rise from death as well—just as you will no doubt rise from death—and let me share in the Messianic kingdom." His prayer had basically the same content as what the King himself will say one day: "Then the King will say to those on his right [i.e., the righteous], 'Come, you who are blessed by my Father, *inherit the kingdom* prepared for you from the foundation of the world'" (Matt. 25:34).[28] The Messianic kingdom is the ultimate Eden, the ultimate paradise—not in heaven, but in God's renewed world. This is what Revelation 2:7 and 22:1–2 clearly indicate: paradise lies beyond the resurrection. The criminal could have prayed: "Jesus, remember me when you come into paradise, that is, the Messianic kingdom" (cf. "For the Lord comforts Zion; he comforts all her waste places and makes

---

26. Ratzinger's assertion is rather weak: "What exactly the good thief understood by Jesus' coming in his kingly power, and what he therefore meant by asking Jesus to remember him, we do not know" (2011), 212.

27. Luce (1933), *ad loc.*

28. This verse, too, has been misunderstood as a reference to "heaven"; see https://www.biblehub.com/ commentaries/matthew/25-34.htm.

her wilderness like Eden, her desert like the garden of the Lord; joy and gladness will be found in her, thanksgiving and the voice of song," Isa. 51:3).

Jesus' answer is noteworthy. He says as it were, "You will indeed have a share in my kingdom to come, that is, in the ultimate Eden, in the eternal paradise. But in addition to this, even today,[29] that is, before the sun has set,[30] you will have a foretaste of it, in some way or another" (although this is not further explained). Ultimate paradise is so clearly a notion connected with the Messianic kingdom and with the new heavens and new earth that it would be quite amazing if we had to accept that Jesus suddenly, and exceptionally, was giving here a description of the intermediate state as such. The righteous do not "go to paradise" when they die because paradise exists in the resurrection state. But in some way or another, the righteous who have passed away are "with Christ" already now, and this itself is a foretaste of paradise; it is "paradisal" in nature. Think of the terms I have used earlier, in addition to foretaste: advance, anticipation, prelude, overture. We must now examine this point a bit more closely.

5.2.2 "With Christ"

Notice that the emphasis in Jesus' answer to the crucified criminal is not on the question *where* departed believers are, but *with whom* they are. They are "with Christ" (Phil. 1:23). In the resurrection, this will be the case to a much fuller extent than in the intermediate state, but already now our deceased loved ones are "with Jesus," abiding in his shadow (cf. Ps. 91:1), and that is "best of all" (GNV). Do not ask for any more details because tradition will probably whisper into your ears all kinds of details about the hereafter that in fact belong to the world to come and the age to come (cf. §1.3.2 on supersessionism).

Please note that, in the Bible, places as such never have glory in

29. Gk. *sēmeron* , "today," is said first in order to put the emphasis on it.
30. Godet (1889), *ad loc.*; Bruce (1979), 641.

themselves, and are never holy as such. Only the Triune God has glory, only he is intrinsically holy. "Holy ground" (Exod. 3:5) is holy only because God is there with his holiness; there is nothing special about the ground as such. The tabernacle and temple were holy only because God dwelt there. Heaven is holy (Deut. 26:15) only because God dwells there. Thus, wondering to what "glorious *place*" believers are heading comes from a mindset that is mistaken from the outset.[31] The glory or holiness of a place is determined by the presence of God, or of the Son of God. What the Lord basically told the criminal is this: "You ask me not to forget you. But I won't have a chance to forget you, for as of today you will be forever with me, in my presence, under my protection, both in the intermediate state and in the resurrection state. And where I am is Eden, is paradise. Although in the fullest sense, Eden or paradise belongs to the world to come (Rev. 22:1–2), you will be *with me*, and that in itself is already an anticipation (foretaste, prelude, overture, anticipation) of the Eden to come."

As F. Godet wrote, "[I]t is not in heaven that one finds God, but in God one finds heaven."[32] It is an error to think of paradise as a place of delight *apart from Christ*. Just as in his person he is the tree of life, in a sense we could even say that in his person he is paradise. Paradise is magnificent because God, or the Son of God, is there. But perhaps it is even more correct to say that, wherever God, or the Son of God, is, there is paradise. The point is not that the departing believer is going to a certain magnificent "place," marvelous descriptions of which have often been given; his prayer is rather, "Into *your* hands I commit my spirit [my breath, my very life, *myself*]" (Ps. 31:5), as the dying Jesus did (Luke 23:46), and the dying Stephen did too: "Lord Jesus, receive my spirit" (Acts 7:59).

The Greek prepositions used for "with" in the expression

---

31. It reminds us of the Muslim paradise, *Jannah*, which contains many pleasures and delights, but Allah is not mentioned at all (*Qu'ran*, surah 76:12–22).
32. Godet (1879), on John 14:1–3.

"with Jesus" differ. In Luke 23:43, the Greek phrase is *met' emou*, that is, not only in my company (which is rather *syn emoi*) but sharing with me in the blessings.[33] In Philippians 1:23 the Greek phrase is *syn Christōi*, "with Christ," in his presence. In 2 Corinthians 5:8 the Greek phrase is *pros ton kyrion*, which, first, indicates a direction ("exchange exile for homecoming," MSG). Second, the Greek preposition may be *pros* as in John 1:1–2 and 1 John 1:2, that is, a reference to intimate fellowship[34] (also cf. Mark 6:3, Gk. *pros*, "with us," implies being acquainted with each other, a confidential being together).

Because of this being "with Jesus," the resurrection state—of which the intermediate state is anticipation and foretaste—is blissful in particular because of the presence of Christ. It is a profound mistake to imagine the blissful condition of the righteous in eternity as a place of pleasure cut off from Christ. It will be glorious *because* it will be a dwelling "forever with the Lord." If he were not in paradise, if he—forgive me the ugly supposition—were in hell, then hell would be glorious, not paradise.

A. Hoekema rightly said about being "with Christ" that this is all that Paul knows about the intermediate state.[35] J. van Genderen quoted an unmentioned author: "After all, the important thing is not the splendour of heaven, but the Savior in heaven."[36] Yet, we are allowed to think about the glorious implication of this being "with Christ," as did J. Verkuyl: "Paradise—that word reminds us of an overture, of preliminary rest and peace, of sabbatical stillness, of the soft light of God's love, of the mild shadow under God's protecting hand. The core of paradisal life is formed by the words 'with me.'"[37]

---

33. Plummer (1922), *ad loc.*; Matter (1965), 33.
34. Hughes (1962), 178 note 53; Barnett (1997), 271 note 26.
35. Hoekema (1979), 104.
36. Van Genderen and Velema (2008), 837.
37. Verkuyl (1992), 453.

5.3   The "Third Heaven"
5.3.1   God's Dwelling-Place?

In 2 Corinthians 12:2–4 there is an apparent connection between paradise and the "third heaven":

> I know a man in Christ [Paul is referring to himself] who fourteen years ago was caught up to the third heaven—whether in the body or out of the body I do not know, God knows. And I know that this man was caught up into paradise—whether in the body or out of the body I do not know, God knows—and he heard things that cannot be told, which man may not utter.

What does "paradise" mean here? The problem is that we do not know anything more about what the Apostle Paul understands by "paradise" here than what the text tells us. It is the only time he uses the word in his epistles. Expositors have often thought that this refers to the intermediate state, but the text says nothing of the kind; the idea arose only because of traditional biases concerning the hereafter (Interim Theology: "going to heaven when you die").

The "third heaven" is usually understood as that which comes "after" the first heaven (the sky with its clouds) and the second heaven (the firmament with the stars).[38] Or perhaps these are counted as one: the sky with clouds and stars, and in this case, the second heaven might be something like the "heavenly places" in Ephesians (1:3, 20; 2:6; 3:10; 6:12[39]). Or perhaps the "third heaven" is what in the Old Testament is sometimes called the "heaven of heavens" (Deut.10:14; 1 Kings 8:27; 2 Chron. 2:6; 6:18; Neh. 9:6; Ps. 68:33; 148:4). In addition, Mark 11:10 ("the highest [heavens]"), Ephesians 4:10 ("far above all the heavens"), and Hebrews 4:14 ("passed through the heavens") suggest that there are various heavens, al-

---

38. So Pickering (n.d.), 29, 77; cf. Deut. 10:14; 1 Kings 8:27; 2 Chron. 2:6; 6:18; Neh. 9:6; Ps. 68:33; 148:4.

39. An "intermediate heaven," to which Satan also has access.

though the Greek plural noun *ouranoi* is possibly a Hebraism related to the Hebrew dual form *shamayyim* ("heavens," often rendered in the singular). If Jesus is "exalted above the heavens" (Heb. 7:26), and at the same time is "in" heaven,[40] there must be lower heavens as well as a heaven where he is now seated on the throne of God.[41] In the face of all these possibilities, the precise meaning of the expression "third heaven" within the framework of 2 Corinthians 12 remains uncertain.

A more literal translation of verse 4 says, "[H]e heard inexpressible words [Gk. *rhēmata*], which it is not lawful for a man to utter." Thus, Paul heard "words" in this paradise, of which he tells us two things: he is not *able* to express (formulate) these words, and he is not *allowed* to express them. But who is , or who are uttering these words? Expositors are vague on these things, and understandably so. But if these words that Paul heard *cannot* and *may not* be repeated, perhaps they came from God himself. And this might mean that the expression "third heaven" refers to God's own dwelling place (although even "the heaven and heaven of heavens cannot contain him," 2 Chron. 2:6 KJV). God is the One who "sits in the heavens" (Ps. 2:4); his "throne is in heaven" (11:4; cf. 103:19; Isa. 66:1; Matt. 5:34; Acts 7:49; Heb. 8:1; Rev. 4:2). Compare this statement as well: "The heavens are the LORD's heavens, but the earth he has given to the children of man" (Ps. 115:16).

And paradise? Maybe here it is nothing more than a description of the Edenic character of God's dwelling place.[42] The Apostle was caught up to this place—whether in the body or out of the body—there to catch a glimpse of things and words so magnificent that he could not express them. But these are no doubt things that *will* be revealed one day in the "world to come."

---

40. Eph. 6:9; Col. 4:10; Heb. 9:24; 1 Pet. 3:22; cf. 1 Thess. 1:10; 4:16.
41. Westcott (1950), on Heb. 4:14 as well as 7:26.
42. In this view, the meaning might not be too far removed from the celestial Eden mentioned in Ezekiel 28; see Ouweneel (2020), §§2.2 and 2.3. This heavenly Eden is older and more magnificent than the earthly garden of Genesis 2–3.

5.3.2 More Details

Zoroastriansm and Jewish literature[43] [both] speak of seven heavens, and we encounter this and similar notions among the Church Fathers as well (Irenaeus, Tertullian, Clement of Alexandria, Origen, Epiphanius, and Augustine). However, the Bible does not speak of such a thing. On the contrary, the Apostle Paul speaks of such an elevated matter that we can hardly imagine four more heavens beyond his "third heaven."[44]

Please note that we must not read into the text some primitive worldview about various heavens above the earth. Rather, what matters here is the awareness of the distinction between the physical-immanent heaven and heaven in the transcendent sense.[45] If Paul was caught up to the "third heaven," we suppose this to mean that he was caught up to the presence of the glorified Christ. This is more that Augustine suggested, namely, that the "third heaven" would be nothing more than the contemplation of God;[46] in my view, such a description leaves out of consideration the element of being "caught up," physically or otherwise.

Regarding whether the "third heaven" in verse 2 is the same as paradise in verse 4, opinions have always been widely divided.[47] Some have claimed that Paul was speaking here of two occasions of being "caught up," others that he was speaking here of two stages in one event of being "caught up," first to the "third heaven," then to paradise, which, in this case, would either be higher than the "third heaven," or the highest or central place in the "third heaven." Still others have claimed that the "third heaven" and paradise are

---

43. E.g., *Apocalypsis Mosis* 35:2; 2 Enoch 20:1 (www.scribd.com/doc/3678772/ The-Book-of-the-Secrets-of-Enoch-WR-Morfill; see the extensive explanation by R. H. Charles in this linked document, xxx–xlvii); *Ascensio Isaias* 3:11.

44. Cf. Irenaeus, *Adversus Haereses* 2.30.7; cf. Grosheide (1959), 341.

45. Hughes (1962), 434.

46. Augustine, *De Genesi ad litteram* 12.

47. De Vuippens (1925), 98; Grosheide (1959), 341–42; Hughes (1962), 435–36; Bernard (1979), 109, who pleads for identity.

identical.

It is quite conceivable—though we cannot prove it—that Paul was starting here from a presupposition similar to the one found in 2 Enoch 8:1–3:

> And those men took me thence, and led me up on to the third heaven, and placed me there; and I looked downwards, and saw the produce of these places, such as has never been known for goodness. And I saw all the sweet-flowering trees and beheld their fruits, which were sweet-smelling, and all the foods borne [by them] bubbling with fragrant exhalation. And in the midst of the trees that of life, in that place whereon the Lord rests, when he goes up into paradise.[48]

The matter is important because, *if* paradise and the third heaven are identical here, and *if* paradise here is the abode of believers who have passed away, then this is the only place in the Bible telling us that "heaven" is the place where believers go when they die. But notice the two enormous *ifs*! Yet, F. Grosheide said without hesitation: "*The third heaven* is the place where the blessed [i.e., deceased believers] are,"[49] even though a little later he said: "Paul does not say who are dwelling in the *paradeisos*, he does not even say that people or angels, souls or bodies are sojourning there."[50] Irenaeus had written centuries earlier:

> Paradise had been prepared for the righteous, those who have the Spirit; in which place Paul too, when he was caught up, heard words that are unspeakable as far as we are concerned in our present condition. . . . There, those who have been caught to that place will stay until the consummation, as a prelude to immortality.[51]

This is far more than can be proven from the text.

In paradise Paul "heard things that cannot be told, which man

---

48. https://www.sacred-texts.com/bib/fbe/fbe115.htm.
49. Grosheide (1959), 340.
50. *Ibid.*, 342.
51. *Adversus Haereses* 5.5.1.

may not utter." The things he heard apparently were not fit for human ears on earth, *or* they were intended for him alone. It is suggestive to think here of the conversations of believers who had passed away, but of course this is pure speculation. They could just as well be words of angels, or words of God himself, possibly uttering a personal message for Paul himself.

5.4   The "Building from God"
5.4.1   Two Interpretations

In 2 Corinthians 4:18–5:8, the Apostle Paul says,

> [W]e look not to the things that are seen but to the things that are unseen. For the things that are seen are transient, but the things that are unseen are eternal. For we know that if the tent that is our earthly home is destroyed, we have a building from God, a house not made with hands, eternal in the heavens. For in this tent we groan, longing to put on our heavenly dwelling, if indeed by putting it on we may not be found naked. For while we are still in this tent, we groan, being burdened—not that we would be unclothed, but that we would be further clothed, so that what is mortal may be swallowed up by life. . . . We know that while we are at home in the body we are away from the Lord. . . . [But] we are of good courage, and we would rather be away from the body and at home with the Lord.

Paul literally spoke in 5:1 of "our earthly house of the tent" (cf. the KJV), that is, "our earthly tent-dwelling" (cf. "this tent," v. 4). By this, he means his mortal body, using a metaphor comparable to the "jars of clay" in 4:7, and to the way Peter spoke of his body ("this tent") in 2 Peter 1:13–14. It is the human corporeal mode of existence, as fragile and temporary as a tent, the "mortal body" (Rom. 8:11). It is "this corruptible/mortal" (1 Cor. 15:53–54 KJV), which is "destroyed" at death (2 Cor. 5:1) or "put off" (2 Pet. 1:14).[52] Of Jesus, we read that the Word became flesh and "dwelt"

---

52. Wendland (1954), 170–71, who sees in this passage the transition of the one mode of existence to the other, exaggerates in saying that the text does

(Gk. *eskēnōsen*, from *skēnē*, "tent") among us, that is, he pitched his tent among us (John 1:14 EXB); he dwelt among us in the tent of his human body. The apocryphal book Wisdom 9:15 says, "[A] perishable body weighs down the soul, and this earthy tent burdens the thoughtful mind" (RSV).

As the tent (tabernacle) in the wilderness gave way to the temple in the Promised Land, similarly the believer's "earthly tent" gives way to a heavenly temple, "a building from God, a house not made with hands, eternal in the heavens."[53] On the basis of this comparison, we cannot conclude anything else but that when speaking of this "eternal house," Paul meant the resurrection body. When our mortal body is broken down—that is, when we die—we "have" (are entitled to, hope for, possess the sure promise of) the resurrection body, although we will receive it [only] at the resurrection.[54]

Some have seen the comparison in a different light: Abraham "lived in tents," but he "was looking forward to a city that has foundations, whose architect and builder is God" (Heb. 11:9–10). This is not the resurrection body, but the heavenly city; compare Luke 16:9, where the "earthly tent" is opposed to the "eternal dwellings." Hence the expression "not made with hands"is not meant to suggest that the "earthly tent" *is* "hand-made," but to underscore the transcendent nature of the heavenly dwelling, that it is not of the present creation.[55]

It is understandable that, if the latter interpretation is correct,[56]

---

not refer to death. What else could the "destruction" of the body in verse 1 be?

53. Thornton (1956), 119.
54. Ambrose (d. 397); Sevenster (1955); Hughes (1962), 163; Ridderbos (1975), 501; Bernard (1979), 65; Osei-Bonsu (1991), 178; Barnett (1997), 257–59.
55. Grosheide (1959), 141; cf. Heb. 9:24; also see Mark 14:58, where a temple made with hands is replaced by a temple not made with hands.
56. Other proposed but much less likely interpretations include: the "building of God" is (a) the church, (b) the new Jerusalem, (c) the heavenly temple of the Lord's presence, (d) an eternal body, which the believer received at baptism (a being invested with Christ).

some have thought here of the intermediate state, namely, the dwelling place of deceased believers.[57] P. Hughes and P. Barnett rightly saw as a disadvantage of this approach that the word "house" in 2 Corinthians 5:1 would then have been used in two different ways.[58] The earthly, temporary house, that is, the mortal body, is exchanged for a heavenly, eternal building; this can only be the resurrection body. The direct sequel of the passages, that is to say, the passage following this verse, underscores this interpretation, although here again the exegesis is debatable. Verse 4 explains:

> For while we are still in this tent, we groan, being burdened—not that we would be unclothed, but that we would be further clothed [or, clothed about, clothed extra] beyond what we already are clothed with; Gk. *ependusasthai*], so that what is mortal may be swallowed up by life.

Here, the metaphors of house and tent are exchanged for that of clothing. Without discussing the matter extensively, I would suggest that the phrase "further clothed" refers to the resurrection, when "this perishable body" will "put on" (Gk. *endusasthai*) the imperishable, and "this mortal body" will "put on immortality" (1 Cor. 15:53).[59]

5.4.2 The Intermediate State?

The argument of 2 Corinthians 5:1–8 (being "at home with the Lord") seems to fit the notion of the heavenly dwelling. Some agree with the interpretation of John Calvin, who combined the views: the passage (specifically v. 2) means that "the blessed condition of the soul after death is the commencement of this *building*, and the

---

57. Ephraem (d. 373); Herveius (twelfth century); Thomas Aquinas (d. 1274); Tasker (1958), *ad loc.*; Schlatter (1987), 271–73; Hodge (1994), *ad loc.*; Stanley (2008), *ad loc*

58. Hughes (1962), 165; Barnett (1997), 258n15.

59. So Hughes (1962), 168–69; Bernard (1979), 65; Barnett (1997), 261; *contra* Bavinck, *RD*, 4:618, who thought of a "robe" that the deceased receives immediately at death.

glory of the final resurrection is the consummation of it."[60] Thus, in verses 2–4 we have an anticipation of the resurrection, whereas in verses 6–8 Paul may have been thinking of the intermediate state. Paul would thus have been presenting to us a clear continuity: as soon as believers leave their present body behind at death, they "have" a building of God, which is first their heavenly dwelling in the intermediate state, and the new, glorified body in the resurrection state.

Other interpreters have also searched for continuity, but in a different direction; they tried to combine the exegesis of the resurrection body with the present meaning of "having" by thinking of a kind of "spiritual body" that believers would possess in the intermediate state, and which would be transformed into the new, glorified body.[61] One might think here of the eyes, the bosom, the finger, and the tongue that the dead possess according to Luke 16:23–24. However, we should not read too much "corporeality" into this, as follows from 2 Corinthians 5:8: Paul uses here the Greek phrase *ek tou somatos*, which literally means, "out of/outside the body." The notion of what has been called an "intermediate body" or an "ethereal" body is speculative, and usually presupposes the body-soul dichotomy.[62] More careful, therefore, are the suggestions by F. Prat, who understood the "building from God" to refer to being clothed with heavenly glory,[63] and by F. Grosheide, who viewed it as the "heavenly [mode of] existence," here being opposed to the earthly mode of existence.[64]

No matter how one interprets 2 Corinthians 5:1–2, in verses 6–8 the reference can hardly be to anything other than the interme-

---

60. Calvin (1849), *ad loc.*
61. This view has been defended by A. B. Bruce, R. H. Charles, T. F. Torrance, F. F. Bruce (1971), 469–70, W. D. Davies (1980), 318, M. J. Harris (1983, 1990); and M. Thrall (1965), 1:389–92.
62. Cf. Bavinck, *RD*, 4:618–20.
63. Prat (1926/27), quoted in Harris (1976), 349.
64. Grosheide (1959), 142; cf. *RD*, 4:619.

diate state.[65] Two conditions are compared here: on the one hand, being "at home in the [present] body" (this is the earthly tent-house of v. 1), that is, not at home "with the Lord" but on earth; on the other hand, our being (or becoming) "at home with the Lord" (Gk. *endemesai*, "to dwell," to be at home), after we have come "away from" our earthly body (Gk. *ekdemesai*, "to dwell outside," to get away from). In the intermediate state, believers are "unclothed" (v. 4, without their earthly tent or robe, i.e., their mortal body), but "at home with the Lord," in some preliminary or anticipatory form.

The most mysterious here is verse 3: ". . . if indeed by putting it on we may not be found naked." An initial possible exegesis reads this as spiritually "naked," that is, as being an unbeliever: a person will receive the glorious body from heaven only if he is a true believer (cf. KJV, and see Rev. 3:17–18; 16:15; also Matt. 22:11; 1 John 2:28).[66] A second possible reading of the verse is: if we have really put on the robe of the resurrection body, the Lord at his appearance will not find us naked, that is, in a disembodied state.[67] A third possibility is that "naked" indeed means "without a body," but in a different way, as for instance in the CEV: "We want to put it on like clothes and not be naked" (cf. also the GNV).[68] A fourth interpretation is the one of the CEB: ". . . since we assume that when we take off this tent, we won't find out that we are naked." This is supposed to mean that when believers have put off their mortal bodies in the intermediate state, they are not really "naked." This reminds us of what was quoted above from Thrall, Prat, and Grosheide.

5.4.3 Ambiguity

Regarding Paul's desire to "be at home with the Lord," we seem to discern a certain ambiguity. On the one hand, he groans, being bur-

---

65. Cullmann (1962), 238–39.
66. This is the view of, e.g., Grosheide (1959), 144–45, Berkouwer (1972), 58, and Bernard (1979), 66.
67. Hughes (1962), 169; cf. Barnett (1997), 262.
68. Cf. Ridderbos (1975), 502.

dened (v. 4), because (at death) he does not wish to be "unclothed" (i.e., putting off the mortal body). Rather, he wishes to be "further clothed" in that, at the Parousia, he immediately puts on his resurrection body, "over" his mortal body, so that "this corruptible" puts on "incorruption," and "this mortal" puts on "immortality" (1 Cor. 15:53) without having had to die first. In this interpretation, there is no contradiction between 1 Corinthians 15 and 2 Corinthians 5, as some have presumed.[69] In short: Paul does not wish to die, but would rather continue to live until the Parousia, so that there would be no putting off, but only a putting on.

On the other hand (v.8), Paul does wish to end his sojourn in the body in order to enjoy being with the Lord. Not dying and being alive at the Parousia is great; but in a sense it is even greater, more wonderful, to die and thus to be "at home with the Lord." This tension is similar to the one we find in Philippians 1:21–24, where Paul's concern for the churches plays a role in his considerations. But even there, dying is gain in comparison with our present existence because being with Christ is far better. In 3:10–11 he desires to be like Christ in his death, in order *in this way* to attain the resurrection from the dead, just as Christ did. What is the greater privilege: to be alive at the moment of the Parousia (1 Thess. 4:15), or to be like Christ in the way that he, through death, attained the resurrection? As John Bernard put it: "Even if we must die before the Second Advent, we would say, we are content, for this absence from the body will be presence with Christ . . . , though the glory of that Presence shall not be fully manifested until the Day of the Parousia."[70]

Here again, we are struck by the fact that the New Testament does not expand on the intermediate state at all; we hear only that it consists in being "with Jesus" (Luke 23:42–43), being "with Christ"

---

69. Knox (1939), 128–30; Davies (1980), 308–32; in opposition to this, see Ridderbos (1975), 500–501; Erickson (1998), 1187.
70. Bernard (1979), 67.

(Phil. 1:23), and here "being with the Lord." Even 2 Corinthians 5:9—"So whether we are at home or away, we make it our aim to please him"—does not supply us with any information about the experiences of the believers in the intermediate state. Duffield and Van Cleave suppose that this verse tells us that believers make it their aim to please the Lord also in the intermediate state.[71] However, this cannot be the intention of the verse, for verse 10 shows us that the most important point in pleasing the Lord is what believers have done *in the body*.[72] Thus, verse 9 does not speak of "being at home with the Lord," as in verse 8, but of being at home in the body (v. 6). It says that, whether we are in our mortal body at the Parousia, or whether we through death have come "away from the body" (v. 8), as long as we remain on the earth, we endeavor to please the Lord.

In addition to 2 Corinthians 12:2–4, chapter 5:1–8 is the only other passage in Scripture where the word "heaven" in some way might be understood in connection with the intermediate state, and then only if, in verses 1–2, we think not (only) of the resurrection body but (also) of the abode of deceased believers. A third possible passage might be Acts 7:55–59, where Stephen sees "the heavens opened, and the Son of Man standing at the right hand of God" (v. 56), and prays, "Lord Jesus, receive my spirit." This might be interpreted to mean, "Let me be where you are." For the rest, the believer's heavenly destiny is always connected with [Christ's] resurrection.[73]

Some Christians argue as follows: Jesus is in heaven, deceased believers are "with Jesus," therefore, deceased believers are in heaven. This is rather simplistic. Jesus is at the same time also with the believers on earth (Matt. 28:20). Jesus dwells in believers' hearts (Eph. 3:17; cf. John 14:23). We are the church of him who fills the

---

71. Duffield and Van Cleave (1996), 554.
72. Hughes (1962), 179.
73. E.g., Phil. 3:20; Heb. 3:1; 1 Pet. 1:[3-]4.

universe (Eph. 1:22–23). He is God (the Son) who is in heaven as well as in Sheol and in the uttermost parts of the sea (Ps. 139:7–10). For the claim that deceased believers are "in heaven," we need more solid evidence than this argument provides.

5.5   "Falling Asleep"
5.5.1   Luke 8:52–55

In discussions about the intermediate state, the terms "sleeping" and "falling asleep" often play a significant role. After Stephen had been stoned, he "fell asleep" (Acts 7:60). This means that he died; his blood was shed (22:20); he was buried immediately (8:2). When the Apostle Paul says that Jesus appeared to five hundred brothers, he added that some of these "have fallen asleep" (1 Cor. 15:6); a little later he spoke of those "who have fallen asleep in Christ" (vv. 18, 20; cf. also v. 51; 7:39 KJV). At these and other places, "falling asleep" clearly means "dying": "those who have fallen asleep" are the same as the "*dead* in Christ" (1 Thess. 4:13–16; cf. 1 Cor. 15:35, "How are *the dead* raised?"). These deceased persons include Old Testament believers: Peter spoke of "the fathers" who "fell asleep" (2 Pet. 3:4; cf. Matt. 27:52), and Paul spoke of David who "fell asleep" (Acts 13:36). Just as the opposite of "dying" is "living," the opposite of being "asleep" is being "awake" (1 Thess. 5:10).

The Greek verb used is *koimaomai*, "to sleep" or "to put to sleep" or "to fall asleep." Outside the Bible as well, the verb means "to die" or "to be dead," apparently because a dead body resembles a sleeping body: both are at rest, with the eyes closed. In the New Testament, the verb is limited to believers who have died. Just as the sleeping person will awaken at a certain moment, the deceased believer will "awaken" at the resurrection of the righteous (Acts 24:15).

Interestingly, the Greek verb *koimaomai* lives on in the French word *cimetière* and the English word *cemetery*. These words come from the Latin *cemeterium*, which is derived from the Greek *koimētēri-on*, "sleeping place, dormitory." A cemetery is a place for people who have "fallen asleep," that is, who are dead.

Sometimes, the Greek verb used is *katheudō*, "to fall asleep" or "to sleep" (e.g., Matt. 9:24 and parallel passages). Jesus used this verb when he made a remarkable *contrast* between being "dead" and being "asleep." Consider the episode recorded in Luke 8:52–55 (cf. Matt. 9:23–25; Mark 5:39). In the house of Jairus,

> all were weeping and mourning for her [i.e., his daughter], but he said, "Do not weep, for she is not dead but sleeping." And they laughed at him, knowing that she was dead. But taking her by the hand he called, saying, "Child, arise." And her spirit returned, and she got up at once.

Jesus' language is mysterious because (a) Luke had already told us "she was dying" (v. 42); (b) the messengers told Jairus, "Your daughter is dead" (v. 49); (c) all the people in the house "knew" she was dead; and (d) her spirit had left her. Moreover, if she had not been dead, Jesus would have awakened her only from a literal sleep, and there would have been no miracle.

Now what about the statement "she is not dead"? The most satisfactory explanation seems to be that Jesus makes an anticipatory statement: the girl was now "asleep" (i.e., dead), but within a few moments she was going to return from death. Perhaps we have a similar situation in Acts 20, where a young man was "taken up dead," but Paul said, "Do not be alarmed, for his life [literally, soul] is in him," which I take to mean, his life is returning to him *right now*.

Coming back to the daughter of Jairus, we understand the Lord to have said that, indeed, her body was physically dead, but her spirit (her personality) was still alive, and that this spirit would return very soon to the body (notice the phrase, "her spirit returned"). The word "alive" may seem a strong term here, but indeed, Jesus himself told us that to God all those who are dead live (Luke 20:38). Moreover, compare Song 5:2, "I slept, but my heart was awake," which is taken to mean that the bride was dreaming. This is the notion of a "sweet sleep" (Prov. 3:24), a sleep with sweet dreams.

When believers pass away, they enter into a state of "sweet sleep."

Apparently, Jesus wished to contradict the conviction of all those people in that house. To them, death was an irreversible process; at best, one could hope that the little girl would "rise again in the resurrection on the last day" (cf. John 11:24). In fact, the people present were making preparations for the child's funeral. Jesus seemed to be saying, "The child is not dead in the definitive sense *you* give to the term; stop preparing to bury her, for she is on the brink of returning to life." She is "only" sleeping; she will soon wake up. *Jesus* would wake her up, in the same quick and easy way a sleeping person is awakened.

The way Jesus used the term "sleeping" here is not entirely identical to the expression "falling asleep" or "being asleep" that we have found elsewhere. The "dead in Christ" are asleep, from the moment they died until the time of their resurrection. But by way of exception, here Jesus made a *contrast* between being "dead" and being "asleep": the girl is not dead—as one is dead who must wait for the resurrection—but only sleeping for a few more moments. The single contrast between "death" and "sleeping" in Luke 8 is the exception that confirms the rule. In *all* the other cases, the two expressions are equivalent: deceased believers are "asleep," that is, "dead." Therefore, we cannot make the general statement that the New Testament always distinguishes between death and "being asleep."

5.5.2   John 11:11–15

We turn now to John 11, where Jesus himself *identified* being asleep and being dead. This is the general rule in the Bible: the "dead" in Christ are "asleep." They *are* physically dead, but their death is "only" like a "sleep." In John 11, we find another passage in which Jesus used the term "asleep" in a somewhat mysterious way. Jesus and his disciples were on their way to Bethany because Lazarus was ill. He told them:

"Our friend Lazarus has fallen asleep, but I go to awaken him." The disciples said to him, "Lord, if he has fallen asleep, he will recover." Now Jesus had spoken of his death, but they thought that he meant taking rest in sleep. Then Jesus told them plainly, "Lazarus has died, and for your sake I am glad that I was not there, so that you may believe. But let us go to him" (John 11:11–15).

Again, there is no doubt that the person involved was truly dead. Jesus himself said so. And when they arrived in Bethany, they found this to be truly the case (vv. 21, 32, 39). Nor can there be any doubt that Lazarus' being "asleep" and Jesus going to "awaken" him amounted to saying that Lazarus was "dead" and that Jesus was going to "raise" him from the dead.

The way the disciples misunderstood Jesus is quite unsurprising. When, after a period of severe illness, the patient falls asleep, this is a sign that they are beginning to recover. As the apocryphal book Sirach says (31:2), "[S]erious illness will chase sleep away" (CEB). In John 11:4, Jesus had said, "This illness does not lead to death," which apparently meant that death would not have the last word in this case. The disciples took this to mean that either Lazarus would be healed in the natural way, or Jesus would go and heal him in a miraculous way. On the way to Bethany, when Jesus told them that Lazarus had fallen asleep, they saw this as the beginning of his healing. In a sense this was correct: Jesus *was* going to "heal" him, but in the sense of raising him from death.

In fact, the disciples should have known better. When Jesus said emphatically, "I go to awaken him," they should have understood that there had to be a deeper meaning in this journey to Bethany than simply going there to "awaken" a sick person who was soundly asleep. Therefore, Jesus plainly told them that Lazarus had died. From this, they should have been able to conclude that Jesus was going to raise him from the dead.

The idea of "awakening" a dead person is enhanced by the

way Jesus "cried out with a loud voice, 'Lazarus, come out!'" (John 11:34). It reminds us of the way the disciples shouted to Jesus to wake him up from sleeping when they were in a boat (Luke 8:24), or the way Delilah woke Samson by shouting (Judg. 16:14). At the resurrection of the "dead in Christ," there will be a "cry of command," the "voice of an archangel," and the "sound of the trumpet of God" to wake them up (1 Thess. 4:16; cf. 1 Cor. 15:52).

5.5.3   About Metaphors

In recent decades, much light has been shed on the role of metaphors in the Bible. Their role is enormous. They are often misunderstood because people have tried to eliminate biblical truths by claiming that this or that is "only" a metaphor. No, there are great truths in the Bible that apparently can be expressed *only* in the form of metaphors. A simple example: a father is literally a male who has begotten one or more children through intercourse with one or more women. God is a Father metaphorically in the sense that believers are his "children" (also a metaphor); he is not a father literally because he is not a male, and he has no intercourse with women. Nonetheless, his Fatherhood, though metaphorical, is very *real*. In a sense it is perhaps more real than human fatherhood because a human father can be said to be a mere image of God's Fatherhood.

Similarly, there is literal death, which is physical death. But there is also metaphorical "death": (a) the condition of sinful, unconverted humans (Eph. 2:1); (b) the condition of believers who are spiritually lethargic (Eph. 5:14); (c) the eternal condition of the wicked after their resurrection ("second death," Rev. 21:8). Again, the fact that these descriptions are metaphorical in no way negates their full and serious *reality*. In a sense, the "second death" is even more fully and seriously real than physical death.

Similarly, the phrases "falling asleep" or "being asleep" have both a literal and a metaphorical meaning. The literal meaning is found in many passages.[74] The metaphorical meaning involves either a low spiritual condition ("sleep") of followers of Jesus (Mark 13:36; Eph. 5:14), or the dying or being dead of believers (see above). Again, claiming that "being asleep" is a metaphor never suggests that it is *only* a metaphor. The phrase reflects a deep spiritual reality, even though it is expressed in metaphorical language

---

74. E.g., Gen. 41:5; Judg. 4:21; 1 Sam. 26:12; 1 Kings 18:27; Jonah 1:5; Matt. 8:24; 28:13; Mark 14:37; Luke 8:23.

6

REAL AND SUPPOSED PLACES IN THE AFTERLIFE

In my Father's house are many rooms.
If it were not so,
would I have told you that I go to prepare a place for
you?
And if I go and prepare a place for you,
I will come again
and will take you to myself,
that where I am you may be also.

John 14:2–3

Ich habe Lust zu scheiden
Und mit dem Lamm,
Das aller Frommen Bräutigam,
Mich in der Seligkeit zu weiden.
Flügel her!
Ach, wer doch schon im Himmel wär!

> I wish to depart,
> and with the Lamb,
> the all-righteous Bridegroom,
> to feast in blessedness.
> Bring me wings!

Ah, if I were only in heaven![1]

Wer weiß, wie nahe mir mein Ende?

[*Who Knows How Near My End Is?*]

Bach cantata BWV 27

Unknown poet

6.1   Real Abodes
6.1.1   The Souls under the Altar

In Revelation 6:9–11 we read:

> When he [i.e., the Lamb] opened the fifth seal, I saw under the altar the souls of those who had been slain for the word of God and for the witness they had borne. They cried out with a loud voice, "O Sovereign Lord, holy and true, how long before you will judge and avenge our blood on those who dwell on the earth?" Then they were each given a white robe and told to rest a little longer, until the number of their fellow servants and their brothers should be complete, who were to be killed as they themselves had been.

The "souls" (disembodied personalities[2]) of those who have died as martyrs because of their witness to the faith are viewed here "under the altar." Presumably this is because they have given their lives as a sacrifice to God.[3] In the Old Testament, the blood of sacrificial animals was poured out at the foot of the altar of burnt offering (Exod. 29:12; Lev. 4:7–34). This blood is identified with the "soul" as the life principle in the biological sense (Lev. 17:10, 14)—another of the many biblical meanings of the word "soul." Therefore, these martyrs, who have given their blood for the sake of God and the Lamb, are viewed here at the foot of the altar (also cf. Gen. 4:10). The Apostle Paul compares his approaching martyr's

---

1. An interesting confusion of death and resurrection: feasting with the Bridegroom will occur at the Parousia, *not* at death.
2. We ought not to introduce here the Platonic notion of the immortal soul; see extensively, chapter 8.
3. See Ouweneel (1988), 243–45.

death to a sacrifice as well (Phil. 2:17; 2 Tim. 4:6; cf. also Rom. 12:1).

The passage is important because apparently it is not all peace, joy, and bliss in the hereafter. If we may generalize the quoted passage, we may say that deceased believers are well aware of the terrible things that have happened to them, and that their oppressors are still avoiding their coming retribution. Thus, these believers are aware of what is happening on earth, and of what ought to happen there. In connection with this, Revelation 14:13 is important: "'Blessed are the dead who die in the Lord from now on.' 'Blessed indeed,' says the Spirit, 'that they may rest from their labors, for their deeds follow them!'"[4] There has been much speculation about the phrase "from now on." Does it mean from the time of the fulfillment of this vision? Or from the time when John wrote this? Or from the moment of the deceased person's death? I suggest a connection between Rev. 14:13 and Rev. 6:9–11: the multitude of martyrs is complete in 14:13, their trials lie behind them, and they are happy, for since their resurrection, their disembodied souls are no longer "under the altar" but they have risen from the dead, and enjoy the bliss of heaven (cf. 20:4). At last, their complete rest has arrived.

In the intermediate state, the deceased can still be concerned with what is happening on earth. We see this also with Dives, who is worried about the destiny of his five biological brothers (Luke 16:27–28). And Abraham is also aware of his distant descendant, Moses, and the things he wrote (long after Abraham), and of his still more distant descendants, the prophets and their writings. These things refute the notion expressed occasionally that the deceased dwell in blessed ignorance concerning conditions on earth, or concerning the things they had experienced during their own lives. The deceased do know about their own earthly history (Matt. 7:22); their works follow them (Rev. 14:13). The dead pagan kings mockingly greet the dead king of Babylon in Hades (Isa. 14:9); they

---

4. See *ibid.*, 117–18.

know who he is, what he has done, and what he is going to experience in Sheol. And, if we may interpret Luke 16:9 this way, the friends whom the righteous person formerly had treated well receive him in the "eternal dwellings," happy to reward him. Hebrews 12:1 could also be taken to mean that the deceased believers are able to follow the course of living believers on earth.

G. van Niftrik spoke of a real *working* together with what God is doing on earth; as he put it (beginning by quoting the words of Jesus):

> "My Father is working until now, and I am working" (John 5:17). Soon we will work with God in a new way. He does not want to do it without us. Covenant history is continued. This creation must be brought to consummation and glorification. . . . [Deceased believers] are going to *work* with God for the complete permeation of the earth by heaven. This is their bliss.[5]

The author's claim would be acceptable were we to replace the phrase "deceased believers" with the phrase "risen believers."

The question has been widely debated regarding how a deceased person can possibly be "wrapped in a robe" (Samuel in 1 Sam. 28:14), or receive a robe in the hereafter (Rev. 6:11) before his or her body has been raised, because souls are mentioned later in Revelation 20:4. John Walvoord belonged among those who assumed that, between death and resurrection, these "souls" employ a temporary body, because a robe cannot clothe an immaterial spirit.[6] However, Walvoord's talk of an immaterial soul or spirit showed that he too was influenced by the ancient body-soul dualism (see chapter 8). That the deceased in Luke 16:23–24 have eyes, a bosom, fingers, and a tongue is no more problematic than that they receive a robe, all of which is metaphorical. The "souls" in Revelation 6:9 need not be immaterial souls any more than the eight "souls" in

---

5. Van Niftrik (1970), 144.
6. Walvoord (1966), 134–35.

Noah's ark were (1 Pet. 3:20)—since in such instances, the term "souls" simply means "persons."

6.1.2 The "Prison"

In 1 Peter 3:18b–20 we read of

> . . . Christ . . . being put to death in the flesh but made alive in the spirit, in which [or the Spirit, in whom] he went and proclaimed to the spirits in prison, because they formerly did not obey, when God's patience waited in the days of Noah, while the ark was being prepared, in which a few, that is, eight persons, were brought safely through water.

Without entering into all the exegetical issues present in these verses (for a discussion of these, see §6.2.1), we limit ourselves here to the word "prison" (Gk. *phulakē*, from *phulax*, "guard, watchman"). The term recalls Isaiah 24:22, "They [i.e., the wicked] will be gathered together as prisoners in a pit [or, dungeon]; they will be shut up in a prison, and after many days they will be punished."

The interpretation of this phrase "the spirits in prison" is among the most debated matters in New Testament studies, more debated than 2 Corinthians 5:1–8 (§5.4).[7] The history of interpretation exhibits two main options. The disobedient "spirits in prison" are either the disembodied personalities of those who perished in the Noahic Flood and are kept in Hades, or they are the fallen angels of Genesis 6:1–4 in their "prison," or their semi-human offspring, who perished in the Flood. In the former case, the "prison" is the same as Hades, the abode of the wicked between their death and their resurrection. In the second case, the "prison" is the same as the underworld (Gk. *tartaros*), the place where certain fallen angels are kept (see following section).

The proclamation by the Spirit of Christ occurred either in the days of Noah, or between Jesus' death and resurrection, or after his resurrection. In the former case, verses 19–20 must be read more

---

7. See Ouweneel (2007a), 147–48.

161

or less as follows: ". . . in which [Spirit] he [i.e., Christ] *at the time, in Noah's days,* went and proclaimed to the people whose spirits are *at present* in prison, the people who *formerly* did not obey, when God's patience waited in the days of Noah." Indeed, Genesis 6:3 speaks of the Spirit through whom God spoke and acted in those days. F. Spitta understood these to be the fallen angels ("sons of God") of Genesis 6:1–4, who hear Christ announcing their judgment.[8] Others thought, and still think, these were the wicked in the days of Noah, to whom, through Noah, the Spirit preached in vain.[9]

H. Bavinck has argued that not only is there no gospel preaching to the dead in "prison" in 1 Peter 3:19–20 (and 4:6), but also that this would be an incongruity:

> Did he at that time go physically to hades? When did he do that? How long did he stay there? And suppose all this were possible— however unlikely it is as such—who then is conducting the preaching in hades on an ongoing basis after this time? Is there a church in the underworld? Is there an ongoing mission, a calling and ordination to ministry?[10]

Those who believe verse 19 referred to an event that occurred between Jesus' death and resurrection conclude that verse 21c contains the first mention of Jesus' resurrection, whereas verse 18c would speak of his existence as a disembodied spirit.[11] This interpretation does not work, because the expression "made alive" in verse 18 cannot possibly refer to a stage before the resurrection (cf. 1 Cor. 15:22).[12] Therefore, there appears to be no basis in the text for identifying a descent into Hades of Christ between his death

8. Spitta (1890), *ad loc.*
9. Augustine; *SYN ad loc.*; Grant (1902), 161–63; Kelly (1923), 200–205; "many Reformed," according to Greijdanus (1931), 62; more recently and quite extensively, Grudem (1988), 157–61, 203–39.
10. Bavinck, *RD*, 4:631.
11. So Hart (1979), 68.
12. Elsewhere the being "made alive" of believers is equated with their being "raised up" (Eph. 2:5–6).

and resurrection, despite the statement in the Apostles' Creed (see further §6.2.1). We should rather think of the ascension of the risen Christ (cf. v. 22), at which time it was possible that he proclaimed his triumph over the fallen angels,[13] or over the wicked who had already died, including Noah's contemporaries, who were introduced here in 1 Peter 3 as examples.[14]

6.1.3 *Abyssos* and *Tartaros*

In Luke 8:31 we hear of the Greek *abyssos*, the "abyss,"[15] down into which the exorcised demons did not wish to be sent. The parallel passage, Matthew 8:29, identifies this as a place where they would be "tormented before the time," namely, the time of their definitive judgment. Apparently, for demons the abyss is comparable with what Hades is for deceased unbelievers: a kind of "detention center" of punishment and torment before the ultimate judgment, which will presumably occur before the "great white throne" (Rev. 20:11-15; see §11.2.4).

We hear about this abyss in Revelation 9:1–2 and 11 as well; the latter verse speaks of the "angel of the abyss," called Abaddon (Heb. for "destruction" or "underworld") or Apollyon (Gk. for "destroyer"); we read more about this in Rev. 11:7, 17:8, 20:1 and 3. Generally speaking, this appears to be a place where certain apostate angels are kept. But in Revelation 11:7 and 17:8 it is "the beast" rising from the abyss, and this "beast" is both the Roman Empire and the head of this Empire. It is possible that the term "abyss" is used here only to indicate the satanic origin of this "beast."

Romans 10:7 is the only passage where the Greek word *abyssos* seems to refer to the abode of the dead: "'. . . or 'Who will descend into the abyss?' (that is, to bring Christ up from the dead)."[16] Ap-

---

13. So Blum (1981), 241–43.
14. So Greijdanus (1931), 62–64; Hommes et al. (1946), 489.
15. *TDNT* 1:9–10; *DNTT* 2:205.
16. Cf. Ps. 107:26, especially in the Septuagint (where it is 106:26): ". . . that lift them high into the heavens; then, to the abyss, they descend."

parently, here descending into the abyss was the same as descending into Sheol or Hades. In the Septuagint, *abyssos* is the usual rendering of Hebrew *t'hom*, the "deep" or "primeval ocean," mentioned in Genesis 1:2. Psalm 71:20b says, "[F]rom the depths [Heb. *mitt'homot* (from *t'hom*); Septuagint: *ek tōn abyssōn*] of the earth you will bring me up again," that is, you will make me return from Sheol.[17] According to rabbinic tradition, Sheol lies under the *t'hom*.

In 2 Peter 2:4 we find the interesting Greek verbal form *tartarōsas*, that is, "cast them into hell [Gk. *tartaros*]" (CEB: "cast into the lowest level of the underworld"; CJB: "gloomy dungeons"). Most translations have something like "cast down to hell," which is definitely mistaken because the text was speaking in the past tense, whereas being cast down into hell belongs to the future (Rev. 20:10–15). This *tartaros* is something like a "detention center" for fallen angels, where they have been "committed to chains of gloomy darkness to be kept until the judgment" (2 Pet. 2:4; cf. vv. 9, 17; 3:7). This is comparable to what Jude 6 tells us about angels who "did not stay within their own position of authority,"[18] and who are "kept in eternal chains under gloomy darkness[19] until the judgment of the great day" (see again §11.2.4).

From the time of Homer, the Greeks understood Tartarus to be a place of special divine punishments, and this idea was adopted in the ancient Jewish literature that was written in Greek.[20] The Septuagint uses *tartaros* in Job 40:20b (v. 15 NETS): "But when it [i.e., Behemoth (v. 15), a supernatural power[21]] went up on a steep mountain, / it brought gladness to the quadrupeds in Tartarus."

---

17. Here, this means a return from trouble; in another context, it might be a reference to the resurrection.
18. Those who did not limit themselves to the responsibilities granted to them, and left the place assigned to them; Blum (1981), 390.
19. Gk. *zophos*, the gloomy darkness of the nether world, also the nether world as such.
20. Bauer (1971), 1594; Strachan (1979), 134–35; Josephus, *Contra Apionem* 2.240; *Sibylline Oracles* 2.302; 4.186.
21. Ouweneel (2003), 221.

And in Job 41:23–25 (vv. 31–33 NETS):

> It [i.e., Leviathan, another higher power[22]] makes the deep boil like a caldron
>
> and regards the sea as a pot of ointment
>
> and Tartarus of the deep [Gk. *abyssos*] as a captive.
>
> [*it reckoned the deep* [Gk. *abyssos*] *for a promenade.*]
>
> There is nothing on earth like it,
>
> made to be mocked at by my angels.
>
> Everything high it sees,
>
> and it is king over all that are in the waters.

In 1 Enoch 20:2, the place of punishment for the apostate is identified by the Greek word *Gehenna* (the New Testament word for "hell"), and the one for fallen angels by the Greek word *tartaros*.

6.2   The *Limbus Patrum*

6.2.1   "Descended Into Hell"

The exegesis of 1 Peter 3:18–20 given in §6.1.2 is linked directly to the well-known and heavily debated words of the Apostles' Creed: Jesus "descended into hell [the nether world; Gk. *katelthonta eis ta katōtata*; Lat. *descendit ad inferna*]." The Greek word *katōtata* means "depths, lower places"; the expression is related to what we find in Ephesians 4:9, "the lower parts [Gk. *katōtera*] of the earth." Similarly, the Latin word *inferna* ("nether world, underworld, realm of the dead") comes from *inferus*, "being under [i.e., often: being in the underworld]" (cf. "inferior"). In Italian (*inferno*), Spanish (*infierno*), and French (*enfer*), the word *infernum* (singular) or *inferna* (plural) came to mean "hell," a rendering that has strongly enhanced all the confusion related to the rendering "descended into hell" instead of "descended into the underworld."

Peter's quotation from Psalm 16:10, "[Y]ou will not abandon my soul to Hades, or let your Holy One see corruption" (Acts 2:27), clearly suggests that, between his death and resurrection, Jesus was

---

22. *Ibid.*, 215, 221, 281, 316–17, 325; cf. Ouweneel (2008), 47–48, 59.

in Hades. But what do we mean by this? There are at least four explanations to which we must pay attention.[23]

(a) Here, the word "Hades" is the rendering of Hebrew *sh'ol* (Sheol), which need not mean anything more than the grave (see §4.3); the word "corruption" in Acts 2:27 supports this interpretation. God did not "leave" Jesus in (or "abandon" him to) the grave where he would have undergone the corruption of his body; he raised him from the grave.

(b) Jesus descended into Hades (the nether world, the realm of the dead) in order to break the power of hell and Satan. Jesus became Man in order "that through death he might destroy the one who has the power of death, that is, the devil" (Heb. 2:14). After this dethronement of Satan, it is Jesus who holds the "keys of Death and Hades" (Rev. 1:18). Joseph Ratzinger put it this way: Jesus' descent into Hades was symbolized in his baptism, signifying his ". . . knocking and flinging open the gates of the abyss"; his descent

> is a descent into the house of the evil one, [a] combat with the "strong man" (cf. Lk 11:22[; Matt. 12:29]) who holds men captive [Heb 2:14–15]. . . . Throughout all its history, the world is powerless to defeat the "strong man"; he is overcome and bound by one yet stronger, who, because of his equality with God, can take upon himself all the sin of the world . . . .[24]

(c) Jesus descended into Hades in order to preach the gospel to the pagans and unbelievers there. This is suggested by the NOG: he "went to proclaim his victory to the spirits kept in prison" (1 Pet. 3:19), and also by Phillips: "It was in the spirit that he went and preached to the imprisoned souls of those who had been disobedient in the days of Noah" (vv. 19, 20a). In both cases, interpretation (d) is also possible.

---

23. See Ouweneel (2007b), 410.
24. Ratzinger (2007), 20.

(d) Jesus descended into Hades in order to liberate the believers who had died before him. This teaching is found among Roman Catholic and Reformational theologians, and nowadays also among Evangelicals.[25] Its roots are found in the writings of the Church Fathers, namely, in the idea of the (Latin) *Limbus Patrum*, literally: "edge (border) of the fathers" (a place "bordering" on hell), that is, the alleged abode of the Old Testament believers, which since the death of Christ is supposed to be unpopulated. A famous example of this teaching is found in the Gospel of Nicodemus II.9–10.[26]

Regarding this teaching, J. MacCullough wrote that from the second century, no doctrine was better known or more popular than this one, including the descent into Hades, the victory over death and Hades, the preaching to the dead and the release of souls, and this popularity kept increasing.[27] J. Sanders noted that the doctrine of Christ's descent into hell (read: Hades!) and the release of the souls from it was established by the end of the first century; the only unanswered question involved the identity of the persons released.[28]

P. Hughes thought he knew the answer to this question. Without argument or proof, he asserted (in reference to 2 Cor. 12:4): "If our Lord descended to hades, it was to liberate the souls of the just who had been awaiting His triumph and thence to lead them to the heavenly Paradise won for them through His conquest on the cross."[29] This view in its elaborate form is constructed with the following arguments:[30]

(a) Jesus personally descended to Hades in order to "lead a host of captives"; this is adopted from Ephesians 4:8, which is a quotation from Psalm 68:18. Here, much is being deduced from the

---

25. Regarding this, see Ouweneel (2009a), 307–309.
26. www.masterandmargarita.eu/archieven/nicodemus.pdf.
27. MacCullough (1930), 45.
28. Sanders (1992), 183–84.
29. Hughes (1962), 436.
30. Prince (2006); (1995), 463–64; Duffield and Van Cleave (1996), 551–52.

words, "Thou hast ascended on high, thou hast led captivity captive" (KJV), which is taken to mean "thou hast led captives," as modern translations usually render it: "You ascended on high, leading a host of captives in your train" (ESB).

Comment: Paul himself did not make this deduction at all; on the contrary, it hardly fits into his argument (see below).

(b) Jesus spent three days and three nights in "the heart of the earth" (Matt. 12:40).

Comment: This does not refer to some abode—Hades or Paradise—where Jesus would have sojourned; basically, it means nothing more than that he spent this period in the grave.

(c) Jesus took all the just from Hades, and took them to "Paradise." Psalm 16:10 and its quotation in Acts 2:27 ("you will not abandon [Gk. *enkataleipō*[31]] my soul to Hades") are adduced as evidence that, between his death and resurrection, Jesus was indeed in Hades.

Comment: As we have seen, this might not mean anything more than that he was in the grave, or in the realm of death; many translations indeed have the word "grave" in Acts 2:27.

(d) These righteous ones supposedly were the saints who, after Jesus' resurrection, came out of their graves and appeared to many in Jerusalem (Matt. 27:52–53).

Comment: This identification is pure speculation; the text suggests nothing of the kind (see further in §6.2.3).

Part of this ancient view is echoed in the explanation by Joseph Ratzinger that we cited in (b) above.

6.2.2 Further Comments

The core question is whether it is correct to say that, until the death of Christ, Old Testament believers had lived in darkness. To demonstrate this, reference is sometimes made to Job: ". . . before I go—and I shall not return—to the land of darkness and deep

---

31. Bauer (1971), 427.

shadow, the land of gloom like thick darkness, like deep shadow without any order, where light is as thick darkness" (10:21–22); ". . . if I hope for Sheol as my house, if I make my bed in darkness . . ." (17:13; Eccl. 11:8). The idea is that Jesus released the righteous from this place of darkness by leading them to Paradise at his resurrection or ascension.

Against this view of Christ's victory, a number of serious objections must be put forward. First, we cannot consider Job as someone experienced with Sheol, for he had never been there *and* he was speaking as a desperate man. Scripture is indeed inspired (2 Tim. 3:16), but Job was not inspired; not everything a believer says is of the Spirit.[32] Moreover, the Hebrew word *sh'ol* means little more than "grave" (see §4.3), and there darkness does indeed reign.

Second, after having died, Lazarus went to recline "in Abraham's bosom" (Luke 16:22)—this was before Christ's triumph—and from the response of Dives we certainly do not get the impression that the abode of Abraham and Lazarus was dark and gloomy.

Third, the promise made to the criminal on the cross (Luke 23:43)—no matter how it is interpreted (see §5.2)—was to be fulfilled on that very same day, and not three days later at Jesus' resurrection.

Then there is the weak interpretation of Ephesians 4:8–10. As we saw, here Paul was freely quoting Psalm 68:18, "You ascended on high, leading a host of captives in your train and receiving gifts among men, even among the rebellious, that the LORD God may dwell there [i.e., on Zion])." Theodore of Mopsuestia (c. 400) was among the earliest to posit the idea that the captives would be redeemed people. G. von Harless suggested that the text is about people who, while on earth, had been bound in sins.[33] E. König, F.

---

32. The theological term *inspiration* never refers to persons, but to Scripture (2 Tim. 3:16); see extensively Ouweneel (Forthcoming-b).
33. Harless (1834), *ad loc.*

Delitzsch, and others believed that these are souls that were held in Hades.[34] However, our first observation is that the notion of leading Old Testament believers on high does not fit the context of either Ephesians 4:8–10 or Psalm 68:18. The topic of the righteous ones being caught up is completely absent, and we have no basis for reading it into the text, contrary to the intentions of David and Paul.

Second, it is exegetically unacceptable to view the captives as God's own people; the context clearly points to *enemies* who have been taken captive; compare the CEB: "You ascended the heights, leading away your captives, receiving tribute from people, even from those who rebel against the LORD God's dwelling there" (cf. Judg. 5:12, "Arise, Barak, lead away your captives"). Nor can we twist the argument in Ephesians 4:8–10 by identifying these people as captives of God's *enemies*, who were released by Christ.[35] No, Paul's application of the point was that Christ "has gained the victory over hell and world, has borne all curse and guilt of his people, has brought about a full atonement for them," as S. Greijdanus put it.[36] Therefore, K. Wuest understands the "captives" to have been demons who tried to stop Jesus in his ascension.[37]

F. F. Bruce said of it:

[T]he passage has served as one of the few biblical proof-texts for the harrowing of hell—the idea that between his death and resurrection Christ invaded the abode of the dead and released the men and women of God who, from Adam onward, had been held fast there, thus "leading captivity captive." No explanation is offered in this *pesher* [i.e., "interpretation"] of the multitude of captives taken by the conqueror in Ps. 68:18; but the words would refer more naturally to prisoners-of-war from the enemy army than to the conqueror's

---

34. König (1927), *ad loc.*; KDC, 6:261–62.
35. Salmond (1979), 324.
36. Greijdanus (1925), 87.
37. Wuest (1977), 98–99.

rightful subjects who had been released from the enemy leader's unwelcome control.[38]

In summary, the cumulative force of a number of speculative interpretations of passages that by themselves are already complicated cannot produce a reliable theological hypothesis. We *can* say, though, that Ephesians 4:8–10 underscores the idea of a triumphal procession that Christ has made after his victory over Satan and his powers, comparable with 1:20–22, Colossians 2:15, and 1 Peter 3:22. However, this is something very different from some kind of "release" of Old Testament believers, a "bringing them up" from some dark underworld to the light of Paradise. There is no biblical evidence for this notion, no matter how many orthodox theologians may have defended it.

6.2.3   The Saints Risen [Raised] at Jesus' Death

In §6.2.1, I mentioned the saints who, after Jesus' resurrection, came out of their graves, and appeared to many in Jerusalem (Matt. 27:50–53). Often, the doctrine of the *Limbus Patrum* and of Old Testament believers being brought up from the darkness at Jesus' resurrection are related to the passage just mentioned:

> Jesus cried out again with a loud voice and yielded up his spirit. And behold, the curtain of the temple was torn in two, from top to bottom. And the earth shook, and the rocks were split. The tombs also were opened. And many bodies of the saints who had fallen asleep were raised, and coming out of the tombs after his resurrection they went into the holy city and appeared to many.

This strange passage has understandably led to vigorous debates.[39] Multiple exegetical questions arise here: What "saints" are intended here? All Old Testament believers, or only a few? If the

---

38. Bruce (1984), 344.
39. In addition to France (2007), *ad loc.*; see also D. Wenham (1973), 42–46; Senior (1976); J. W. Wenham (1981); Wright (2003), 632–36; and Pawson (2004), 179–85.

latter, which few? How could they have been raised at the moment of Jesus' death, but left their graves only after his resurrection? What happened after the events related in the text to these resurrected believers? Did they return to their graves? Did they live on earth for a time, and then die again? Or did they ascend to heaven, as did the risen Jesus? To what people did they appear? How public were these appearances? Why does Matthew not tell us a little bit more about this remarkable event?

I see five possible ways of approaching this difficult passage.

(a) We must not take the word "raised" here too literally, but rather assume that these saints appeared to people in the spirit, or in a temporary body of some kind, like Samuel in 1 Samuel 28:11–16 and Moses during the transfiguration on the mount (e.g., Mark 9:4–5), or like the three "men" (three angels, or the LORD with two angels) who visited Abraham in Genesis 18.

Response: This interpretation is unlikely, since the combination of the words "raised" and "bodies" never points to anything other than a genuine resurrection.

(b) F. Grosheide, too, thought of the previous possibility, and gave it this twist: this did not involve "an actual resurrection but the fact that God, in order to reveal the great significance of the death (not the resurrection) of Christ, took for a certain time the bodies of godly people from the earth, which had been split by the earthquake, and showed them to many."[40]

Response: This interpretation faces the same objection as the previous one. This event involved not a deceased Moses or Samuel appearing briefly to only a few people, but *resurrected* people appearing to a large number of people.

(c) These raised saints received their old bodies again, just like the three raised persons in the Old Testament, the three in the Gospels, and the two in Acts (see §2.2), which implies that, after a peri-

---

40. Grosheide (1954), 439.

od of time, they passed away again.

Response: This interpretation is unlikely, for the word "to appear" is used for angels and the risen Jesus,[41] but never for raised people who, like Lazarus, returned to their old bodies, and afterward died again.

(d) At the moment of Jesus' death, the resurrected ones received new, glorified bodies, just as Jesus himself did three days later.

Response: This interpretation is doubtful, for in this case these deceased would have received their resurrection bodies before Jesus received his, which would then have meant that Jesus is *not* the "firstfruits" of the deceased (cf. 1 Cor. 15:20, 23)[42]—unless interpretation (e) is correct.

(e) We must read the text differently: ". . . the earth shook, and the rocks were split. The tombs also were opened [at Jesus' death]. And many bodies of the saints who had fallen asleep were raised [at Jesus' resurrection], and coming out of the tombs after his resurrection. . . ."[43] This approach solves the problem of how these saints could have stayed in their graves for three days *after* having been raised.

Response: It is also possible that they spent these three days somewhere outside the city, unseen by others.[44] The objection against this proposed way of reading the text is that the series of verbs in the Aorist tense is interrupted abruptly, and the obvious link is broken between opening the graves and raising the saints.

Unfortunately, we must conclude that, because of the extreme brevity of the passage and the lack of parallel accounts and similar events, we are left with more questions than answers. The best we can say is that, perhaps, possibility (e) is the least unlikely.

---

41. Mark 16:9; Luke 24:34; Acts 9:17; 13:31; 26:16; 1 Cor. 15:5–8; cf. Acts 1:3.
42. Pawson (2004), 182.
43. Wenham (1981); Carson (1984), 581–82 sympathizes with this exegesis.
44. France (2007), 1082.

6.3 Purgatory

6.3.1 The Basis for this Doctrine

Protestant readers should not think that they can quietly omit reading this section! They should reflect on these three passages before reading any further. First, in his Sermon on the Mount Jesus speaks of being "put in prison": "Truly, I say to you, you will never get out until you have paid the last penny" (Matt. 5:27). Second, we find the same metaphor in the parable on forgiveness: ". . . in anger his master delivered him to the jailers [literally, torturers], until he should pay all his debt" (18:34). Third, consider this: "If anyone's work is burned up, he will suffer loss, though he himself will be saved, but only as through fire" (1 Cor. 3:15).

Is there a place in the afterlife where a person can make restitution for certain serious trespasses in the past, and thus be saved, as the first two passages might suggest? Or is there a salvation that is reached only "through fire," as the third passage might be taken to suggest?

The place known as "purgatory" is ostensibly a place where people are "purged" (cleansed, made ready for heaven) after death. The English term is better than the Dutch term *vagevuur* and the German term *Fegefeuer*, meaning literally "purging fire." These two latter terms place too much emphasis on the aspect of "fire," thereby leading us to think of hell,[45] whereas the Latin word *purgatorium* (from *purgare*, "to cleanse") indicates much better that this is a place of catharsis, or purification—a refinery rather than a prison.[46]

In the Roman Catholic view, purgatory is a place where, or a condition in which, the souls of those who have died in a state of grace undergo a limited amount of suffering in order to do penance for unatoned daily sins, and for their mortal sins insofar as these

---

45. Matt. 5:22; 18:9; Mark 9:43; cf. the "eternal fire," Matt.18:8; 25:41; Jude 7; also cf. the "lake of fire," Rev. 19:20; 20:10, 14–15; 21:8.
46. Rahner (1978), 462.

have already been forgiven through confession or a perfect contrition, but not yet expiated.[47] After this purging, the soul is allowed into heaven. The doctrine was formally promulgated by Pope Innocent IV (c. 1250), and confirmed and underscored by the Second Council of Lyon (1274), the Council of Florence (1439), and the Council of Trent (1545–1563).

In the writings of Roman Catholic theologians such as Karl Rahner we find some healthy modification of this doctrine.[48] But this does not change the fact that the Second Vatican Council firmly confirmed this doctrine "regarding this vital fellowship with our brethren who are in heavenly glory or having died are still being purified."[49]

The first Bible passage that Roman Catholics use in support is 1 Corinthians 3:12–15:

> Now if anyone builds on the foundation with gold, silver, precious stones, wood, hay, straw—each one's work will become manifest, for the Day will disclose it, because it will be revealed by fire, and the fire will test what sort of work each one has done. If the work that anyone has built on the foundation survives, he will receive a reward. If anyone's work is burned up, he will suffer loss, though he himself will be saved, but only as through fire.

The Dutch Wikipedia article, apparently written by a Roman Catholic, says of this passage: "Protestants interpret it differently because they do not accept the doctrine of purgatory."[50] It seems to me that the reality is instead the very opposite: Protestants do not accept the doctrine of purgatory because to them this passage

---

47. An unforgiven mortal sin cannot be expiated in purgatory; those who die in a state of mortal sin go to hell forever, according to Roman Catholic doctrine. There is much in this view of expiation that we cannot agree with, but that is not our subject right now.
48. Rahner (1978), 461–62.
49. *Lumen Gentium* 7 (http://www.vatican.va/archive/hist_councils/ii_vatican_council/documents/vat-ii_const_19641121_lumen-gentium_en.html).
50. nl.wikipedia.org/wiki/Vagevuur.

means something quite different.

It is noteworthy that the Eastern Orthodox have always reject-ed this doctrine, too.[51] As I once told a Catholic theologian and friend, with tongue in cheek: "Every doctrine that is defended by only one denomination is necessarily wrong." Of course, this holds for *every* denomination, or group of closely related denominations; it is only "with all the saints" that we begin to "comprehend" God's truth (Eph. 3:18).[52] Doctrines that only Catholics affirm include those of the immaculate conception of Mary and of purgatory, both of which I believe to be false.

6.3.2 Various Aspects

At the beginning of the previous section I quoted Matthew 5:26 and 18:34. Roman Catholics understand these verses to teach that, in the hereafter, it is possible to do penance for certain sins. And they believe that Matthew 12:32 ("whoever speaks against the Holy Spirit will not be forgiven, either in this age or in the age to come") suggests that, in the hereafter, there is still the possibility of forgive-ness, as long as no blasphemy against the Holy Spirit is involved.[53] Protestants argue that these passages do not teach anything resem-bling a doctrine of purgatory, which at best is being read into them by those who already believe in it.

Roman Catholics are not persuaded by this objection.[54] They argue that the early church developed the doctrine of purgatory, and, according to Jesus' promise, it was being guided into the truth by the Holy Spirit (John 16:13). Roman Catholics do not believe in purgatory primarily "because it is in the Bible," but because the church has taught it from a very early time—and the church can-

---

51. See Shenouda III, *Why Do We Reject Purgatory?* (orthodoxwiki.org/Purgatory).
52. Cf. Ben Zoma, "Who is wise? He who learns from everyone," with an appeal to Ps. 119:99 (Pirkei Avot 4:1).
53. This argument is found in Pope Gregory the Great (McGrath [2017], 441).
54. See Ouweneel and De Korte (2010), 46–47.

not err, because it is led by the Spirit. Biblical arguments, such as the ones mentioned, function in an *a priori* manner for Protestants; but they function in an *a posteriori* manner for Roman Catholics, as an afterthought to confirm what the church has been teaching all along.

Moreover, the logic is typically scholastic: if God *can* do something, and for logically compelling reasons *must* have done it, then it is in the spirit of Scripture to assume that he *did* it. Thus, there *must* be a purgatory in order to prepare souls for heaven, and therefore it *must* exist. Actually, Protestant scholasticism exhibits its own examples of this type of thinking (e.g., if there is an eternal counsel of election, there must also be an eternal counsel of reprobation).

There is another side as well. We must be careful when appealing to various Church Fathers and leaders, who supposedly defended this doctrine. Perhaps some of them did nothing more than assume a kind of cleansing before the judgment seat of Christ, when many believers will see the "wood, hay, and straw" in their lives burned away before they can enter glory. Our first reply is that this event will occur at or after the Parousia (cf. Matt. 25:31; Rev. 20:12–15), not at the time a believer dies. Our second observation is that such a purging does not imply the existence of a certain *place* where such a cleansing would occur during a certain *time*. Actually, the entire idea of a purgatory is part of a mistaken interim theology ("going to heaven when you die"). If the latter is mistaken, the idea of a purgatory is mistaken as well.

There is even less of a basis for assuming that believers who have remained behind would be able, through financial or other means, to shorten this time in purgatory for their relatives and friends. Think of the well-known discussion about indulgences between Martin Luther and his opponents (Johann Tetzel[55] and others).

---

55. His mantra was "As soon as a coin in the coffer rings, / the soul from purgatory springs" (Ger. *Sobald das Geld im Kasten klingt, die Seele in den Himmel springt!*).

Protestants cannot accept the doctrine of purgatory because it is not biblical. But they are not allowed to attach false associations with it. For instance, J. Heyns suggested that this doctrine is directly related to the Roman Catholic doctrine of good works,[56] and J. Verkuyl asserted that purgatory is a denial of the message of radical grace.[57] These suggestions overlook the fact that the New Testament teaches many times that, while standing before the judgment seat of Christ, believers definitely must account for their *works*,[58] and that there will be *rewards* for our good works,[59] but also a cleansing with regard to defective works (1 Cor. 3:12–15). H. Berkhof criticized the Reformation on this point:

> [The Reformation] imagined a sudden, radical transformation after the judgment, usually without giving it further theological reflection and without connecting it with the struggle for sanctification on earth. . . . [1 Cor. 3:15 suggests] that Paul thought of more than an abrupt re-creation of man; salvation is accompanied by a painful becoming aware of one's own failures on earth which signify both punishment as well as purification ("fire"). Among the classic ecclesiastical models, the Reformational model is entirely unique in its sharp rejection of a process of purification that transcends death].[60]

6.3.3 The *Limbus Puerorum*

Let me add here another remarkable example of the logic similar to what I just described: if God *can* do something, and for logically compelling reasons *must* have done it, then it is in the spirit of Scripture to assume that he *did* it. This example involves the de-

---

56. Heyns (1988), 400.
57. Verkuyl (1992), 455.
58. Rom. 2:16; 14:10; 1 Cor. 4:4–5; 2 Cor. 5:10; cf. 1 Cor. 1:8; Gal. 6:4–5; Phil. 1:10; 2:16.
59. Rom. 2:6–10; 1 Cor. 3:8, 14; Rev. 2:23; 22:12.
60. Berkhof (1986), 493–94; the words within brackets appear in the Dutch original of the 2nd edition [", die zowel straf als loutering betekent ('vuur'). Onder de klassieke kerktypen staan de reformatorische geheel alleen in hun scherpe afwijzing van een louteringsproces over de dood heen."]).

velopment of the idea of the *Limbus Puerorum* or *Infantium*, that is, the "limbo [a place 'bordering' on hell] of children" who have died before having been baptized. Logic dictated the following steps in the argument:

(a) These children cannot go to heaven, for Jesus said: "[U]nless one is born of water and the Spirit, he cannot enter the kingdom of God" (John 3:5). The "water" was taken to mean the water of baptism, and the "kingdom of God" was taken to mean heaven. Another supposed proof-text is Mark 16:16, "Whoever believes *and is baptized* will be saved," from which verse baptism is taken to be an indispensable condition of salvation. This is why Roman Catholics have always baptized their newborn babies as soon as possible after their birth (and many early Protestants did too).

(b) These children cannot go to hell, either, for they have not yet committed sins (this is true, but we must not forget that the sinful *nature* as such is sufficient for being eternally condemned).

Conclusion: For these young deceased children there must be an abode that is neither heaven nor hell; a place neither of supernatural bliss (perhaps only of natural joys) nor of torment. This is what was called the *Limbus Infantium* or *Puerorum*. Hints of it have been found in the writings of Church Fathers such as Augustine, Jerome, and Gregory the Great.

In 2007 the Roman Catholic Church, under the guidance of Pope Benedict XVI, downgraded this doctrine to a mere possible theological opinion. Since then, the entire concept of the *Limbus Puerorum* has played a minimal role in Roman Catholic thinking; the tendency is to assume that unbaptized children who die young may nevertheless be saved by God on the basis of Jesus' work of redemption.

How would Protestants solve the problem mentioned here? Hyper-Calvinists take *predestination* as their starting point: babies who died young were either predestined by God for salvation, or reprobated. In the former case these children die in a regenerated

179

state, thanks to immediate regeneration, that is, a rebirth without the mediation of God's Word.[61]

Neo-Calvinists take the *covenant* as their starting point; they generally teach that children of believing parents are included in the covenant of grace, and therefore they are saved when they die young; but children of unbelieving parents are not.[62]

Personally I believe that *all* children who die young are saved. They do have original sin, but Christ paid the price for this on the cross (Rom. 8:3; 2 Cor. 5:21). When Jesus speaks of little children, he says, "[[T]he Son of man has come to save that which was lost" (Matt. 18:11 NKJV). But when he speaks of those who can be held responsible for their deeds, he says, "[T]he Son of Man came *to seek* and to save the lost" (Luke 19:10). They must be sought because, through their evil deeds, they have wandered away from God (cf. Isa. 59:2, "your iniquities have made a separation between you and your God"). Those who, from God's viewpoint, must be sought are the same as those who, from the human viewpoint, must repent and convert.

The Bible argues several times that children are not punished for the sins of the fathers,[63] so the conclusion from this seems obvious that neither can the eternal destiny of children who die young depend on the faith or unbelief of the parents. Young children have a special place in the grace of God, independent of any covenant relationship that might be involved.[64] Children cannot be held accountable for their knowledge of creation or of their conscience (Rom. 1:19–20; 2:15), so that *they* may be "excused" (1:20b.). The wicked are judged "according to their works";[65] the "resurrection

---

61. Cf. Heyns (1988), 306–307.
62. Cf. Canons of Dordt I.17 (Dennison [2008], 4:125); also see De Groot (1952), 36; cf. 226–39.
63. Deut. 24:16; 2 Kings 14:6; 2 Chron. 25:4; Jer. 31:29v.; Ezek. 18:20.
64. See, e.g., Ps. 8:2; Matt. 18:3; 19:13–15; 21:16.
65. Rom. 2:6; 2 Cor. 11:15; 2 Tim. 4:14; Rev. 2:23; 18:6; 20:12–13; cf. John 3:19–20; Rom. 14:10–12; 2 Cor. 5:10; Jude 15.

of judgment" is for "those who have done evil" (John 5:29). But children who die young *have* not done any evil; they have not committed wicked deeds. They will face no judgment seat of God because they will have nothing to account for.

In Jonah 4:11 we see God's concern for children who are too young to be held accountable, an episode that definitely does not involve covenant children: "[S]hould not I pity Nineveh, that great city, in which there are more than 120,000 persons who do not know their right hand from their left, and also much cattle?" That children are mentioned in the same breath with cattle is remarkable; animals, too, share in the consequences of the Fall, but they are just as unaccountable for their deeds as young children are. Why should both groups perish with, and because of, the wicked? The only difference between the two groups is that children will exist forever, whereas animals will not.

6.4   The Father's House
6.4.1   What Is It?

"Let not your hearts be troubled. Believe in God; believe also in me. In my Father's house are many rooms. If it were not so, would I have told you that I go to prepare a place for you? And if I go and prepare a place for you, I will come again and will take you to myself, that where I am you may be also" (John 14:1–3). Among important eschatological questions that must be asked regarding this passage, the first is this: What is the Father's house?

I am astonished at the attempt by many expositors to smuggle the intermediate state into this verse. For thousands of Christians, it seems self-evident that their deceased beloved ones are in the "house of the Father," although the verse does not suggest any connection between the Father's house and the intermediate state. On the contrary, Jesus speaks here specifically of his personal coming.[66] We realize that his coming does not always refer to his

---

66. Cf. Gaebelein (2012), *ad loc.*; *contra* Dods (1979), 822 and many others.

Parousia, his return on the clouds of heaven. Thus, he himself said in verse 18: "I will not leave you as orphans; I will come to you." This has been understood correctly by many expositors to refer to Jesus' coming in the person of the Holy Spirit, called the "Helper" in verse 16 and the "Spirit of truth" in verse 17. This is not strange: the Spirit *is* the Spirit of Jesus (Acts 16:7), the Spirit of Jesus Christ (Phil. 1:19), the Spirit of Christ (Rom. 8:9; 1 Pet. 1:11), the Spirit of God's Son (Gal. 4:6). In a comparable sense, Jesus says in verse 23: "If anyone loves me, he will keep my word, and my Father will love him, and we will come to him and make our home with him."

However, since John 14:3 speaks of a "taking *to myself*," that is, he is not just coming *to us* but taking us to be *with him* in the Father's House, Jesus is apparently not referring to Acts 2, but to the day his church is caught up into heaven (cf. 1 Cor. 15:51–54; Phil. 3:20–21; 1 Thess. 4:13–17). Jesus is not speaking of the death of an individual believer but of taking the church as a whole to himself; note the plural Greek pronoun *humeis*, "you (my people)."

Compare the difference between this and the account of Lazarus and Dives. When Lazarus died, we hear only that angels came and carried him to the bosom of Abraham (Luke 16:22). We may conclude that when a believer passes away, God sends his angels ("ministering spirits sent out to serve for the sake of those who are to inherit salvation," Heb. 1:14) to take up him or her. But taking up the church in its totality is done by Jesus in person:

> *The Lord himself will descend from heaven* with a cry of command, with the voice of an archangel, and with the sound of the trumpet of God. And the dead in Christ will rise first. Then we who are alive, who are left, will be caught up together with them in the clouds to meet the Lord in the air, and so we will always be with the Lord (1 Thess. 4:16–17; italics added).

Moreover, "*from* it [i.e., heaven] we *await* a Savior, the Lord Jesus

Christ, who will transform our lowly body to be like his glorious body" (Phil. 3:20–21). The Father's house will be an abode, not of deceased and disembodied saints but, of *risen* and *glorified* saints.

6.4.2 "Preparing a Place"

A second exegetical point in John 14:1–3 involves the precise meaning of Jesus "preparing a place." Some believe that this refers to Jesus' work on the cross, through which he has prepared a place for his own in the Father's house.[67] This interpretation appears to be obvious, but a strong objection can be leveled against it. Jesus "goes" and "comes again," and in the meantime he is "preparing a place." This can be explained meaningfully only if he is not speaking of going to the cross but of going to the same place from which he will also return. This is explicitly stated in verse 28: "You heard me say to you, 'I am going away and I come to you.' If you loved me, you would have rejoiced, because I am going to the Father" (also cf. v. 12; 16:7, 10, 17, 33, 36). Thus, Jesus' statement in John 14:2–3 can mean only that he was going to the Father's house.

Perhaps Jesus is comparing himself here with a servant who is sent ahead in order to prepare lodging for the night.[68] Compare also the language of the girl in Song 8:2 to her friend, "I would lead you and bring you into the house of my mother." It is possible, too, that Jesus was thinking here of the same thing expressed by the Targum in 1 Chronicles 17:9, "I will appoint a prepared place for my people, and they will dwell in their places, and be disturbed no more" (for the latter phrase cf. John 14:1, "Let not your hearts be troubled").

Now in what way can we understand that Jesus has prepared a place in the Father's house? Did he not prepare a place there for his people on the cross? No, this is not at all self-evident. Through his work of atonement, Jesus has cleansed his people from their sins, has prepared forgiveness for them, and has reconciled them with God. But this does not at all imply that they are now entitled to a

---

67. E.g., Gaebelein (2012), *ad loc.*
68. Dods (1979), 822.

place in the house where the Father and the Son and the Holy Spirit dwell, where they have dwelt from eternity.[69] Adam and Eve were not even entitled to such a place; the prospect that lay before them was to live eternally on earth. But Jesus *did far more than restore what Adam and Eve had lost*. Jesus granted to his followers eternal life, that is, fellowship with the Father and the Son (cf. John 17:3, 21–23). This eternal life is the life that was with the Father, and came down in the person of Jesus, the Father's Son (1 John 1:1–4; see further in chapter 9).

Taken this way, we may say that eternal life is living in the Father's house. And at present, the abode of the Triune God is also for all those who have received this eternal life, that is, who have received the Son himself as their life (1 John 5:11–13). As well as the Father and the Son come to dwell *with them* (John 14:23), that is, on earth, similarly they are privileged to come and dwell *with the Triune God*, that is, in his heavenly house. If, by rebirth and faith, they have become partakers of the divine nature (2 Pet. 1:14), and if they have thus been "created after the likeness of God" (Eph. 4:24), they are at home there where God himself is at home. When, after his death and resurrection, the Son entered the Father's house as the glorified *Man*, this implied that glorified human beings who have received the life of the Father's house also have their place there, and after the resurrection will enter there.[70]

6.4.3   Link to John 2:16?

A third question that arises among interpreters is whether the Apostle John was suggesting a connection between John 2:16 ("[D]o not make my Father's house a house of trade") and 14:2 ("In my Father's house are many rooms"). Despite a small difference

---

69. Yet, I would not speak here of an *uncreated* habitation of the Triune God, as some have done, because what can be uncreated other than God himself? I would instead suggest that the Father's house has been created by God from eternity, just as we speak of the "eternal generation" of the Son.
70. Grant (1897), 577; cf. *SYN, ad loc.*

(Gk. *oikos* in 2:16 and *oikia* in 14:2), it is almost inconceivable to me that such a link would be absent.[71]

As soon as we accept such a connection, we must assume that, in 14:2, Jesus is referring to the heavenly temple,[72] of which the earthly temple in 2:16 was a physical reflection. This assumption sheds special light on the expression "many rooms" (mansions, habitations). In the temple of Solomon there were "chambers,"[73] which in the temple of Ezekiel 40–44 can be recognized even more readily as priestly chambers (41:6–11; 42:1–14): rooms where the heavenly priests dwell and perform their priestly service. In this context, it is interesting that the word for "room" in John 14:2, Greek *monē*, in later Greek acquired the meaning "monastery."[74] The Father's house is like an immense "monastery," where God's people live in heavenly "cells," permanently serving God (also see §§12.3.4 and 12.3.5).

If this is a proper interpretation, we must view in the "many rooms" of John 14:2–3 the priestly chambers that belong to the earthly temple as well as the heavenly one. In "my Father's house" there are "many rooms" for the heavenly priests, who will forever perform their "temple service," that is above all, their sacrifices of praise and worship. God's servants will "worship" (AMPC: "pay divine honors to him and do him holy service") him for all eternity (Rev. 22:3–5).

In this way, the expression "preparing a place" may become clearer: "Thus it was necessary for the copies of the heavenly things to be purified with these rites, but the heavenly things themselves with better sacrifices than these. For Christ has entered, not into holy places made with hands, which are copies of the true things, but into heaven itself, now to appear in the presence of God on our behalf" (Heb. 9:23–24). The blood of Christ cleanses not only

---

71. See Grant (1897), 576; Gaebelein (2012), *ad loc.*
72. Cf. Rev. 3:12; 7:15; 11:19; 14:15, 17; 15:5–6, 8; 16:1, 17.
73. 1 Chron. 9:26, 33; 23:28; 28:11–12.
74. Cf. Lat. *monasterium,* and the English derivation "monk."

God's people of their sins, but also the way into the heavenly sanctuary. This was already depicted in the action of the high priest who, on the Day of Atonement, entered the Most Holy place and sprinkled the blood of the sacrifice in front of, and on, the mercy seat on the ark (Lev. 16:14–15).

This is what the writer of Hebrews declares to be the case already today,

> Therefore, brothers, since we have confidence to enter the holy places by the blood of Jesus, by the new and living way that he opened for us through the curtain, that is, through his flesh, and since we have a great priest over the house of God, let us draw near with a true heart in full assurance of faith, with our hearts sprinkled clean from an evil conscience and our bodies washed with pure water (cf. 10:19–22).[75]

These are two different things: cleansing from sins does not automatically entail entrance into God's presence in the heavenly sanctuary. However, Jesus not only bore the sins of his people but he also prepared a place for them in the "Father's house," the heavenly temple, so that they are now entitled to dwell there for all eternity with the Triune God.

---

75. Regarding the Old Testament sin offering, cf. Ouweneel (2009a), 105–109.

7

DEVIATING DOCTRINE

[The rich] are to do good, to be rich in good works,
    to be generous and ready to share
thus storing up treasure for themselves as a good
foundation for the future,
    so that they may take hold of that which is truly
    life.
O Timothy,
    guard the deposit entrusted to you.
Avoid the irreverent babble and contradictions of
what is falsely called "knowledge,"
    for by professing it some have swerved from the
    faith.

1 Timothy 6:18–21

Ach schläfrige Seele, wie? ruhest du noch?
    Ermuntre dich doch!
Es möchte die Strafe dich plötzlich erwecken
    Und, wo du nicht wachest,
    Im Schlafe des ewigen Todes bedecken.

    Oh, sleepy soul, what? Do you still rest?
    Arouse yourself now!
        Judgment might abruptly awaken you

and, were you not aware,
envelop you in the sleep of eternal death.[1]

Mache dich, mein Geist, bereit
[*Make Yourself Ready, My Soul*]
Bach cantata BWV 115
based on Johann Burchard Freystein (1695)

7.1   Reincarnation
7.1.1   What Is It?

When I gave lectures in Germany about eschatology, the question would occasionally arise as to what I thought of "the rebirth" (Ger. *Wiedergeburt*). I would begin my response with an exposé on John 3 and the like, until somebody made clear to me that the person who had asked the question was really asking about reincarnation! Quite a different matter altogether. It is rather confusing and embarrassing when our opponents use the same terms that we use (having adopted them from the Bible), but attach very different meanings to them.

The term "reincarnation" means "renewed incarnation," that is, assuming a physical body again. It is the doctrine of the "wheel of rebirth" or "wheel of existence," or the "transmigration of souls": after a person's death, his soul is not going to some eternal abode but "transmigrates" to another, newborn human being, or to an animal. Not only do millions of Hindus and Buddhists adhere to this doctrine, but in the Western world, theosophists, anthroposophists, and many spiritists do as well. Belief in reincarnation appears also in the Kabbalah, and therefore is widely adhered to by Hasidic and other Orthodox Jews. This is astonishing because, as I hope to show, there is not a trace of it in the Jewish Bible. Nonetheless, great rabbis such as Isaac Luria (d. 1572) and the Vilna Gaon (d.

---

1. Here, several meanings of "death" are combined: the sleep (false rest) a person may experience; if he does not awaken from this, he will experience the "sleep" of eternal death.

188

1797) have explained and defended it. The latter wrote a commentary on the book of Jonah, whose story he viewed as an allegory of reincarnation (Jonah experiencing death in chapter 2, and rising as a new person in chapter 3). Often, reincarnation is viewed as part of a developmental process, in which the soul, perhaps after thousands of reincarnations, finally attains its goal: merging into the cosmic soul, the world spirit, the All, "God."

Christian systematic theology had to deal with belief in reincarnation ever since the teaching entered Christian thought.[2] Thus, the early Christian writer who has been accused most frequently of views of reincarnation was Origen (d. c. 253). Adherents of the doctrine of reincarnation mention him as *the* example of early Christians who believed in reincarnation, but claim that the early church suppressed this belief, especially during the Fifth Ecumenical Council, which was held at Constantinople (553).[3] However, in reality there is no unequivocal evidence that Origen believed in reincarnation; at any rate, he was condemned as a heretic for very different reasons. But even if he had believed in reincarnation, this does not change the core question for any orthodox Christian: Is there any support for this belief in the Bible? I am convinced that the answer must be: Not in the least.

In the next two sections I will mention the Bible passages that are usually adduced by adherents as evidence of reincarnation. I must say in advance that I am ashamed to mention some of them because they obviously have nothing to do with reincarnation. But I mention them only because they have been appealed to by adherents.[4]

---

2.   See Ouweneel (1978, 327–30).
3.   See reluctant-messenger.com/origen1.html.
4.   See reluctant-messenger.com/origen3.html; Howe (1987); MacGregor (1989); for good refutations, see, e.g., www.comparativereligion.com/reincarnation3.html.

7.1.2 Proof-texts from the Gospels

(a) *Matthew 11:14* ("[I]f you are willing to accept it, he [i.e., John the Baptist] is Elijah who is to come") and *17:12–13* ("'I tell you that Elijah has already come, and they did not recognize him, but did to him whatever they pleased. So also the Son of Man will certainly suffer at their hands.' Then the disciples understood that he was speaking to them of John the Baptist"). Reincarnationists conclude from these passages that John the Baptist must have been a reincarnation of the prophet Elijah.

Response: From Luke 1:17 it is clear that John was not Elijah *in person*, but that he was meant to go out "in the spirit and the power of Elijah," that is, with similar characteristics in his ministry. Moreover, Jesus makes clear that John "was" to be Elijah only on the condition that the people would accept him as Messiah's herald and forerunner. Therefore, after his ministry had been rejected, John could truthfully say that he was *not* Elijah (John 1:21; cf. vv. 5–11). This means that the prophecy concerning Elijah still had to be fulfilled (Mal. 4:5–6; cf. Rev. 11:3–12). Moreover, it would hardly fit with belief in reincarnation that Jesus called John "Elijah" just after the disciples had seen the actual Elijah on the Mount of Transfiguration (Matt. 17:1–8). There they had seen Moses and Elijah, not Moses and John the Baptist; this means that, in the hereafter, Elijah still existed as Elijah. Moreover, even if John were indeed Elijah in person, this could hardly be evidence for reincarnation because Elijah had never died but, without dying, had been caught up to heaven (2 Kings 2:11). Thus, there could be no question of the soul of a dead person transmigrating to another body.

(b) *Matthew 16:13–14* ("'Who do people say that the Son of Man is?' And they [i.e., his disciples] said, 'Some say John the Baptist, others say Elijah, and others Jeremiah or one of the prophets'"). Reincarnationists assert that apparently the disciples, *or* the people they quote, believed in reincarnation; that is, some believed that Jesus was the reincarnation of John the Baptist, or of Elijah, or

190

of Jeremiah, or of another great prophet.

Response: In reality, the disciples were merely expressing the Jewish expectation of their time that the prophets mentioned would one day return in person. That is, John was supposed to come to finish his work that had been interrupted so prematurely; Elijah in order to prepare the way of the Messiah (cf. Mal. 4:5); and Jeremiah to bring back the ark that he had hidden in a cave (cf. 2 Macc. 2:1–12).[5] Such Jewish hopes are not mentioned in the Bible, apart from Malachi 4:5.

(c) *Matthew 26:52* ("[A]ll who take the sword will perish by the sword"); *Revelation 3:10* ("[I]f anyone is to be slain with the sword, with the sword must he be slain"). Reincarnationists emphasize that in practice *not* all who take the sword perish by the sword. They believe that, therefore, these statements can be true only if the speakers were thinking of previous lives in which it had happened or subsequent lives in which it was still going to happen.

Response: This is a highly speculative and unnecessary interpretation. It is far more obvious to assume that only a simple, general principle is given: what a person sows they must also reap (cf. Jer. 15:2; Gal. 6:7).

(d) *Mark 10:29–30* ("[T]here is no one who has left house or brothers or sisters or mother or father or children or lands, for my sake and for the gospel, who will not receive a hundredfold now in this time, houses and brothers and sisters and mothers and children and lands, with persecutions, and in the age to come eternal life"). According to reincarnationists, a person can have a hundred mothers only if, through reincarnation, they are born many times from different mothers.

Response: It is evident that Jesus is speaking of what his followers receive in "this time," not in previous or in subsequent lives: their spiritual family will take the place of their physical family that they had left. In such a spiritual family one can have many "moth-

---

5.   Bruce (1979), 222.

ers" (cf. John 19:27; Rom. 16:13; 1 Thess. 2:7).

(e) *John 3:3* ("[U]nless one is born again he cannot see the kingdom of God"). Reincarnationists often render "reincarnation" as "rebirth": the deceased person is reborn in a different body. Every passage where this or a similar term occurs[6] is therefore used by them as support.

Response: But if reincarnationism was current in Jesus' days, how could Nicodemus, who was a highly qualified Bible teacher (see John 3:10), assume that Jesus was speaking about a new *physical* birth? Moreover, careful examination of the passages mentioned shows that they are referring to the transition from the old world to the new world (Matt. 19:28), or from a person's old state to a new state (John 3:3–7; Titus 3:5; 1 Pet. 1:3, 23), and in both cases this is once-in-a-lifetime affair.

(f) *John 9:2* ("Rabbi, who sinned, this man or his parents, that he was born blind?"). Reincarnationists suggest that this question implies that the blind man might have sinned in a previous life, and that it thus presupposes belief in reincarnation as a common thing for Jesus and the disciples.

Response: In reality, the question reflects a rabbinic belief, based especially on Genesis 25:22 (the infants "struggling together" in Rebekah's womb), that children can sin already in their mother's womb.[7] Compare John 1:9, ". . . the true Light which gives light to every man coming into the world" (NKJV), according to some suggesting that a person can be given light already when they are yet in their mother's womb. The disciples may also have believed that the soul is pre-existent (cf. Wisdom 8:20 [CEB], "[B]ecause my soul was already dignified, it entered a spotless body").[8] It is also possible that the disciples were simply confused, or believed that the punishment for a sin could precede that sin.[9] At any rate, there is not the

6. Matt. 19:28; Titus 3:5; 1 Pet. 1:3, 23.
7. Strack and Billerbeck (1922), 2:528–29.
8. Morris (1971), 478; cf. Ouweneel (2008), 116.
9. Dods (1979), 782.

slightest reason to think of reincarnation here.

7.1.3   Proof-texts from Other New Testament Books

(a) *1 Corinthians 15:36–44* ("What you sow does not come to life unless it dies. And what you sow is not the body that is to be, but a bare kernel, perhaps of wheat or of some other grain. But God gives it a body as he has chosen, and to each kind of seed its own body. . . . It is sown in dishonor; it is raised in glory. It is sown in weakness; it is raised in power. It is sown a natural body; it is raised a spiritual body. If there is a natural body, there is also a spiritual body"). For reincarnationists, the biblical concept of "resurrection" is the same as reincarnation: the deceased person "rises" in the form of another person. Reincarnationists see in Paul's description a treatise on the various bodies that the one soul can successively inhabit.

Response: The simple reality is, of course, that the resurrection is the rising again of the very same dead body that the deceased has left behind (cf. Rom. 8:11)—in a glorified state—not the reception of a different body.

(b) *Hebrews 9:27* ("[I]t is appointed for man to die once, and after that comes judgment"). Reincarnationists read this such that, at death, a person is judged, and on the basis of the verdict the soul is placed in a subsequent body.

Response: This is reading into the text an already existing belief, which is not contained in the text at all. In the light of the entire Scripture, the verse cannot tell us anything other than that, at death, the eternal destiny of a person is determined once and for all: they will go to be "with Christ," or they will go to Hades.

(c) *James 3:6* ("The tongue is set among our members, staining the whole body, setting on fire the entire course of life [Gk. *trochon tēs geneseōs*], and set on fire by hell"). For reincarnationists, the "course of life" (AMPC: the "wheel of birth," ASV: the "wheel of nature") is the same as what they call the "wheel of rebirth" or "of existence" (cf. Eccl. 1:4–9).

Response: But how can this "wheel" be "set on fire"? What we have here is the "course of nature" (DARBY), the "course of our existence" (GNT), the "course of life" (HCSB), and so on. It has nothing to do with reincarnation.

(d) *Revelation 12:5* ("She gave birth to a male child, one who is to rule all the nations with a rod of iron, but her child was caught up to God and to his throne"). Reincarnationists believe this to mean that the deceased (?) child can rule the nations only if, through reincarnation, the child returns to the world.

Response: The simple reality of the entire New Testament is, of course, that Jesus has died, is risen (in the same body! Rom. 8:11), has ascended to heaven, and from there will return on the clouds of heaven, in order to begin his Messianic rule.

(e) There are several Bible passages that point to the pre-existence of Christ as the eternal Son of God.[10] Reincarnationists suppose that these prove that humans have known a different mode of existence before their birth.

Response: This is a mistake, first, because these verses are true *only* of Christ himself; they cannot be applied to any ordinary human being. Second, pre-existence is something basically different from reincarnation. The latter is a soul moving from one body to another. Pre-existence, however, refers to a person—the Son of God—who has existed since eternity, and at a certain moment (the "fullness of time," Gal. 4:4) takes on a human body (Heb. 2:14), and thus becomes a human being (John 1:14).

Our general conclusion must be that, negatively, there is not the slightest basis in the Bible for the doctrine of reincarnation; it is in conflict with everything we know about the intermediate state and the resurrection state. Positively, the Bible tells us a very different story about the destiny of individual people and of the world as a whole.

To state the matter in one sentence: redemptive history is a strictly linear process—from creation through Fall and redemp-

---

10. E.g., John 1:1–3; 17:5, 24; 1 John 1:1–4; Gal. 4:4.

tion to the consummation—whereas the doctrine of reincarnation makes redemptive history a cyclical matter.

7.2 Psychopannychia

7.2.1 A Complicated Debate

The word "psychopannychia" means literally something like "all-night soul condition." The word was coined by John Calvin, in his very first theological publication.[11] He intended it to mean the "all-night-*vigil* of the soul," that is, the wakefulness of the soul between death and resurrection. In practice, the word acquired the opposite meaning: the "all-night-*sleep* of the soul." This is the way the term is now commonly used. The doctrine of soul sleep in the intermediate state rejects the idea of a conscious or wakeful continuation of existence between death and resurrection. It was defended by many Anabaptists and Socinians, and today, in a number of varieties, is preached by Seventh Day Adventists and Jehovah's Witnesses,[12] but also by some Reformed theologians (see below). In 1967, this doctrine played a key role in the division among the Reformed Churches in the Netherlands (Liberated) through some controversial books by pastors B. Telder (d. 1980) and C. Vonk (d. 1993).[13]

To illustrate how complicated the debate is, look at this sentence by Calvin: "The Anabaptists commonly all do hold opinion that the souls being departed from the body do no more live until the day of the resurrection" (Fr. *Les Anabaptistes tiennent tous communement, que les ames estans departies du corps, ne vivent point, iusques au iour de la Resurrection*).[14] At least two matters mentioned here deserve to be questioned. First, Calvin ardently and frequently defended the Greek scholastic body-soul dualism, and phrased the problem in the language of this dualism: "souls that have left the body."

---

11. Calvin (1534); regarding this subject, see Balke et al. (2009), 43–45, and more extensively Balke (1999).
12. Lewis and Demarest (1996), 451–52.
13. Telder (1960, 1963); Vonk (1969).
14. Quoted in Balke (1999), 304.

Second, is the issue really whether souls in the intermediate state "live"? Is this not a misleading term? The issue is whether the human personality after death is in a kind of coma, or has some form of awareness or consciousness.

In evaluating this issue, we must be careful with the term *living*. The human personality, whether of a believer or an unbeliever, continues to exist in some way or another after physical death. This may be an important reason why Jesus said of God regarding deceased believers: "Now he is not God of the dead, but of the living, for all live to him" (Luke 20:38). However, especially in the case of an unbeliever I do not see how this continuing existence could ever be called *living*. Jesus says, "Whoever believes in me, though he die, yet shall he live." But the term "living" cannot be generalized, as if all existing is "living." On the contrary, unbelievers are spiritually dead (Eph. 2:1; Col. 2:13), and when they have been raised, they are still called the "dead" (Rev. 20:12), and they will soon enter the "second death" (v. 14).

But even of deceased believers it is clearly said that they are "dead." The Bible never says that only their bodies died, whereas their souls were still alive. Dorcas "became ill and died" (Acts 9:37), not just her body died. Epaphroditus "was ill, near to death . . . he nearly died for the work of Christ" (Phil. 2:27, 30), not just his body. "Be faithful unto death" (Rev. 2:10), not just the death of your body. At the Parousia, the "dead in Christ" will rise (1 Thess. 4:16), not just their dead bodies. Paul asks, "How are the dead raised? With what kind of body do they come?" (1 Cor. 15:35). Here "the dead" cannot be "dead bodies," for Paul's very question is with what body *they*—"the dead"—will come.

However, in this discussion, one always faces an "on the one hand" and an "on the other hand"; for instance, James says, "[T]he body apart from the spirit is dead" (2:26). There is the constant tension here, caused not by the body-soul *dualism* but rather by the *duality* of the personality and human corporeal existence (the earthly "tent," 2 Cor. 5:1; 2 Pet. 1:13–14). John 19 does not tell us that Jesus' body was dead, but that *Jesus* was dead (v. 33). But when it comes to his burial, we hear that Joseph of Arimathea asked for the *body* of Jesus (v. 38), and after he had received it, he wrapped this *body* in cloths (v. 40). But then, when it comes to the actual burial, we read of the tomb: ". . . they laid *Jesus* there," not just his body (v. 42). There is the dual*ity*, but as soon as we might be tempted to turn this into a dual*ism*, we hear things like this: *Jesus* died, *Jesus* was buried; but also: *Jesus* was in Hades (Acts 2:27; according to some: 1 Pet. 3:19), and *Jesus* was in paradise (Luke 23:43). We will have to live with the mystery, which appears also in Luke 16:22–23: *Dives* died, not just his body; *Dives* was buried, not just his body; and *Dives* lifted up his eyes in Hades, not just his soul. It does not take us any closer to the truth if we try to simplify things by introducing here a Greek body-soul dualism. However, the same passage clearly shows—against the psychopannychians—that Dives, just like Lazarus, continued to exist after his physical death in a form of wakefulness. Although introducing Greek dualism does not help us understand this, rejection of any form of dualism does not allow us to dismiss this fact. This is what we must now investigate somewhat more closely.

7.2.2 Biblical Arguments

Let us consider some of the arguments of the psychopannychians.

(a) *Ecclesiastes 9:5* ("[T]he living know that they will die, but the dead know nothing, and they have no more reward, for the memory of them is forgotten") and *verse 10* ("[T]here is no work or thought or knowledge or wisdom in Sheol, to which you are going").

Response: It is always a bad sign when theologians take their starting point in dark and difficult Bible passages, and on the basis of them annul the significance of clear and obvious Bible passages. Thus, on the basis of Ecclesiastes 9:5, all passages that imply a certain consciousness or wakefulness after death[15] are dismissed as irrelevant. Ecclesiastes is clearly a writing in which the author has decided to look no further than at what is "under the sun," an attitude that he abandons only near the end of the book. He has limited himself to empirical observation, and in that case, obviously, a corpse "knows nothing."[16] We find the same sentiment in Job: "[A] man dies and is laid low; man breathes his last, and where is he? . . . If a man dies, shall he live again?" (14:10, 14). What dogmatician would stake his conclusions about the intermediate state or the resurrection on such verses? Job's irresolute question, "If a man dies, shall he live again?" must be answered with a thundering "Yes!"

(b) Compare the perspective of *Psalm 115:17* ("The dead do not praise the LORD, nor do any who go down into silence"; cf. 6:5; 30:9; 146:4) and *Isaiah 38:18–19* ("Sheol does not thank you; death does not praise you; those who go down to the pit do not hope for your faithfulness. The living, the living, he thanks you, as I do this day"). This again seems to suggest that the dead are unconscious.

Response: Here again, we must remind ourselves of the veil that hangs over the intermediate state in the Old Testament. In verses like the ones mentioned, Sheol means little more than the grave. Moreover, it is an empirical given that (buried) corpses do not praise and give thanks to God (or to the idols). Those who wish to investigate the matter of the intermediate state and of a possible consciousness of the deceased will have to consult the New Testament where we receive much more light on the matter of the intermediate state. Who would prefer to live by the question marks (the dusk) of the Old Testament instead of living by the exclamation marks (the clear light) of the New Testament?

(c) Death is a sleep, and the dying of believers is called a "falling asleep" (see §5.5 for references and discussion). The verb "to sleep" suggests a lack of awareness of the things going on around

---

15. Already dealt with: Isa. 14:9–10, 16–17; Luke 16:19–31; 23:43; Phil. 1:23; Rev. 6:9–11.
16. Hough (2000), 20–22.

the person.

Response: The terms "sleep" and "falling asleep" refer to the tranquil appearance of the dead person, who lies with eyes closed; they look as though they are asleep.[17] The terms do not tell us anything about their consciousness; I already quoted Song 5:2, "I slept, but my heart was awake." Just as the sleeping person can dream very actively and realistically, the person "fallen asleep" could very well have a conscious existence in the hereafter. We must be careful especially with the term *"soul* sleep" (*psych-* in "psychopannychia"; cf. Dutch *zielenslaap* and Ger. *Seelenschlaf*). It is the *person* who "falls asleep" (John 11:11; Acts 7:60), not just his soul, certainly not if "soul" is taken here in any Platonic or Aristotelian-Thomistic sense (see next chapter).

If we had to choose here between body and soul, we would say that the body is asleep, rather than the soul. This is because Matthew 27:52 speaks of the *bodies* of the "saints who had fallen asleep," and Acts 13:36 tells us of the David who had "fallen asleep" that *he* (that is, his body, not his continuing personality) "saw corruption." 1 Corinthians 15:20 speaks of those who have "fallen asleep" who will follow Christ in his resurrection, a fact that pertains to their bodies, not their souls.[18] The Old Testament expression "sleeping in the dust of the earth" (Dan. 12:2; cf. Job 7:21; 20:11; Isa. 26:19) clearly refers to (especially) the bodies of those who have died.

(d) 1 Thessalonians 4:13 ("[W]e do not want you to be uninformed, brothers, about those who are asleep, that you may not grieve as others do who have no hope") supposedly does not presuppose any intermediate state; otherwise Paul would have comforted believers with the reassurance that believers would again see their beloved who had "fallen asleep."

Response: This argument entirely ignores the actual sadness of

---

17. Berkhof (1981), 763.
18. Grant (1889), 99–100; of course, we are not using the term "soul" here in the sense of the Platonic "immortal soul" (see extensively chapter 8).

those left behind. They were not worrying about whether they would again see their beloved ones after death, but about whether their beloved ones would be present at the Parousia (cf. vv. 15–16). They were not concerned about the intermediate state but about the post-Parousia state. Paul's focus in the entire first letter to the Thessalonians is never on the intermediate state at all, but constantly on the Parousia and what was to follow it.[19]

(e) Passages such as Luke 16:19–31 are strongly metaphorical, and therefore tell us nothing about the intermediate state.

Response: This is a logical error. In the same way, people have argued that the book of Revelation is strongly symbolical, and that therefore the episode in Revelation 6:9–11 (the "souls under the altar"; see §6.1.1) cannot be used as evidence for conscious existence after death. Metaphors definitely do tell us something about the reality they describe. There is a conscious existence after death, even if this can be described only in metaphorical language.

(f) Psychopannychians claim that conscious existence after death can be defended only on the basis of the body-soul dichotomy.

Response: This is an important point because it involves two standpoints that are diametrically opposed. We are made to believe that we must choose between the only two options available: either Greek scholastic body-soul dualism, or psychopannychia. In reality, I believe that this is comparing apples and oranges. From an anthropological viewpoint, I am much closer to Telder and Vonk than to scholastically influenced theologians, whose anthropology was developed in terms of the thinking of Plato, Aristotle, and Thomas Aquinas (and, I must add, the Reformers). Yet, in my view, Telder and Vonk and so many others have gone to the other extreme. Notice again that in Luke 16:22–23, "he" (the *person*) dies, "he" (the *person*) is buried, and "he" (the *person*) lifts up his eyes in the hereafter (see §5.1). This kind of formulation cuts off all dichotomy at the

19. See 1 Thess. 1:10; 2:19; 3:13; 4:15–16; 5:2–3, 23.

roots, yet, Lazarus and Dives clearly exist in a conscious manner in the hereafter, no matter how metaphorically this is being described.

(g) In Luke 23:43, we must translate: "Truly, I say to you today, you will [sometime in the future] be with me in paradise."

Response: Apart from the New World Translation of the Jehovah's Witnesses, I know of no Bible translation that renders this verse this way. This is a typical example of distorting a Bible verse in order to fit it into one's own beliefs (the New World Translation contains many more such examples). People do not see that in such a rendering, the word "today" has become totally superfluous. In contrast with this, in the common renderings it is precisely the word "today" which is of vital importance. The criminal expressed his hope that—in my words—at the Parousia Jesus would not forget him (see §5.2). This Parousia could still be far away; indeed, even today the Parousia has not yet occurred. Contrary to this, Jesus assured the man that he would be "with Jesus" that very same day. The "with me" (Gk. *met' emou*) suggests partnership, fellowship, intimacy, which excludes any form of unconsciousness.[20] David Pawson rightly wondered what kind of comfort the converted criminal could have enjoyed if he was supposed to believe that on that same day he would enter into a kind of coma[21] (which in fact has lasted to this very day).

(h) In Acts 2:34 ("David did not ascend into the heavens") it is flatly denied that David is "in heaven" (cf. John 3:13, "No one has ascended into heaven").

Response: From the context it is evident that Peter was in no way referring to the intermediate state, but was drawing a parallel with the *risen* Jesus who, in his resurrection body, had ascended into the heavens. This had not happened to David. Of course not, David had not even been raised from the dead yet, let alone ascended to heaven. But this is not to deny that he is "with Christ," with all the

---

20. Plummer (1922), *ad loc.*; Geldenhuys (1983), 615n15.
21. Pawson (2004), 201.

bliss that this involves. The argument that our opponents use here might at best make an impression upon people who are used to speaking of "going to heaven when you die," which is part of a mistaken Interim Theology.

7.2.3   Positive Counterarguments

To the eight assertions mentioned in the two previous sections, I would add a few positive considerations in support of my position.

(1) How can being deceased and being "with Christ" be "gain" (Phil. 1:21),[22] and be "far better" (v. 23; GNT, "best of all") if there is no conscious existence after death? Why would being in a "coma" (Pawson) "with Christ" be better than living consciously on earth, in fellowship with the Lord? As J. J. Müller put it,

> [There is] no mention here of an intermediate state of unconscious-
> ness or sleep of the soul in which Christ's presence would not be
> experienced; and also no thought that he would be with Christ only
> after the resurrection. Such an immediate being-with-Christ is far bet-
> ter than the continuance of the earthly life.[23]

True enough, one should not attempt to deduce too much concerning the intermediate state from a single passage like Philippians 1:21–23,[24] but neither can one deduce from it some form of soul sleep.

(2) A sleeping body is an understandable metaphor, but a sleeping soul, no matter how this phrase is understood, is hardly conceivable, and a sleeping spirit even less. We read in 1 Peter 3:19 about the "spirits" in "prison" (see §6.1.2), but we also read of the "spirits of the righteous made perfect" (Heb. 12:23), "perfection"

---

22. It is quite artificial when Telder (1960), 93–94, thinks here of gain "for Christ, for his name and sake and church"; cf. the refutation of this idea by Grant (1889), 117; Berkouwer (1972), 53–55; Ridderbos (1975), 507; Van Genderen and Velema (2008), 832.
23. Müller (1984), 63.
24. Matter (1965), 33–34.

referring here to the resurrection (cf. 11:40).[25] Whether the Bible refers to "spirits" in the intermediate state, or to "spirits" in the resurrection, in all these cases *conscious* spirits are meant. The word "spirit" need not have any other meaning here than it has generally in the New Testament.[26] In Luke 23:46, Jesus commits his "spirit" to the hands of the Father, and in Acts 7:59 Stephen commends his "spirit" to the Lord. The human spirit is almost always active, even during dreaming periods. Why would this human spirit have characteristics in the intermediate state different from those it has in the pre-death and the post-resurrection condition?

(3) How could the *deceased* Moses appear on the Mount of Transfiguration, and speak with Jesus about his departure (Luke 9:31), if he were in a state of soul sleep?[27] The text does not say that this was merely a vision. Moses as well as Elijah was really with Jesus on the mount. But I cannot grasp how we could imagine that, for this occasion, Moses had been awakened from his sleep, in order to be put to sleep again after the event.[28] Moses' *spirit*—his Ego, his personality—was very much conscious, whereas in the meantime his *body* was quietly asleep in the grave that God had prepared for him (Deut. 34:6). In an analogous way, it can be said of deceased Old Testament believers that, to God, they all "live" (Luke 20:38).

(4) How could it be said that the souls of the martyrs, who are "under the altar," complain about their situation (Rev. 6:9–11), if we must believe that they are in a kind of coma? It is as Calvin said about the Anabaptists who "in the place of the white robes, would give pillows to the souls to make them sleep" (Fr. *au lieu de robes blanches, donnent des coussins aux ames pour les faire dormir*).[29]

---

25. Grant (1889), 116.
26. See, e.g., Mark 2:8; 8:12; Luke 1:47; Acts 17:16; 1 Cor. 5:4; 14:14–15; 16:18; 2 Cor. 2:12; 7:13; cf. Ouweneel (2008), 114–16.
27. The same holds for the Samuel who appears even though he is dead in 1 Sam. 28.
28. Grant (1889), 122.
29. Quoted in Balke (1999), 305.

(5) Calvin also referred to John 5:24, which states that the believer "does not come into judgment, but has passed from death to life." Calvin argued that "in the middle of death, our spiritual life shall not be interrupted" (Fr. *C'est que au milieu de la mort nostre vie sprituelle ne sera point interrompue*).[30] That is, if we are spiritually awake before our physical death, and if we are spiritually awake after our resurrection, it may be supposed that we will be awake between our death and resurrection.

7.3   Spiritism
7.3.1   Is It Allowed?

By "spiritism" we understand the consultation of the dead, or the doctrine that deems such consulting of the dead possible and desirable. The two questions that arise here are, first, is such a consulting of the dead *appropriate* for a biblical believer? And second, is such a consulting at all *possible*?[31]

On the first question, the Bible is quite clear: "A man or a woman who is a [spiritistic] medium or a necromancer [i.e., someone consulting the dead] shall surely be put to death" (Lev. 20:27; cf. v. 6; 19:31). "There shall not be found among you anyone . . . who practices divination or tells fortunes or interprets omens, or a sorcerer or a charmer or a medium or a necromancer or one who inquires of the dead, for whoever does these things is an abomination to the LORD" (Deut. 18:10–12). Nonetheless, such people were regularly found in Israel. In his time, King Saul had "cut off the mediums and the necromancers from the land" (1 Sam. 28:9). King Manasseh did the reverse: he "used fortune-telling and omens and dealt with mediums and with necromancers" (2 Kings 21:6).

Today we no longer stone spiritists—but this does not mean that the wickedness of this evil has diminished in the eyes of the Lord. No Christian should ever get involved in this type of divina-

---

30. *Ibid.* Nevertheless, Balke did criticize Calvin's body-soul dualism and his notion of the soul's "immortality" (*ibid.*, 320–22).
31. See, e.g., *RD*, 4:623–25; Ouweneel (1978), 23–125.

tion and fortune-telling.

In Isaiah 8:19, the prophet says, "And when they say to you, 'Inquire of the mediums and the necromancers who chirp and mutter,' should not a people inquire of their God? Should they inquire of the dead on behalf of the living?" The Hebrew word for "mediums" here is *ovot*, singular *ov*, a word that is perhaps related to *ov* in the sense of "wineskin" (Job 32:19), and might thus refer to the "chirping and muttering" that we just read about. This is supposed to mean the hollow cries of what are alleged to be the spirits of the dead. The Hebrew word *ov* refers to the divining spirit (supposedly the spirit of a dead person, a "familiar spirit") dwelling in certain people, and subsequently may refer to these mediums themselves. The Hebrew *ovot* are mediums, necromancers (1 Sam. 28:3; 2 Kings 21:6). We read in 1 Samuel 28:7 of a "possessor of a familiar spirit" (Heb, *ba'alat-ov*), in short: a medium.

The Hebrew language also uses the term *yid'onim* (from the root *y-d-'*, "to know"), that is, the "knowing ones," the "wise," in the sense of fortune-tellers, necromancers. The "knowing one" is the spirit in the medium, or it is the medium in his or her own person; this spirit possesses some sort of supernatural knowledge. The Hebrew terms *ov* and *yid'oni* are often mentioned together,[32] because in antiquity, spiritism was the main means of fortune-telling (divination). The Septuagint uses the Greek word *engastromythos*, which means someone equivalent to a "ventriloquist," a term whose meaning is quite different today.

7.3.2 Is It Possible?

On the first question—is it allowed?—Scripture is quite clear. Each form of divination, including spiritism (necromancing), is forbidden because it entails a consultation of the "spirits," which are basically evil spirits (demons), not good spirits (angels). It is to enter into contact with the supernatural world, the world of spirits and

---

32. Lev. 19:31; 20:6, 27; Deut. 18:11; 1 Sam. 28:3, 9; 2 Chron. 33:6; Isa. 8:19; 19:3.

demons, instead of consulting the Lord (see again Isa. 8:19, "should not a people inquire of their God?").

Isaiah 59:2 says that iniquities make a separation between God and humans. If therefore a person despised God, and yet wishes to consult the supernatural world, he will find the path to God closed (unless he repents), so that the only path still open is that other one, leading to the world of the powers that are hostile toward God. Please note that this is the world of demons and unclean spirits, and never a world of the spirits of the dead. The Bible may speak of the pagans inquiring "of the idols and the sorcerers, and the mediums and the necromancers" (Isa. 19:3), but this does not mean that the Bible deems that it is *possible* to really contact the spirits of the dead. It refers to what pagans intend to get (information from the dead), but this does not mean that they in fact get it. The dead are in the hereafter; they are not available for consultation by the living.

In §4.4.2 we investigated the story of King Saul at Endor, where he came to consult with the deceased prophet Samuel (1 Sam. 28). This story forms the exception confirming the rule. In my view, as we have seen, the most plausible explanation of this event is that Samuel did indeed appear, but *not* through the activity of the medium; hence, her frightened scream the moment Samuel appeared. This was not what she had expected, and thus it was not something that she herself, with her tricks, had brought about. The story therefore does not supply us with any proof that consulting the dead is indeed possible. It is far more obvious to assume that spiritism is either pure deceit (illusionism) by cunning magicians, or that it is indeed a form of making contact with the supernatural world. However the contact is *not* with the spirits of the dead, but with demons who present themselves as the spirit of the dead, and thereby deceive people.[33]

---

33. See Ouweneel (1978, 330).

7.4 "Sweet Death"
7.4.1 "Sweet Hour of Death"

In the previous chapters, we have investigated what happened during "The Great Shift": the Christian hope involving the Parousia, the resurrection, and the new heavens and new earth, gave way to a new hope: the believer's "sweet death," which takes them immediately to Paradise, to glory, bliss, and blessing. The realization of the former hope lies further away in the future, whereas the realization of the latter hope is much closer. The former hope is global and cosmic, while the latter hope is strictly individual. Where the latter hope is cherished more and more, the former hope disappears into the background. Believers begin to focus entirely upon their death, which, because of what will follow, becomes more and more a "sweet death."

Because of the popularity of the music of Johann Sebastian Bach, his cantata texts are better known than many of the old writings of Pietism, Puritanism, and the Second Reformation. Let me therefore quote once more from these German texts. An excellent example is cantata BWV 161, "Come, you sweet hour of death" (Ger. *Komm, du süsse Todesstunde*). It is a cantata for the sixteenth Sunday after Trinity (the seventeenth Sunday after Pentecost). The Gospel reading for that Sunday is from Luke 7:11–17, about the raising of the son of the widow of Nain. What a wonderful occasion to dwell on the promise of resurrection! However, interestingly, the cantata is hardly about this wonderful topic of resurrection at all, but rather about "sweet death"!

The text is by Salomon Franck, a pietistic poet of Bach's time, whose poems must have pleased Bach, given his frequent use of them. Although Bach belonged to mainstream Lutheran orthodoxy, the private library he left behind shows that he was also interested in the writing of the Pietists, or pietistically influenced orthodox Lutherans.

Take the first aria, which I present here in my own translation:

Komm, du süße Todesstunde,
  Da mein Geist
  Honig speist
    Aus des Löwen Munde;
Mache meinen Abschied süße,
  Säume nicht,
  Letztes Licht,
    Daß ich meinen Heiland küsse.

Come, you sweet hour of death,
  when my spirit
  will feed on honey
    out of the lion's mouth [Judg. 14:8];
make my farewell sweet,
  tarry not,
  final light,
    that I may kiss my Savior.

Not: come, sweet Lord, come soon!—but: come, sweet death, because it will take me to the Lord.

The following recitative continues the topic:

Pale death is my rosy dawn,
  with this rises for me the sun
    of glory and heavenly delight.
Therefore I sigh truly from the depths of my heart
  for the last hour of death alone.
    I desire to pasture soon with Christ.
    I desire to depart from this world [namely,
  through death].

In the cantata, this recitative is followed by an aria, saying in part:

My longing
  is to embrace my Savior

and to be with Christ soon.
Although to mortal ash and earth
I shall be ground through death,
the pure radiance of my soul
will then blaze like the angels.

Here, the soul is like a Phoenix set free, the bird rising from the ashes, not at the believer's resurrection, but at her physical death.

It is only in the next recitative of the same cantata that we find a hint of the resurrection, followed immediately by another reference to "sweet death":

My cool grave shall be covered with roses
until Jesus shall reawaken me,
until His sheep
shall be guided to the sweet pasture of life,
since death does not separate me from
Him.
Therefore break forth, O joyous death-day,
therefore strike, O final hour!

I read this as follows: I look forward to my resurrection, but before I arrive there, I will have to die first; so let my death come as soon as possible!

The chorale continues :

Wenn es meines Gottes Wille,
Wünsch ich, daß des Leibes Last
Heute noch die Erde fülle,
Und der Geist, des Leibes Gast,
Mit Unsterblichkeit sich kleide
In der süßen Himmelsfreude.

If it is my God's will,
I wish that the weight of my body

209

might even today occupy the earth,
and that the spirit, the body's guest,
clothe itself in immortality
in the sweet joy of heaven.

The text is rather confusing, because these latter words suggest that the poet believes one is blessed with immortality and heaven immediately after death, although the cantata text also refers to the resurrection. Yet, typical terms of the future Messianic age, such as the "sun" (the "sun of righteousness" in Mal. 4:2) and being clothed with immortality (1 Cor. 15:53–54) are attached here to the believer's death.

Also notice the expression "the spirit, the body's guest," which betrays the Platonic idea of the spirit lodging in the body for a while, until it is set free from it through death. See what was said above concerning the Phoenix set free.

The final chorale refers to the resurrection again, as if to draw one's final attention to this glorious fact, yet it ends with death again. In a free rendering: "If I one day will be raised by Christ, and will shine like him in heavenly joy and delight, what do I care about death [now]?" The way to bliss is through death; so let me die, the sooner the better!

In summary, we find this double tone in the text: dying is good, for it brings a double blessing: first, the delights of the intermediate state, and second, the joys of the resurrection state. But we must add that the first blessings, being tangible and nearby, usually have the priority. Let me therefore finish with this recitative from cantata 27, "Who knows how near my end is!" (Ger. *Wer weiß, wie nahe mir mein Ende*; also a cantata for the sixteenth Sunday after Trinity):

Mein Leben hat kein ander Ziel,
Als daß ich möge selig sterben
Und meines Glaubens Anteil erben.
Drum leb ich allezeit

Zum Grabe fertig und bereit,
Und was das Werk der Hände tut,
Ist gleichsam, ob ich sicher wüßte,
Daß ich noch heute sterben müßte:
Denn Ende gut, macht alles gut!

My life has no other goal,
than that I might die happy
and inherit my faith's portion;
Therefore I live constantly
prepared and ready for the grave,
and whatever deeds my hands might do
are the same to me, as if I knew for sure
that even today I must die:
for to end well, makes everything well!

7.4.2   In Summary

Many of Bach's cantata texts contain such pietistic overtones. Whether Lutheran or Reformed, when it comes to Pietism—in the Netherlands, the Second Reformation, and in Britain, and later in North America, Puritanism—there is hardly any difference: when I die, I will receive my heavenly inheritance, so what more do I want? So, Lord, let me experience this "sweet death" as soon as possible, so that there is no delay in my entering into my heavenly inheritance!

I reckon that this kind of "sweet death-ism"belongs to the erroneous teachings that I am seeking to refute in the present chapter. *This* is not the proper hope of Christians for the future. *Their* hope involved the Parousia of Christ, and the resurrection of believers, and the Messianic state. "Sweet death-ism" did not characterize the way the apostles lived and thought, nor did the early church fathers live and think this way either (as far as we can assess). It was "The Great Shift" of the fourth century that brought this enormous change. This is where the deepest roots of this deviant teaching

211

must be sought: the Christian hope basically moved from the glorious Parousia to the believer's "sweet death."

In summary, these are the four "-isms" identified in this chapter:

(a) *Reincarnationism* (§7.1) is wrong: at physical death, there is no such thing as a soul moving (transmigrating) to some other body.

(b) *Psychopannychism* (§7.2) is wrong: at physical death, there is no such thing as a soul falling in a kind of coma.

(c) *Spiritism* (§7.3) is wrong: after physical death, there is no such thing as a soul roaming around to be called upon according to the whims of mediums.

(d) The notion of what I am calling *"sweet death-ism"* (§7.4.1) is wrong: at physical death, there is no such thing as a soul entering a world of ultimate bliss; only the resurrection will introduce the *glorified human* into such a world. Christians look forward to the Parousia, not to the intermediate state.

The shared factor in these four false "-isms" is the notion of the "soul" that constitutes a supposed substance distinct from, and independent of, the body's substance. It is time to look somewhat more carefully at this notion; this awaits us in our next chapter.

8

THE PROBLEM OF
BODY AND SOUL

Now may the God of peace himself
sanctify you completely,
and may your whole spirit and body and soul
be kept blameless at the coming of our Lord Jesus
Christ.
He who calls you is faithful;
he will surely do it.
1 Thessalonians 5:23–24

Wohl uns, daß unser Glaube lernet,
Im Geiste seinen Gott zu schauen.
Ihr Leib hält sie gefangen.
Des Höchsten Huld befördert ihr Verlangen,
Denn er erbaut den Ort,
Da man ihn herrlich schaut.

> O fortunate we,
> for our faith teaches,
> to behold our God in the Spirit.
> Their bodies hold them prisoner.
> The Highest's favor fulfills their desire,
> for He builds the place where He can be

gloriously beheld.[1]
Höchsterwünschtes Freudenfest
[*Most Highly Desired Festival of Joy*]
Bach cantata BWV 194
Unknown poet

8.1 The Human Personality
8.1.1 Anthropological Errors

My philosophical dissertation at the Free University of Amsterdam (1986) was on philosophical anthropology. My supervisor was the Reformed philosopher and theologian Andree Troost, professor of philosophy at that University. In discussing anthropological problems with him, I remember how, one day, I pointed to Heidelberg Catechism Q&A 57:

> *57. What comfort do you receive from the "resurrection of the body"?*
> That not only *my soul* after this life shall be *immediately* taken up to Christ its Head (Luke 23:43; Phil. 1:21–23), but also that this my body, raised by the power of Christ, shall be *reunited* with my soul, and made like the glorious body of Christ (1 Cor. 15:53–54; Job 19:25–27; 1 John 3:2) (italics added; see §1.2.3).[2]

I asked how he (Troost), who was so familiar with the dangers of the Greek scholastic body-soul dualism, could possibly accept such a statement.

Troost replied that, if this were a theological treatise, he would reject it. But the Catechism is not formulated in theological language but in ordinary, everyday language, which all church members must be able to understand. I protested that the *underlying thoughts* never-

---

1. Note that the spirit of the living believer is imprisoned within the body, which is an example of Greek scholastic body-soul dualism; cf. §2.1.1]; when, at death, the spirit will be set free, the spirit will be able to freely behold the Lord with delight.
2. *RC*, 2:782.

theless stemmed from Greek scholasticism, which he had to admit, of course. But he replied that it is not easy to explain to a broad church audience what happens at the resurrection without referring to some form of duality within the human being. The Apostles Paul and Peter did something similar when they wrote about the "tent" (i.e., the body) they would soon put off (2 Cor. 5:1, 4; 2 Pet. 1:13–14), which *I* had to admit, of course. Just as I also had to admit that Jesus distinguished between the body that could be killed by other people and the soul that could not (Matt. 10:28). And I also had to admit that James pointed to the body being dead without the spirit (2:26). This is what I call the biblical *duality* with the human being, to be sharply distinguished from the Greek scholastic body-soul *dualism*. This distinction is what I will explain in this chapter.

Theological discussions about the hereafter have been heavily burdened by this body-soul dichotomy, which soon entered Christian thought, and played a great role in patristic and medieval Christian thinking. Back in §§1.2.2 and 1.2.3, we took note of the fast-spreading conviction that the "immortal soul substance" goes to "heaven," whereas the mortal body substance dies. The Bible says that the *person* dies, but dualistic theology says that only the *body* dies; the "soul" "survives" this death. In the resurrection, the body is raised, and is "united" to the soul.

This splitting of a person into two "substances"—body and soul—which together were thought to constitute the human being, was the first error. Some authors (especially because of 1 Thess. 5:23, but also Heb. 4:12 [NABRE], "penetrating between soul and spirit") preferred a trichotomy (three-part person) to a dichotomy (two-part person). This complicated the problem still more: how are the three "substances" of body, soul, and spirit, related, and how are they split up at physical death, and how do they reunite at the resurrection?

The second error to be mentioned was also borrowed from the Greek philosophers. It was the idea that the immaterial soul (and/or spirit) is far more important than the material body, and that death therefore implies a liberation of the soul/spirit from the prison of the body (see above, in §§1.2.3, 2.1.1, and 2.1.2). This led to the *practical*—but not necessarily theological—idea that, strictly speaking, dying was greater than rising, because its result was greater. At death, the soul/spirit is set free from the prison of the body, whereas at the resurrection the liberated soul was reunited to the (resurrected) body. The soul had to return to its prison, no matter that in the meantime this had become a glorified body. Yet, the basic error remained: the spiritual is higher than the physical. This was one of the ideas of Neo-Platonism, and because Augustine was influenced to some extent by this school of thought, we find the same idea in his writing too.[3] It is no wonder that Calvin was influenced by it, as well, as we saw in §2.1.1.

8.1.2   The Unity of the Human Person

The two above-mentioned errors provided enormous momentum for what I have called "The Great Shift" (§1.2.2): in the fourth century, Christian hopes shifted away from the Parousia and the resurrection—which had been their focus during the preceding centuries (see §12.1.2)—and toward an increased focus on dying and "going to heaven". [In this way] Interim Theology displaced Parousia theology. In this chapter, we will briefly investigate the anthropological changes that were part of "The Great Shift." I have formulated my anthropology in several other publications;[4] here I shall limit myself to those aspects that will help us understand what was at stake during "The Great Shift," and how it influenced Christian expectations, and we will endeavor to refute the underlying errors.

In opposition to every type of dichotomy or trichotomy, we must begin with the assertion that the human person is an absolute *unity*. All human feelings, thoughts, imaginations, decisions, and so

---

3.   See, e.g., R. A. Markus in Armstrong (1967), chapter 22.
4.   See Ouweneel (1984; 1986; 2008; 2015).

on, find their deepest *radical* (or root)[5] unity in the human Ego. When we say things like, "*I* feel, *I* think, *I* want," this is the same as saying that feelings, thoughts, and decisions of the will are (immanent) functions of the (transcendent) human Ego. The latter is the center or focal point on which the entire person converges. The use of many metaphors (root, focal point, convergence, etc.) provides us a clue to a certain incapacity or embarrassment when we speak of this Ego, because we cannot conceptualize the latter (enclose it in concepts); we can only form ideas of it.[6] From the earliest times, this Ego has been referred to as soul, spirit, heart (in its figurative sense), personality, personal center, and so on, both in the Bible and in paganism.

The terms that we use are not all that important as long as we are not caught in either of two dangerous snares: either the snare of functionalism (or reductionism), or the snare of psycho-physical dualism. Functionalism means that one of the "functions" of immanent human existence is absolutized, and all other functions are reduced to it (hence the term "reductionism"). Well-known examples are materialism ("everything is physical") and spiritualism, or psychic monism ("everything is spirit; matter is illusory"). But rationalism must also be mentioned: humans are primarily considered to be *rational* beings, so that the postulated "soul" is specifically the *rational* (or, *reasonable*) *soul*, as it has been called by Aristotle (Gk. *psychē logikē*; Lat.: *anima rationalis*).

The other great danger is that of psycho-physical dualism. One form of it is declaring the soul (or the spirit, or the Ego, etc.) to be a certain distinct "part" of a person,[7] instead of identifying the Ego with the human personality as such, or with the focal point of the total human being. The Hebrew and Greek words for "soul" have many meanings (see the following section); but in the emphat-

---

5. From Lat. *radix*, "root."
6. For this terminology, see Ouweneel (2014).
7. This was also argued by Heyns (1988), 119; Visscher (1937), 91, called the *nephesh* ("soul") an "independent essence."

ic meaning in which I use the word here, I would not say that I *have* a soul (in addition to other parts), or that I *consist* of a soul along with other parts, but that I *am* a soul. The first time the word "soul" in reference to a human person appears in the KJV is in Genesis 2:7:[8] "[T]he LORD God formed man of the dust of the ground, and breathed into his nostrils the breath of life; and man became a living soul." The man did not *receive* an (immortal) "soul," he *became* a living "soul" in a way no animal is a "living soul," namely, by being "breathed into" by God himself.

Viewing the heart or the Ego as a "constitutive part" of the human being is rooted in pagan thinking.[9] This view is unbiblical: the human heart is not a "thing" or a "part," but, as I said, rather a "focal point," which can no more be severed from the entire person than the center of a circle can be severed from the circle, or the focal point of a lens can be severed from the lens. In this "point"—this heart—the person experiences the unity of their entire human being; here, all aspects and structures of their humanity come together as the spokes converge on the axle of a wheel. Although we should not read philosophy into any Bible verse, I venture to quote Proverbs 4:23 here: "Keep your heart with all diligence, for out of it spring the issues of life" (NKJV); this verse teaches that all functions of human life find their origin in the heart.

8.1.3   "Soul" and "Spirit" in the Bible

In a brief survey, let me mention some of the meanings that the words "soul" and "spirit" can have in the Bible.[10] I do this to unmask the error of those who select only one meaning and declare this to be the definition of "soul" or "spirit." There are many

---

8. We find the Hebrew term for "soul" in Genesis 1:20–21, 24 and 30, "living soul" (i.e., living creature; in this case: various types of animals).

9. See Ouweneel (1984), §2.2.2; (1986), chapters 5 and 6. By "pagan" I understand all that falls outside the Jewish-Christian tradition and has not been influenced by the latter. Not every pagan idea is *a priori* necessarily mistaken, but it must definitely be critically examined.

10. See Ouweneel (1986), §5.3.2.

shades of meaning, as is usually the case with terms in everyday language, where they often do not have single, univocal meaning as they do in the sciences. Therefore, it is quite mistaken to limit terms like "soul" and "spirit" to one or two meaning(s) among multiple possibilities (see the following section).

(1) *Biotic meanings:*

(a) In fact, the basic meaning of the two Hebrew words *nephesh* and *ruach*, as well as the Greek *psychē* and *pneuma*, is "breath," while *ruach* and *pneuma* can also mean "wind"; but other words for "breath" are usually used in the Bible.

(b) In addition to "breath," the word "blood" directly involves "life" in the biotic sense: when the breath or the blood of a person leaves her body, the person dies. It is said that the "soul" is both the blood and *in* the blood.[11]

(c) Both "soul" and "spirit" can refer to biotic life in general, not only in humans but also in animals (for *ruach*, see, e.g., Eccl. 3:19, 21). The "soul" is more typically biotic life than the "spirit"; therefore, it can be said of humans and animals that they *are* living "souls" (Gen. 1:20–21, 24, 30 Darby), that is, "living creatures," but never that they *are* "spirits" (except in the case of disembodied persons[12]). In an expression such as "the soul dies" (Ezek. 18:4, 20), the meaning of "soul" is the entire human person seen from the biotic point of view. In a passage such as Hebrews 4:12, the word "soul" might have to do more with the biotic-psychic aspect of life, and the word "spirit" more with the spiritive aspect of life (see point [2]), but this is just one of several possible interpretations. At any rate, such a verse does not provide the slightest ground for assuming a trichotomous anthropology.

(2) *Perceptive-sensitive meanings:* The Hebrew words *nephesh* and *ruach* indicate many kinds of feelings, such as hatred, pain, grief,

---

11. Gen. 9:4; Lev. 17:10–14; Deut. 12:23.
12. Luke 24:37, 39; Heb. 12:23; 1 Pet. 3:19; cf. Luke 23:46; Acts 7:59.

dismay, impatience, jealousy, inner unrest, torment, despondency, rage, bitterness, irritation, dread, arrogance, and so on; also think of hunger and thirst (Deut. 12:15, 20–21; many times in Prov.), and of sexual desire (Gen. 34:3, 8; Jer. 2:24). Similarly the Greek words *psychē* and *pneuma* can refer to many types of feeling, but often in direct reference to the spiritive aspect (see point [3]), and especially the relationship to God (see under [4]).[13] In Paul's writings, the *psychē* has an especially biotic and psychic meaning, whereas *pneuma* refers more to the spiritive, the more typically human. Thus, the unbeliever is *psychikos* (dominated by the *psychē*), and the Spirit-led believer is *pneumatikos*: dominated by the *pneuma* (1 Cor. 2:14–15), in the sense not of some "immortal spirit," but of the human spiritive life, or especially of the Holy Spirit working within human spiritive life.

(3) *Spiritive meanings*: In the light of point (2), we may say that the focal point of the new life in Christ seems to be in particular the human spirit (Rom. 8:16, the Spirit bearing witness with our spirit). In 1 Peter, *psychē* is the entire human personality (1:9, 22; 2:25; 3:20; 4:19), whereas the *pneuma* is the spirit of a dead person (3:19). More specifically we find the following spiritive meanings of *ruach* and *pneuma*:

(a) Reason: grasping, reflecting, understanding.[14]
(b) Imagination: figuring, inventing, designing.[15]
(c) Will: wanting, choosing, deciding.[16]

(4) *Transcendent meanings* (the Ego or personality): Commonly, for this meaning it is the word "heart" that is used, but sometimes also the word "soul" in its most emphatic meaning (e.g., Matt. 10:28; Rev. 6:9) and the word "spirit" in its most emphatic meaning (e.g., Heb. 12:23; James 2:26; 1 Pet. 3:19).

---

13. Cf. Mark 12:30; 14:34; John 10:24; 12:27.
14. E.g., Deut. 34:9; Job 32:8; Ps. 77:6; Isa. 29:24; Dan. 5:14; 6:4; Mark 2:8; 1 Cor. 2:11.
15. E.g., Exod. 28:3; 1 Chron. 28:12; Ezek. 11:5; 20:32.
16. E.g., Exod. 35:21; Job 32:18; Isa. 19:14; Ezek. 13:3; 1 Cor. 4:21; 2 Tim. 1:7.

Of course, in the Bible, these various meanings of "soul" and "spirit" overlap somewhat. But the conclusion we may safely draw is that the explicit and exclusive transcendent meaning of "soul" and "spirit" in the sense of the Ego or the personality is quite rare. In other words, there is virtually no basis for the idea of an "immortal soul" or "spirit" in the Bible, because in the great majority of cases "soul" and "spirit" have biotic, psychic, and spiritive meanings; that is, these are simply overlapping aspects of the *immanent* human corporeal mode of existence, which ceases at physical death. Only rarely do "soul" and "spirit" have the *transcendent* meaning of the human Ego or personality.

8.2   Substantialism[17]

8.2.1   Naïve Anthropology

The Bible does not speak of a "soul" or "spirit" as a concrete thing, traditionally called a *substance*, or as an independently existing, essentially immutable thing. Nor does it speak of a person as "consisting" of two or three "parts."[18] Greek scholastic dichotomy and trichotomy have become so powerful that the verse quoted at the beginning of this chapter (1 Thess. 5:23) is commonly taken to mean that a person consists of three "parts." Similarly, Matthew 10:28, Hebrews 4:12, James 2:26 and similar texts are often understood to suggest that a person consists of two or three "parts." However, these passages never speak of "parts"; they describe the totality of human existence in ordinary, everyday language. Spirit and body and soul are not little "parts" of a person any more than heart, soul, strength, and mind are "parts" of a person in Luke 10:27 ("love the Lord . . . with all your heart/soul/strength/mind"[19]). Speaking like this is nothing but an unpleasant effect of

17. See extensively Berkouwer (1962), 216–23.
18. Carey (1977), 29.
19. The Greek word for "mind" is *dianoia*, related to *nous*. Although the human *nous* or *noos* ("mind") plays a considerable role in the New Testament (e.g., Luke 24:45; Rom. 7:23, 25; 12:2; 1 Cor. 14:14–15; 2 Thess. 2:2), *and* although the Greek philosopher Anaxagoras had given it an important

ancient pagan substantialism. Tertullian, for example, called body and soul two "sister substances."[20]

An additional problem is that the natural sciences are accustomed to using rigidly defined terms; as a consequence, in our scientistic era, many theories, especially in charismatic circles, about what "soul" and "spirit" are supposed to mean in the Bible[21] must be called superficial and poorly considered. For such a theology, a few favorite Bible passages are picked, and the many passages where "soul" or "spirit" means very different things are neglected.

One such naïve saying, popular among Pentecostals and Charismatics, is this one: "I am a spirit being who has a soul and lives in a body."[22] None of these three phrases is correct, as the present chapter will show. First, if I *am* a "spirit being" (whatever this being is), how could one ever speak of "my (or one's) spirit," sometimes in juxtaposition with "my (or one's) soul"?[23] Second, if I can say only that I *have* a soul, how can persons often be referred to in the Bible as *souls*?[24] Third, if I live in a body, then this body is not part of me; how then can it be said of so many *persons* that *they* were buried, not just their bodies?[25]

The fact is that both "soul" and "spirit" can each mean *many* different things in the Bible, just as in everyday parlance (see previous section). But in the theories just mentioned, only one meaning is selected and presented as *the* biblical meaning of soul and spirit, respectively. The resulting theories are superficial, naïve, and far

---

place in his anthropology, it hardly ever played as great a role in Christian philosophical and theological anthropology as did soul, spirit, and body.

20. *De anima* 52; see Pannenberg (1991), 2:182–83; cf. 2:282–83.
21. The Internet gives us numerous examples, too many to mention..
22. See, e.g., https://www.awmi.net/reading/teaching-articles/spirit-soul-and-body/ and https://mitchhorton.com/pauls-model-of-man-i-am-a-spirit-i-have-a-soul-and-i-live-in-a-body/.
23. Job 7:11; Isa. 26:9; Mark 2:8; Luke 1:46–47; Rom. 1:9; 1 Cor. 14:14–15; 2 Cor. 2:13; 1 Thess. 5:23; Heb. 4:12.
24. Ezek. 18:20; Acts 2:41; 1 Pet. 3:20; Rev. 18:13.
25. Luke 16:22; John 19:42; Acts 2:29; 5:6, 9–10; 8:2.

more Greek than biblical, even though their proponents seem to be unaware of this. Often, these proponents lack a philosophical or an academic theological training, which would, at the very least, have taught them about the pagan background of such theories. But part of the problem within theology itself is that there is too much thoughtless repetition, too little independent thinking. If Augustine, Calvin, and the creeds say A, how dare you think it is B?[26]

Consider the entire discussion about whether a person is dichotomous (with two constitutive parts: soul/spirit and body) or trichotomous (with three constitutive parts: soul, spirit, and body). The simple answer is that both views are radically mistaken; both have been produced by the very same pagan substantialism, which is fundamentally erroneous.[27] In the Bible, the unity of the person is so important that a person simply cannot be a sum of two or three or more parts.[28] At most we may discern various aspects, that is, various viewpoints under which we may consider the totality, unity, and coherence of the person.

8.2.2   What/Who Is Buried?

Sometimes, the Bible does speak in the form of a *duality* ("twoness") of the (transcendent) Ego and the (immanent) body, especially in connection with death, but we may never identify this as a *dualism* (antithesis) of two *substances*. The Apostle Paul tells us that the human Ego dwells in a "tent," the body, which is "destroyed" at physical death (2 Cor. 5:1). The Apostle Peter speaks of being in a "tent," knowing that shortly he will have to "put off" his "tent" (2 Pet. 1:13–14 NKJV). The Apostle James said that "the body apart from the spirit is dead" (2:26). Jesus spoke of those who can kill the

---

26. There may well be a formal difference, but certainly no practical difference, between the authoritative power of tradition in both Roman Catholicism and Protestantism.

27. Bavinck (1920), 22, did not object to the term "dichotomy." Although Berkouwer (1962), 200–201 spoke of "parts," he radically rejected both dichotomy and trichotomy, *ibid.*, 207–23.

28. For extensive arguments, see Ouweneel (1984; 1986).

body but not the soul (Matt. 10:28). Such everyday *practical* speaking is far removed from the *theoretical* idea of two distinct substances, namely, the soul (spirit, heart, Ego) and the body, between which a kind of unity must then be sought.

The meaning of this practical parlance is clearly shown in cases where the Ego is bound equally to the personality and to the body, such as in cases where it is not just the body but the *person* that is buried. John 19 says that the body of Jesus was buried (John 19:38, 40), but also that *Jesus* was buried (v. 42), meaning the very same thing. The Bible says that Lazarus, Dives, David, Ananias, Sapphira, and Stephen, not just their mortal remains, were buried (Luke 16:22; Acts 2:29; 5:6, 9–10; 8:2). In the Bible, which is a practical book, it is equally correct to say that a certain person put off his body (which is buried) as to say that this *person* was buried, because every form of theoretical substantialistic dualism is foreign to the Bible.

One of the consequences of substantialistic dualism has always been that, as we have seen, under the influence of Hellenistic thinking the soul was viewed as more important than the body. Traces of this are found in the writings of church fathers like Augustine, who were influenced by Neo-Platonism. In the case of the deceased person, people have unbiblically referred to the corpse by speaking of burying the mortal remains, referring to the mortal stuff that remains after the immortal soul has left the body. Think of sentences like this one: "This is no longer Father, but only his mortal remains; Father himself is in heaven."

Nothing is more typically pagan than such talk about the "mortal remains" of the dead. This is *never* the way the Bible speaks about the dead; you need think only of the way the patriarchs spoke of their dead: in Genesis 23, Abraham wished to bury his dead wife, not just her "remains." "Isaac breathed his last, and he died and was gathered to his people" (35:29), in which there is little difference between saying *he* was buried and saying *he* went to be with his ancestors (see §4.2.3). Jacob buried *Rachel* (Gen. 35:19; 48:7), not just her "remains." And concerning himself, he said, "I am to be gathered to my people; bury *me* with my fathers in the cave that is in the field of Ephron the Hittite" (49:29).

8.2.3 The "Inferiority" of the Body

In all forms of ascetism and many forms of mysticism, we find a condescending way of speaking about the body, a way that is utterly unbiblical. Think of the negative attitude toward sexuality in large parts of the church; this attitude has continually formed the primary reason for legitimizing celibacy: the asexual state is better than the sexual state (with a false appeal to 1 Cor. 7). The Apostle Paul says the contrary; he even speaks of

> deceitful spirits and teachings of demons, through the insincerity of liars whose consciences are seared, who forbid marriage and require abstinence from foods that God created to be received with thanksgiving by those who believe and know the truth. For everything created by God is good, and nothing is to be rejected if it is received with thanksgiving, for it is made holy by the word of God and prayer (1 Tim. 4:1–5).

The reason for forbidding marriage as well as certain foods was apparently the heretics' manner of looking with condescension at everything that is material-physical.

The New Testament speaks of marriage and sexuality in a very positive way.[29] Paul emphasized that believers must put their *bodies*—not just their spirits or souls—in the service of God (Rom. 6:13, 19; 12:1), that is, their entire personalities. Paul called this *body*—not the soul or the spirit—a temple of the Holy Spirit (1 Cor. 6:19). The doctrine of the resurrection in particular contradicts all Greek contempt for the body (cf. the Athenians' response to Paul's message of the resurrection in Acts: "[W]hen they heard of the resurrection of the dead, some mocked. But others said, "We will

---

29. Matt. 19:4–6; 1 Cor. 7; Eph. 5:22–33; 1 Pet. 3:1–7.

hear you again about this" (17:30–32).

For the sake of clarity, the "body" (Gk. *sōma*) must be distinguished here from "flesh" (Gk. *sarx*). In some cases, the latter term is a neutral reference to the body, such as in this phrase: Christ "was manifest in the flesh" (1 Tim. 3:16), that is, revealed himself in a body of flesh and blood.[30] However, the Greek term *sarx* can also refer to the fragile, perishable body subject to sin,[31] and hence to the sinful nature as such.[32] As far as I am aware, this is never the case with the Greek term *sōma*.[33]

Let me add one more consideration. The notion of an "immortal soul/spirit" was read into the Bible because early Christian thinkers were deeply impressed with Greek thinking on this point; as a consequence, they began to search for these Greek views in the Bible. Justin Martyr in his *Apologies* and Augustine are two examples of early Christian thinkers who believed that there were seeds of Christianity present in Greek philosophy. They also claimed that the divine Logos had illuminated thinkers like Socrates, Plato, and Aristotle, and even that Aristotle was a forerunner of Christ in secular matters, just as John the Baptist had been in sacred matters. In modern times, Roman Catholic thinker Karl Rahner spoke of "anonymous Christians."[34] In his *Divine Comedy*, Dante Alighieri placed people like Homer, Horace, Virgil, and Ovid in the first (and least bad) circle of Hell (or Limbo), and the pagan Emperor Trajan in Paradise.

In the light of this widespread phenomenon of honoring the Greeks, it is no wonder that their views on body and soul were considered to be sacrosanct and divinely inspired. After this, it was easy

---

30. See also John 1:14; Rom. 4:1; 2 Cor. 5:16; Gal. 4:13; Phil. 1:24.
31. Isa. 40:6; Matt. 26:41; Rom. 7:5; Gal. 1:16.
32. Rom. 7:26; 8:3–9, 12–13; Gal. 5:13, 16–17; Heyns (1988), 121.
33. In Rom. 6:6, where we find the phrase "body of sin," the Greek word *sōma* either refers to the body that is the instrument of sin (we sin with our eyes, ears, hands, feet, etc.; see AMPC), or it has a figurative meaning (PHILLIPS: "tyranny of sin," TPT: "stronghold of sin").
34. See D'Costa (1985) and Clinton (1998).

enough to read these Greek views into the Bible. *There is no heresy that could not be read into the Bible*, to mislead simple souls. This commitment extends to the point where modern orthodox Protestant theologians become very defensive when one denies and discredits notions such as the body-soul dualism, the immortal soul, and anthropological dichotomy or trichotomy, as well as psychocreationism or traducianism. This defensiveness arises especially because certain elements of these notions are present in their creeds and catechisms (see the examples mentioned in the following sections).

8.3   Scholastic Dualism in the Past
8.3.1   Patristic and Thomistic Dualism

The Athanasian Creed tells us that, if a person does not believe what it says, they "can not be saved." One of the things it says is that Christ is "perfect God, and perfect Man, of a reasonable soul [Latin text: *anima rationali*] and human flesh subsisting. . . . For as the reasonable soul and flesh is one man; so God and Man is one Christ." So, the Creed is saying that if a person does not accept the (nonbiblical!) Aristotelian concept of the *anima rationalis*, they cannot be saved! In his treatise "On the Morals of the Catholic Church" (Lat. *De Moribus Ecclesiae Catholicae*), Augustine wrote: "Man, then, as viewed by his fellowman, is a rational soul with a mortal and earthly body in its service."[35]

The Bible does not teach or presuppose any form of anthropological *dualism*; at best it presupposes a certain *duality*, a bipolarity. In this duality, these two poles do not form an antithesis, for the human heart is nothing but the concentration point *of all the human functions themselves*, including the physical and biotic functions. In other words, the functions do not stand dualistically opposite the heart, the Ego, but are functions *of* the heart. This is never a duality of something mental (in the sense of the Aristotelian *anima rationalis*) as opposed to something material-physical, for both the mental

---

35. Augustine, (n.d.-2), 1.27.52.

and the physical are strictly immanent. The only duality that I believe is acceptable on a biblical basis is that of the *transcendent* (with its unity, fullness, totality, convergence) and the *immanent*-empirical (with its diversity, brokenness, divergence).

In scholastic theology, it was particularly the great medieval philosopher-theologian Thomas Aquinas who elaborated the Aristotelian concept of the soul, while at the same time adapting it to biblical demands, for instance, by claiming that it was an immortal soul.[36] In this view, the soul, spirit, or heart is nothing but a totality of hypostatized[37] *immanent* human (psychic-spiritive[38]) *functions*. When this view speaks of the "unity of body and soul," this is no more than the *secondary* unity of two primarily distinct, even contrary immanent function complexes: a mental (psychic-spiritive) and a natural (physical-biotic) function complex—two essentially different substances or things, for which a secondary unity must be sought.[39] Please notice the difference between this and the duality just mentioned. This is never a *dualism* of two antithetical immanent function complexes, but a duality involving *all* immanent functions, on the one hand, and the transcendent heart or Ego or personality, on the other hand. There cannot be any antithesis here because the functions are functions *of the heart*, and the heart is the concentration point and integration point *of the functions*.[40]

One of the consequences of Thomistic dualistic thinking was the issue of how the (Aristotelian) "rational soul" (Lat. *anima rationalis*)—a highly unfortunate confusion between the transcendent

---

36. I do not work this out here; see my earlier anthropological work, especially Ouweneel (1984; 1986).
37. The word "hypostasized" means "turned into a substance," into some independent "thing," distinct from other substances in the human mode of existence.
38. A term I have coined to refer to the higher modal functions of humanhood, from the logical to the pistical modalities; see more extensively, Ouweneel (2015).
39. Vollenhoven (1933), 33; Gehlen (1950).
40. See briefly, Ouweneel (2015) and extensively, Ouweneel (1986), §5.2.2.

Ego and the immanent-rational—originated in the human being. Thus, a *wrong* view can create problems whose solutions are necessarily equally wrong. Thomas presented a "psychocreationism," according to which the body is formed in the natural way from a pair of parents, whereas the "rational soul" (Lat. *anima rationalis*) is created separately by God and placed in the human body. In contrast with this, *traducianism* teaches that, with the seed of the parents, the soul is "traduced"(or transmitted by generation) to the child. Roman Catholic anthropology adheres to psychocreationism, Lutheran anthropology to traducianism. Both are utterly mistaken because both are rooted in the same mistaken Thomistic, dualistic thinking.[41] If the starting point is wrong, the outcome can never be right; "the diseased tree bears bad fruit" (Matt. 7:17).

8.3.2   Dualism among Early Reformed Theologians

The father of Reformed theology, John Calvin, followed Augustine in teaching that in Philippians 1:23, Paul is testifying that death is a separation of body and soul: we will be with Christ when our soul is severed from the body.[42] Of course, Paul said nothing of the kind. Calvin spoke of the human "immortal soul" as the "noblest part" (Lat. *nobilior pars*) of humans,[43] in line with Neo-Platonism, and, along Aristotelian Thomistic lines, he saw this "immortal (rational)" soul as the seat of the intellect and the will, and "separate from the body" (Lat. *a corpore separatum*)," the latter being nothing but a "perishable house of clay."[44] In his *Institutes*, Calvin freely wrote of the "immortal" and "rational" human "soul" or "spirit."[45]

Calvin's successor in Geneva, Theodore Beza, was the man who introduced the study of Aristotelian logic and metaphysics at the

---

41. Cf. Berkouwer (1962), 292.
42. Calvin (1965), *ad loc*
43. Calvin (1960), 1.15.2. Regarding this problem of the "immortality of the soul" with all its eschatological implications, see extensively Van Leeuwen (1955) and Berkouwer (1962), chapter 7.
44. See the criticism by Berkhof (1986), 185.
45. Calvin (1960), 1.15 *passim*.

Calvinist universities as the necessary foundation for theological education.[46] Since that time, Reformed theology has gradually been led back into the arms of medieval scholasticism, from which John Calvin had at least partially liberated it. For centuries, the remains of scholastic thought continued to influence Reformed theology, as can be seen in the Reformed confessions (see examples in §1.2.3).

The Second Helvetic Confession, written in 1566 by Heinrich Bullinger, was the most famous Reformed confessional document, second only to the Heidelberg Catechism. In chapter 7 we read:

> We say also that man consists of two, and those divers substances in one person; of a soul immortal (as that which being separated from his body, neither sleeps nor dies) and a body mortal, which notwithstanding at the last judgment shall be raised again from the dead, that from henceforth the whole man may continue for ever, in life or in death.[47]

The Annotations of the Dutch States Translation (1637) offer evidence of this scholastic dualism when they refer, for example, in 1 Corinthians 15:45 to the human "reasonable and immortal soul."[48]

The Reformed theologian Gisbertus Voetius, representative of the Second Reformation, was so thoroughly convinced of the significance of Aristotle for Christian thinking that, in his battle with the French philosopher René Descartes (who was living in the Netherlands at the time), he argued that to oppose Aristotle was the same as to oppose Christianity.[49] Voetius called Aristotle "our" philosopher—and the consequences of this thinking continue to poison Reformed theology to this very day. Broad segments of traditional Protestant thinking, from Anglican to Evangelical, are still locked in the grip of Greek scholastic thought.

Another great representative of the Second Reformation, Wil-

---

46. See Kickel (1967).
47. Dennison, *RC*, 2:820) cf. the Belgic Confession Art. 18, 19, 34, and 37.
48. Haak (1918), *ad loc.*
49. See, e.g., Cohen (2008), 19–20, 162–75.

helmus à Brakel, a student of Voetius, published in 1700 his work entitled *The Christian's Reasonable Service*,[50] in which he fully defended the scholastic anthropological dualism of the two substances, namely, the immortal soul and the mortal body, as well as the fallacy of psychocreationism, the division of body and soul at physical death, and the reunion of body and soul at the resurrection. He taught that at death the souls of deceased believers are immediately taken up to God "in the third heaven" (cf. §5.3), and there they already enjoy everything that they will enjoy forever after the reunion of body and soul. This leads one to ask: Who needs more examples? Virtually all traditional Protestant theologians, at least until the twentieth century, have uncritically repeated this Greek scholastic paradigm.

To underscore the idea of the "rational and immortal soul," people quote Genesis 2:7 (God "formed man of the dust of the ground, and breathed into his nostrils the breath of life; and man became a living soul"; KJV). This is a verse into which many scholastic theologians have read the notion of an "immortal soul." In reality, the verse says about the "soul" only that "man *became* a living soul" (KJV), that is, a "living being" (ESV). This confronts any thinking person with a riddle: How can a verse telling us how the first man *became* a (Hebrew) *nephesh* be twisted to say that the first man *received* a ("rational, immortal") *nephesh*. What God actually did was to breathe into this man the "breath of life" (Heb. *nishmat chayyim*). This biblical "breath of life" has nothing to do with the Aristotelian Thomistic rational, immortal soul.

8.3.3 Dualism among Later Reformed Theologians

Abraham Kuyper viewed body and soul as two (not three) substances,[51] strongly pleading for the psychocreationist view,[52] and

---

50. Brakel (1992), see especially 1:chapter 10.
51. *DD* 1:63; 1892, 2:206–207.
52. Kuyper (2019), 462; see also (1892), 1:49. Cf. extensively, Visscher (1937), 113–33, 162–68, who called psychocreationism the "Reformed doctrine" (162).

thus fully presupposing Platonic and Aristotelian Thomistic dualism. Many Reformed theologians have followed Kuyper in this, such as W. Geesink, who also provided numerous quotes from Calvin to support his views.[53] It is astonishing how much Calvin managed to derive from Genesis 2:7,[54] and how much Geesink managed to derive from Calvin. All these theologians show what happens when a theory thought to be unassailable, even though it is adopted from paganism, is read into the Bible (in addition to Gen. 2:7, for instance into Eccl. 12:7, Matt. 10:28, 1 Thess. 5:23, Heb. 4:12, 12:9, and James 2:26).

In reality, Scripture contains no dualism of a rational, immortal soul and a material, mortal body. Other well-known Reformed theologians who succumbed to the same scholastic body-soul dualism were J. C. Sikkel[55] and H. Bavinck,[56] although the latter was more moderate, and avoided using terms like "substance" and "rational soul."

L. Berkhof, too, wrestled with the matter, condemning the extremes of scholastic dualism, yet clearly leaning toward it.[57] It seemed virtually impossible to break free from this age-old theologoumenon, especially because many sought its basis in the confessions and catechisms. This was why the scholastic Reformed theologian V. Hepp insisted that criticism of substantialistic dualism had to be condemned as *"decidedly anti-confessional"* and *"unconditionally at odds with the Reformed confession."*[58] He could not imagine for a moment that the confessions themselves could be mistaken at various points, a thought that for many theologians to this day appears to be frightening. Once again, when it comes to the power of tradition, there is no practical difference between Roman Catholics and

---

53. Geesink (1925), 268–91.
54. And others have as well, such as Leupold (1942), 117, and Rice (1975), 103.
55. Sikkel (1923), 146.
56. *RD*, 2:554–62.
57. Berkhof (1981), 206–12.
58. Hepp (1937), 40–41, 79.

traditional Protestants.

8.4   Modern Developments

8.4.1   Evangelicals

With Evangelical theologians such as Lewis Sperry Chafer we see similar struggles, in particular when he had to choose between psychocreationism (defended earlier by Charles Hodge) and traducianism (defended earlier by William Shedd), or between dichotomy and trichotomy.[59] Unfortunately, he failed to discern the underlying Greek scholastic tradition, which was more pagan than biblical. If he had, he would not have felt compelled to choose between these two false options.

Another Evangelical example is James G. S. S. Thomson, who told us that, according to the Old Testament, at death "the body remained on earth; the *nephesh* passed into Sheol; but the breath, spirit, or *ruach*, returned to God, not Sheol."[60] He was overlooking these facts: first, Sheol usually refers to nothing more than the grave: and, second, *nephesh* and *ruach* can mean many things in the Old Testament. This is the familiar error of limiting terms like *nephesh* and *ruach* to just one or a few of their many possible meanings in the Bible.

Many other theologians enthusiastically continued the age-old conflict between dichotomy (defended, for example, by Augustine) and trichotomy (defended, for example, by Clement of Alexandria and Origen, and more recently by A. Murray,[61] G. H. Pember,[62] A. R. Fausset,[63] W. Nee,[64] and many others, who often repeat uncritically what they have read from other Protestant authors). Very few theologians have had the courage or wisdom to critically examine

---

59. *ST* 2,chapters 13 and 14.
60. J. G. S. S. Thomson in Henry (1962), 271.
61. Murray (1984), 159–60; cf. 193.
62. Pember (1975), 76–77.
63. Fausset in Jamieson et al. (1871), 3:469.
64. http://www3.telus.net/trbrooks/The_Spiritual_Man.pdf. This (unfortunately dreadful) book was the only one that Watchman Nee wrote personally; all his other books were based on his sermons and compiled by others.

the underlying philosophical presuppositions. They clearly demonstrated the power of a philosophical tradition, especially when it is assumed that the creeds, confessions, and catechisms validate that tradition.

Even in the twentieth century, Reformed theologian K. Dijk expressed difficulty with the notion of the immortal soul,[65] yet he maintained the idea of the division between body and soul at physical death, as well as the mistaken idea that, at death, the believer's soul goes to the house of the Father. The rest of his book is devoted to "heaven" as the place where believers will be during the intermediate state. South African theologian P. S. Dreyer dryly called the book "a nice example of modern Protestant scholasticism"[66]—and this is exactly what it is.

8.4.2 A Change for the Better

However, things have changed in the twentieth century. H. Ridderbos[67] and B. Oosterhoff[68] flatly rejected any scholastic dualism. G. Berkouwer rejected the conflict between psychocreationism and traducianism as a "fruitless dilemma" and a "dead-end conflict."[69] He clearly exposed the origin of the conflict as coming from scholastic substantialism.[70] J. Douma as well as M. J. Paul et al. also rejected the notion of the immortal soul.[71]

A. Hoekema rejected both dichotomy and trichotomy.[72] S. Fowler viewed the underlying Greek scholastic substantialism as a pernicious intrusion of pagan philosophy into Christian thought, and a serious hindrance to understanding the full riches of the gos-

---

65. Dijk (1955), chapter 1.
66. https://www.ajol.info/index.php/hts/article/view/147615/137119.
67. Ridderbos (1975), 100–107.
68. Oosterhoff (1972), 101–102.
69. Berkouwer (1962), chapters 6 and 8; see also Cullmann (1962), 66–68; Prenter (1967), 272–74; Ladd (1974), 457; Heyns (1988), 124, Van Genderen and Velema (2008), 356–57, Spykman (1992), 238.
70. Berkouwer (1962), 342–43; cf. 318.
71. Douma (2004), 17–18; Paul et al. (2004), 39n9.
72. Hoekema (1986), 209, 318, 326, 342–43.

pel.[73] The latter is especially important: we are dealing here not with a collateral subject interesting only to connoisseurs, but with a matter of vital importance to Christianity, because any form of dualism threatens the *radicality* of both the Fall (how did the Fall affect both the soul substance and the body substance?) and redemption (how does redemption affect both the soul substance and the body substance?).[74]

Unfortunately, other modern theologians still think along the old lines. Pentecostal theologians Duffield and Van Cleave defended a dichotomy against a trichotomy, spoke of the resurrection as the union of the spirit with a glorified body, and defended traducianism,[75] as if no recent debates of these topics had occurred. M. Erickson also preferred traducianism. Although he refused to choose between a dichotomy and a trichotomy, he still continued to speak of persons consisting of a material and an immaterial element.[76] The most regrettable component in his view was his rejection of anti-substantialism because he associated it with existentialism.[77] However, anti-substantialism and existentialism in and of themselves have nothing to do with each other.

Existentialism is an obsession that we detect more frequently in Erickson's views. For instance, in the field of bibliology, where critics accused fundamentalists of rationalism, Erickson immediately suspected the influence of existentialism (as a form of irrationalism[78]). His logic appeared to be that because we know existentialism to be wrong, the rationalism under attack must ipso facto be right.[79] Such simplifications of serious problems are of no great help.

73. Fowler (1981), 3–4.
74. See Ouweneel (2008), §§6.4.3 and 12.2.
75. Duffield and Van Cleave (1996), 140–44.
76. Erickson (1998), 538–57.
77. Other rather recent defenders of substantialistic dualism are Smythies and Beloffs (1989); Foster (1991); Moreland and Ciocchi (1993).
78. Or, more correctly, existentialism is (or was) a rational attempt to emphasize the significance of the irrational.
79. Erickson (1982), 391.

Just to make sure, let me add here that not every rejection of a (substantialist) dichotomy or trichotomy automatically deserves our endorsement, because sometimes such rejection has led , on the one hand, to physicalism or materialism, or, on the other hand, to a psychic monism or spiritualism. Moreover, the rejection of any form of dualism has sometimes led to the denial of the intermediate state, as happened with P. Althaus, G. van der Leeuw, B. Telder and C. Vonk (see §7.2).[80] This is to throw out the baby with the bathwater. Instead, we should maintain that a person does indeed continue to function after their physical death, but to maintain this, we need no ancient or modern anthropological dualism.

8.5   The Human Unity
8.5.1   The End of Substantialism
Today, both the scholastic body-soul dualism and the body-soul-spirit trichotomy have become totally untenable, for reasons arising not only from philosophy and theology, but also from the natural sciences. In the light of modern scientific research, not a single psychic-spiritive activity of the Ego (or the heart, the soul, the spirit, or whatever people call it) can occur apart from physico-physiological processes. In other words, such activities cannot, and do not, proceed from different substances that are separable from each other. Our psychic-spiritive activity proceeds from the transcendent Ego and functions in *all* immanent aspects of cosmic reality. Within our empirical reality, there is no thinking, feeling, or willing apart from the influence of our physical condition and the physiological activities of the body.[81]

Thus, there is no longer any scientific room for the old view of mechanistic matter-substance, which is supposedly independent of the soul. Matter-substance has been expelled by dynamic views of intensive interactions on the biotic, psychic, and spiritive levels. To

---

80. Berkouwer (1962), 249–55.
81. Cf. Ouweneel (1984), especially §§2.3.2, 4.2, 4.3, and 6.2.2; see also Pannenberg (1991), 2:182.

put it sharply: within our immanent reality, it is impossible for humans to say a prayer or words of praise within their hearts without an exchange of potassium and sodium ions on both sides of their brain cell membranes.[82]

Ancient substantialism, which was unbiblical, has been definitively replaced by functional approaches. A rational soul (or spirit) that functions independently of physical-biotic processes is now inconceivable. Similarly, the idea of a material substance, that is, some "ground-matter" that under all circumstances would remain the same, is also inconceivable. Even stable particles such as electrons can be destroyed when photons are produced, and they can be created from photons. Even the most stable particles, the neutrons, can be destroyed through collisions with their anti-particles, during which their energy is turned into light. Matter is no longer a substance but rather condensed energy. If matter can no longer be called a "substance," then certainly neither can the soul, the spirit, or the heart.

Every notion of anthropological dichotomy or trichotomy is based on a *theoretical* separation between two or three immanent function complexes, a physical-biotic complex (the "material body") and a psychic-spiritive complex (the "rational, immortal soul"), or a psychic (the "soul") and a spiritive function complex (the "spirit"). In practice, such a separation is inconceivable because of the total interdependence and interwovenness not only of these two or three complexes, but of *all* immanent aspects and structures of the human mode of existence. Keep in mind that a duality is never a *dualism* between two *immanent* function complexes, but a *duality* between, on the one hand, the *entire immanent* human mode of existence and, on the other hand, the *transcendent-religious* concentration point of that existence: the Ego, the heart, the transcendent human personality. I call it "religious" because it is in their hearts that

---

82. If I remember correctly, I found this statement somewhere in the writings of British natural scientist and creationist Arthur Ernest Wilder-Smith.

people are oriented toward God—or toward idols, for that matter. Compare the highly interesting—and difficult—statement in Ecclesiastes 3:11: God "has put eternity[83] into man's heart" (GW: "He has put a sense of eternity in people's minds"; AMP: "a sense of divine purpose").

In summary, modern Bible teachers who are still defending anthropological dichotomy or trichotomy have no basis for their position; they are philosophically mistaken, they are theologically mistaken, they are scientifically mistaken, and worst of all: they are biblically mistaken. Nevertheless, the Internet provides numerous defenses of such dichotomies or trichotomies. The slogan, "I am a spirit, I have a soul, I live in a body," is endlessly repeated by people who, apparently, have difficulty thinking for themselves.

8.5.2 Biblical Aspects

In contrast to the entire traditional substantialist dualism, which is rooted in pagan thought, Christian theology needs a fundamentally different approach, one rooted in Jewish-Christian thought. The "body," the "tent" that is "put off" at physical death, is not a material substance, but the *entire* immanent human mode of existence. The soul that continues to function after physical death is not a substance, containing the higher immanent (psychic-spiritive) functions. Rather, it is the transcendent human Ego: the "heart" (in the sense of Prov. 4:23) or the "inner self" (in the sense of 2 Cor. 4:16).

We now understand why the entire dilemma of traducianism and psychocreationism must be rejected because it is based on the substantialistic body-soul dualism. In Genesis 2:1, we are told that the *entire* creation was *finished*; there is no room for advocating the ongoing creation of human souls, as psychocreationism teaches.

---

83. It is amazing in how many different ways the Heb. word ʿolam in this verse has been rendered: "the world," "ignorance," "the desire to know the future," "the past," "past and future," "the timeless." The central idea is that in contrast with animals, people have the capacity to ponder the time and the place in which they are living.

God has "made of one blood all nations of men" (Acts 17:26 KJV), which means from *all human beings*, not just from the bodies of human beings. All humans descend from Adam, not just the bodies of all humans. Verses like Matthew 10:28 ("both body and soul") and James 2:26 ("the body apart from the spirit is dead") do not say that humans are *dichotomies* of body and soul substances. And 1 Thessalonians 5:23 ("your whole spirit and body and soul") and Hebrews 4:12 (soul and spirit are distinct) do not say that humans are *trichotomies* of spirits, souls, and bodies. These things are read into the text by Christians who—usually unconsciously—have already accepted the Aristotelian Thomistic paradigm. At most, we can say that every person is a unity, in which various aspects may be discerned, which, of course, is not explained any further in the verses mentioned. This *unity* comes from Adam and Eve.

Let us remember that, because of this very transcendence of the human heart, the coherence of the immanent human mode of existence and the transcendent heart is basically a mystery for us. As G. C. Berkouwer put it:

> There is no science, and no theology, which can unveil for us this mystery of man. This does not mean an under-evaluation of science and theology, but rather an understanding of their meaning and their limits. Man, who no longer understands himself, can again understand this mystery only from the viewpoint of the divine revelation in Jesus Christ.[84]

He called the human being *homo absconditus* ("hidden human"),[85] as a parallel with *deus absconditus*, the "hidden God."

A. Hoekema located the mystery of humanity especially in the fact that humans are both creations and persons.[86] I take this to mean that the term "creation" entails *distance* between God and hu-

---

84. Berkouwer (1962), 309.
85. *Ibid.*, 20.
86. Hoekema (1986), 6.

mans: He is the Creator, while they are creatures. But the term "person" entails *similarity* between God and humans: they have been created in the image and after the likeness of God.

In summary, we can say, first, that the Christian philosophical anthropology[87] presented here resists every form of functionalism (the absolutization of particular immanent functions). This is true especially of the most dangerous of all functionalisms, *logicism*, which absolutizes human reason, belief in the autonomy of reason, the view that humans are above all rational (or reasonable) beings, and therefore exalting the highest aspect in a person, the soul, which is necessarily the rational (or reasonable) soul.

Second, a Christian anthropology distinguishes various aspects and structures in the immanent human mode of existence,[88] but additionally it discerns the fact that the essence of humanity cannot be captured in any one of these aspects and structures, nor in any (hypostasized) complex of immanent functions. The human essence surpasses this entire immanent diversity, without, however, being separate from it, or standing dualistically opposed to it as a distinct substance.

Third, it maintains that "the human being as such" (humanity in itself) does not exist, but the essence of human beings can be understood only from their relationship to their (true or pretended) Origin, that is, it can be understood only through religious self-knowledge. In doing so, no "human being *as such*" is secondarily related to God, but this relationship *itself* belongs to the essence of a human being, as is expressed in the biblical phrase "image of God."[89] This has also been called the "eccentricity" of humans,[90] which I choose to understand as the fact that the human center lies

---

87. Greatly inspired by Reformational anthropology, especially represented by Herman Dooyeweerd (1984); cf. Ouweneel (1986).
88. See again, Ouweneel (2015).
89. *CD* 3/2:78, 132–202; Polman (1956), 247; Berkouwer (1962), 22–23, 34–35.
90. Plessner (1928).

not within the person but "eccentrically" in one's transcendent-religious relationship to God (or to idols).

Fourth, true knowledge of humanity does not come through Christian anthropology as such. Rather, it comes as true *self*-knowledge, possible only through the regenerating power of, and illumination by, the Holy Spirit in the human *heart*, through the working of God's Word in the *heart*, and through a living faith in Jesus Christ (his person and his work) with the entire *heart*. The results of this knowledge will become evident in the entire immanent-functional life of such a person.

8.5.3   What Happens at Physical Death?

Let us now summarize what we have been considering, with a direct application to what happens to the human mode of existence at the moment of physical death. Basically, I have described three main views.

(a) *Substantialistic dualism:* Humans consist of two substances, called the soul substance (basically the rational soul) and the body substance. According to some, there are three substances, including the spirit. At physical death, these two (or three) are divided: the body goes to the grave, and the soul or the spirit goes to the hereafter. At the resurrection, the soul/spirit is re-united with the body, which is now the resurrection body. The advantage of this view is its simplicity: you have two (or three) parts, which are temporarily divided but later reunited. Throughout the centuries, Christians adhering to this view have firmly believed that this is the biblical view, without having any idea of its real origin.

(b) *Monism:* A person consists of one substance only, or, if one wishes to avoid the word "substance," a person is an essential and existential psycho-physical unity, which cannot be divided. One can also say that this unity is either totally physical (materialism) or totally psychic (spiritualism). At physical death, nothing could possibly be divided, and thus, the entire person goes to the grave. This person is raised at the resurrection, when the one person, now glo-

241

rified, rises from the grave. In more modern times, some Christians who have—rightly—rejected substantialistic dualism, have firmly believed that their monism, and the concomitant pyschopannychia (see §7.2), were the only acceptable alternative.

(c) Some Christians may be unable to believe there could be a third option. Yet, I believe there is, and it is the one I am defending in this book. It is a Christian philosophical anthropology that rejects every form of dualism, but also every form of *immanent* monism. In opposition to these views, this Christian philosophical anthropology accepts the notion of a duality—not a dualism!—not of two immanent function complexes, but of the transcendent Ego and the entire immanent human mode of existence (the so-called "function mantle"). At physical death, the latter immanent mode of existence, the "body," is put off entirely, but the transcendent Ego, the human personality, continues to exist after this physical death in a way that we cannot further analyze or understand. The Bible does not explain it, because the Bible is never preoccupied with philosophical puzzles. The Bible expresses what we have been saying here by means of very ordinary expressions like "putting off" one's "tent," or by saying that the same *person* who is buried is also the *person* who lifts up their eyes in the hereafter. In other words, the *entire* person dies, in the sense that the body that is destroyed at and through death *is* the person in the structural whole of their immanent appearance. *And* the *entire* person continues to exist after this death, in the sense that the Ego that keeps existing *is* that same person in her transcendent unity and fullness.[91]

Interestingly, Reformational philosopher K. J. Popma believed that the *entire* person dies but at the same time continues to exist in the hereafter *with both body and soul*, that is, including the "function mantle."[92] He was very careful not to say more than he could possibly account for, yet he believed there must be some form of "bodi-

---

91. Dooyeweerd (1984), 3:89.
92. Popma (1958), 2:195; cf. 1:73, 111–12.

ly" existence for humans after physical death. In this way, he could account for such bodily aspects as the eyes, the bosom, the finger, and the tongue of Dives, of Lazarus, and of Abraham in Luke 16:23–24. However, the problem with Popma's view is to determine how there can be a *dying* function mantle, and yet an active function mantle in the hereafter. We leave the matter here, because Popma himself recognized that we can only speculate on these things. G. Berkouwer rightly said, "There is no one who does not grope for words to express this mystery."[93]

---

93. Berkouwer (1962), 263.

9

ETERNAL LIFE[1]

[Y]ou [Father] have given him [i.e., the Son] authority
over all flesh,
to give eternal life to all whom you have given him.
And this is eternal life,
that they know you, the only true God,
and Jesus Christ whom you have sent.

John 17:2–3

Also hat Gott die Welt geliebt,
Daß er uns seinen Sohn gegeben.
Wer sich im Glauben ihm ergibt,
der soll dort ewig bei ihm leben.
Wer glaubt, daß Jesus ihm geboren,
Der bleibet ewig unverloren,
Und ist kein Leid, das den betrübt,
Den Gott und auch sein Jesus liebt.

> God so loved the world,
> that He gave us His Son.
> Whoever gives himself to Him in faith
> shall afterwards live with Him eternally.

---

1. For several publications on eternal life, which I have found to be profitable,
    I refer to http://biblecentre.org/content.php?mode=8&cat=6#eternallife.

Whoever believes that Jesus was born for him,
will never be lost,
and no sorrow will trouble him
who loves God and also His Jesus.

Also hat Gott die Welt geliebt
[*God So Loved the World*]
Bach cantata BWV 68
Salomo Liscow (1675)

9.1   Life in Christ
9.1.1   "Asleep in Jesus"

In 1912, Abraham Kuyper published a collection of meditations entitled *In Jesus ontslapen*.[2] It is a remarkable book. All the traditional errors that we are trying to refute in the present book are found throughout these meditations: the Greek scholastic body-soul dualism, the idea that John 14:2–3 (the "house of my Father"), Romans 7:24 ("Who will deliver me from this body of death?"), and Hebrews 12:23 (the "spirits of the righteous made perfect") describe the believer's death and the intermediate state, the idea that the "kingdom of heaven" is "heaven" in the intermediate state. Moreover, as so many other authors have done, Kuyper transferred many characteristics of the resurrection state and the Messianic kingdom to the intermediate state.

An element that we have not yet discussed is the promises to the "conquerors" (or those who "overcome") in Revelation 2 and 3, all of which Kuyper applied to the intermediate state: the tree of life, the hidden manna, the white stone, ruling over the nations, the white garments, and the "city of my God, the new Jerusalem." All of these are attained and received as soon as the believer enters the intermediate state. In reality, however, these promises characterize the resurrection state; as a key to this claim, compare the "conquerors" (or those who "overcome") in Revelation 15:2, "I saw what

2.   English translation: *Asleep in Jesus: Meditations* (1929).

246

appeared to be a sea of glass mingled with fire—and also those who had conquered the beast and its image and the number of its name, standing beside the sea of glass with harps of God in their hands."

An element that I had not yet found elsewhere is Kuyper's appeal to a remarkable expression in Zechariah 3:7, where the Lord God tells the high priest Joshua: "I will give you places to walk among these who stand here." Many translations (ERV, EXB) and expositors think here of angels. However, without adducing any arguments, Kuyper interpreted the latter group as referring to the departed saints in the intermediate state among whom Joshua would receive a place after his death.

This interpretation is just as invalid as the way some expositors have applied Psalm 23:6 to the intermediate state: "I shall dwell in the house of the LORD forever." In the Old Testament, the house of the LORD is the temple (thus many times from 1 Kings to Ezra); as the selfsame David wrote, "One thing have I asked of the LORD, that will I seek after: that I may dwell in the house of the LORD all the days of my life, to gaze upon the beauty of the LORD and to inquire in his temple."[3] It is shocking to see how easily such passages are transferred to the intermediate state without the slightest basis.[4]

Returning to Kuyper, we note his description of the believer's physical death as "the passageway to eternal life, which goes through the gate of death."[5] This view of eternal life, which we will examine in this chapter, ties in with the ancient (Roman Catholic and Protestant) tradition of applying the term "eternal life" to the intermediate state. During "The Great Shift," the eschatological focus moved increasingly away from the Parousia to physical death. In this process, eternal life came to mean the afterlife, when a person

---

3. Ps. 27:4; cf. 84:4; 87:1, 3, 10; 92:13; 116:19; 118:26; 122:9; 134:1; 135:2.
4. See several of the older expositors (https://www.biblehub.com/commentaries/psalms/23-6.htm).
5. Kuyper (1929), 83, 85.

moved through physical death to the eternal state, including both the intermediate state and the resurrection state. A clear example is the Heidelberg Catechism Q&A 42, "Our death is . . . only a dying to sin and an entering into eternal life (John 5:24; Phil. 1:23; Rom. 7:24–25)."[6] In obituaries, we read that a person has passed away "in the hope of eternal life" (cf. Titus 1:2; 3:7), which, given the context, apparently means that the person hoped to go to heaven at his or her death. It may come as a surprise to some that the Bible speaks of eternal life in quite different ways.

In his work entitled *The Imitation of Christ* (see §1.3.2), Thomas à Kempis wrote: "Are not all laborious things to be endured for the sake of eternal life? It is no small thing, the losing or gaining the Kingdom of God. Lift up therefore thy face to heaven."[7] Here, the author has linked both the kingdom of God (cf. §1.4.1) and eternal life to the intermediate state, as dozens of other Christian writers have done. At a later point à Kempis wrote: "Thou commandest that I draw near to Thee with firm confidence, if I would have part with Thee, and that I receive the food of immortality, if I desire to obtain eternal life and glory."[8] Here again, eternal life is identified with life in glory, specifically life in the intermediate state. Is this the way the Bible speaks of it?

Many, both Roman Catholics and Protestants, have thought that "entering eternal life" (cf. Matt. 18:8–9; 19:17) is the same as entering heaven when one dies.[9] Roman Catholic authors Van Doornik et al. put it in simple words: "Heaven means eternal life," which for them includes the intermediate state.[10] However, nowhere in the New Testament is such a link made. As we will see more clearly in

---

6. *RC*, 2:779.
7. 3.47.4 (http://www.gutenberg.org/cache/epub/1653/pg1653.txt).
8. *Ibid.*, 4.1.2.
9. See Ouweneel (Forthcoming-a), §11.8.1 in connection with the kingdom of heaven.
10. Van Doornik et al. (1956), 445); in the same section they also identify the intermediate state as the "kingdom of heaven" (see §1.4.1).

the course of the present chapter, the eschatological dimension of eternal life *is always linked to the Messianic kingdom, and with the subsequent eternal state.* We will return to this point later in the chapter; let us first consider what (spiritual) life means in general.

9.1.2   The New Life

In the Bible, the phrase "eternal life" has a specific meaning, one that is usually quite different from the meaning it has acquired in ordinary Christian language. In the New Testament, regeneration (God granting people a new nature, Titus 3:5) and being made (spiritually) alive (God granting people new life; Eph. 2:1, 5; Col. 2:13) are closely related.[11] The person who is reborn, that is, has been made alive, possesses (spiritual) *life* from God: he or she "has passed from death to life" (John 5:24). The person who has come to Jesus "has life" (cf. v. 40; cf. 6:33, 35, 51, 53). Not only this, but, Jesus in person *is* this life: "In him was life, and the life was the light of men" (1:4). "I am the resurrection and the life. Whoever believes in me, though he die, yet shall he live" (11:25). "I am the way, and the truth, and the life. No one comes to the Father except through me" (14:6). The person who receives him, receives life: "Because I live, you also will live" (v. 19); the believer "has life in his name" (20:31): "Whoever has the Son has life; whoever does not have the Son of God does not have life" (1 John 5:12).

The Apostle Paul knew this notion of Christ as the believer's life, too: ". . . always carrying in the body the death of Jesus, so that the life of Jesus may also be manifested in our bodies" (2 Cor. 4:10). Here the word "death" is the Greek word *nekrōsis*, which actually means "putting to death." Elsewhere, Paul says, "I have been crucified with Christ. It is no longer I who live, but Christ who lives in me. And the life I now live in the flesh I live by faith in the Son of God" (Gal. 2:20). And again: "For you have died, and your life is

---

11. See Ouweneel (2009b), chapters 2 and 3.

hidden with Christ in God. When Christ who is your life appears, then you also will appear with him in glory" (Col. 3:3–4); ". . . the promise of the life that is in Christ Jesus" (2 Tim. 1:1).

The fact that this life from God involves eternal life is obvious from a similar verse in Titus 1: ". . . in hope of eternal life, which God, who never lies, promised before the ages began" (v. 2). John, too, speaks of such a divine promise: "And this is the promise that he [i.e., God] made to us—eternal life" (1 John 2:25). In his eternal counsel, before death had entered the world (cf. Rom. 5:12), God had promised to grant eternal life to the righteous. We will investigate in the present chapter what this entails.

For a proper understanding of the rest of this chapter, it is important to see that the expression "Christ your [or, our] life" has a double meaning.[12] First, we know that the term "life" refers to the life principle in living organisms; it is what makes them alive. There are different life principles; for instance, there is vegetative life, animal life, and human life. Yet, they have this in common, that plants, animals, and humans are all living organisms; the life principle is manifested in each category, though in different ways. To say that something is alive is to say that it contains the life principle. Something that does not contain this life principle is either dead (that is, it *has* lived), or inanimate (that is, it has never lived). The regenerated person has come to "life," which is the same as saying that he or she has received a spiritual "life principle" that makes, and keeps, him or her "alive." Since the resurrection and glorification of Jesus and the pouring out of the Holy Spirit, this new, spiritual, supernatural life in the believer has a concrete name: Jesus Christ. Even the newly reborn person, the infant in the faith, can say: Christ lives in me, which is to say: Christ is the new life principle in me.

However, this is very different from the other meaning that the term "life" can have, such as in the expression, "[T]o me to live

---

12. Cf. *TDNT* 2:832–75, especially 865–72; *DNTT* 2:475–83.

is Christ" (Phil. 1:21): Christ is the content, the meaning, and the purpose of my life. This second meaning of "life" refers to life as a form of existence; people "lead" a certain life: they may prefer life in the village to life in the city (or vice versa), they may lead the life of a wretch, or the life of a prince. The Apostle Paul said, "Brothers, I have lived my life before God in all good conscience up to this day" (Acts 23:1). With this second meaning of the term, we can speak of the beginning or end of someone's life (Heb. 7:3; 11:22), and about "rising to a better life" (11:35), that is, attaining a better existence than one had here on earth.

Every infant in the faith can say, "Christ is my life," that is, he is the new life principle in me (which is the first meaning of "life"). This is simply stating an objective fact. However, the statement "To me to live is Christ" (which is the second meaning of "life") is something very different. It is the statement of Paul as a mature, experienced Christian, who had chosen to lead a life that was full of Christ. When he said, "To me to live is Christ," he had behind him a life in which he had proven the truth of this confession. At that very moment, he was in prison because of publicly serving Christ. This is comparable with what is said of the "fathers" in Christ, namely, that they "know" him, that is, were in close relationship with him (1 John 2:13–14). That was a sufficient description of them; Christ was the full content of their existence.

9.2 Life = Eternal Life?
9.2.1 Connection and Distinction

Is this "life" in its transcendent-religious meaning the same as eternal life (Gk. *zōē aiōnios*)?[13] This seems to be obvious because the life we are speaking of is life from God, and it is life that will last eternally. Indeed, in the writings of the Apostle John, the meanings of these two notions seem to overlap because John often mentions the two terms in the same context. For instance, Jesus says, "Whoever

---

13. Regarding this subject, see Ouweneel (1976).

believes in the Son has eternal life; whoever does not obey the Son shall not see life, but the wrath of God remains on him" (John 3:36; cf. 5:24, 39–40; 6:53–54).

In a similar way, John says in his first letter: "That which . . . we looked upon and have touched with our hands, concerning the word of life—the life was made manifest, and we have seen it, and testify to it and proclaim to you the eternal life, which was with the Father and was made manifest to us . . ." (1 John 1:1–2). "And this is the testimony, that God gave us eternal life, and this life is in his Son. Whoever has the Son has life; whoever does not have the Son of God does not have life. I write these things to you who believe in the name of the Son of God, that you may know that you have eternal life" (5:11–13).

Or consider this example from Paul's writings. In one chapter (Rom. 6) he speaks of "newness of life" (v. 4), the "life" that the believer lives to God (v. 11), the fact that believers have been "brought from death to life" (v. 13), *and* that the "free gift of God is eternal life in Christ Jesus our Lord" (v. 23). It is not easy to claim that "eternal life" in the latter verse is something different from "life" in the earlier verses. We might only presume, on the basis of verse 22 (". . . its end, eternal life"), that in Paul's view there is an eschatological dimension to "eternal life," as we will see later (§9.3.1[14]). All these passages suggest that "life" in the spiritual sense in which John and Paul write about it, can hardly be very different from what the same Apostles call "eternal life," just as "God" is not different from "the eternal God" (Gen. 21:33; Deut. 33:27; Isa. 40:28; Rom. 16:26).

Nevertheless, John seems to suggest a highly interesting distinction. The regeneration mentioned in John 3 involves primarily a new nature, but this also obviously implies new life. In order to be able to enter the kingdom of God, a person needs new life from God. However, in verse 12 we find a remarkable transition to a passage that involves eternal life: "If I have told you earthly things and you do not believe, how can you believe if I tell you heavenly things?" Leon Morris sees two possible explanations for this mysterious verse: either the discussion with Nico-

14. Cf. Gal. 6:8; 1 Tim. 1:16; 6:12; Titus 1:2; 3:7; also see Jude 21.

demus involves the "earthly things," while the "heavenly things" refer to Jesus' higher teaching, which is not given here, *or* the discussion with Nicodemus involves the "heavenly things," while the "earthly things" refer to Jesus' earlier teaching.[15] In both cases, Jesus supposedly refers to teaching that in John's Gospel is not given to us in any explicit form at all. Merrill Tenney explains the "earthly things" as teaching that is given in a metaphorical form, while the "heavenly things" involve teaching that is given in an abstract form.[16] Indeed, the metaphor of wind refers to something earthly, but this does not imply that the teaching concerned is "earthly."

The view of Marcus Dods seems the most acceptable: the "earthly things" are such things as the ones of which Jesus had spoken: things that are verified in human, earthly experience, the need of a spiritual birth and the results thereof.[17] Rebirth was a change that is undergone in this earthly life. The kingdom of regenerated people would be established here on earth, during the Messianic kingdom (which is not "heaven"; see §1.4.1). In contrast with this, the heavenly things are matters that are not open for human observation, matters that belong to the invisible world, to the nature and the counsels of God.

This seems to me a proper approach. However, Dods does not indicate what those heavenly things might be. Therefore, we must go one step further: the "heavenly things" are those that belong to the place from which Jesus himself had descended: Jesus, the Son of God who had become Son of Man. This is hinted at in the verse that follows: "No one has ascended into heaven except he who descended from heaven, the Son of Man" (v. 13); I appreciate the added phrase found in certain manuscripts: "No one has ascended to heaven but He who came down from heaven, [that is,] the Son of Man *who is in heaven*" (NKJV). This has little to do with the counsels and the ways of God, as has been suggested by Dods; we should

15. Morris (1971), 222.
16. Tenney (1981), 48.
17. Dods (1979), 715; cf. Godet (1879), *ad loc.*; Bouma (1927), 53.

not introduce here all kinds of Pauline elements. Rather, we must search in the remainder of John 3.

9.2.2 Eternal Life Is Heavenly

In the context of John 3, the "heavenly things" are the things that belong to heaven, *and in the person of Christ have descended on earth*, as we have just seen in 1 John 1:3, ". . . the eternal life, which was with the Father and was made manifest to us," namely, in the person of the Son. This "eternal life" is exactly what is discussed by Jesus in the following verses in John 3: "And as Moses lifted up the serpent in the wilderness, so must the Son of Man be lifted up, that whoever believes in him may have *eternal life*. For God so loved the world, that he gave his only Son, that whoever believes in him should not perish but have *eternal life*" (vv. 14–16; italics added).

I venture the thesis that regeneration, including the reception of new life, belongs to the "earthly things" (as Dods also claims). This is especially the case because rebirth is viewed here as the entrance into the kingdom of God, which, as we have seen, is emphatically a kingdom on earth.[18] In contrast with this, eternal life belongs to the "heavenly things," as the life of heaven, which in the person of Christ has descended to earth. As S. Prod'hom wrote, "'Heavenly things' were not part of the revelation of the Old Testament; they belong to the domain of eternal life."[19] This is very true; *God* dwells in heaven, but the Old Testament blessings of humanity all belong to this earth, being linked in particular with the Messianic kingdom. The contrast between heaven and earth is well maintained: "The heavens are the LORD's heavens, but the earth he has given to the children of man" (Ps. 115:16).

In order to reveal to humans the "heavenly things," and give them a share in them, Someone had to descend from heaven and bring them to the earth, so to speak. As C. Bouma put it, "Nobody can reveal these heavenly things other than he [i.e., Christ], 1:18.

---

18. See Ouweneel (Forthcoming-a), §2.3.1.
19. Prod'hom (1924), 42–43.

This is because, to this end, one must have been in heaven, which is true of no one on earth other than of him *who descended from heaven.*"[20] In other words, from verse 12 onward, "Jesus proceeds to tell Nicodemus of the *heavenly things.*"[21] Christ descended from heaven (John 3:13), and had to be lifted up on the cross (v.14), in order that repentant sinners would be able to receive eternal life. The new life of regeneration is earthly insofar as it gives access to the earthly kingdom of God. Eternal life is heavenly because it is the life of heaven—*not of the intermediate state*—but heaven in the sense of the "Father's house" (cf. 14:1–3), the life that in the person of the Son descended to this earth. The "kingdom of heaven" is a kingdom *on earth* (§1.4.1), which belongs to this earth, but which is ruled from heaven. Eternal life belongs to heaven, to the Father's house, but has descended to earth. As we have seen in §6.4, the house of the Father is entered by believers *not* at their physical death, but at the Parousia: Jesus will come in person, in order to take his people to the sphere to which eternal life belonged, from where it had descended in Jesus Christ, and where it will be enjoyed by believers in their resurrection state.

9.3 Paul on Eternal Life

9.3.1 Life and Eternal Life

In the writings of the Apostle Paul, the distinction between the life of regeneration and eternal life is more obvious. Paul speaks of "life" as a present possession,[22] and sometimes also as an eschatological reality.[23] See, for instance, this statement: ". . . our Savior Christ Jesus, who abolished death and brought life and immortality to light through the gospel" (2 Tim. 1:10). Here "life" might be viewed as the believer's present possession, but alongside "immor-

---

20. Bouma (1927), 53.
21. A. J. Macleod in Davidson (1954), 871.
22. In addition to the examples already given, see Rom. 5:18; 6:4; 8:6, 10; Gal. 2:19; 5:25.
23. Rom. 5:17; 6:8; 2 Cor. 13:4; 2 Tim. 2:11.

tality" it definitely seems to refer to the resurrection.[24]

However, when Paul speaks of eternal life, he always seems to do so in an eschatological context: "He will render to each one according to his works: to those who by patience in well-doing seek for glory and honor and immortality, he will give eternal life" (Rom. 2:6–7). "But now that you have been set free from sin and have become slaves of God, the fruit you get leads to sanctification and its end, eternal life" (6:22). "For the one who sows to his own flesh will from the flesh reap corruption, but the one who sows to the Spirit will from the Spirit reap eternal life" (Gal. 6:8). Paul speaks of "grace" that reigns "through righteousness leading to eternal life through Jesus Christ our Lord" (Rom. 5:21). He also speaks of "those who were to believe in him [i.e., Christ] for eternal life" (1 Tim. 1:16), and of the "hope of eternal life" (Titus 1:2; 3:7).

This eschatological dimension in his speaking of eternal life is not at all linked to the ancient Roman Catholic and Protestant thinking that "entering eternal life" (cf. Matt. 18:8–9; 19:17) is the same as entering heaven when one dies (see §9.1.1). Nowhere in the New Testament is such a link made; the connection is the undiluted fancy of authors saturated with Interim Theology. Rather, the eschatological dimension of "eternal life" is always linked to the Parousia, with the resurrection state, and in certain cases clearly with the Messianic kingdom.

It is exactly the same in the Gospels; when they refer to "inheriting eternal life,"[25] this always refers to the Messianic kingdom (see more extensively in §9.4.1). The same is true when Paul uses the expression: "Or do you not know that the unrighteous will not inherit the kingdom of God? Do not be deceived: neither the sexually immoral, nor idolaters, nor adulterers, nor men who practice homosexuality, nor thieves, nor the greedy, nor drunkards, nor revilers, nor swindlers will inherit the kingdom of God" (1 Cor.

---

24. Towner (2006), 472.
25. Matt. 19:29; Mark 10:17; Luke 10:25; 18:18.

6:9–10; cf. Gal. 5:21; Eph. 5:5). "I tell you this, brothers: flesh and blood cannot inherit the kingdom of God" (1 Cor. 15:50). These passages definitely do not refer to "going to heaven"—no matter what the classical expositors committed to Interim Theology have claimed[26]—but to the "world" and "age to come," the Messianic kingdom on earth.

9.3.2 Practical Realization Now

For the Apostle Paul, eternal life is not just a future blessing, which today is beyond our grasp. On the contrary, he calls upon Timothy to spiritually appropriate this eschatological promise already now: "Fight the good fight of the faith. *Take hold of the eternal life* to which you were called and about which you made the good confession in the presence of many witnesses" (1 Tim. 6:12; italics added). Compare what Paul says later in verse 19: ". . . thus storing up treasure for themselves as a good foundation for the future, so that they may *take hold* of that which is truly life." This is striving to live in the light and the power of the "age to come" already today (Mark 10:30).

It is like a person who knows that one day he will inherit a certain estate, although at present he possesses none of it yet (see Gal. 4:1 for this type of metaphor). He may walk around the estate, he may rejoice in the thought that one day he will be the owner, although today he is not yet the owner. He may even walk around to become acquainted with his future property, and this is a good and wise thing: he is preparing himself for his future task. On the day he receives his inheritance, no part of it will be strange to him; on the contrary, he will know every corner of it. Nor will his task be new to him because he will have imagined himself undertaking this task many times. In my view, this is what believers do when "taking hold" of (future) eternal life.

---

26. See, e.g., John Gill on Gal. 5:21, ". . . shall not inherit the kingdom of God; by which is meant the heavenly glory, called a 'kingdom', because of the grandeur and magnificence of that state" (http://biblehub.com/galatians/5-21.htm).

I must mention immediately that "inheriting eternal life" has also been linked to the intermediate state, that is, inheriting is "going to heaven when you die," especially through a mistaken reading of 1 Peter 1:4, which speaks of "an inheritance that is . . . kept in heaven for you" (see more extensively §12.2.2 below). In such a view, the notion of "inheriting eternal life" also strengthens the mistaken notion that "eternal life" refers to the intermediate state. However, compiling mistaken conclusions seldom leads to correct theories.

Later in this chapter, we will see that Paul was certainly aware of the significance of eternal life as a present possession. However, he never uses the terminology that is so common in John's writings: the believer "has" (i.e., possesses) eternal life.[27] We will return to this. But for now, we can outline the differences between the Apostles John and Paul with regard to eternal life as follows. These differences are not absolute; they simply identify different focuses in John's and Paul's ministries, respectively.

(a) John speaks about eternal life mainly as a present possession (one exception is John 4:36, "gathering fruit for eternal life"; another is 12:25, "whoever hates his life in this world will keep it for eternal life"), whereas for Paul, eternal life is a blessing belonging to the future (although this is not always equally clear, as in Rom. 6:23). It seems to me that 1 Timothy 6:12 is not a real exception because Paul speaks of taking hold of something that in itself is still eschatological. *Neither for John nor for Paul does an eschatological blessing (i.e., one belonging to the future)ever refer to the intermediate state.* Linking eternal life with "going to heaven when you die" is purely biased imagination.

(b) John links eternal life especially with "heaven" in the sense of the Father's house (1 John 1:1–3; cf. John 14:1–3), which—I cannot repeat this often enough—is never linked to the intermediate state (see §6.4). Paul links eternal life especially with the heaven-

27. John 3:15–16, 36; 5:24, 39; 6:40, 47, 54; 1 John 3:15.

ly kingdom of Christ that will be established on earth. The latter is in line with the use of the expression "eternal life" in the synoptic Gospels to describe inheriting the kingdom. Yet, this distinction is not very absolute either: there may be a clear relationship between the Father's house and the Messianic kingdom in the sense that they both involve the enjoyment of the same divine life. At least—and this is the pivotal point—*all these refer to post-resurrection realities.*

One important difference is that some people will enjoy eternal life *on earth*, in their present bodies, in which they will be alive at the moment of the Parousia; this is presumably what those speaking of "inheriting eternal life"[28] or "inheriting the kingdom" (Matt. 25:34; cf. 5:5) in the Gospels were thinking of (see more extensively, §9.4). Others will enjoy eternal life during the Messianic kingdom *from the heavenly side*, that is, in their glorified resurrection bodies; these are the ones who look forward to the "heavenly city" and the "heavenly country," namely, in the "world to come," during the "age to come."[29] Remember: Hebrews *never* speaks of the intermediate state; its future references are all linked to the Messianic kingdom.

(c) John is occupied especially with how the life of heaven (i.e., the house of the Father, 14:2–3) can be brought down to the earth, and can dwell in believers. Paul is occupied especially with how earthly people can become heavenly citizens (Phil. 3:20), that is, how they can receive a share in the future heavenly kingdom, that is, "inherit eternal life." John's basic question is: How can eternal life be brought into people? Paul's basic question is: How can people be brought into eternal life? In other words: John wonders how heaven can be brought into people, Paul wonders how people can be brought into heaven (which always means in the resurrection state, never in the intermediate state).

Here again, the distinction is not absolute: the central question for both Apostles, as I see it, is how a connection can be forged

---

28. Matt. 19:29; Mark 10:17; Luke 10:25; 18:18.
29. Heb. 11:10, 16; 12:22–24; 13:14; cf. 2:5; 3:1; 6:4–5; 8:5; 9:23; 10:1.

between the life of heaven (the Father's house, the heavenly side of the future Messianic kingdom) and beings who, by nature, are so very earthly. The answer is that only in Christ can heaven and earth be connected; that is, only in him, very earthly humans not only receive forgiveness and salvation but become heavenly beings, in resurrection bodies made fit for heaven and for eternity.

9.4   Eternal Life in Its Future Sense in the New Testament
9.4.1   The Synoptic Gospels

The life of the future (Messianic) age is the life of the [Messianic] age, which is identical with eternal life in the Old Testament sense (Ps. 133:3, "life forevermore"; Dan. 12:2, "wake to everlasting life"). As Jesus explains, "Truly, I say to you, there is no one who has left house or wife or brothers or parents or children, for the sake of the kingdom of God, who will not receive many times more in this time [i.e., the present age[30]], and in the age [Gk. *aiōn*] to come eternal [*aiōnios*] life" (Luke 18:29–30). This linguistic connection between "age" and "eternal" is not obvious in English (nor in Latin: *saeculus* and *aeternus*), but it is obvious in Greek: *aiōn* and *aiōnios* (and in Dutch: *eeuw*[31] and *eeuwig*). In the Hebrew or Aramaic that Jesus spoke, the connection must have been equally clear. "Eternal life" (Heb. *chayyē ʿolam*, Dan. 12:2[32]) is the life that belongs to, is characteristic of, the "age to come" (Heb. *ʿolam habba*), the Messianic age. Jesus was speaking here of eternal life in entire agreement with the Old Testament passages and with Jewish custom.[33]

Not only he, of course, but also his Jewish contemporaries understood "eternal life" in this eschatological-Messianic way. First, there was the Torah expert. "And behold, a lawyer stood up to put him to the test, saying, 'Teacher, what shall I do to inherit eternal

---

30. Cf. Gal. 1:4; 1 Tim. 6:17; Titus 2:12; Heb. 9:9
31. Interestingly, English *age* and Dutch *eeuw* ("age, century") come from the same root as the Greek word *aiōn*.
32. In Ps. 133:3 the Heb. is *chayyim ʿad-haʿolam*, which basically means the same thing.
33. Cf. Morris (1971), 227.

life?"' (Luke 10:25). This is essentially the same as asking: What do I have to do to receive my share in the "age to come," that is, what do I have to do to receive my inheritance in the coming Messianic kingdom? It is *not* like asking: What do I have to do in order to get to heaven when I die?[34] As far as we can assess, no Jews were occupied with that question (they lived before "The Great Shift"); their eyes were focused on the coming of Messiah and his kingdom. Very telling are these two expressions in Luke 2: Simeon, Anna, and all the godly in Israel were "waiting for the consolation of Israel" (v. 25) and the "redemption of Jerusalem" (v. 38), in short, they were waiting for the Messianic age, whose earthly center would be Jerusalem (e.g., Isa. 2:2–4; Zech. 14:8–20).[35]

It was the same with the rich young ruler, another Jewish man, who asked Jesus, "Good Teacher, what must I do to inherit eternal life?" (18:18). He could just as well have asked, "What must I do to inherit the kingdom?" (Matt. 25:34; cf. 5:5). Entirely in line with this, the criminal on the cross asked Jesus, "[R]emember me when you come into your kingdom" (23:42), that is, when your kingdom arrives, at the beginning of the Messianic age (the "age to come"), do not forget me; let me have a share in it (see §5.2.1). Also when Jesus speaks to Nicodemus about entering the kingdom of God (John 3:5), he essentially means the same as what the lawyer, the ruler, and the criminal asked him about, and what any Jew could have asked him about: What is needed to reach the age (or, world) to come—the Messianic age, the world of the Messiah—and have a share in it?

For every pious Jew, this was the most important question of

34. Cf. Bengel's *Gnomon*: receiving eternal life is receiving the "kingdom of heaven" (Ger. *Himmelreich* = heaven) (https://biblehub.com/commentaries/mark/10-17.htm).
35. Interpreters committed to amillennialism, supersessionism, and Interim Theology spiritualize such passages. In my view, in the Bible the term "Israel" *always* means "Israel," and never "the church," despite passages like Rom. 2:28–29, 9:6, and Gal. 6:16. Regarding these and many other passages, see Ouweneel (2019), especially chapters 3 and 6.

life: How do I receive an inheritance in the Messianic kingdom? What must I *do* for that? We should not dismiss this "doing" all too quickly—as if it necessarily arises from a legalistic attitude—because this emphasis clearly reverberates in the New Testament letters:

> Now the works of the flesh are evident: sexual immorality, impurity, sensuality, idolatry, sorcery, enmity, strife, jealousy, fits of anger, rivalries, dissensions, divisions, envy, drunkenness, orgies, and things like these. I warn you, as I warned you before, that those who do [or, make a practice of doing] such things will not inherit the kingdom of God (Gal. 5:19–21; cf. 1 Cor. 6:9–10; Eph. 5:5).

In the same vein, Jesus simply told both the lawyer and the ruler to follow God's commandments. This is what he told his disciples as well: How do you acquire subjects for his kingdom? Make them my disciples by baptizing them and by "teaching them to observe all that I have commanded you" (Matt. 28:18–20). Teach them the "law" of the kingdom (James 2:8), which is a "law of liberty" (1:25; 2:12), that is, the law that is fitting for the kingdom of freedom that God will institute. In this respect, there is no difference between the Old Testament and the New Testament: *keeping the Torah is the condition for entering the kingdom.*[36] From the New Testament, we learn more clearly that this is possible *only* through regeneration, faith, and the power of the Holy Spirit, but this does not change the principle: "If you love me, you will keep my commandments. . . . Whoever has my commandments and keeps them, he it is who loves me" (John 14:15, 21a). "Owe no one anything, except to love each other, for the one who loves another has fulfilled the law" (Rom. 13:8). "Bear one another's burdens, and so fulfill the law of Christ" (Gal. 6:2). "I am stirring up your sincere mind . . . that you should remember the predictions of the holy prophets and the commandment of the Lord and Savior through your apostles" (2

---

36. Ps. 15:1–5; 24:3–8; Isa. 33:14–17.

Pet. 3:1–2). And so on.

Jesus told Nicodemus that regeneration is the condition for entering the kingdom of God (John 3:3, 5), but this cannot be separated from the human responsibility and response of obedience. In Matthew 25, Jesus gave a rather different answer, which does not conflict with the previous one: the wicked "will go away into eternal punishment, but the righteous into eternal life" (v. 46). The born again and the righteous are identical groups. The truly righteous (Heb. *tsaddiq*) is one who *lives* righteously due to the new, divine life that is in him or her. See a little earlier in the chapter:

> Then the righteous will answer him, saying, "Lord, when did we see you hungry and feed you, or thirsty and give you drink? And when did we see you a stranger and welcome you, or naked and clothe you? And when did we see you sick or in prison and visit you?" And the King will answer them, "Truly, I say to you, as you did it to one of the least of these my brothers, you did it to me (Matt. 25:37–40).

These are the ones to whom the King says, "Come, you who are blessed by my Father, inherit the kingdom prepared for you from the foundation of the world" (v. 34).

To the Messianic kingdom, that is, the "age to come," belongs the life of that age, that is, a blessed existence and functioning under the blessed rule of the Messiah, in peace and righteousness. As the prophet says,

> For out of Zion shall go forth the law [Heb. *Torah*, divine instruction], and the word of the LORD from Jerusalem. He shall judge between many peoples, and shall decide disputes for strong nations far away; and they shall beat their swords into plowshares and their spears into pruning hooks; nation shall not lift up sword against nation, neither shall they learn war anymore; but they shall sit every man under his vine and under his fig tree (Micah 4:2–4; see also Isa. 33:14–17).

The Messianic kingdom is for "everyone who has been recorded for life in Jerusalem" (Isa. 4:3), and for "all who were waiting for the redemption of Jerusalem" (Luke 2:38). It is for the "poor in spirit" (Matt. 5:3; cf. Isa. 57:15; 66:2), and for "those who are persecuted for righteousness' sake" (Matt. 5:10).

9.4.2 The Gospel of John

In John's Gospel, eternal life is usually viewed as a present possession of believers, but sometimes we find the phrase used with an eschatological meaning:

> Do you not say, "There are yet four months, then comes the harvest"? Look, I tell you, lift up your eyes, and see that the fields are white for harvest. Already the one who reaps is receiving wages and gathering fruit for eternal life, so that sower and reaper may rejoice together (John 4:35–36; cf. the same metaphor in Gal. 6:8, "reaping" eternal life, like bringing in a harvest).

Later in John, we read: "Whoever loves his life loses it, and whoever hates his life in this world will keep it for eternal life" (12:25; CJB: "will keep it safe right on into eternal life"). In the latter verse, the expression "this world [Gk. *kosmos*, not *aiōn*]" seems to suggest another world, a "world to come," although this expression does not occur in John's writings. It is the cleansed world that John the Baptist referred to (1:29). What comes closest is the coming "kingdom" in John's other large book: Revelation (cf. 11:15; 12:10).

In John's writings (apart from the book of Revelation), the eschatological meaning of eternal life is the exception more than the rule.[37] If John emphasizes eternal life as a present possession,[38] this implies that, for those who belong to Jesus, the *present* "age" is already fully Messianic, so to speak. John 3:3–5 implies entering the Messianic kingdom already today, namely, through regeneration. Therefore, John can say, "Children, it *is* the last hour" (1 John

---

37. Cf. "life" and "living" in 2:7, 10; 7:17; 20:4; 21:6; 22:1–2, 14, 17, 19, even though the phrase "eternal life" is never used.

38. John 3:15–16, 36; 5:24, 39; 6:40, 47, 54; 1 John 3:15.

2:18), that is, the Messianic age is already becoming full reality. This is comparable with Hebrews 6:5, where the "powers of the age to come" are to some extent a spiritual reality already today. "For the kingdom of God does not consist in talk but in power"—already now (1 Cor. 4:20). The kingdom of God is "a matter of . . . righteousness and peace and joy in the Holy Spirit"—already now (Rom. 14:17).

The eschatological meaning of eternal life underscores that redemptive terms have, in addition to an individual significance, also a collective and cosmic significance, which is at least as important as the individual one. One day, the entire (renewed) cosmos will share in eternal life, so to speak. Eternal life is not just the personal possession of redeemed individuals. Rather, it is the life that will characterize and dominate the entire kingdom of God:

> Come, let us return to the LORD; for he has torn us, that he may heal us; he has struck us down, and he will bind us up. After two days he will *revive* us; on the third day he will raise us up, that we may *live before him*. Let us know; let us press on to know the LORD; his going out is sure as the dawn; he will come to us as the showers, as the spring rains that water the earth" (Hos. 6:1–3; italics added).

Such words remind us of John's Gospel: "[W]hoever drinks of the water that I will give him will never be thirsty again. The water that I will give him will become in him a spring of water welling up to eternal life" (4:14). "Whoever believes in me, as the Scripture has said, 'Out of his heart will flow rivers of living water'" (7:38). And as the prophet Isaiah says:

> With joy you will draw water from the wells of salvation. And you will say in that day: "Give thanks to the LORD, call upon his name, make known his deeds among the peoples, proclaim that his name is exalted. Sing praises to the LORD, for he has done gloriously; let this be made known in all the earth. Shout, and sing for joy, O inhabitant of Zion, for great in your midst is the Holy One of Israel" (Isa. 12:3–6).

9.5 Realized Eschatology
9.5.1 "Giving and Having"

In his writings, John describes eternal life as a present spiritual possession with the Greek verbs *didōmi*, "to give," and *echō*, "to have."
We find "to give" in John 10:28 ("I give them eternal life, and they
will never perish, and no one will snatch them out of my hand")
and in 1 John 5:11 ("And this is the testimony, that God gave us
eternal life, and this life is in his Son"). "To have" is found in at
least the following passages: ". . . that whoever believes in him may
have eternal life. For God so loved the world, that he gave his only
Son, that whoever believes in him should not perish but *have* eternal
life."[39] The believer "has eternal life abiding in him" (3:15); he has it
"in himself" (cf. John 6:53).

This having means not just that a person is entitled to eternal
life, or that he or she has an admission ticket to eternal life. This is
in contrast with the Heidelberg Catechism Q&A 58, which explains
eternal life as follows:

> 58. What comfort do you receive from the article "life
>   everlasting"?
>
> That, inasmuch as I now feel in my heart the beginning of
> eternal joy (2 Cor. 5:2–3), I shall after this life possess com-
> plete blessedness, such as eye has not seen, nor ear heard,
> neither has entered into the heart of man (1 Cor. 2:9), there-
> in to praise God forever (John 17:3).[40]

This is a double mistake: first, according to John, eternal life involves something that the believer possesses already in the present.
Second, eternal life is never linked to what comes "after this life,"
that is, in the intermediate state.

In John's writings, believers do not have merely an admission
ticket to eternal life, they *have* eternal life. As surely as believers

---

39. John 3:15–16; also see v. 36; 5:24; 6:40, 47, 54; 1 John 5:13; 3:15.
40. *RC*, 2:782; see Ouweneel (2016), *ad loc.*

already share in Christ, as surely as they possess the Holy Spirit, just as surely they already possess eternal life. 1 John 3:15 in particular is very clear about this, although the statement stands in a negative context: "Everyone who hates his brother is a murderer, and you know that no murderer has eternal life abiding in him." Conversely, this means that true believers actually do have eternal life *abiding* (Gk. *menō*) in them. This "abiding" is just as real and genuine as in the following verses in the same letter: "[W]hoever says he abides in him. . . ."[41] If eternal life is "abiding" in a person, no person, no power, can take it away from him or her (cf. John 10:27–28).

The believer possesses eternal life only and exclusively in Christ. As far as people's physical life is concerned, they are independent; they are not dependent on other beings for it (except on God's providential power; cf. Heb. 1:3). But with a branch in a vine it is different. Such a branch has no life apart from the vine; if it is separated from the vine, it will wither, and consequently remain fruitless (John 15:1–7). Similarly, believers do not possess eternal life apart from Christ. Jesus told the spiritual leaders of Israel: "You search the Scriptures because you think that in them you *have eternal life*; and it is they that bear witness about me, yet you refuse to come to me that you may have life" (5:39–40; italics added). They did not understand that merely searching the Scriptures, no matter how noble this is in itself, brings a person no eternal life. The searcher needs a vital[42] relationship with Christ.

Jesus Christ *is* (in person) eternal life. He said, "I am . . . the life" (John 11:25; 14:6). John says that eternal life is in God's Son; whoever has the Son, has life (1 John 5:11–12). "[W]e are in him who is true, in his Son Jesus Christ. He is the true God and eternal life" (v. 20). Paul says that the "life of Jesus . . . [is] manifested in our mortal flesh" (2 Cor. 4:10–11); Christ is "your life" (Col. 3:4).

---

41. 1 John 2:6; also see vv. 10, 14, 27; 3:9, 24; 4:12; cf. vv. 15–16.
42. "Vital" is an appropriate term here because it comes from Lat. *vita*, "life."

Not a single spiritual, eternal blessing, nor a single material, earthly blessing, such as the blessing of the future Messianic age, can be received and enjoyed apart from Christ and his work, for He is God's "Yes" and "Amen" to all his promises (2 Cor. 1:20).[43]

For the Apostle John, through the coming of Christ eternal life is *realized* eschatology:[44]

> That which was from the beginning, which we have heard, which we have seen with our eyes, which we looked upon and have touched with our hands, concerning the word of life—the life was made manifest, and we have seen it, and testify to it and proclaim to you the eternal life, which was with the Father and was made manifest to us . . . (1 John 1:1–2).

By revealing the name of the Father here on earth, Jesus can say: "[T]his is eternal life, that they know you, the only true God, and Jesus Christ whom you have sent" (John 17:3); that is, to know God *as the Son knew him*, namely, as the eternal Father of the eternal Son, and to know Jesus *as God knew him*, namely, as the eternal Son of the eternal Father.

9.5.2 Future versus Present

Whereas in Paul's writings, which connect with the Old Testament and the synoptic Gospels,[45] the eschatological (future Messianic) dimension of eternal life is prominent, for John, eternal life is mainly a present spiritual reality. It is a *heavenly* matter (see again John 3:12), brought down in Jesus (1 John 1:1–4), and granted to the believers now. It is the life of the Father's house (cf. John 14:2–3), which believers will enjoy in the resurrection state, but it has been granted to them already now through regeneration and the gift of the Holy

---

43. I. Coulibaly in Adeyemo (2006), 1401.
44. This term must not be confused with the idea that the kingdom of God is already being realized here and now, thereby displacing all end time views; see Ouweneel (Forthcoming-a), §11.5.
45. Also see Jude 21, "[K]eep yourselves in the love of God, waiting for the mercy of our Lord Jesus Christ that leads to eternal life."

Spirit. In summary, at Jesus' first coming, the life of the Father's house descended in his person, and through faith became, and still becomes, the possession of every believer; at Jesus' second coming, believers are taken up into the Father's house, where this eternal life came from, and where it is at home.

In the Reformed creeds, eternal life is exclusively a future matter; in this respect, they are very Pauline, so to speak, but hardly Johannine. Earlier I referred to the Heidelberg Catechism (see §9.5.1); let me also quote the Belgic Confession here. God intended "that through [Christ] we might obtain immortality and life eternal" (Art. 20);[46] ". . . every man who is earnestly studious of obtaining life eternal . . ." (Art. 34).[47] These are future references, too. See also the Canons of Dordt (I.9): "Therefore election is the fountain of every saving good, from which proceed faith, holiness, and the other gifts of salvation, and finally[!] eternal life itself, as its fruits and effects, ..."[48] No doubt, *the authors of these documents are thinking (primarily) of the intermediate state.* Little room exists for a biblical understanding of eternal life, which has the following three aspects (the intermediate state *not* being one of them). It exists:

(a) as a present possession, in the Johannine sense;

(b) as the life of the future Messianic kingdom (see the Gospels and Paul); or

(c) as the life of the Father's house (see John again).

As soon as the features of the Messianic kingdom, as well as those of the Father's house, are applied to the intermediate state, confusion abounds, from which we never will get a clear picture of eternal life.

According to the Apostle Paul, believers will one day enter eternal life; according to John, eternal life has already entered believers, even if its fullness lies in the future, that is, not in the intermediate

---

46. *RC,* 2:435.
47. *Ibid.,* 2:445.
48. *Ibid.,* 4:123.

state but in the resurrection state, when believers will have entered the house of the Father.

Apparently, Paul linked eternal life especially with a heavenly *place* and *position*, which is essentially the resurrection state; John linked it especially with divine *relationships* and *fellowship*, which have become a reality already now, and will find their complete fulfillment in that same resurrection state.

9.5.3   John and Paul

In summary, the Apostle Paul is particularly (although not exclusively) focused upon the glorified Man Christ Jesus at the right hand of God.[49] Perhaps this was especially because Paul, while he was still Saul of Tarsus, had encountered him in this glory.[50] Thus, Paul associates eternal life with heaven because Christ is there; the believer's true spiritual life is "hidden with Christ in God" (Col. 3:3), where Christ is: at the right hand of God. Please notice again, this is never "heaven" as the intermediate state, but "heaven" in the resurrection state—but as a spiritual reality heaven's eternal life may dwell in the believer's heart already now, as in the expression "Take hold of eternal life" (1 Tim. 6:12, 19).

The Apostle John, however, is focused on eternal life as it was first with the Father, and then as it descended to people on earth in the person of the Son, in order that believers would enjoy fellowship with the Father and the Son (1 John 1:1–5). Perhaps this was especially because John, who referred to himself as the "disciple whom Jesus loved,"[51] had enjoyed fellowship with Jesus when he was "in the bosom of Jesus" (13:23 ESV note), just as the Son had been in the bosom of the Father (1:18 ESV note).

The Apostles were not impersonal messengers; on the contrary, they were personally involved in what they preached. Paul focused

---

49. Rom. 8:34; Eph. 1:20; Col. 3:1; cf. Heb. 1:3, 13; 8:1; 10:12; 12:2.
50. See, in addition to the account of his conversion in Acts 9:1-19, Acts 22:14–15 and 18, also 1 Cor. 9:1.
51. John 13:23; 19:26; 20:2; 21:7, 20.

upon Jesus *as he had seen him*. John focused upon Jesus *as he had experienced him*. Each one proclaimed the message as a true witness, that is, according to what he had heard, seen, looked upon, and touched (cf. 1 John 1:1).

Paul explained how people can one day receive a place in heavenly bliss, that is, receive eternal life (in the resurrection state, not the intermediate state). John explained how eternal life, that is, the life of heaven, can receive a place in people. Paul's ministry takes people on earth into eternal life in heaven (as something to be realized after the Parousia and the resurrection). John's ministry takes eternal life in heaven into people on earth as a present possession (as something to be *fully* realized only after the Parousia and the resurrection). Both aspects of the gospel are equally important; they complete one another in an extraordinary way—a way that, unfortunately, is little understood.

Since the Garden of Eden, the new life that God grants through regeneration is always essentially the same *divine* life. However, there is an enormous difference in the way in which, and the extent to which, this life can be manifested, as explained by both John and Paul. Chemically, charcoal and diamond are essentially the same substance, namely, carbon. But in character and value they are totally different. Through regeneration, Abraham, Moses, David and so many others, possessed life from God. But the great difference is that this life has now been *revealed* in its true fullness (1 John 1:1–3) because the eternal *Father* has been revealed in and through his Son, Jesus Christ. This is abundant life (John 10:10), life in its richest and most glorious form, the life of the Father's house itself, the life that is inherent to the eternal fellowship of the Father, the Son, and the Holy Spirit. Both John and Paul give this life a name, as we have seen: basically, it is Christ himself.

After his discussion with Nicodemus, Jesus entered more deeply into this matter in his conversation with the Samaritan woman: "[W]hoever drinks of the water that I will give him will never be

271

thirsty again. The water that I will give him will become in him a spring of water welling up to eternal life" (John 4:14). This water is the Holy Spirit, as is evident from John 7:38–39. No believer had possessed this Spirit dwelling permanently in him or her until Jesus rose.[52] By the power of the Spirit, the life that through regeneration dwells in the believer comes to full blossom in the knowledge and enjoyment of eternal life: the life in the "heavenly places," as Paul would put it (Eph. 1:3), in and with the risen and glorified Christ, in the fellowship of the Triune God: "that they may be one even as we are one, I in them and you in me" (17:22–23; cf. 1 John 1:1–4).

Summarizing, we see that the Bible links eternal life:

(a) with the present spiritual state of believers;
(b) with the (post-Parousia) Messianic kingdom; or
(c) with the (post-Parousia) Father's house.

In contrast to traditional Christianity, the Bible never links eternal life with the intermediate state.

---

52. Cf. John 7:39; 14:16; 20:22; also see, e.g., Rom. 8:9; 1 Cor. 6:19; Eph. 1:14.

THE EDEN STORY

A History of Paradise, from its Demise to its New Rise

WILLEM J. OUWENEEL

Also Available from the Author

10

AFTER THE HEREAFTER

Now I saw a new heaven and a new earth,
for the first heaven and the first earth had passed
away.
Also there was no more sea.
Then I saw the holy city, New Jerusalem,
coming down out of heaven from God,
prepared as a bride adorned for her husband.
And I heard a loud voice from heaven saying,
"Behold, the tabernacle of God is with man,
and He will dwell with them, and they shall be His
people.
God Himself will be with them and be their God.
And God will wipe away every tear from their eyes;
there shall be no more death, nor sorrow, nor crying.
There shall be no more pain,
for the former things have passed away."
                                        Revelation 21:1–4 (NKJV)

Zion hört die Wächter singen,
das Herz tut ihr vor Freuden springen,
sie wachet und steht eilend auf.
Ihr Freund kommt vom Himmel prächtig,
von Gnaden stark, von Wahrheit mächtig,

ihr Licht wird hell, ihr Stern geht auf.
Nun komm, du werte Kron,
Herr Jesu, Gottes Sohn!
Hosianna!
Wir folgen all
zum Freudensaal
und halten mit das Abendmahl.

Zion [i.e., the bride of Christ] hears the watchmen sing,
her heart leaps for joy within her,
she wakens and hastily arises [Matt. 25:6–7].
Her glorious Friend [i.e., the Bridegroom] comes from heaven,
strong in mercy, powerful in truth,
her light becomes bright, her star rises.
Now come, precious crown,
Lord Jesus, the Son of God!
Hosannah!
We all follow
to the hall of joy
and hold the [Lamb's] evening meal together [Rev. 19:6–9].[1]

Wachet auf, ruft uns die Stimme
[Awake, Calls the Voice to Us]
Bach cantata BWV 140
Philipp Nicolai (1599)

10.1 God's Tabernacle

10.1.1 The "Tabernacle of the Testimony"

Revelation 21:3 says. "And I heard a loud voice from the throne

---

1. This time not a description of "going to heaven," but a beautiful portrait of the Parousia, though with supersessionist overtones (Zion is the church).

saying, 'Behold, the dwelling place [or tabernacle] of God is with man. He will dwell with them, and they will be his people, and God himself will be with them as their God." Probably the correct reading for "people" is the Greek singular *laos*, underscoring the point that there will no longer be a diversity of nations (Gk. *ethnē*); there will be only God's people. The division into many different nations originated after Noah's Flood as a consequence of the sin of the wicked, rebellious unification attempt of Babel (Gen. 10:5, 32; 11:1–9). In God's new world, there will be no more distinction between the nations, including Israel. When the blessing of God spreads one day to all nations, that is, all believers of the Old and New Testaments, all earthly, temporary differences will disappear. There will be just "people" in the sense of human beings, that is, the righteous ones from every century and from every part of the former world.

What actually *is* the "new heaven" that is mentioned in Revelation 21:1? Is it the dwelling place of God? In line with Genesis 1:1 ("the heavens and the earth," referring to the entire cosmos), and the reference to it in, for instance, Acts 4:24 and 14:15, we think instead of the renewed cosmos. The announcement of the renewal of "heaven and earth" is made in both the Old and the New Testaments.[2] I suppose that it will be pointless to wonder whether God's people will dwell *either* in the new heaven *or* on the new earth, because the new world will be one. The upper and the lower "stories" of this new world will be connected as it were by a ladder like Jacob's ladder, "set up on the earth, and the top of it reached to heaven," on which the saints will be "ascending and descending" (cf. Gen. 28:12; also see John 1:51 about angels ascending and descending).

Of more interest for our present purpose is how we must understand "God's dwelling place (tent, tabernacle)." The Greek root is *skēn-*, from which *skēnē* and related words have been derived,

---

2. Isa. 65:17; 66:22; Matt. 5:18; 24:35; 2 Pet. 3:13; Rev. 20:11; 21:1.

which are the usual words for "tent."[3] In Hebrews 8–9 it is the word for the tabernacle (*tabernaculum* is Latin for "tent") of Israel in the wilderness, the tent of God, in which his glorious presence (the *Shekhinah*, as the rabbis called it) dwelt since the events recorded in Exodus 40.[4]

In order to understand the meaning of *skēnē* in Revelation, let us look first at chapter 13:6, "[The beast] opened its mouth to utter blasphemies against God, blaspheming his name and his dwelling [Gk. *skēnē*], that is, those who dwell in heaven." There is a slight preference for this reading, that is, to view the Greek word *kai* ("and") as a later insertion.[5] Yet, I would not easily wish to discard the *kai* reading, as we find it in the KJV: ". . . his tabernacle, and them that dwell in heaven." In other words, I am suggesting that we differentiate between the tabernacle and the inhabitants of heaven. The former would be the heavenly place of worship, or the entire heaven as a place of worship. As could be expected, traditional expositors such as John Gill see in these heavenly inhabitants (also) deceased believers: "angels and saints departed, who are in heaven."[6] In other related places, such as Revelation 11:12, expositors have seen the intermediate state as well, and even speak of the "heavenly church," the part of the church that is already "in heaven."[7]

Heaven is a place of worship, as Revelation 15:5 says, "After this I looked, and the sanctuary of the tent [Gk. *skēnē*] of witness in heaven was opened." Here, we read of the heavenly "temple" as the place of God's dwelling as well as the place of heavenly worship. In 11:19, we find the "ark of the covenant" (cf. Deut. 31:26),

---

3. Matt. 17:4 par.; Luke 16:9; Acts 7:43–44; 15:16; 2 Cor. 5:1–4; Heb. 11:9; 2 Pet. 1:13–14; Paul was a tentmaker (Gk. *skēnopoios*, Acts 18:3).
4. Exod. 40:34–35 (cf. 13:21–22; 14:19–24; 16:10; 19:9, 16:10; 24:15–18).
5. Metzger (1975), 746–47; cf. Ouweneel (1990), 91.
6. https://biblehub.com/commentaries/revelation/13-6.htm; also cf. Jamieson-Fausset-Brown on the same page.
7. Geneva Study Bible (https://biblehub.com/commentaries/revelation/11-12.htm); cf. §3.2.2 on the "militant" and "triumphant" church.

while the expression "tent of witness (testimony)" in 15:5 reminds us of the "ark of the testimony."[8] The entire terminology is adopted from the Old Testament tabernacle terminology. The tabernacle was called "tabernacle of the testimony" because it housed the "ark of the testimony, "and the ark was called this because it contained the "testimony," namely, the two tablets of stone on which the Ten Commandments were written.[9]

10.1.2   The Feast of Booths

The first mention of *skēnē* in Revelation is this: "For this reason, they [i.e., the great multitude] are before the throne of God; and they serve Him day and night in His temple; and He who sits on the throne will spread His tabernacle over them" (7:15 NASB). In all four passages from Revelation that we have mentioned, *skēnē* seems to be a metaphorical reference to the tabernacle in the wilderness, when the glorious presence (the *Shekhinah*) of YHWH dwelt in the midst of his people of Israel.[10] But now we must add that *skēnē* also reminds us of the Feast of Booths (Lev. 23:34), in earlier translations called the Feast of Tabernacles.

Let us first look at Revelation 21:3. This verse seems to say that God's *Shekhinah*, his holy, glorious splendor, will dwell amid God's people in his new creation, as it once did in the tabernacle in the wilderness and the temple in Jerusalem. It also reminds us of the orderly arrangement of the camp of Israel in Numbers 2, where we find the tabernacle in the middle, and all the tribes of Israel arranged around it. Similarly, in God's new world we find all his people around him, and he himself dwelling in their midst. However, there is another association evoked by the mention of the tabernacle in Revelation 21:3, and this is, as I said, the Feast

---

8.   Cf. "tabernacle of the testimony" (e.g., Exod. 38:21) and "ark of the testimony" (e.g., Exod. 25:22).

9.   Exod. 25:16; 31:18; 32:15; 40:20.

10. In addition to Exod. 40:34–38, see 29:45–46; Lev. 26:11; Num. 5:3; 35:34; Deut. 12:11; 14:23; 16:2, 6, 11; 23:16; 26:2; see Ouweneel (1988), 259n18 and references.

of Booths. The LXX renders the Hebrew word *sukkah* ("booth" or "tabernacle") as *skēnē*. In John 7:2, the Greek word for "Feast of Booths" is *skēnopēgia*, in which one easily recognizes the word *skēnē*. During this feast, the Israelites lived in booths (huts, small cabins) for an entire week, and invited each other into their booths in order to celebrate together how they once dwelt in booths (huts, tents) for forty years during their wilderness journey, on their way to the Promised Land (Lev. 23:43).

The passage in Revelation that reminds us most of the Feast of Booths is chapter 7:9–17 (NASB), where we find a multitude of believers from every nation and all tribes and peoples and tongues. The palm branches mentioned in verse 9 constitute the first reference to the Feast of Booths (Lev. 23:40; see also Neh. 8:15, "Go out to the hills, and bring olive branches and wild olive branches, myrtle branches, palm branches and branches of other leafy trees, to make booths, as it is written"). One might conclude that the reference to the palm branches in Revelation 7:9 is rather obscure, unless they are intended as a clue to draw our attention to the Feast of Booths.

The second reference is Revelation 7:15, which says that God will "spread His tabernacle [or tent, booth] over them [i.e., his people]." The idea may be here that God's new world will be like one enormous Feast of Booths for all his people worldwide, during which God will dwell in the greatest "booth" (or "tabernacle") of all, and will graciously and lovingly "spread" it over all his people, so that they will be his guests and friends forever.

10.1.3 Three References

There are three New Testament passages that shed light on this resemblance of God's new world to the Feast of Booths. The first is the passage about the transfiguration of Jesus on the Mount, where Peter exclaimed: "Master, it is good that we are here. Let us make three tents [booths, tabernacles, Gk. *skēnas*], one for you and one for Moses and one for Elijah" (Luke 9:33). Of course, Peter was not thinking of canvas tents; where would he have found the material for them on that mountain? He was thinking of booths made of tree branches that he would be able to find there. It is as though Peter liked the scene[11] before him so much that he tried to retain it, as if the entire company of six persons on that mount—three of them in a glorified state—could enter immediately into the great festival of God's new world.

But the other meaning of *skēnē* is also suggested in that same scene, namely, that of God's tabernacle among his people, where his *Shekhinah* dwelt. This is because the story as it is told in Luke 9 continues as follows (v. 34): "As he [i.e., Peter] was saying these things, a cloud came and overshadowed them, and they were afraid as they entered the cloud." This cloud reminds us of the *Shekhinah*, especially because of the term "overshadowed" (Gk. *epeskiazen*). The latter is a clear reference to Exodus 40:35, "Moses was not able to enter the tent of meeting [i.e., the tabernacle] because the cloud settled on [LXX: *epeskiazen*, more accurately: overshadowed] it, and the glory of the Lord filled the tabernacle." Like the various passages in the book of Revelation, Luke 9 evokes in our minds at the same time both meanings of "tabernacle," which constitute two aspects of God's new world: his dwelling place will be in the midst of his people, and he will spread his "booth" over them in a protective and cherishing way.

The second passage is John 7, where we find the only reference to the Feast of Booths in the New Testament: "Now the Jews' Feast of Booths was at hand" (v. 2). The highlight of the feast was "the last day of the feast, the great day" (v. 37), the day of the water libation ritual. The water ceremony entailed carrying water from the Pool of Siloam to the Temple Square where it was solemnly poured out before God as a prayer for new rain. It was presumably during this ceremony that Jesus shouted: "If anyone thirsts, let him come to me and drink. Whoever believes in me, as the Scripture has said

---

11. Interestingly, the English word "scene" comes from Greek *skēnē* ("tent"), mentioned in the text.

[cf. Isa. 12:3], 'Out of his heart will flow rivers of living water.' Now this he said about the Spirit, whom those who believed in him were to receive, for as yet the Spirit had not been given, because Jesus was not yet glorified" (vv. 37b–39). These "rivers of living water" that Jesus mentioned flow from the hearts (literally, bowels) of believers, but in Revelation the metaphor has a broader eschatological range, linked to the new world that God will create: "Then the angel showed me the river of the water of life, bright as crystal, flowing from the throne of God and of the Lamb" (Rev. 22:1;[12] cf. v. 17, "[L]et the one who is thirsty come; let the one who desires take the water of life without price").

There is no reference to booths in John 7, but there *is* a link to Revelation 7, where we find God's people lovingly overshadowed by his *skēnē* (v. 15b), and where the text continues: "They shall hunger no more, neither thirst anymore; the sun shall not strike them, nor any scorching heat. For the Lamb in the midst of the throne will be their shepherd, and he will guide them to *springs of living water*, and God will wipe away every tear from their eyes" (vv. 16–17; italics added). In the Old Testament, the Elim oasis is a wonderful picture of God's new world, where we find both elements: the palm trees and the living water: ". . . Elim, where there were twelve springs of water and seventy palm trees" (Exod. 15:27).

The third passage about the Feast of Booths involves Jesus entering Jerusalem on Palm Sunday:

> The next day the large crowd that had come to the feast heard that Jesus was coming to Jerusalem. So they took branches of palm trees and went out to meet him, crying out, "Hosanna! Blessed is he who comes in the name of the Lord, even the King of Israel!" And Jesus found a young donkey and sat on it, just as it is written, "Fear not, daughter of Zion; behold, your king is coming, sitting on a donkey's colt!" (John 12:12–15).

---

12. Cf. also Ezek. 47:1–12; Joel 3:18; Zech. 14:8, although the meaning here in Rev. 22:1 might be literal, referring to the earthly temple and the holy city during the Messianic kingdom.

Of course, Easter is not the Feast of Booths; yet, the branch-es of palm trees used by the crowd are remarkable, as well as the two eschatological references. One is from Psalm 118: "Save us, we pray,[13] O LORD! . . . Blessed is he who comes in the name of the LORD!" (vv. 25–26). Some expositors have linked Psalm 118 with the Feast of Booths, and have viewed it as a procession song. These three, Psalm 118, Palm Sunday, and the Feast of Booths unani-mously point to God's new world.

The other prophecy that is quoted in John 12 is from Zechariah 9:9, "Rejoice greatly, O daughter of Zion! Shout aloud, O daughter of Jerusalem! Behold, your king is coming to you; righteous and having salvation is he, humble and mounted on a donkey, on a colt, the foal of a donkey." Here again, the passage in its original context is clearly eschatological, that is, reaches far beyond John 12 to the Messianic kingdom:

> [H]e [i.e., the Messiah] shall speak peace to the nations; his rule shall be from sea to sea, and from the River [i.e., Euphrates] to the ends of the earth. . . . On that day the LORD their God will save them, as the flock of his people; for like the jewels of a crown they shall shine on his land. For how great is his goodness, and how great his beauty! Grain shall make the young men flourish, and new wine the young women (Zech. 9:10, 16–17).

10.2 God's New World
10.2.1 Features

There are several features of God's new world in Revelation that deserve closer attention, and will help us once again to distinguish sharply between the intermediate state and the resurrection state. For instance, take this statement:

> He [God] will wipe away every tear from their [i.e., his people's] eyes, and death shall be no more [cf. 20:14], neither shall there be mourn-

---

13. The four Hebrew words for this phrase are *Hoshiʿah na*, which in the Greek of John 12:13 changes to *Hosanna*.

ing, nor crying, nor pain anymore, for the former things have passed away. And he who was seated on the throne said, "Behold, I am making all things new" (Rev. 21:4–5).

Of course, in the intermediate state there are no more tears and pain either, as we may suppose—but death is still there; believers exist in a state of (physical) death; they cannot be called alive (they come to life only in the resurrection; Rev. 20:4–5). Revelation 21 is clearly about the post-resurrection world.

It is scarcely possible to form a picture of God's new world; our words and imagination fail to describe the new heavens and the new earth. It is like describing a river landscape or a mountain vista (things that cannot be held) to a person born blind. Therefore, we speak of the new creation almost exclusively in metaphors: a wedding, a supper, a city with golden streets, a feast (Rev. 19–21). These have been drawn from our experience. As H. Berkhof put it: "This imagery on the one hand infinitely magnifies what is uplifting and gladdening in this world, and on the other hand completely expels other elements which are just as much part of our world, elements such as sorrow, confusion, and sin."[14] And a bit later, he wrote regarding eternal life:

> Should not the dogmatician here yield to the poet? It is true, imagery is the language that comes closest to what eternity is, together with the language of music. Hence the best verbalizations of eternal life are found in [Johann Sebastian] Bach and [George Frederic] Handel[15] and in a number of church songs and Christian hymns. In comparison, the conceptual language of dogmatics is bound to be always meager and dry.[16]

---

14. Berkhof (1986), 526.
15. Of course, the texts that Bach and Handel used were usually written by other people. Here, for Bach, Picander (C. F. Henrici) or Salomon Franck, and for Handel, Thomas Morell should have been mentioned.
16. *Ibid.*, 537.

There is hardly any other way to describe the new world than in a negative manner: the emphasis lies on what will be found *no more*, which in itself is already quite an encouragement. If we had to summarize world history in five words, we could hardly find more appropriate words than the five just quoted: tears, death, mourning, crying, and pain (v. 4). These are the characteristics of the present world since the Fall, and it will stay this way until the Parousia.

In Revelation 7:17 it was announced that God will wipe away every tear from the eyes. This lovely picture reminds us of the mother who wipes the tears from the eyes of the crying child (cf. Ps. 56:8 on the preciousness of the tears of God's people). We might speak here of the maternal feature of God's love. He says explicitly to his people: "As one whom his mother comforts, so I will comfort you."[17] Of course, it does not necessarily mean that believers enter eternity with literal tears on their glorified faces. Nor are these tears of remorse that must be wept before the judgment seat of God. What it does mean, I think, is that for God's children, the bliss of eternity will put an end to all grief. Tears, death,[18] mourning, crying, and pain belong to the "former things" (Rev. 21:4; cf. Isa. 25:8); among the "new things" (v. 5) they will no longer occur.

The prophet says, "[E]verlasting joy shall be upon their heads; they shall obtain gladness and joy, and sorrow and sighing shall flee away" (cf. Isa. 35:10; 51:11). According to the summary of H. Berkhof, eternal bliss implies the eradication of sin, the abolition of what is provisional, unveiled communion with God (the "contemplation" of God), perfected community, the perfected society, the absolute unity of freedom and love, the centrality of Christ, and the world that will be healed, including nature.[19]

10.2.2 The Conquerors

In God's new world, his people will not be like Adam, who began

---

17. Isa. 66:13; cf. 49:15; Ps. 131:2; Luke13:34b.
18. Cf. Isa. 25:8; 1 Cor. 15:54; Rev. 20:13–14.
19. Berkhof (1986), 538–39.

in a "state of innocence," but will be those who have tasted all the misery resulting from sin. It is for this very reason that they are now perfectly able to enjoy all that God has prepared for them. They will be happy in God, whereas Adam thought he could become happier through disobedience to God. The best possible world is the one where God can be present with all his holiness and glory, and can be at rest. In Isaiah 43:24, the LORD says to Israel, "[Y]ou have burdened me with your sins; you have wearied [or in other translations: troubled, tired] me with your iniquities." As long as sin still reigns in this world, God cannot find perfect rest. The Lamb will need to cleanse the cosmos of its stain of sin (John 1:29).

Thousands of years of history will have demonstrated the unrest, trouble, and weariness that sin has brought into this world. Through the eternal life that is in them, redeemed humans will at last experience the contrast between the unrest that sin brought into this world, and the full rest that will descend upon the world. The world will finally correspond with God's thoughts, a world full of people who will be in perfect unity with each other, and with God.

"And he said to me, 'It is done [Gk. *gegonen*, or, It has happened]!'" (Rev. 21:6) This statement had been made earlier in connection with the judgments (16:17). Now peace and righteousness can be definitively established; the old world is finished, and a new, perfect world is breaking through. Every prophecy has been fulfilled, every divine promise has been realized, every enemy has been defeated. This has become possible because of the Lord and Savior who cried on the cross: "It is finished [Gk. *tetelestai*]" (John 19:30). It is his work, and nothing else, that has made God's new world possible. "For the Son of God, Jesus Christ, whom we proclaimed among you, . . . all the promises of God find their Yes in him. That is why it is through him that we utter our Amen to God for his glory" (2 Cor. 1:19–20).

"I am the Alpha and the Omega, the beginning and the end"

(Rev. 21:6). This is the everlasting God, who is the origin and goal of all that exists: God "declaring the end from the beginning and from ancient times things not yet done, saying, 'My counsel shall stand, and I will accomplish all my purpose'" (Isa. 46:10). This being the beginning and the end, the first and the last, the Alpha and the Omega [the first and the last letter of the Greek alphabet], is not only characteristic of (the Triune) God (Rev. 1:8), but also specifically of Jesus Christ, the Son of God (1:17; 2:8; 22:13; cf. Isa. 41:4; 44:6; 48:12).

"To the thirsty I will give from the spring of the water of life without payment" (Rev. 21:6c). This principle remains valid. The verse speaks of the one who "thirsts for God" (Ps. 42:2; 63:1), who ardently longs for him who is the origin, foundation, meaning, and goal of their existence. Those who "seek" God (cf. Acts 17:27; Heb. 11:6) will find the spring (or fountain) of the water of life.[20] The promise is included in Revelation 21 to indicate how a person can become a partaker in the everlasting bliss that is presented here. On the road of faith there are two goals: that of the "conquerors" (or, "overcomers," v. 7) and that of the "losers," that is, the pagans and the nominal Christians (v. 8). Jesus came into this world to tell us about this wonderful life, eternal life (see the previous chapter),[21] and revealed to us the source of this life: the love of God (John 3:16). In the Bible, the gospel is often presented from the viewpoint of God's righteousness, of repentance and conversion, as well as from the viewpoint of the love of God, who longs for the salvation of sinners. Here instead, we find the longing of *humans*, thirsting[22] for true life, for the love of God, who is the spring of eternal life: "[T]o those who by patience in well-doing seek for glory and honor

---

20. Cf. Rev. 22:17; Ps. 36:8–9; 42:1–2; 63:1; Isa. 12:3; 55:1; Jer. 2:13.
21. See also Ouweneel (2009b), 99–109.
22. Of course, it is true to say that God himself creates this thirst in these people (cf. Phil. 2:13), but this does not eliminate human responsibility and initiative.

and immortality, he will give eternal life."[23]

"The one who conquers will have this heritage, and I will be his God and he will be my son" (Rev. 21:7). God granted this promise—"he will be my son"—for the first time to David with reference to the latter's son Solomon (2 Sam. 7:14). This word, or passage, is quoted with reference to Christ (Heb. 1:5) as well as with reference to his followers (2 Cor. 6:18). The eternal Son of God became a human, in order that humans could and would become sons of God.[24]

Notice that this is the only time in John's writings where the Apostle uses the Greek term *huios* ("son") for believers (other times he uses the Greek words *tekn[i]on* or *paidion*, "child"). This is all the more remarkable because the title "son of God" (Lat. *filius Dei*) was the common title of the Roman emperors, the world conquerors of that time. Here, the follower of Christ, as a "son of God," has sided with the Lamb who had been rejected by an evil world. The "son of God" has remained faithful to the Lamb in all tribulations, has triumphed over all circumstances, and in God's new world will be on the side of the glorified Lamb, just as he had been on the side of the rejected Lamb:

> [B]ehold, on Mount Zion stood the Lamb, and with him 144,000 who had his name and his Father's name written on their foreheads . . . they were singing a new song before the throne. . . . No one could learn that song except the 144,000 who had been redeemed from the earth. It is these who have not defiled themselves with women, for they are [spiritual] virgins. It is these who follow the Lamb wherever he goes. These have been redeemed from mankind as firstfruits for God and the Lamb, and in their mouth no lie was found, for they are blameless (Rev. 14:1–5; for their purity, cf. 2 Cor. 6:17–18; Rev. 18:4).

---

23. Rom. 2:7; cf. Ps. 42:2; 63:1; 143:6; Isa. 55:1.
24. Ouweneel (2009b), 114–16.

10.2.3 The Losers

Unfortunately, there are also the losers: "But as for the cowardly, the faithless, the detestable, as for murderers, the sexually immoral, sorcerers, idolaters, and all liars, their portion will be in the lake that burns with fire and sulfur, which is the second death" (Rev. 21:8). The "cowardly" are those who have never dared to confess the name of Jesus. They have the "spirit of fear," not the Spirit of power, love, and self-control (cf. 2 Tim. 1:7). Those who are not *confessors* of Jesus can never be true *followers* of Jesus because Jesus himself, in the hour of greatest peril "in his testimony before Pontius Pilate made the good confession" (1 Tim. 6:13). In their minds, such false Christians may have sided with Jesus, but in their public testimony they side with his enemies, and will perish with them. There is no true believer who is not a Christ confessor.[25]

These losers—these lost ones—should possibly be viewed in contrast with the conquerors (those who overcome) of verse 7, so that the text may not refer to the wicked in general, but (especially) to nominal Christians: the *cowardly* (who fear persecution, and therefore do not confess the name of Christ; Matt. 10:32–33; 13:21), the *faithless* (or unbelievers; pseudo-believers, who have denied the faith under the persecution), the *detestable* (or those committing abominations, those who have been following the "abominations and impurities" of the beast and the prostitute of Rev. 17:4; cf. the *idolaters*), and so on.[26] However, it is true that, from the "detestable" onward, the description also applies to non-believers in general. In Revelation, the cowardly (or, fearful) are specifically those who bow down before the image of the beast (13:14–15; 14:9, 11), whereas the faithful are those who have conquered (or overcome) the beast and its image (15:2). The "murderers" may be especially those who have persecuted the faithful (cf. 9:10), and the "liars" those who, out of fear and hypocrisy, have denied the truth of God.

25. Rom. 10:9–10; cf. Matt. 10:32–33; Luke 12:8; John 12:42.
26. Mounce (1977), 375.

In the Bible, we rarely encounter a simple division between believers and unbelievers. Rather, the division is between the righteous and the wicked, because it is through the *behavior* of people that they display what is really in their *hearts*. Therefore, Revelation 22:14–15 says,

> Blessed are those who wash their robes, so that they may have the right to the tree of life and that they may enter the city by the gates. Outside are the dogs[27] and sorcerers and the sexually immoral and murderers and idolaters, and everyone who loves and practices falsehood.

The Apostle Paul is very clear about who will be allowed into God's new world:

> Or do you not know that the unrighteous will not inherit the kingdom of God? Do not be deceived: neither the sexually immoral, nor idolaters, nor adulterers, nor men who practice homosexuality, nor thieves, nor the greedy, nor drunkards, nor revilers, nor swindlers will inherit the kingdom of God (1 Cor. 6:9–10).

"I warn you, as I warned you before, that those who do [wicked] things will not inherit the kingdom of God" (Gal. 5:19–21). "For you may be sure of this, that everyone who is sexually immoral or impure, or who is covetous (that is, an idolater), has no inheritance in the kingdom of Christ and God" (Eph. 5:5).

There is no third option. *In the end*, every human being is either a righteous person or a wicked person, a servant of God or a rebel against Christ. Just as there will be God's new world, there will also be the "lake of fire," where "the smoke of their torment goes up forever and ever, and they have no rest, day or night" (cf. 14:11; see the next chapter). *In the end*, every human being is either on the side of the Lamb or one who fights against the Lamb. He or she is either an overcomer or a loser; there will be no neutral party in between.

---

27. Possibly the male prostitute or the whoremonger; see Deut. 23:17–18.

A person will either live with the Lamb in the new Garden of Eden (Rev. 2:7; 22:1–2), or lament with the dragon in the lake of fire (12:9; 20:2, 10).[28] It is the Lamb or the dragon. It is the garden or the lake. The contrasting imagery of Revelation is quite impressive; stated in ordinary language, it will be life or death; light or darkness; love or hatred.

10.3 Special Bible Passages
10.3.1 Revelation 20:14 and 21:5, 8

In this book on the afterlife, we have investigated what are the biblical meanings of "death" (§§2.3 and 2.4). Now we arrive at this remarkable statement: "Then Death and Hades were thrown into the lake of fire. This is the second death, the lake of fire" (Rev. 20:14). Here "death" is the *condition*, and "Hades" is the *place* of the dead (§4.3). At their physical death, those who are spiritually dead go to Hades, and in the end they themselves, but also Death and Hades as such, find their everlasting end in the lake of fire. The latter is also a *place*, while the *condition* in which the wicked will exist is described as the "second death" (Rev. 2:11; 20:6, 14; 21:8). Humans will be complete beings only when they are no longer disembodied personalities, but have a resurrection body. In the case of the righteous, this is a glorified body (1 Cor. 15:51–55; Phil. 3:20–21); in the case of the wicked, even after their resurrection they will still be called (spiritually) dead (Rev. 20:12).

A complete person is an embodied person. Therefore, physical death is an abnormal, temporary condition, and Hades is a temporary place. They belong to the post-Fall world, and do not fit into the ultimate conditions that God has designed. Therefore, they are thrown into the lake of fire, and in this way forever abolished. After the wicked have been raised, they will possess bodies again, and thus, as Matthew 10:28 says (cf. 5:29), with "body and soul," they are cast into hell. This verse does not imply a body-soul dualism

---

28. See extensively, Ouweneel (2020).

in the Greek scholastic sense, but simply tells us that the most our enemies can do is to end our physical lives, but they cannot affect our personalities. Only God can cast the entire embodied personality into hell.

"Behold, I am making all things new" (Rev. 21:5). The old form of everything that belonged to the first creation will have ended. Of course, we are referring to empirical creation here. The angels have indeed been created (Col. 1:16; cf. Ezek. 28:14–16) but do not belong to the material creation that the text is referring to. They live in their own sphere. And of course, the Creator himself is not involved either. But we must remember that, in a certain sense, even believers are not involved, because they have already taken part in the new creation as far as their personalities are concerned: "Therefore, if anyone is in Christ, [such a person] is a new creation. The old has passed away; behold, the new has come" (2 Cor. 5:17).

"For neither circumcision counts for anything, nor uncircumcision, but [what counts is whether a person is] a new creation" (Gal. 6:15).

The believer has "put on the new self, created after the likeness of God in true righteousness and holiness" (Eph. 4:24); ". . . the new self, which is being renewed in knowledge after the image of its creator. Here there is not Greek and Jew, circumcised and uncircumcised, barbarian, Scythian, slave, free; but Christ is all, and in all" (Col. 3:10–11).

In the present world, which is the old (post-Fall) world, there are those who already spiritually partake of the new creation. One day, they will no longer be the exception—new creatures functioning within an old world, with all the injuries and distress that belong to such an unnatural situation—because God's entire world will be a new creation. In the present creation, believers no longer belong to "the cosmos," that is, the world in its present state, whose ruler is Satan (John 12:31; 14:30; 16:11): "[T]hey are not of the world [Gk. *kosmos*]" (John 17:16), even though their bodies *are* still part of the old creation.[29]

10.3.2   Hebrews 12:25–29

At this point we must consider in some detail Hebrews 12:25–29:

> See that you do not refuse him who is speaking. For if they [i.e., the
> Israelites] did not escape when they refused him who warned them
> on earth, much less will we escape if we reject him who warns from
> heaven. At that time his voice shook the earth, but now he has prom-
> ised, "Yet once more I will shake not only the earth but also the heav-
> ens" [Hag. 2:7]. This phrase, "Yet once more," indicates the removal
> of things that are shaken—that is, things that have been made—in
> order that the things that cannot be shaken may remain. Therefore
> let us be grateful for receiving a kingdom that cannot be shaken, and
> thus let us offer to God acceptable worship, with reverence and awe,
> for our God is a consuming fire.[30]

The writer of the letter to the Hebrews tells us about the "re-
moval [and replacement by something else]" (Gk. *metathesis*[31]; cf.
7:12) of "all things," that is, the transformation of all perishable
(material) things into imperishable ("neo-material") things. All
things that were linked to the old creation will give way to the newly
created things. This does not exactly mean that the new creation will
replace the old creation. Just as our *present* body will be raised (Rom.
8:11), and the new body will be very different from our present
body, so too there will be continuity and discontinuity between the
"old things" and the "new things." *This* world will be renewed, but
the new world will relate to the old world as the ear of wheat relates
to the seed of wheat (cf. 1 Cor. 15:27–38). The old world will be
shaken, and a new world will emerge from it, as the ear does from

---

29. Rom. 8:11, 23; 2 Cor. 5:1–2; Phil. 3:20–21.
30. Heb. 12:25–29; cf. Deut. 4:24; Isa. 33:14; Lam. 2:3.
31. In modern linguistics, *metathesis* is the transposition of letters and syllables
    in a word or words.

the seed.[32] And just as one who has seen only wheat seeds cannot imagine what the head of wheat might look like—despite the continuity between the two—so too at present we cannot imagine what the new world might look like—despite the continuity between the two. We will say with the Queen of Sheba: "Behold, the half was not told me" (1 Kings 10:7)—another example of a verse that traditionally has mistakenly been applied to the intermediate state.[33]

The new world that will be formed by God's hands will be a "kingdom that cannot be shaken." There is no cyclical pattern here; that is, there is no new world, or even new world*s*, appearing *after* the new world to come. There are only two breaks: the Fall, which changed the pure created world into a sinful world, and the transformation, which will change the present world into God's new and definitive world.

The writer of Hebrews mentions still another connotation evoked by the word "shaking." When God spoke from Mount Sinai in a lofty, majestic way, it was like a word of thunder which made the earth tremble.[34] However, for his new world, God will speak a much mightier word and once more, there will be a shaking, but this time not only the earth will be shaken, but also the celestial things (not the dwelling place of God, but the entire empirical cosmos). To illustrate this, the writer referred to Haggai 2:7, quoted from the LXX. The prophet Haggai spoke of the shaking of heaven and earth as the introduction to the Messianic kingdom, as many other prophets have done.[35] However, in the use that the writer of Hebrews makes of this quotation he goes far beyond the primary meaning. He spoke not only of the introduction of the Messianic

---

32. See also John 12:24: "[U]nless a grain of wheat falls into the earth and dies, it remains alone; but if it dies, it bears much fruit."

33. Matthew Henry seems to do so (https://biblehub.com/commentaries/1_kings/10-7.htm).

34. Exod. 19:18; cf. Judg. 5:4–5; Ps. 18:8; 68:7–8; 77:19; 114:4, 7; Hab. 3:6; see Ouweneel (1982), 2:90.

35. Zech. 14:4–5; Matt. 24:29; Rev. 6:12–14; 11:13; 16:18.

kingdom but also of the ultimate arrival of the new heavens and the new earth. This is a "shaking" that involves a complete transformation of creation.

The "shakable" things (Heb. 12:27) have been made by God (cf. 3:4b). They belong to the first creation, which was *able* to be "shaken," and indeed *was* "shaken" through the Fall, and therefore in the end cannot remain: "You, Lord, laid the foundation of the earth in the beginning, and the heavens are the work of your hands; they will perish, but you remain; they will all wear out like a garment, like a robe you will roll them up, like a garment they will be changed" (Heb. 1:10–11; cf. Ps. 102:25–27). The first creation *could* be shaken, and indeed it was, and will be; God's new creation *cannot* be shaken. Genesis 1 was God's first word; God's commanding order for the transformation of the first creation into the new one will be his last word.

10.3.3 2 Peter 3:7–18

We turn next to consider 2 Peter 3:7–18:

> [T]he heavens and earth that now exist are stored up for fire, being kept until the *day of judgment* and destruction of the ungodly. . . . [T]he *day of the Lord* will come like a thief, and then the heavens will pass away with a roar, and the heavenly bodies will be burned up and dissolved, and the earth and the works that are done on it will be exposed. Since all these things are thus to be dissolved, what sort of people ought you to be in lives of holiness and godliness, waiting for and hastening the coming of the *day of God*, because of which the heavens will be set on fire and dissolved, and the heavenly bodies will melt as they burn! But according to his promise we are waiting for new heavens and a new earth in which righteousness dwells. . . . To him be the glory both now and to the *day of eternity*. Amen (2 Pet. 3:7, 10–13, 18b; italics added).

Long ago, in the days of Noah, the earth underwent a "water immersion," so to speak (vv. 5–6), while, at the end of our present

world, it will undergo a "fire immersion." Through the waters of
the Flood, Noah reached, as it were, a new, purified earth, an event
compared with baptism (cf. 1 Pet. 3:20–22). Similarly, the old earth
will go through the fire (cf. Luke 3:16; 12:49–50), and in this way be
transformed into a new earth.

This passage is the answer to the question of the mockers (2 Pet.
3:3–4): ". . . scoffers will come in the last days with scoffing, following their own sinful desires. They will say, 'Where is the promise of
his coming [Gk. *parousia*]? For ever since the fathers fell asleep, all
things are continuing as they were from the beginning of creation.'"
In his reply, Peter did not adopt the same Greek word *parousia*, or
a similar term; instead, he speaks of the "day of the Lord" (Gk.
hēmera kyriou, v. 10), that is, the day of his judgment, beginning with
the Parousia, when the mockers, among all the wicked of world history, will have to account for their mocking and other evil works.[36]

In this passage, the Apostle Peter spoke of no fewer than four
"days," the first of which, the "day of judgment" (Gk. *hēmera kriseōs*,
v. 7), I assume to be the day of the Parousia, or the age beginning
with the Parousia. This is no different from the second day mentioned, the "day of the Lord," although millennialists might like to
include in this term the entire period of the Messianic kingdom.[37]
They might even refer to verse 8, where Peter says that "with the
Lord one day is as a thousand years, and a thousand years as one
day" (cf. Ps. 90:4), and thus connect the day of the Lord with the
thousand-year reign of Revelation 20:1–6.

These things do not concern us now. For the moment, it is
enough to distinguish the "day of the Lord," which, in my view,[38] is
different from "the day of God" (Gk. *tou theou hēmera*, v. 12) and the
"day of eternity" (Gk. *hēmera aiōnos*, v. 18) (the latter two days I take

---

36. Cf., e.g., Isa. 13:6, 9; Jer. 46:10; Ezek. 30:3; Joel 1:15; 2:1, 11, 31; 3:14;
    Zeph. 1:7, 14; Acts 2:20.
37. See the verses in the previous note, plus Isa. 58:13; Ezek. 13:5; Amos 5:18,
    20; Obadiah 1:15; Mal. 4:5.
38. I am relying on Grant (1902), 189–90.

to be identical). The "day of the Lord" would thus be the day of the Parousia and of the Messianic kingdom, whereas the "day of God" is the everlasting "day" of the new heavens and the new earth. If we see the sabbath day—the seventh day of the week—fulfilled in the "day of the Lord," the "day of God" (or the "day of eternity") corresponds with an eighth "day," which is at the same time the first day of a new "week," to which there will be no end (cf. John 20:26, and see §12.2.3).

It is important to carefully examine verses 10 and 12 here. Verse 10 says, "[T]he day of the Lord will come like a thief, and then the heavens will pass away with a roar, and the heavenly bodies[39] will be burned up and dissolved, and the earth and the works that are done on it will be exposed." If we take Revelation 20:1–6 and 21:1–8 literally, we know that this "burning" and "dissolving" will occur only at the end of the "day of the Lord." This is *followed* by the "day of God," if we may understand verse 12 this way: ". . . the day of God, because of which the heavens will be set on fire and dissolved, and the heavenly bodies will melt as they burn." That is to say, *in view* of the "day of eternity" the former creation will be dissolved, and give way to God's new world. If I am interpreting the text correctly, the "day of the Lord" will *end* with the old creation dissolving, which is the *beginning* of the "day of God," or the "day of eternity." After the seventh day of world history, there will be an everlasting eighth day.

The last word of 2 Peter 3:10 is "exposed" (ESB; Gk. *eurethēsetai*, literally "will be found"). It is understandable that later scribes have replaced this difficult word by a much more easily understandable term: *katakaēsetai*, "will be burned up" (not to be confused with the earlier word "burned up" in this verse, Gk. *kausoumena*). A number of modern translations are more exegetical than literal, such as the MSG ("the earth and all its works exposed to the scrutiny of Judg-

---

39. Gk. *stoicheia*; these are indeed either the celestial bodies, or the four elements of antiquity: earth, air, fire, and water; cf. Ouweneel (2008), 83–86, and references there.

ment") and the NIV ("the earth and everything done in it will be laid bare").[40]

10.4   The Apostle Paul
10.4.1   1 Corinthians 15:23–28

When everything that belongs to the first creation is gone, the new heavens and the new earth will arrive, and the everlasting, unchangeable final state will emerge. This is what the Apostle Paul has to say about it:

> But each in his own order: Christ the first fruits, then at his coming those who belong to Christ. Then comes the end, when he delivers the kingdom to God the Father after destroying every rule and every authority and power. For he must reign until he has put all his enemies under his feet. The last enemy to be destroyed is death. For "God has put all things in subjection under his feet." [Ps. 8:6] But when it says, "all things are put in subjection," it is plain that he is excepted who put all things in subjection under him. When all things are subjected to him, then the Son himself will also be subjected to him who put all things in subjection under him, that God may be all in all" (1 Cor. 15:23–28).

We have seen in Revelation 21 that, in the new heavens and the new earth, it is only (the Triune) God who is mentioned, together with his people. This is further explained in 1 Corinthians 15:23–28. A specific chronological order is being described here:

(a) Christ is the "firstfruits," that is, the first person to be raised from the dead, the "firstfruits" of the great harvest of resurrection.

(b) The mention of Jesus' resurrection is followed by a first "then" (Gk. *epeita*), referring to his Parousia, when his people will be raised from the dead (i.e., at least almost two thousand years after [a]).

(c) After this, there is a second "then" (Gk. *eita*), referring to "the end," which is apparently the time of the arrival of the new

---

40   Cf. Greijdanus (1931), 146; Strachan (1979), 145; Blum (1981), 286.

heavens and the new earth. Between the first and the second "then," millennialists place the Messianic kingdom, that is, the thousand years of Revelation 20:1–6. Amillennialists accept only a very short time between the first and the second "then." Again, this does not concern us right now; for the moment, we are interested in the eternal state. One day, the reign of the Son of Man will come to an end. This will occur when all his promises are fulfilled, all his rights have been satisfied, and all his enemies have been destroyed.

(d) When all Christ's enemies, and even death itself have been destroyed (see Rev. 20:14), the Son of God will hand over the kingdom to his Father, who had given it to him in the first place (cf. John 5:22–29).

(e) After this, it will be "[the Triune] God" who will be "all and all," which is the same as saying "everything in all his creatures." This does not mean that Jesus Christ will no longer have any role. Daniel 7:14 says, "And to him [i.e., the Son of Man of v. 13] was given dominion and glory and a kingdom, that all peoples, nations, and languages should serve him; his dominion is an everlasting dominion, which shall not pass away, and his kingdom one that shall not be destroyed" (cf. 2:44). To be sure, we must often relativize the words for "eternal" in the Old Testament, but the language here is quite strong. The Nicene Creed also says, "He will come again in glory to judge the living and the dead, and his kingdom will have no end." So how can Christ hand over the kingdom to God, and still be in charge? The answer, as I see it, is that he will no longer rule specifically as the Son of Man, but as God the Son he remains forever the King of kings and the Lord of lords (cf. Rev. 19:16 with 1 Tim. 6:19).

The consequence is important: if the text says, "*God* will be all in all," this is undoubtedly the Triune God: Father, Son and Holy Spirit.[41] None of the persons of the Godhead can do anything apart from the other two, and this will remain true in eternity.

---

41. Cf. Ouweneel (2007b, 272, 292–93).

It is said of God's servants, that is, the righteous ones from all the ages of world history, that "they will reign forever and ever" (Rev. 22:5). This strong language means that believers will also be included in God's reign forever: "For if, because of one man's trespass, death reigned through that one man, much more will those who receive the abundance of grace and the free gift of righteousness reign in life through the one man Jesus Christ" (Rom. 5:17; cf. Eph. 1:11). As the Bridegroom is forever one with his bride, also in his rule, so too, God is forever associated with his people, even in his rule of the world.

10.4.2 1 Timothy 4:1–4

G. C. Berkouwer has dealt with the ancient theological question about whether in their (eternal) "contemplation of God" (Lat. *visio Dei*) believers will still have need of the earth. In other words, what room is there still for a new earth, if heaven seems to be sufficient for the saints?[42] The question is quite understandable: if believers "go to heaven when they die" (as in Interim Theology, dominant since "The Great Shift"), why and for what purpose would they need the earth in their eternal future?

For instance, E. Böhl is quite outspoken on the matter: "A visible heaven and a material earth will not be necessary at all anymore because the blessed ones will be with the Lord in their glorified bodies."[43] Such ideas are hardly conceivable apart from "The Great Shift" and Interim Theology. If, at the resurrection, the saints would have to return" from heaven to the earth to receive their glorified resurrection bodies, that might sound like a regression, even though ultimately it will be a renewed earth. Such expositors, especially those who identify the (beginning of the) eternal heavenly blessings with the intermediate state, totally ignore the materiality— albeit a glorified materiality to be sure—of the resurrection

---

42. Berkouwer (1972), 28–288; also see (1963), chapter 5.
43. Böhl (2004), 611; cf. Bach cantata BWV 75: the believer "has, when what is earthly has disappeared, found himself and God."

body, and thus of the eternal environment in which glorified humanity will dwell.

Once we realize this fact, it becomes senseless to ask whether glorified people will dwell in the new heavens or on the new earth, for since Genesis 1:1, "heaven and earth" are the usual description of all empirical reality (see §10.1.1, and recall what is written there about Jacob's ladder). And in eternity this will be a *renewed* totality of all empirical reality.

Those who think along the lines of Böhl will need to avoid, while they are still on earth, falling into total asceticism, as if "seeing God" (Lat. *visio Dei*) by definition excludes all earthly and material pleasures. King Hezekiah wished very much to be healed in order to be able to "see" the Lord "in the land of the living," because in his death he would *not* be able to "see" the Lord (Isa. 38:10–11). In church history, the longing for the contemplation of God has led to much unhealthy asceticism and mysticism, including despising the earthly and material, and forbidding certain good things, including marriage. As we have seen (§8.1.2), the Apostle Paul warned about

> deceitful spirits and teachings of demons, through the insincerity of liars whose consciences are seared, who forbid marriage and require abstinence from foods that God created to be received with thanksgiving by those who believe and know the truth. For everything created by God is good, and nothing is to be rejected if it is received with thanksgiving, for it is made holy by the word of God and prayer (1 Tim. 4:1–5).

It is the "worldly" (i.e., sinful and demonic) things that hinder the contemplation of God, *not* God's own good creation ("heaven and earth"). God is contemplated not only in the spiritual things but also in all the good things that he has created. This is true both for the present world and for the world to come. Actually, "spiritual" and "material" do not exclude each other at all. The body that is raised is a "spiritual body" (1 Cor. 15:44), yet it will be made of the matter of the new creation. It will be a body with flesh and bones, that is, a body that can be touched,[44] and that is able to take in food.[45]

Our goal is not reaching "heaven," either in the intermediate state or in the resurrection state, but our goal is reaching the "new heavens *and the new earth*." This will be a world that will be both spiritual and material. Believers are on their way, not to an immaterial (ghostly) world but to a world of new matter; even though it is a new kind of matter, to be sure, it is still real matter. What is inferior is not matter as such, as the ancient Greeks claimed, but only matter that has been affected by sin. One day, God will cleanse and renew the sinful world, giving us not a matterless world but, a *material* world that has been freed from the stain of sin and death. The Lamb of God will not abolish this material cosmos, but will remove sin from it (John 1:29).

Many Christians have been influenced by Interim Theology, and thus have learned to focus their hope on "going to heaven when they die." In this heaven, they will exist in a disembodied state, as if this is their actual, God-intended eternal future. The more that such Christians think like this, the more they will, consciously or unconsciously, begin to despise all that is material and somatic in this world. One Greek scholastic error (the blessed soul, freed from the body) is thus worsened by another Greek scholastic error (a matterless eternity). Believers must instead look forward to the house of the Father, which will be like the royal palace, or priestly temple,[46] of the Triune God in the midst of his new, very spiritual and very material world.

---

44. Matt. 28:9; Luke 24:39; John 20:17, 20, 27.
45. Luke 24:42; John 21:5, 13; Acts 10:41 (also 1:4 in certain translations).
46. The Hebrew word *hekhal* means both "palace" and "temple"; see, e.g., Ps. 29:9, where a Dutch translation has "palace," and all English translations have "temple"; and Ps. 45:14, where YLT has "temple," and most other translations have "palace."

11

ETERNAL JUSTICE

And the sea gave up the dead who were in it,
  Death and Hades gave up the dead who were in
them,
and they were judged, each one of them,
 according to what they had done.
Then Death and Hades were thrown into the lake
of fire.
  This is the second death, the lake of fire.
And if anyone's name was not found written in the
book of life,
  he was thrown into the lake of fire.

Revelation 20:13–15

Der Heiland ist gesetzt
In Israel zum Fall und Auferstehen.
Der edle Stein ist sonder Schuld,
Wenn sich die böse Welt so hart an ihm verletzt,
Ja, über ihn zur Höllen fällt,
Weil sie boshaftig an ihn rennet
Und Gottes Huld und Gnade nicht erkennet!
Doch selig ist
Ein auserwählter Christ,

Der seinen Glaubensgrund auf diesen Eckstein leget,
Weil er dadurch Heil und Erlösung findet.

The Savior is destined
in Israel for destruction and resurrection
[Luke 2:34].
The noble stone has no flaw;
even if the evil world
injures itself so sorely upon it
[Isa. 8:14; 1 Pet. 2:8],
indeed, hurtles over it to hell,
this is because it wickedly runs at it
and God's grace
and mercy will not recognize!
Yet blessed is
a chosen Christian,
who grounds his faith upon this cornerstone
[1 Pet. 5:1–8],
since through this he will find salvation and
redemption.[1]

Tritt auf die Glaubensbahn
[*Step upon the Path of Faith*]
Bach cantata BWV 152
Salomon Franck (1715)

11.1   The Eternal Destiny of the Wicked
11.1.1   The Last Judgment

The New Testament refers to the judgment seat of God (Rom. 14:10), which appears to be the same as the judgment seat of Christ (2 Cor. 5:10). Both expressions were used by the Apostle Paul. Jesus himself told us that

---

1.   An interesting combination of various meanings of Christ the "stone," evoked by Simeon's remark about Jesus being appointed to bring about a "fall" (Luke 2:34).

the Father judges no one, but has given all judgment to the Son, that all may honor the Son, just as they honor the Father. . . . And he [i.e., the Father] has given him [i.e., the Son] authority to execute judgment, because he is the Son of Man. Do not marvel at this, for an hour is coming when all who are in the tombs will hear his voice and come out, those who have done good to the resurrection of life, and those who have done evil to the resurrection of judgment (John 5:22–23, 27–29).

First, there is the resurrection of a group of the dead, then there is a trial of this group before the judgment seat. That is, these sessions never involve disembodied people, but only people with resurrection bodies (see below).

In Acts 17:31, the Apostle Paul said that God "has fixed a day on which he will judge the world in righteousness by a man whom he has appointed; and of this he has given assurance to all by raising him from the dead." Here, the emphasis is on judgment because he was speaking to unbelieving Gentiles. In a similar speech by the Apostle Peter (3:19–21), though, the emphasis is on the "times of refreshing" and the "time for restoring all the things," because he was speaking to Israel, the people of God, even though they had betrayed the Son of God. Indeed, the Parousia will mean eternal judgment for some, and eternal salvation for others. Both of these aspects are elaborated in the book of Revelation, for instance, in chapter 14. In verses 1–5 we read about the redeemed, who are as-sociated with, and followers of, the Lamb. But in verses 14–20, we find the Parousia in described in terms of its judgment character. We hear of the "harvest of the earth," which entails the gathering of the good element (the wheat), but also the burning of the chaff and the stubble.[2] After this, we hear of "treading the winepress"

---

2. Cf. Mal. 4:1; Isa. 17:4–6; 18:5; Jer. 51:33; Hos. 6:11; Joel 3:13; Matt. 13:30–43; Mark 4:29. Cf. as a contrast the "harvest" being gathered in the *present time* through the preaching of the gospel (Matt. 9:37–38 par.; John 4:35–36).

(Rev. 14:18–20), which always seems to refer to complete destruction.[3]

Traditionally, the church has spoken of "the Last Judgment" in connection with the Parousia. For instance, the Apostles' Creed says, "Jesus Christ, [...] who [...] is seated at the right hand of God the Father, the Almighty One, from where he will come to judge the living and the dead" (Lat. *Iesum Christum . . . qui . . . sedet ad dexteram Dei Patris omnipotentis, inde venturus est iudicare vivos et mortuos*). Many understand the text to be saying that, at his Parousia, Christ will judge both the living and the dead at the same time. However, the New Testament never says such a thing (and, strictly speaking, the Apostles' Creed and the Nicene Creed do not either). It only says that Christ, in a general sense, is "appointed by God to be judge of the living and the dead" (Acts 10:42), and "Christ died and lived again, that he might be Lord both of the dead and of the living" (Rom. 14:9), and ". . . Christ Jesus, who is to judge the living and the dead" (2 Tim. 4:1), and people "will give account to him who is ready to judge the living and the dead" (1 Pet. 4:5).

Jesus will judge all people who ever lived. But this does not necessarily mean that everyone will be judged *at the same time*, namely, immediately after the Parousia. First, Matthew 25:31–46 only speaks of the nations that will be alive at the moment of the Parousia; the dead are not mentioned. Second, from the millennialist point of view—which I am not discussing here, but am mentioning only in passing—deceased believers rise at the Parousia, but the wicked who are in the graves will rise no sooner than a thousand years *after* the Parousia (Rev. 20:4–6, 11–15). In between is the thousand-year Messianic kingdom (see §11.3 on the first and the second resurrection in Rev. 20:4–6). Let us now look at this matter somewhat more closely.

---

3. Isa. 24:13; 63:2–3; Jer. 25:30; Lam. 1:15; Joel 3:13; Rev. 19:15.

11.1.2 Traditional Views

The traditional view identifies only one Last Judgment, that is, the judgment of all people who have ever lived, in one single session. This doctrine yielded a frightening prospect for many people, especially during the Middle Ages. Numerous painters have sought to depict its horrors, such as Michelangelo Buonarroti in the Sistine Chapel (Vatican City), Giorgio Vasari in the Duomo (cathedral) of Florence, Fra Angelico (now in the San Marco museum, Florence), and especially Hieronymus Bosch in various horrific paintings, for example the triptych *The Last Judgment* in Bruges (Belgium), ascribed to him or to his school.

The horrors of the Last Judgment were intensified by the Latin text of the Requiem mass, and it was always a gratifying task for composers to set the text to music as dramatically as possible.[4] This was true especially of the *Dies Irae* ("Day of Wrath"), a poem possibly written by Thomas of Celano (thirteenth century), friend and biographer of Francis of Assisi. The poem says, among other things:

The day of wrath, that day

will dissolve the world in ashes [2 Pet. 3:12], . . .
When therefore the Judge will sit,
whatever lies hidden will appear:
nothing will remain unpunished [Luke 8:17; 12:2].
What then will I, poor wretch [that I am], say?
Which patron will I entreat,
when [even] the just may [only] hardly be sure [cf. 1 Pet. 4:18]?[5]

The harsh language reminds us of Zephaniah 1:14–16:

The great day of the LORD is near, near and hastening fast; the sound

---

4.   Great examples are the Requiems by Wolfgang Amadeus Mozart, Antonin Dvořák, Hector Berlioz (*Grande Messe des Morts*), and Giuseppe Verdi (*Messa da Requiem*).
5.   https://en.wikipedia.org/wiki/Dies_irae.

of the day of the LORD is bitter; the mighty man cries aloud there. A day of wrath is that day, a day of distress and anguish, a day of ruin and devastation, a day of darkness and gloom, a day of clouds and thick darkness, a day of trumpet blast and battle cry against the fortified cities and against the lofty battlements.

After the Middle Ages, during the Reformation, the shrill atmosphere finally changed. Martin Luther said in a sermon (1533): "The 'papists' succeeded in making us almost scared to death of Christ, and viewed him only as Judge. It was concealed that he is the Redeemer. . . . Christ comes for the wicked as Judge. However, be not afraid, but raise your heads because your redemption is drawing near [Luke 21:28]."[6] In other words, learn to look forward to his coming, because for *you* he will come not as the cruel Judge, but as the Redeemer.

The righteous have nothing to fear at the judgment seat of Christ; on the contrary, they may even look forward to it, for they will finally know their own hearts as the Lord has known them,[7] and they will fully realize how many sins have been forgiven them (cf. Luke 7:47). There will be greater rewards for some, and smaller rewards for others,[8] there will be different "crowns" (more literally, "wreaths").[9] Only the wicked should be afraid of the Last Judgment. How often Jesus' words have been forgotten: "Truly, truly, I say to you, whoever hears my word and believes him who sent me has eternal life. He *does not come into judgment*, but has passed from death to life" (John 5:24; cf. 3:18, 36). To be sure, believers *will* appear before the judgment seat of God, or Christ (Rom. 14:10; 2 Cor. 5:10), but not to be *condemned*.

---

6. Quoted in Van Genderen (1998), 85.
7. Cf. 1 Chron. 28:9; 29:17; Ps. 7:9; Jer. 11:20; 17:9–10; 1 Cor. 13:12; Rev. 2:23.
8. 1 Cor. 3:12–15; 4:3–5; 2 Cor. 5:10; Gal. 6:3–8.
9. 1 Cor. 9:25; 2 Tim. 4:8; James 1:12; 1 Pet. 5:4; Rev. 2:10; 3:11; the metaphor refers to the ancient games, such as the Olympic Games.

11.2   The Courtroom Hearings

11.2.1 Not during the Intermediate State

That there is one judgment seat of Christ does not necessarily mean that there will be only one judgment session before this seat. Every city has its own courthouse, but in this one courthouse many different trials occur. The same is true for the judgment seat of Christ. If I understand the Bible correctly, there are at least *four different trials* before this same judgment seat, each with a different character, with different defendants, and occurring at different times.

Please note that there is no such hearing during the intermediate state; there is no biblical basis for the idea that immediately at death, a person appears before the judgment seat of Christ.[10] I do not know of any trial mentioned in the Bible that involves disembodied people. Once again we are dealing with an unpleasant consequence of Interim Theology, a confusion between what happens at death and what happens at the Parousia.

The verse usually quoted here is Hebrews 9:27, "[I]t is appointed for man to die once, and after that comes judgment." But this does *not* say, "*Immediately* after death, a person appears before the judgment seat of Christ." I believe that the Greek phrase translated "after" (*meta de touto*) can be interpreted in one of two ways. First, it may be understood to mean that immediately at death, a person's destiny is fixed once and for all, without a formal trial. This is like the story of Lazarus and Dives, where we do not hear of a trial either. Instead, Lazarus went immediately to the bosom of Abraham, and Dives immediately to Hades. Second, the phrase may be an indefinite "after": at some (possibly considerable) time after physical death—namely, in the resurrection state—every human being will appear before the judgment seat of Christ, and even then they will not all appear at the same time.

---

10. *Contra* Van Doornik et al. (1956), 440.

11.2.2 The First Trial

First, there is the court hearing involving glorified believers at the Parousia: "Why do you pass judgment on your brother? Or you, why do you despise your brother? For we will all stand before the judgment seat of God" (Rom. 14:10; cf. 2 Cor. 5:10); this will apparently occur in *heaven*. There will be *one* group at this first trial: the saints of all ages, from Adam to the saints who are alive on earth at the time of the Parousia. There can also be only *one* outcome: eternal salvation (cf. John 5:24). In other words, the eternal salvation of believers is no longer at stake. How could it be otherwise? They will be standing before the throne in their resurrection bodies, which will be as glorious as that of Christ himself (Phil. 3:20–21). Perhaps we may add that they are standing there clothed in white garments wearing golden crowns on their heads (Rev. 4:4). And the One sitting on the throne is their Lord and Savior, who once gave his blood in order to redeem them.

Thus, the question may arise: Why do they face a judgment at all? The reason is that there will be different rewards, according to the faithfulness of each (see above):

> Each one's work will become manifest, for the Day will disclose it, because it will be revealed by fire, and the fire will test what sort of work each one has done. If the work that anyone has built on the foundation survives, he will receive a reward. If anyone's work is burned up, he will suffer loss, though he himself will be saved, but only as through fire" (1 Cor. 3:13–15).

In the language of Luke 19 (the parable of the ten minas) we state it this way: the Master says to the one, "[Y]ou shall have authority over ten cities," and to the other: "[Y]ou are to be over five cities" (vv. 17, 19). The difference will be based on the faithfulness and devotion of each servant. Apparently, the reference is to the fact that the believers will reign together with Christ during the "thousand years" (Rev. 20:4–6). "If we have died with him, we will

310

also live with him; if we endure [the oppressions and persecutions as he did], we will also reign with him" (2 Tim. 2:11–12).

Recall as well the different "crowns" or "wreaths" mentioned in §11.1.2. There will be the "imperishable wreath" (1 Cor. 9:25, for those who have "run" well), the "crown of righteousness" (2 Tim. 4:8, for those who have lovingly longed for the Parousia), the "crown of life" (James 1:12; Rev. 2:10, for those who have died as martyrs for the Lord), the "crown of glory" (1 Pet. 5:4, for those who have faithfully exercised leadership amid various hardships), and more generally, the "golden crowns" (Rev. 4:4, for *all* believers, if we accept the view, together with many other expositors, that the "twenty-four elders" are representatives of the risen and glorified believers).

11.2.3 The Second Trial

Second, there is the court hearing involving the living nations (Matt. 25:31–46), which apparently will take place on *earth*, immediately after the Parousia, with the Son of Man sitting on his "throne of glory" (v. 31). There are *two* groups here: the "sheep" (the righteous) and the "goats" (the wicked), each with a different destiny. For the righteous, there is the "kingdom" that the Father has prepared for them (v. 34), or "eternal life," which is the blessed life of the kingdom (v. 46). For the wicked, there is the "eternal fire" (v. 41), also called the "eternal punishment" (v. 46). But these are the ultimate judgments; the first issue to be decided is: What people are worthy to enter the Messianic kingdom that God has prepared for them, and that they will enjoy under the blessed rule of the Messiah?

Interestingly, there is only one criterion for being allowed entrance into the Messianic kingdom: a person's attitude toward the people called the "brothers" of the King (v. 40), that is, the "least" of the hungry, the thirsty, the naked, the sick, and the prisoners. As one might put it: the "Lazaruses" of the story in Luke 16:19–31. Here, the gospel has been reduced to its very core; as James 1:27 put it: "Religion that is pure and undefiled before God the Father is this: to visit orphans and widows in their affliction, and to keep oneself unstained from the world." What the righteous did to such people, they did for Christ, even if they never knew him or his gospel.[11] See also James 2:5, "Listen, my beloved brothers, has not God chosen those who are poor in the world to be rich in faith and heirs of the kingdom, which he has promised to those who love him?"

Usually, the picture given in Matthew 25 is precisely the way many Christians imagine that the Last Judgment will be. But remember, *there are no resurrected people at this judgment*, but only the nations that are alive on earth when the King appears. In other words, this is only one out of the four trials that I believe we must distinguish. In addition, for the wicked this cannot be their *final* judgment. If I understand the passage correctly, the "sheep" will enter the kingdom, and the "goats" will die, and will be raised after the Messianic kingdom arrives, in order to undergo the trial described in the next section.

11.2.4 The Third Trial

Third, there is the court hearing involving the fallen angels, also called the angels of Satan (Matt. 25:41; Rev. 12:7, 9), who are clearly identical with the unclean spirits, the demons (cf. Luke 11:18). Satan is the "prince of the power of the air" (Eph. 2:2); this "power" involves the "rulers," the "authorities," the "cosmic powers over this present darkness," the "spiritual forces of evil in the heavenly places" (6:12).

These demonic powers know that there will be a time of judgment for them. Amazingly enough, they knew about that prospect even when Jesus was on earth, and that this time had *not* yet come; therefore, they asked not to be tormented *before* the time set for their judgment (cf. Matt. 8:29). Perhaps they also know that the "eternal fire" has been prepared by God primarily for the "devil and his angels" (25:41).

---

11. For further details on this complicated matter, see Ouweneel (2012), §12.6.

It seems there are demons who are able to move around in relative liberty until the very last moment (cf. Matt. 12:43–45); these are the demons that can take "possession" of people (who thus become "possessed"). And there are other demons who at present are already imprisoned: "God did not spare angels when they sinned, but cast them into *Tartarus* [see §6.1.3] and committed them to chains of gloomy darkness to be kept until the judgment" (2 Pet. 2:4; cf. Jude 1:6). Some had linked this group of angels with the "sons of God," who, some time before Noah's Flood, intermingled with women (Gen. 6:1–4).

The final destiny of all demonic, Satanic powers is the lake of fire (cf. Rev. 20:10). Interestingly, in some way or another, the righteous will be involved in this judgment of the angels if we understand 1 Corinthians 6:3 correctly: "Do you not know that we are to judge angels?" In addition, consider this verse, where Paul tells the believers: "The God of peace will soon crush Satan *under your feet*" (Rom. 16:20).

This idea of believers taking part in the divine judgment is also encountered in Matthew 19:28, where Jesus told his disciples: "Truly, I say to you, in the new world, when the Son of Man will sit on his glorious throne, you who have followed me will also sit on twelve thrones, judging the twelve tribes of Israel" (cf. Luke 22:30).

Notice that the wicked people in the lake of fire are not being tormented by demons, as so many medieval presentations portrayed the event. On the contrary, Satan and his demons themselves will be tortured in hell. Jesus tells us that the "eternal fire" was "prepared for the devil and his angels" in the first place (Matt. 25:41); that is, they will not be the tormentors, but rather the most severely tormented.

11.3   The Fourth Trial

11.3.1   The Resurrection of the Wicked

Fourth, after the "thousand years" there will be the court hearing involving the dead who had no part in the "first resurrection." In-

313

deed, there are two resurrections, the first and the second (Rev. 20:4–6), a "resurrection of life" and a "resurrection of judgment" (John 5:29); there will be a "resurrection of the righteous" and a "resurrection of the unrighteous" (Acts 24:15). In between are the "thousand years."[12]

I am not saying that everything in Revelation is chronological— for apparently it is not—but events described in the last chapters are chronological, as indicated by the repeated phrases "Then I heard" or "Then I saw." The chronological order is this (see further in §12.1.1):

(a) "Then I heard": the marriage supper of the Lamb (19:6-10).

(b) "Then I saw" (2x): the Parousia, where Christ descends from heaven with the glorified saints (19:11–21).

(c) "Then I saw" (2x): the "thousand years," beginning with the first resurrection, that of the righteous (20:1–10).

(d) "Then I saw": after the "thousand years", the second resurrection, that of the wicked (20:11–15).

(e) "Then I saw": the appearance of the new heavens and the new earth (21:1–8).

The resurrection of the wicked, followed by their judgment before the "great white throne," will take place at an unspecified location ("between heaven and earth"?), and the defendants consist of just *one* group: all the wicked, "great and small" (v. 12), who have died from Cain until the last ones who die just before this judgment occurs.

There is only *one* outcome: the lake of fire, though with different degrees of punishment:

[T]hat servant who knew his master's will but did not get ready or act according to his will, will receive a severe beating. But the one who did not know, and did what deserved a beating, will receive a light beating. Everyone to whom much was given, of him much will

---

12. For more details about this, see Ouweneel (2012).

be required, and from him to whom they entrusted much, they will demand the more (Luke 12:47–48).

Throughout human history, no human being can escape physical death (with one exception: believers who are alive at the moment of the Parousia). Similarly, no human being can escape the resurrection of the dead. At the very end of the first creation, the wicked will be the last to rise from their graves. This is what Job seems to say (if his words indeed imply a resurrection[13]): "But a man dies and is laid low; man breathes his last, and where is he? As waters fail from a lake and a river wastes away and dries up, so a man lies down and rises not again; *till the heavens are no more* he will not awake or be roused out of his sleep" (Job 14:10–12). And more specifically with regard to judgment, Robert Mounce wrote, "[N]o one is so important as to be immune from judgment and no one is so unimportant as to make judgment inappropriate."[14] This refers to the "great and small" who will be raised from death.

11.3.2 The Great White Throne

The dead of whom Revelation 20 speaks will receive a resurrection body, which in their case is *not* a "glorious body" (cf. 1 Cor. 15:43; Phil. 3:20–21), but a body that will last eternally, and that is fit for being thrown into the lake of fire (cf. Matt. 10:28). While living on earth, they were already morally "dead" (Eph. 2:1; Col. 2:13), then they underwent physical death, which, in the context of Revelation 20, may be called the "first death," and finally, after their resurrection, they will be thrown into the lake of fire, which is called the "second death" (vv. 6, 14). This means that these people will have been raised, and yet will remain dead forever. If I understand the biblical data correctly, only the wicked will be standing before the "great white throne" (perhaps apart from the fallen angels, mentioned in §11.2.4). Verse 15a leaves open the theoretical possibil-

---

13. Cf. Hartley (1988), 234–35.
14. Mounce (1977), 365.

ity that there might be persons before the throne whose names *are* "found written in the book of life."[15] But I believe the context shows that this will not really be the case.

"[A]nd books were opened" (Rev. 20:12; cf. Dan. 7:10c). Everything these people had done before they died has been registered, and will be brought into the open.[16] Jewish tradition spoke about books in which all the good and bad deeds of humans have been recorded before God.[17] This does not mean, though, that what matters most is whether good deeds or evil deeds weigh more, as many people (including nominal Christians) think. Decisive will be faith in the God of the Scriptures, and since the coming of Christ, faith in Jesus Christ; these are the believers who are registered in the book of life (vv. 12, 15). The evil works written down in "the books" are only the external features of the hearts' refusal to repent and believe (cf. Jer. 17:9–10; Rom. 2:4–6). God is righteous, also toward unbelievers. He demonstrates black-on-white that they have deserved his judgment, that their names are not written in the book of life, and that therefore they must be cast into the "second death." Whoever has not become part of the world of life belongs forever to the world of death. "And the dead were judged by what was written in the books, according to what they had done" (v. 12). That is, the heaviness of their verdict is determined by the seriousness of their misdeeds (cf. 2:23; 22:12; Luke 12:47–48).

Revelation 20:13 tells us where the dead will come from: "And the sea gave up the dead who were in it, Death and Hades gave up the dead who were in them." For us, sea, death, and Hades are not comparable magnitudes. (Physical) death is the *condition* of the body after death, and Hades (not to be confused with hell!) is the *place* where the unbeliever exists between death and resurrection. These are mentioned together in line with 1:18, where we hear that

15. Cf. Exod. 32:32–33; Ps. 69:28; Dan. 12:1; Rev. 3:5; 13:8; 17:8; 21:27.
16. Cf. Eccl. 12:14; Rom. 2:5–8, 16; 14:9; Acts 10:42; 2 Tim. 4:1; Heb. 6:2; 1 Pet. 4:5; Rev. 11:18; 20:12–15.
17. 4 Esdras 6:20; 1 Enoch 47:3; 90:20; 2 Baruch 24:1; Jubilees 30.

316

Jesus has the keys of them. As we have seen, the Greek term *Hades* is related to the Hebrew term *Sheol*, which can also mean "grave" (§4.3). Therefore, perhaps the text is saying that not only the ordinary graves in the soil of the earth, but also the "seafarers' graves," which literally are no graves at all, will have to give back the dead who are in them.[18] In other words, even where the sea, and also for instance fire or the stomachs of wild carnivores, have entirely destroyed the bodies,[19] God will be able to "give life to mortal bodies" (Rom. 8:11), that is, to produce the resurrection bodies, even if nothing is left of the mortal bodies. After all, in graves themselves, after a number of years nothing more is left of the body than the bones. This will be no impediment to God raising the dead.

Revelation 21:4 confirms once more that "[physical] death shall be no more." Henry Alford argued that, just as there is a second and higher life, so too there is a second and deeper death. Just as after this life there is no more death, so after the second death there will no more be life.[20] The "second death" is continued and conscious existence but not "life" in any proper sense. Just like physical death, "second death" is a *condition*, and just like Hades, the lake of fire is a *place*.

11.4 Hell

11.4.1 *Gehenna*

In the Bible, the word "hell" is a confusing term, especially in the older translations. Unfortunately, the KJV uses the word "hell" as the translation of Hebrew *sj'ol* (Sheol), and of Greek *Hades*, *gehenna* and *tartaros*. It is quite unwise and confusing to render three different concepts with one and the same English word. It has strongly furthered Interim theology: "When you die, you go either to heaven,

---

18. For this interpretation we must take "sea" literally, whereas this cannot be done, e.g., in Rev. 13:1.
19. 1 Enoch 61:5 speaks of people who have been devoured by the fishes of the sea.
20. Alford (1884), 735–36.

or to hell." The Vulgate says in Luke 16:22, *Mortuus est autem et dives, et sepultus est in inferno*, "The rich man died too, and was buried in *infernum*," the latter being the common term for "hell," but here it says, "buried in *infernum*," as if *infernum* here is nothing more than Sheol, the grave. The *Nova Vulgata* (the revision of the Vulgate in modern time), says in verses 22–23, however: *[M]ortuus est autem et dives et sepultus est. Et in inferno elevans oculos suos, cum esset in tormentis,* "The rich man died too, and was buried. And lifting up his eyes in *infernum*, as he was in torments, . . ." This is the way it has been understood for centuries: Dives died, and went to "hell." Instead, the translation *infernum* or "hell" should have been reserved for the Greek word *gehenna*.

After the Reformation, Protestant scholars continued to read the text this way. The Westminster Larger Catechism Q&A 86 says that "the souls of the wicked are at their death cast into hell, where they remain in torments and utter darkness, and their bodies kept in their graves, as in their prisons, till the resurrection and judgment of the great day (Luke 16:23–24; Acts 1:25; Jude 6–7)."[21] This is a double mistake. First, the Bible nowhere says that the wicked go immediately to *gehenna* when they die. Second, the catechism answer clearly betrays the ancient Greek scholastic body-soul dualism. The Bible knows nothing of "souls"—as entities independent of the bodies—that are in hell or in Hades (or in paradise, for that matter).

It may sound amazing to many tradition-formed ears, but *at this moment*, no human being is yet in the Father's house, and *at this moment*, no human being is yet in hell. As we have seen, the righteous will go into the Father's house only at the Parousia, that is, *in their resurrection bodies*, and the wicked will go to *gehenna* only after the judgment before the great white throne, that is, *in their resurrection bodies*. At present, the dead are in the intermediate state. Their eternal destiny has already been fixed (cf. Heb. 9:27), the righteous have the paradisal foretaste of eternal bliss, the wicked have the hor-

---

21. *RC*, 4:317.

rendous foretaste of eternal misery. It is all foretaste, anticipation, prelude, overture, both positive and negative: it is looking forward to blessing, or dreading damnation. It is either the limbo of delight, or the limbo of disaster. But it is not yet the real thing. To reach this ultimate reality, every human being must experience resurrection and pass before the judgment seat of Christ.

11.4.2 The Valley of Ben-Hinnom

The lake of fire in Revelation is the same as what especially in the Gospels is called "hell." Remarkably enough, the Greek word for hell, *gehenna*, is a Hebrew loanword, derived from Aramaic *gēhinnam* and Hebrew *gēy Hinnom*. This is an abbreviation of *gēy ben-Hinnom*, which means "valley of Ben-Hinnom," or "valley of the son(s) of Hinnom."[22] Literally, this refers to a narrow, rocky valley lying south of ancient Jerusalem, mentioned in Joshua 15:8, 18; 18:16. In the days of King Solomon, child sacrifices were offered in the valley to the Ammonite idol Molech, although the name of the valley is not mentioned in this case (1 Kings 11:7). These abominations continued under the Judean kings Ahaz and Manasseh, now with mention of the name of the valley; King Josiah put an end to this practice.[23] Through the prophet Jeremiah, the LORD God strongly protested against these misdeeds,[24] and announced that he himself would burn the corpses of the wicked there.[25]

In the Valley of the Son of Hinnom was the location known as Topheth,[26] the actual sacrificial spot, a burning place, where the sacrifices—animals as well as humans—were burned. Afterward, this Valley became a place where, on a huge stake, rubbish and corpses of animals and despised criminals were burned. In Jewish apocalyptic literature, the all-consuming and constantly burning fire

22. See *TDNT* 1:657–58; *DNTT* 2:208–209; Toon (1986).
23. 2 Chron. 28:3; 33:6; cf. 2 Kings 16:3; 21:6; 23:10.
24. Jer. 19:2, 6, 11–14; 32:35.
25. Jer. 7:31–33; cf. Isa. 31:9; 66:24.
26. Isa. 30:33; Jer. 7:31–32; 19:6, 11–14.

in the Valley of Hinnom, that is, *ge-henna*, became the model for the wicked who had to stay there eternally.[27] As such, the notion of *gehenna* was distinct from the literal Valley of Hinnom. In Isaiah 30:33, we find already the figurative meaning of Topheth: this burning place in which the king of Assyria will eventually perish is hell. The "king" in this verse is possibly the last (eschatological) king of Israel: the false leader hinted at in Isaiah 57:9, where some translations have "king," and others have "Molech": "You journeyed to the king [or, to Molech] with oil and multiplied your perfumes; you sent your envoys far off, and sent down even to Sheol."[28] Just as in Revelation 19, where some identify him with the "false prophet"—helper of the Satanic "beast," this wicked person is destined for hell.

Jesus uses the word *Gehenna* several times;[29] some of his statements show that people are not cast into hell at the time of physical death because Jesus speaks of being thrown into hell *with the body* (Matt. 5:29–30; 10:28). This corresponds with Revelation 20, where the dead are thrown into hell *after* their resurrection and trial, that is, *with* their resurrection bodies. If one would ask people why they think some people are cast into hell immediately at their physical death, the answer is the erroneous translation of Luke 16:22–23 (KJV), "[T]he rich man also died, and was buried; and in hell he lifted up his eyes, being in torments." Consider also Psalm 9:17 (KJV), "The wicked shall be turned into hell."[30] The moment we choose the correct translations ("Hades" in Luke 16, and "Sheol" or "grave" in Ps. 9), no biblical evidence exists that the wicked go to "hell" when they die; they go to "hell" only after their resurrection and trial.

---

27. 1 Enoch 27:1–3; 54:1–3; 56:3–4; 90:26–27; 4 Esdras 7:36; 2 Baruch 59:10; 85:13; Sibylline Oracles 1:103; 2:291; see also the Talmud: tract Berachot 28b.
28. See further in Ouweneel (2012), chapter 8.
29. Matt. 5:22, 29–30 par.; 10:28 par.; 23:15, 33.
30. The NKJV, which corrects some but not all the errors in the KJV, has "Hades" in Luke 16:23, but "hell" in Ps. 9:17.

11.4.3 Details

Apart from the Gospels, the word *gehenna* occurs only in James 3:6, "The tongue is . . . among our members . . . set on fire by hell." The idea of a stake, and thus of fire, was one of the strongest associations that remained connected with the notion of "hell." In Matthew 5:22 and 18:9, Jesus speaks of the "hell of fire" (CEB: "fiery hell"), in Matthew 13:42 and 50 of the "fiery furnace," in Mark 9:43 (cf. v. 48; Luke 3:17 par.) of the "unquenchable fire," and in Matthew 18:8 and 25:41 of the "eternal fire." Jude 7 speaks of a "punishment of eternal fire." In Matthew 25, the "eternal fire" (v. 41) is parallel with "eternal punishment" (v. 46).

In summary, notice the following features:

(a) The Bible clearly shows that the wicked dead ones are in Sheol (which usually simply means the grave), and their personalities are in Hades, that is, in the disembodied state, whereas the wicked with their resurrection bodies will be in *Gehenna* ("hell"). There is no one in Hades *with* a body, and there will be no one in hell *without* a body.

(b) In fact, there *is* no word for "hell" in the Hebrew Old Testament. This is because the notion of the resurrection is very rare in the Old Testament; its view of the future rarely goes any further than Sheol, which is usually no more than the grave, with a few hints at a form of conscious existence in Sheol (see §4.3).

(c) Matthew 23:15 tells us that a wicked person is a "son of hell" (NKJV), that is: a person belonging to, and destined for, hell.

(d) Matthew 25:41 calls hell "the eternal fire prepared for the devil and his angels" (cf. 8:29); therefore, only secondarily is hell the eternal destiny of the wicked as well. I repeat, it is a place where the devil and his angels must suffer just as much as the wicked. If humans must suffer at all there at the hands of others, then this will presumably be a suffering more from each other than from devils (cf. already for Hades: Isa. 14:12; Ezek. 32:21; see §4.4.1).

321

11.5 The Lake of Fire
11.5.1 The Fire

Besides *gehenna*, the other important New Testament expression for "hell" is "the lake of fire" (Gk. *hē limnē tou pyros*, Rev. 19:20; 20:14–15; NABRE: "fiery pool"; NMB: "pond of fire"). Its fuller name is "the lake of fire that burns with sulfur" (19:20), or, "the lake that burns with fire and sulfur" (21:8), or more briefly, "the lake of fire and sulfur" (20:10). The combination of fire and sulfur occurs in 9:17–18 ("killed by the fire and smoke and sulfur") and 14:10 ("tormented with fire and sulfur"), as well as several times in the Old Testament.[31] Sulfur evokes the sharp odor of volcanic activity; in volcanic areas, the yellow substance is found in a natural form. In air, it burns easily. A pool of burning sulfur is very hot and reeks terribly.

We hear about the following persons who are thrown into the lake of fire:

(a) The (Roman) "beast" and the "false prophet" (Rev. 19:20), the political and religious leaders of the (Western) world,[32] directly after the Parousia.

(b) Satan at the end of the "thousand years" (20:10); in the meantime, he will be in the "bottomless pit," the *abyssos* (Rev. 20:1, 3) (see §6.1.3).

(c) (Physical) death and Hades, when they will no longer be needed, because all the dead people of all times will have been raised from death (20:14).

(d) All the wicked who have been raised from death (20:15; 21:8).

The fire metaphor also evokes the smoke metaphor. From the "pit of the abyss," "there went up a smoke out of the pit, as the smoke of a great furnace; and the sun and the air were darkened by

---

31. Gen. 19:24 (cf. Luke 17:29); Deut. 29:23; Ps. 11:6; Isa. 30:33; 34:9; Ezek. 38:22.
32. See Ouweneel (2012), chapters 6, 8, and 12.

reason of the smoke of the pit" (9:2 ASV), and the smoke is mentioned in addition to the fire and sulfur (vv. 17–18). Of the wicked followers of "the beast" we read:

> If anyone worships the beast and its image and receives a mark on his forehead or on his hand, he also will drink the wine of God's wrath, poured full strength into the cup of his anger, and he will be tormented with fire and sulfur in the presence of the holy angels and in the presence of the Lamb. And the smoke of their torment goes up forever and ever, and they have no rest, day or night, these worshipers of the beast and its image, and whoever receives the mark of its name (14:9–11).

Regarding the condemned "great prostitute," too, we hear: "The smoke from her goes up forever and ever" (19:3).

In the descriptions of hell, the fire metaphor is always dominant. The wicked in Hades are described as being "in anguish in this flame" (Luke 16:24), and being in a "place of torment" (v. 28). Earlier attention was given to expressions like the "hell of fire," the "lake of fire," and the "eternal fire." Hebrews 10:27 speaks of "a fearful expectation of judgment, and a fury of fire that will consume the adversaries."[33]

11.5.2 Metaphorical but Real

Fire is a real metaphor for severe torment, but it cannot be taken literally. Fire is the rapid oxidation of certain materials; it is a chemical process of combustion. However, the same material—read: the resurrected bodies of the wicked—cannot be eternally oxidated, eternally transformed by a chemical process. Also consider the fact that the devil and his companions will also be in hell, but they never had bodies. They will be in hell as bodiless spirits—yet they will undergo the same fiery torments.

Moreover, Hades and hell are also described as the "outer dark-

---

33. Also see Matt. 3:10, 12 par.; 7:19; 13:40; John 15:6; 1 Cor. 3:13–15; 2 Thess. 1:8; Heb. 12:29; James 5:3; 2 Pet. 3:7.

ness,"[34] and fire and darkness do not go together.[35] Wisdom 17:21 (CEB) says that "an oppressive night lay all around them [i.e., the wicked], and around them alone. It was a sign of the darkness that was going to receive them." Similarly, Job says of Sheol: ". . . I go— and I shall not return—to the land of darkness and deep shadow, the land of gloom like thick darkness, like deep shadow without any order, where light is as thick darkness."

Saying that fire and darkness are metaphors does not mean that they are "only" metaphors, as if by saying this, one could easily dismiss them. As S. Greijdanus put it, fire is an "earthly metaphor, but one that refers to a horrible reality."[36] It is a reality of something beyond our earthly experience, one that can be described only in terms that we are familiar with from our empirical world, but terms that certainly give us an impression of hell's torments.

In 1 Enoch 107, the punishment of the wicked will be aggravat- ed by the fact that they will be able to see the bliss of the righteous from a distance. This reminds us of Jesus' own words: "In that place [i.e., hell] there will be weeping and gnashing of teeth, when you see Abraham and Isaac and Jacob and all the prophets in the kingdom of God but you yourselves cast out" (Luke 13:28). And about Dives: ". . . in Hades, being in torment, he lifted up his eyes and saw Abraham far off and Lazarus at his side" (16:23). Perhaps the picture of being in "outer darkness" means that the wicked are outside the "house," in the dark and in the cold outer world, in the terrifying perils of the night, whereas they can look through the "windows" into the "house," seeing the righteous at dinner, in

---

34. Matt. 8:12; 22:13; 25:30; cf. 2 Pet. 2:2; Jude 1:6, 14; Geldenhuys (1983), 430.

35. *Contra* Hendriksen (1959), 202–203; a person may receive burns (e.g., by touching hot metal), but fire and darkness are mutually exclusive: where there is fire, there is no darkness—and vice versa. As recently as the nineteenth century, fire was the most important source of light (candle, oil lamp, gas lamp).

36. Greijdanus (1941), 86; cf. Schilder (1932), 40; Geldenhuys (1983), 430.

glowing light, in peace and harmony, in bliss and blessing.[37] This is what Lazarus saw during his short life, lying at the gate of Dives's house, desiring "to be fed with what fell from the rich man's table "(Luke 16:21). And this is what Dives will see forever and ever, lying outside the house of the Father, "desiring to be fed with what will fall from the table of the blessed," so to speak.

Yet, as C. S. Lewis has written, this does not mean that the damned would like to go over to the house, to the light and the delight. As Lewis put it, "I willingly believe that the damned are, in one sense, successful, rebels to the end; that the doors of hell are locked on the inside."[38] In other words, for the wicked, hell will be horrible—but, in a sense, for them heaven would be even more horrible. The worst thing that could happen to the wicked is to be in a place where everyone and everything is worshiping God, where all things are for the honor and glory of God. This is what Lewis meant when he said that the wicked are "successful, rebels to the end." As Lewis also wrote (in my words): If the wicked keep saying all their lives, "My will be done," then God will say to them at the end: "Your will be done. I will take you to a place where I will never bother you again, for all eternity. You will discover how horrible that is, but you will admit that you yourself chose this. I created you with the capacity to make your own choices, and because you are my creature, I respect, and even love, you so much that I will forever respect your choice."

11.6 The Torments of Hell

11.6.1 Remorse

Just as we saw in Luke 16:27–30 with regard to Hades, those tormented in hell have remorse over what has befallen them. Thus, we hear about "weeping and gnashing of teach" in hell.[39] These traits of the hellish sorrows are encountered in the Jewish-Apocalyptic

---

37. France (2007), 319.
38. See Lewis (2003), 183.
39. Matt. 8:12; 13:42, 50; 22:13; 24:51; 25:30; Luke 13:28.

literature as well.[40] The articles in the expression "*the* weeping and *the* gnashing of teach" (correctly included in the ASV) strengthen the fierceness of the scene.[41] Alan High suggested that the weeping points to grief, and the gnashing of teeth to despair;[42] personally, I would also think of rage and remorse.

Please note, "remorse" does not necessarily mean that, if they could, the wicked would love to go to heaven after all; see the close of the previous section. A person can be grieved by the situation they are in, and still believe that in every other situation they would be worse off. For the wicked, darkness is bad, but the true light would be worse; hatred is bad, but true love would be worse; death is bad, but true life would be worse.

It seems that Mark 9:47–48 also points to this remorse: ". . . hell, 'where their worm does not die and the fire is not quenched.'"[43] As the inverted commas in the ESV indicate, this is a quotation, namely, from Isaiah 66:24, "[T]hey shall go out and look on the dead bodies of the men who have rebelled against me. For their worm shall not die, their fire shall not be quenched, and they shall be an abhorrence to all flesh." This verse reminds us also of the apocryphal book Sirach 7:17 (CEB): "[F]ire and worms are the punishment of the ungodly"; and the apocryphal book Judith 16:17, "How terrible it will be for those nations who rise up against my people. The Lord Almighty will take vengeance upon them on the Judgment Day. He will send fire and worms into their flesh, and they will weep forever with the pain." However, these seem to be references to Sheol, rather than to hell (insofar as the authors had already learned to distinguish between the two), where the worms are continually gnawing at the bodies. If we transfer the notion to hell, where the wicked will be *with* their resurrection bodies, this seems instead to

---

40. 4 Esdras 7:93; 1 Enoch 108:3, 5; 2 Enoch 40:12; Ps. Solomon 14:9 (most of these writings originated after Christ, though).
41. Carson (1984), 203.
42. McNeile (1915), *ad loc.*, on Matt. 8:12.
43. So Van Leeuwen (1928), 120.

point to the torments of the damned.

11.6.2 Apart from the Lord

Part of the hellish horrors is also "suffering the punishment of eternal destruction, *away from* the presence of the Lord and from the glory of his might" (2 Thess. 1:9; cf. Phillips, "eternal exclusion"; MSG: "eternal exile").[44] The wicked will hear these awesome words: "Depart *from me*" (Matt. 7:23; 25:41; Luke 13:27). Humans, as God's image-bearers, have been created for relationship and fellowship with God. The breath of even the most wicked person on earth is in God's hand (Dan. 5:23), and God is never far away from them (Ps. 139:5–12). The essence of hell is not just physical pain but the *spiritual* grief of having been severed from one's roots: from God. At the end of §11.5, I argued—with C. S. Lewis—that this is what the wicked in fact wanted all their lives, and will want in eternity. But it seems to me that it is equally true that they will *suffer* on account of this separation, because it is, and will be, against their creational nature. This is the dilemma: the choice between suffering in separation from God and the even greater "suffering"—as the wicked would experience it—of being continually in the presence of God, and thus for the glory of God.

The "outer darkness" is the place of the absolute absence of him who is light (1 John 1:5), and "dwells in unapproachable light" (1 Tim. 6:16)—unapproachable (inaccessible) only for those who persist in their "godlessness," that is, in their living voluntarily without God. And just as horrific as this everlasting separation from God will be their eternal existence with Satan and his angels, as well as with all the other wicked ones, that is, in a place of everlasting hatred, everlasting enmity, everlasting anger, everlasting pride, everlasting strife, everlasting jealousy, everlasting dissension (cf. Isa. 14:9–11; Ezek. 32:18–21). Living apart from God means eternal

---

44. Hendriksen (1959), 201. He undermines his own argument by claiming that God will be in hell too (202).

darkness; living with the devil means eternal fire.[45]

11.6.3 Summary

Gathering all of this together, we see that the Bible tells us very little about the sorrows of the wicked in the lake of fire. Much of the aversion that people have toward hell seems to be based more on the horrendous stories invented about hell than upon the biblical data. One could mention the *Divine Comedy* by Dante Alighieri (d. 1321), the imaginative paintings by Hieronymus Bosch (around 1500), and the novel *A Portrait of the Artist as a Young Man* by James Joyce (1914/1915).[46] And what have preachers done? Think of the famous (or infamous) sermon (1741) delivered by Jonathan Edwards, *Sinners in the Hands of an Angry God*.[47] Nothing of all these horrible stories is found in the Bible. It is especially the picture of demons tormenting people in hell that is totally unbiblical; as we have seen, Satan and his demons themselves belong to the ranks of those who are punished in hell (Matt. 25:41; Rev. 20:10).

Nikolai A. Berdyaev complained (and understandably so) that the idea of hell has been turned into an instrument of religious and moral terrorism, and he argued that because this doctrine worked on people's fear, it kept them in the church; today, however, exciting people's disgust, it rather estranges them from the church.[48] G. C. Berkouwer wrote:

> It is not difficult to understand why the word "hell" has come to be associated only with cruelty and hatred if it is proclaimed without regard for the preaching of the only way out. . . . Is it so surprising then that most people hear in the word "hell" only the sounds of cruelty and hatred, a weapon maintained by "the church" to keep "the world" in line?[49]

---

45. *Ibid.*, 162.
46. Joyce (1994).
47. See www.ccel.org/ccel/edwards/sermons.sinners.html.
48. Berdyaev (1960), 278.
49. Berkouwer (1972), 416, 418.

This is all the more strange, Berkouwer continued, because God's judgment actually does not begin with "the world" (the wicked), but with Christians themselves, already in the present (1 Pet. 4:17).

The essence of the Father's house is not a superficial cafeteria of blessings, joys, and delights, as if we are speaking of an amusement park. Rather, we are speaking of living eternally with the Triune God. Conversely, the essence of hell is not a primitive cafeteria of torments and horrors, as in a medieval house of torture. Rather, it is living eternally apart from the Triune God, that is, being cut off from a person's existential roots. We have seen that places themselves never possess any inherent glory or holiness; they are glorious and holy only if, and when, God is in them. Similarly, places themselves have no profound and lasting horror; they are horrendous only if, and when, God is not in them.

This is the essence of heaven: it is filled with the glory of God, eternally appealing to the human heart and to all the human senses. This is the essence of hell: it is "filled" with the absence of God, so to speak. If a person is bereft of what he or she needs first and foremost—air—he or she will suffocate. If a person is bereft of what underlies and pervades his or her deepest being—God—it will be like an everlasting process of suffocation.

The subject of hell is a complicated doctrinal and theological one. But more than ever it has also become an existential subject, which touches people in a deeply emotional way. No wonder that many have proposed some form of universalism, the doctrine that all people will ultimately be saved. I have extensively discussed this view elsewhere.[50]

Hell has also become a problem for preachers: if there is a hell, where the wicked will be living eternally, how do preachers preach about it? In a threatening way? Today, this has a rather counterproductive effect. In a lenient way, toning down hell or weakening its

---

50. Ouweneel (2009a), §12.2.1; (2012), §14.4.

meaning? That would mean weakening the biblical message. Many preachers solve the problem today by not preaching about it at all. This is understandable, but deeply mistaken. The reality of hell is just as essential to the Christian message as the reality of heaven.

12

EVERLASTING JOY

[W]e impart a secret and hidden wisdom of God,
which God decreed before the ages for our glory.
None of the rulers of this age understood this,
for if they had,
they would not have crucified the Lord of glory.
But, as it is written,
"What no eye has seen, nor ear heard,
nor the heart of man imagined,
what God has prepared for those who love him"—
these things God has revealed to us through the
Spirit.
For the Spirit searches everything, even the depths
of God.

1 Corinthians 2:7–10

Christenkinder, freuet euch!
Wütet schon das Höllenreich,
Will euch Satans Grimm erschrecken:
Jesus, der erretten kann,
Nimmt sich seiner Küchlein an
Und will sie mit Flügeln decken.

. . . Freude, Freude über Freude!
Christus wehret allem Leide.
Wonne, Wonne über Wonne!
Er ist die Genadensonne.

Christian children, rejoice!
Though the kingdom of Hell rages,
and Satan's fury would terrify you:
Jesus, who can save,
takes to Himself His little chicks
and will cover them with His wings.

. . . Joy, joy beyond joy!
Christ wards off all sorrow.
Rapture, rapture beyond rapture!
He is the sun of grace.[1]

Dazu ist erschienen der Sohn Gottes
[*For This the Son of God Appeared*]
Bach cantata BWV 40
Unknown poet

12.1 The Eternal State of the Righteous
12.1.1 Disembodied, Yet Reigning?

To be sure, the Bible does not tell us very much either about the
condition and the activities of the wicked in eternity (see the previous chapter), or about the condition and the activities of the
righteous in eternity. However, what it does say certainly gives us a
definite picture, which will have to satisfy us for the moment. One
reason why the Bible does not tell us more about the eternal state
(Lat. *status aeternus*) of the righteous may be that it is simply too

---

1. Hell and Satan are raging against believers, but Jesus takes them under his
   wings, and will lead them to everlasting joy and delight.

complicated to explain. We do not yet have the eyes that can see what we will see then, the ears that can hear what we will hear then, the nose that can smell what we will smell then, the tongue that can taste what we will taste then, or the imagination to picture it. As the Apostle Paul said, in reference to the Old Testament: "What no eye has seen, nor ear heard, nor the heart of man imagined, what God has prepared for those who love him" (1 Cor. 2:9).

Yet I will endeavor to describe no fewer than twelve different aspects of the eternal state of the blessed. The first seven will be discussed in §12.2. These have a more static nature, describing the condition in which the righteous will dwell in eternity. The last five will be discussed in §12.3; these have a more dynamic nature, describing five specific activities of the believers in eternity.

I will describe the first seven aspects in the form of verbs. William Hendriksen mentioned similar verbs, but astonishingly, he applied all of them to the intermediate state.[2] This is how strong Interim Theology (both Roman Catholic and Protestant) has been, even in the twentieth century. For instance, Hendriksen assumed—and many theologians followed suit and still do—that deceased believers already reign with Christ today, which in my view is not the case at all. Only resurrected saints, in their glorious bodies, will reign with Christ:

> I saw the souls of those who had been beheaded for the testimony of Jesus and for the word of God, and those who had not worshiped the beast or its image and had not received its mark on their foreheads or their hands. *They came to life and reigned with Christ for a thousand years.* The rest of the dead did not come to life until the thousand years were ended. This is the *first resurrection.* Blessed and holy is the one who shares in the *first resurrection!* Over such the second death has no power, but they will be priests of God and of Christ, and *they will reign with him for a thousand years* (Rev. 20:1–4; italics added).

---

2. Hendriksen (1959), 59–60.

12.1.2 An Inescapable Order

Notice the chronological order within the passage just quoted:

(a) The martyrs (as well as all other believers, we may add) are raised from the dead; this is the "first resurrection," namely, that of the righteous, which will occur at the Parousia.

(b) After this, the risen saints reign with Christ during the "thousand years."

(c) After this, there will be the "second resurrection," namely, that of the wicked.

One can escape the power of this passage only on the basis of supersessionism and amillennialism. This is to say: the passage can be argued away only by arguing away the "first resurrection," for instance, by spiritualizing it, as so many expositors have done. Henry Alford, at the time Dean of Canterbury, emphasized that we would be surrendering the principles of exegesis were we to understand by the first and the (implied) second resurrection two completely different things, like a spiritual resurrection and a physical resurrection: "If, in a passage where *two resurrections* are mentioned . . . the first resurrection may be understood to mean *spiritual* rising with Christ, while the second means *literal* rising from the grave;—then there is an end to all significance in language, and Scripture is wiped out as a definitive testimony to anything."[3] Robert Mounce, who quoted this passage, insisted: "If 'they lived' [or, 'came to life'] in verse 4 means a spiritual resurrection to new life in Christ, then we are faced with the problem of discovering within the context some persuasive reason to interpret the same verb [i.e., 'to come to life'] differently within one concise unit. No such reason can be found."[4]

Let me add one more argument. The so-called spiritual resurrection occurs separately for every individual believer (cf. Eph. 2:6; Col. 2:13), whereas the second resurrection will occur simultane-

---

3. Alford (1884), 4, 732).
4. Mounce (1977), 356.

ously. How, then, can the text tell us that there are "a thousand [literal or figurative] years" between the two resurrections, since in this interpretation the "first resurrection" is an event spanning at least two thousand years by now? The claim, then, is that unlike the "second resurrection," the "first resurrection" is not a single event, but individualized for each person. An awkward interpretation like this can be maintained only by supersessionism and amillennialism—which is the commitment of many traditional Protestants to this day (though it is also true that since the twentieth century, more Christians than ever before have turned away from this view).

In my view, Revelation 20:4–6 is one of those passages which are most useful for exposing a mistaken theological paradigm. It is far simpler and far more obvious to explain the passage as it comes to us, at face value. This does not always work, to be sure, but here it works excellently. There are two resurrections in which people "come to life," the first and the second. Both are momentaneous resurrections of physically dead people, namely, the "resurrection unto life" and the "resurrection unto judgment," respectively (John 5:29); the "resurrection of the righteous" and the "resurrection of the unrighteous [the wicked]," respectively (Acts 24:15). This was the view of Apologists like Justin Martyr and Irenaeus,[5] that is, before "The Great Shift" (see §1.2.2). The famous theological representative of "The Great Shift," Augustine, was the first to argue that the first resurrection referred to the regeneration of the soul, whereas the second resurrection was the physical resurrection of both the just and the unjust.[6]

Understanding this process will greatly help us *not* to apply the blessings of the resurrection state to the intermediate state, which is a central issue in this entire book. In other words—and as we near the end of this book it must finally be said—for any supersessionist and amillennialist, it will always remain very difficult to

---

5. See Johnson (1981), 584.
6. *De Civitate Dei* 20.9–10.

surrender Interim Theology because all these topics are closely in-
tertwined. They are part of one and the same theological (specifically Augustinian) paradigm, adhered to by both Roman Catholic
and traditional Protestant theologians, but nevertheless mistaken.
We must go back *before* "The Great Shift" in order to find church
fathers who, in my view, had clearer eschatological views (see the
following section).

12.1.3 Again, the Intermediate State and the Resurrection State

The point of the last chapter in this book is to mention twelve aspects of the believer's everlasting state, and to emphasize the fact
that, indeed, *all of these aspects have been erroneously applied to the intermediate state*. Of course, there are a few similarities between the two,
such as "dwelling" (perhaps 2 Cor. 5:6–8; cf. §5.4) and "resting"
(Rev. 14:13). But the differences between the intermediate state and
the resurrection state far outnumber the similarities. The reason is
simple (as I have already argued several times): during the intermediate state, believers are disembodied, whereas the eternal state
requires their resurrection from death, and their being with Christ
in their glorified bodies.

Recall what was said about "The Great Shift" in the previous
section, and in the early chapters of this book. Since the fourth century of the Christian church, Christian hopes shifted away from the
coming Parousia to what was thought to happen at the believer's
physical death. Elsewhere I have argued what I, along with many
others, see as a main cause of this turn.[7] During the Roman persecutions, from the middle of the first century to the beginning of
the fourth, believers eagerly looked forward to the Parousia and the
Messianic kingdom, out of love for Christ but also to be freed from
their miseries. They were clear about the two resurrections.

However, with the conversion of Emperor Constantine the

---

7. Ouweneel (2012; 2019).

Great (313), and the elevation of Christianity as the state religion of the Roman Empire (380), things changed drastically. Christians felt that now *the Messianic kingdom had already arrived!* The emperor of Rome, and later also the pope of Rome, were thought to be the representatives of Christ's Messianic rule on earth, the church was the "New Israel," and Rome was the capital of the kingdom of Christ. This is what we have called supersessionism, always firmly connected with amillennialism.

Orthodox Christians continued believing in the Parousia during the early Middle Ages, as the Apostles' Creed and the Nicene Creed prescribed. However, the urgency of the Parousia had disappeared. This was because the Messianic peace was identified with the famous *pax Romana* ("Roman peace") and believers assumed that the righteousness of the kingdom had already arrived. In the minds of Christians, the Parousia was shifted to the "end of times," which by definition was very far away. Any remaining Christian *hope* became focused increasingly on the Christian's death, because *this* was now the great change that Christians were looking for. A person's death was inevitable, and, relatively speaking, near. This is why all the characteristics of the Christian's *glorified* state were now transferred to the *intermediate* state.

This "Great Shift" was one of the most drastic—and erroneous—shifts in the entire history of theology and of the Christian church, in a sense far more dramatic than the Reformation. This was true especially for that large part of the Reformation that actually remained very close to the Roman Catholic tradition (except on the points of popery, Mariology, justification by faith, and some other points). Protestant scholasticism was the direct successor to Roman Catholic scholasticism, and soon overtook Protestant theological faculties.

Indeed, these great hermeneutical errors were not corrected by the Reformers at all; they were too busy with other things, especially with the doctrine of salvation. On the point of eschatology, they

337

hardly deviated from the Roman Catholic (that is especially, Augustinian) views.[8] Both Luther and Calvin were thorough Augustinians. As a consequence, hundreds of traditional Protestant theologians simply preached the new eschatology that had been developed in and after the fourth century, and of which Augustine had become the most eminent spokesman, as is clearly shown in his work entitled *The City of God* (Lat. *De Civitate Dei*).[9]

As we turn now to consider the twelve aspects mentioned above, let the reader constantly remember that for a long time now, *these characteristics have been applied to believers in the intermediate state, whereas in reality they belong to the resurrection state or the eternal state.*

12.2 Seven Verbs

12.2.1 Dwelling

We have seen why it is mistaken to apply John 14:1–3, the promise concerning the house of the Father, to the intermediate state (§6.4). We have seen repeatedly that it is vitally important for Interim Theology to apply these verses (also) to the intermediate state, despite the force of the phrase in verse 3, "I come again and take you (to myself)" (Gk. *palin erchomai kai paralēmpsomai*). Until the Parousia occurs, no human being is in the Father's house, except the glorified Jesus himself.

In this house, there are many "rooms," where glorified believers will find their eternal abode, or, as Luke 16:9 puts it, their "eternal dwellings." Jesus will come in person to fetch them from this earth all at once.[10] The house of the Father is not designed for disembodied saints, but only for glorified saints. It will be their eternal home. Whatever aspects remain to be mentioned, this comes first: they will dwell where the Father and the Son have dwelt from eternity.

---

8. The Mennonites did much better with regard to this matter, a point that I am unable to develop here any further.
9. Augustine (n.d.-1).
10. In addition to John 14:2–3, see 1 Thess. 4:13–17; also cf. 1 Cor. 15:51–55; Phil. 3:20–21.

This is the very thing that Jesus requested: "Father, I desire that they also, whom you have given me, may be *with me* where I am, to see *my glory* that you have given me because you loved me before the foundation of the world" (John 17:24). This also indicates that the emphasis is not on *where* the glorified saints will live, but *with whom*. This is a central message in this book, as indicated already in its title: we will be forever *with the Lord*.

To a certain extent, being "with the Lord" is true for the intermediate state, too, of course, as we have seen. Disembodied believers are "with Jesus" (Luke 23:42–43), they are "with the Lord" (2 Cor. 5:8; cf. 1 Thess. 4:17), they are "with Christ" (Phil. 1:23). But here is where the similarity stops. We are not allowed to transfer all that is said about the Father's house to the intermediate state. On the contrary. We can scarcely apply the term "dwelling" to the intermediate state because believers who have died exist in a temporary (disembodied) condition, which is *not* their "home," even less their "eternal home." They are only in the vestibule, in the waiting room, so to speak; they have not yet reached their ultimate abode, which they *cannot* reach without their glorified resurrection bodies.

In the Father's house they will not be merely lodging, but they will really be *dwelling*, because the house of the Father will forever be the house of his children as well (cf. the beautiful verse of 1 John 3:1, "See what kind of love the Father has given to us, that we should be called children of God; and so we are"). They will be "at home" there, just as children born into a family are "at home" in the house of their parents. Because God is their Father, heaven will be forever *their own* dwelling place. In our society, young adults leave their parents' home at a given moment. Spiritually speaking, we will never be as mature as when we are with the Lord—yet, seen from another perspective, we will be like children, forever living with their Father.

12.2.2 Inheriting

Believers are "heirs of God and fellow heirs with Christ" (Rom.

8:17; cf. Eph. 1:9, 14; Rev. 21:7). Inheriting the world entails the coming of the Messianic kingdom, and thus the Parousia and the final resurrection. But notice 1 Peter 1:4, where the Apostle speaks of "an inheritance that is imperishable, undefiled, and unfading, kept in heaven for you." One can understand how clearly this verse has been misunderstood by the Interim Theology of "The Great Shift," as if "heaven" *itself* is this inheritance. Barnes' Notes on the Bible say on this verse: "[H]eaven is spoken of as their inheritance."[11] Many other expositors have spoken similarly. But by what logic? Can they not see the difference between an inheritance "kept in heaven" and an inheritance that *is* heaven (which, incidentally, is an inheritance found nowhere in the Bible)? If I were to say that I have kept a reward for you in my safe—does this mean that my safe *is* the reward?

In connection with the term "inheritance" in 1 Peter 1:4, the Annotations to the Dutch States Translation assert, "This the Apostle says, because many Jews looked for an earthly kingdom under the Messiah."[12] This is an astonishing remark because *this is what all the Old Testament prophets expected as well*, and, as far as we can assess, so did the church fathers before "The Great Shift." One day, he who is the Anointed King of Israel will be king over all the nations.[13] When the apostles ask the risen Jesus: "Lord, will you at this time restore the kingdom to Israel?" (Acts 1:6), he does not reject the question as being mistaken or illegitimate at all,[14] as many expositors have suggested. The only thing he does is tell the apostles that they are not allowed to know *when* this is going to happen. So in fact Jesus is saying: The kingdom *will* indeed be restored to Israel, as

---

11. https://biblehub.com/commentaries/1_peter/1-4.htm.
12. Haak (1918), *ad loc.*
13. Ps. 2; Isa. 9:6–7; 32:1–8; Dan. 7:13–14, 18, 22; Zech. 14; and many other passages.
14. Cf. Jamieson-Fausset-Brown: ". . . they are neither rebuked nor contradicted on this point" (https://www.biblehub.com/commentaries/acts/1-6.htm); cf. the other expositors on this page.

God has promised of old, but only at a time that he has appointed, which you are not allowed to know. This is exactly what Gabriel had told Mary: Your Son "will be great and will be called the Son of the Most High. And the Lord God will give to him the throne of his father David, and he will reign over the house of Jacob forever, and of his kingdom there will be no end" (Luke 1:32–33).

The moment we begin to speculate that heaven as such is our inheritance (cf. also the "inheritance of the saints in light," Col. 1:12[15]), it is only one more step to saying that "heaven" here refers to the intermediate state. In reality, the inheritance is indeed "kept in heaven" for believers, but the *contents* of this inheritance is the universe.[16] This sheds helpful light on Romans 4, where we read of Abraham "that he would be heir [not of heaven, in whatever sense, but] *of the world*" (v. 13; italics added). This promise is extended to all those who are of the same faith as he was (vv. 12–14). Notice again how the Annotations to the Dutch States Translation obscure the clear sense of the text by arguing, first, that "the world" here is the land of Canaan, and second, by declaring that Canaan is a type of "the eternal rest of the believers in heaven."

No—here in Romans 4:13 "the world" is "the world."

This scope of inheritance is also reflected in Ephesians 1:10–11, "[I]n the dispensation of the fullness of the times" God gathers "together in one all things in Christ, both which are in heaven and which are on earth—in Him. In Him also we have obtained an inheritance" (NKJV).[17] As Paul says elsewhere, we are "heirs of God and fellow heirs with Christ" (Rom. 8:17). And what is the inheritance that Jesus has obtained? All things in heaven and on earth,

---

15. Cf. Maclaren (https://biblehub.com/commentaries/colossians/1-12.htm), who refreshingly remarked: "We must begin by dismissing from our minds the common idea... that it [i.e., the inheritance of Col. 1:12] is entered upon by death."

16. Cf. Kelly (1923), 20–22.

17. *Not* "we have *become* [God's] inheritance," or similar renderings, as found in numerous Bible translations.

that is, the entire cosmos: "All authority in heaven and on earth has been given to me" (Matt. 28:18). God's heirs and Christ's co-heirs inherit the world. What can be more obvious than this? One day, Abraham and all who have followed him on the path of faith (including New Testament believers) will rule over the universe. *Not* during the intermediate state but in the resurrection state. Paul says, "[D]o you not know that the saints will judge the world?" (1 Cor. 6:2; AMPC and TLB: "judge and govern the world"; ISV: "rule the world").

This is also the sense of Hebrews 11:10, where we read that Abraham "was looking forward to the city that has foundations, whose designer and builder is God." This is not "heaven," and even less the place where believers go when they die. I am unaware of any passage in Hebrews that refers to the intermediate state; the letter contains not one verse supporting Interim Theology. Hebrews refers to the "world to come" (2:5), to the "age to come" (6:5), and the "city that is to come" (13:14). It is not a city where you *go* (when you die), but a world, an age, a city to *come;* all of this will come *to us,* and this will take place *at the Parousia.* This is the Messianic "(unshakable) kingdom" that is to arrive one day (12:28). Even if Hebrews 11:16 says of the patriarchs, "[T]hey desire a better country, that is, a heavenly one" (v. 16), I am convinced, in line with the entire letter, that the Messianic kingdom is intended, which the glorified saints (including the patriarchs) will experience "from above," so to speak, from heaven, in the resurrection state.[18]

12.2.3 Resting

When it comes to the aspect of resting, we see again a (weak) similarity between the intermediate state and the resurrection state. Revelation 14:13 says, "And I heard a voice from heaven saying,

---

18. How different from, e.g., Matthew Henry's ideas on this verse: "saints, whose home is heaven; . . . pilgrims, travelling toward their home," referring to the intermediate state (https://biblehub.com/commentaries/hebrews/ 11-16.htm).

'Write this: Blessed are the dead who die in the Lord from now on.' 'Blessed indeed,' says the Spirit, 'that they may rest from their labors, for their deeds follow them!'" The first fulfillment is no doubt in the intermediate state because at that point the labors of the believer will be over. However, there can be no doubt that the full realization of this will occur in the resurrection state. One way to understand the expression "their deeds follow them" is that believers will have appeared before the judgment seat of Christ, *which will occur at the Parousia*, and they will have received their rewards and their crowns (or wreaths) (see §§11.1.2 and 11.2.2). Only then will they see the full results of everything they have done for the Lord here on earth.

To be sure, believers in the resurrection state will not be lazy or unemployed; see especially §§12.3.3–12.3.5 below. Yet, it will be a state of eternal rest, saturated with total peace and perfect harmony. They will be doing a relaxed type of work, in perfect leisure. There will be service (§12.3.4), but this service will never entail toil, tension, and trouble, to say nothing of disappointment or failure.

The writer of the letter to the Hebrews wrote, "So then, there remains a Sabbath rest for the people of God, for whoever has entered God's rest has also rested from his works as God did from his" (Heb. 4:9–10). Here again, traditional expositors committed to Interim Theology have understood this as a reference to "heaven." For instance, the Annotations to the Dutch States Translation claim that the rest is "a spiritual and eternal rest."[19] But why would this tranquility of the intermediate state and the resurrection state be called a "*Sabbath* rest"? The Sabbath was the anticipation of the Messianic kingdom. Compare Psalm 92, which is "A Song for the Sabbath," and an anticipation of the Messianic kingdom, in which the enemies will have perished (vv. 7–9), and the righteous will "flourish like the palm tree and grow like a cedar in Lebanon" (v. 12).

---

19. Haak (1918), *ad loc.*

This "Sabbath rest" will be a rest enjoyed not just for believers, but by God's entire creation, as was the case with the first creation, and even for God himself (Gen. 2:2–3).[20] The Sabbath is the "day" of the Messianic kingdom; but the *rest* of that Sabbath will extend to all eternity. Notice that in the story of creation, the "seventh day" (Gen. 2:2–3) is the only day where we do not find the expression, "there was evening and there was morning." Spiritually speaking, it had a beginning, but no ending, merging seamlessly into the "eighth day" of redemptive history, which is called the "day of eternity" (2 Pet. 3:18).

12.2.4 Enjoyment

The Father's house will be a place of everlasting bliss and enjoyment: "Blessed [or more accurately: blissful, happy[21]] are the dead who die in the Lord from now on" (Rev. 14:13). It is the place where tears, mourning, and pain will belong to the past (Rev. 21:4; cf. 7:17; Isa. 25:8). It is the place of laughter, of exuberance, of enthusiasm, and ebullience: "Then our mouth was filled with laughter, and our tongue with shouts of joy; then they said among the nations, 'The LORD has done great things for them'" (Ps. 126:2). It reminds us of Bach's cantata BWV 110, *Unser Mund sei voll Lachens* ("May our mouth be full of laughter"), especially the first aria:

> *Ihr Gedanken und ihr Sinnen,*
> *Schwinget euch anitzt von hinnen,*
> *Steiget schleunig himmelan*
> *Und bedenkt, was Gott getan!*
> *Er wird Mensch, und dies allein,*
> *Daß wir Himmels Kinder sein.*

> Your thoughts and musings,
> soar away now,

---

20. See more extensively, Ouweneel (1982), ad loc.
21. The Greek word is *makarios* ("blissful"), not *eulogētos* ("blessed").

> climb rapidly to heaven
> and consider what God has done!
> He has become human, and for this alone,
> that we might be children of heaven.

Heaven will be a realm of comfort after all the troubles and sufferings that believers have had to endure here on earth (Luke 16:25). It is the place of "the joy of the master" (cf. Matt. 25:21, 23; in the CEV the master says, "Come and share in my happiness"; it is called "everlasting joy" in Isa. 35:10; 51:11). It is the place of the "eternal weight of glory," in contrast with our present (and transient) "light momentary affliction" (2 Cor. 4:17). The Christian gospel is the gospel of the blissful[22] God (1 Tim. 1:11), and the gospel that tells us how to reach the bliss of this God.

Philippians 1:23 indicates that it is "far better" to suffer death and to be "with Christ," and thus to be free of all the troubles and miseries of the believer's earthly existence. In this sense, it seems that enjoyment will also be part of the believer's blessing in the intermediate state. Yet, we should not exaggerate this. Notice again the distinction between the (disembodied) "souls" of the martyrs "under the altar," who are still complaining (Rev. 6:9–11), and the state of the risen saints, who sing the song of Moses and the song of the Lamb (15:2–4). It is the difference—if you will allow me this very earthly picture—between lying in the recovery room after a serious operation, and entering, fully recovered, into one's own home, which has been warmly decorated to gladly receive you.

Take this simple example: I have never read in the Bible about any singing on the part of those existing in the intermediate state, although dozens of pious hymns influenced by Interim Theology happily tell us about it. But I do know about singing on *earth*, during the Messianic age (Isa. 35:10 is a wonderful example), and about singing in *heaven*, in the post-resurrection state (Rev. 5:9; 14:3; 15:3).

---

22. See previous note.

I repeat here this expression of the Apostle Paul: "What no eye has seen, nor ear heard, nor the heart of man imagined, what God has prepared for those who love him—these things God has revealed to us through the Spirit" (1 Cor. 2:9–10). That is, there will be infinite joy in the everlasting state, but it is very difficult to explain *what* believers will enjoy. It will be things that, so far, no eye has seen, nor ear heard, nor the hearts of people imagined. It is like explaining to a person born blind what wonderful landscapes they will see when their eyes are healed, or explaining to a person born deaf what wonderful music they will hear when their ears are healed. We do not even *try* to explain these things; we can only helplessly say: Wait and you will find out—it will be great and wonderful.

Perhaps we must say that it will be the *Lord himself* whom the righteous will enjoy above all. John Calvin wrote that the Lord "will give himself to be enjoyed by them."[23] It will be the ultimate fulfillment of Psalm 34:8, "[T]aste and see that the LORD is good!," a statement quoted in 1 Peter 2:3. In addition to new seeing and hearing, there will be new smelling and tasting and feeling—things that cannot be described at present; words fail us. But one thing we can already say: all of this will center on *him*.

The term "enjoyment" may sound a bit narcissistic, as if this pertains only to what *I* or *we* will enjoy. But in the Bible, enjoyment always occurs in *loving fellowship* with God. It is a *mutual* enjoyment, like that of two believers whose personalities are blended in love (cf. Song 2:16, "My beloved is mine, and I am his"). Here, all taking from the other is balanced by all giving to the other. "It is more blessed to give than to receive" (Acts 20:35)—but when all will give all, then all will receive all.

12.2.5 Understanding

The Father's house will be the place where the righteous will begin to understand many things they have not yet understood, or not

---

23. Calvin (1960), 3.25.10.

yet properly understood, while living on earth. Perhaps this is what Jesus meant when he told Peter: "What I am doing you do not understand now, but *afterward* you will understand" (John 13:7)—but it may also be that Jesus was referring here to the coming of the Holy Spirit in the Day of Pentecost, who would guide the apostles in all the truth (16:13)

At any rate, 1 Corinthians 13:10–12 tells us about eternity: "[W]hen the perfect comes, the partial will pass away. When I was a child, I spoke like a child, I thought like a child, I reasoned like a child. When I became a man, I gave up childish ways." Our understanding of eternal bliss reaches no further than the understanding that a little child has of the approaching holidays.

The text continues: "For now we see in a mirror dimly, but then face to face [i.e., in close communion with the Lord]. Now I know in part; *then I shall know fully*, even as I have been fully known" (italics added). How well has God known me? Perfectly well. How well shall I myself know things in eternity? The answer must again be: perfectly well. With one possible restriction: does this also mean that we will know *God* perfectly well? Or will he in his profoundest being remain eternally beyond our full comprehension? Tradition speaks of the vision or contemplation of God (Lat. *visio Dei*), the comprehension and understanding of God (Lat. *comprehensio Dei*), and the enjoyment of God (Lat. *fruitio Dei*),[24] but the issue involves the extent or range of these three aspects.[25]

One question that arises regularly and suggests that we will know even *less* than we do now is whether we will recognize each other in eternity.[26] The answer is that we will not know *less* than we know now; rather, we will know *more*. Even Dives, who was in Hades, recognized not only Lazarus but Abraham, whom he had never seen in the flesh (Luke 16:24). The inhabitants of Sheol recognize

---

24. *RD*, 4:722.
25. Cf. Van Genderen and Velema (2008), 879–80; see the discussion in §12.2.7.
26. Cf. Hoek (2004), 282–84.

the entering king of Babylon (Isa. 14:12) and the king of Egypt (or Assyria? Ezek. 32:21). What kind of privilege would it be to recline at table with Abraham, Isaac, and Jacob (Matt. 8:11) if people would not be able to recognize these three men? (Think as well of Luke 13:28, where we read that in hell "there will be weeping and gnashing of teeth, when you see Abraham and Isaac and Jacob and all the prophets in the kingdom of God but you yourselves cast out"). On the Mount of Transfiguration, Peter was able to recognize Moses and Elijah immediately, without ever having seen them in the flesh (Mark 9:4–5). What would everlasting glory be without the capacity to recognize all the saints? We would not even be able to recognize *Jesus Christ*, whom we have never met in the flesh either (cf. 2 Cor. 5:16).

For the supposed ignorance of the dead we must not appeal to passages such as Job 14:21, Ecclesiastes 9:5–6 and 10, and Isaiah 63:16—as has been done—where things are viewed from a gloomy, dark perspective. Herman Bavinck suggested that it is "probable" that deceased believers "know as much about the church militant on earth as the latter does about them."[27] I think he is right, aside from his use of the traditional expression "church militant," which presupposes the existence of a "church triumphant" in the intermediate state (see §§3.2.2 and 12.3.5).

One argument that has been put forward against recognizing each other in the hereafter is that, if this were so, we would also be aware of those whose destiny did *not* involve "being with Christ," our relatives and acquaintances, and this would sadden us. My counter-question is this: Would *we* be sadder in the hereafter than the Father and the Son, who will miss many with whom they, while these people were still alive, had pleaded in love to repent and come to faith?[28] Moreover, the bonds "in the flesh" that were precious to

---

27. *RD*, 4:641).
28. Cf. 2 Cor. 5:20 (DRA): "[W]e are ambassadors for Christ, as though God were *pleading* through us: we *implore* you on Christ's behalf, be reconciled to God."

us on earth will no longer be significant as such.[29] In other words, in eternity, we will love our beloved ones more than we ever did on earth—but at the same time, we will love all the other children of God just as much.

12.2.6 Shining

In Matthew 13:43, Jesus says during the interpretation of a parable, "Then [i.e., at the Parousia] the righteous will shine like the sun in the kingdom of their Father." This statement reminds us of Daniel 12:3, "[T]hose who are wise shall shine like the brightness of the sky above; and those who turn many to righteousness, like the stars forever and ever." Even though these verses are primarily references to the Messianic kingdom, one may wonder whether the righteous will ever cease shining. Actually, even today believers must shine to some extent in this world: ". . . blameless and innocent, children of God without blemish in the midst of a crooked and twisted generation, among whom you shine as lights in the world" (Phil 2:15).

All three passages refer to the light-bearers in the sky, especially the stars. If Christ is the Sun (Mal. 4:2), the believers are the stars—not as bright as the Sun, yet bright enough to lighten the night (Gen. 1:16–18; Ps. 148:3). At the same time, we must add that believers will never shine more than when they have received their glorified resurrection bodies.

In the resurrection state, the bride of the Lamb will be invested with the "glory of God" (Rev. 21:9–11). She will be a radiant bride, who, even *after* the "thousand years" since her wedding (19:6–9), will still look like a radiant, luminous bride, "adorned for her husband" (21:2)—as if her wedding were only yesterday. This shining is nothing but reflecting the glory of Christ himself: ". . . the light of the knowledge of the glory of God in the face of Jesus Christ" (2 Cor. 4:6; cf. 3:18, ". . . reflecting the glory of the Lord," as many translations have it).

---

29. Cf. Matt. 12:46–50; 2 Cor. 5:16; see Hendriksen (1959), 68–69.

There is no way that believers in the intermediate state can be said to be shining, although here again many Interim theologians have applied this to the intermediate state.[30] Even though there is a preliminary fulfillment today, in the full sense of the term this shining requires the resurrection body: Jesus "will transform our lowly body to be like his glorious body" (Phil. 3:21). The body "is sown in dishonor; it is raised in glory" (1 Cor. 15:43). The glorious resurrection body will reflect the glorious body of the risen Christ himself. Disembodied saints will have to wait before they can begin shining. They are like electrical sockets that require the lamps to be plugged into them.

12.2.7 Contemplating

The Father's house will be the place where the blessed saints will contemplate the glory of God. It was the will of the Son that, as he himself said, they "see my glory that you have given me because you loved me before the foundation of the world" (John 17:24). "For now we see in a mirror dimly, but then face to face" (1 Cor. 13:12); "we shall see him as he is" (1 John 3:2). "They will see his face, and his name will be on their foreheads" (Rev. 22:4). "Blessed are the pure in heart, for they shall see God" (Matt. 5:8). "Strive for peace with everyone, and for the holiness without which no one will see the Lord" (Heb. 12:14; cf. 1 John 3:6; 3 John 1:11).[31]

At the same time, we must wonder whether this contemplation will consist of seeing God in his essence (Lat. *visio Dei per essentiam*)," as Roman Catholicism teaches.[32] Does God not remain eternally the Invisible One?[33] At least we must say that, even in blessed eternity,

---

30. See various older authors, https://www.biblehub.com/commentaries/matthew/13-43.htm.
31. See also Exod. 24:11; Num. 12:5–8; Deut. 34:10; Ps. 24:6; 27:8; 63:2; 105:4; 2 Cor. 3:18; but see also Exod. 3:6; 33:18–23; Num. 6:24–26; Judg. 6:22; 13:22; Isa. 6:5.
32. Denziger (1997), 1305; regarding this, see Berkouwer (1963), 155–61, 173–82; Berkhof (1986), 539.
33. John 1:18; 1 Tim. 1:17; 6:16; Heb. 11:27; 1 John 4:12.

no creature will ever be able to fathom the depths of God's being. It is said only of the Holy Spirit that he "searches everything, even the depths of God" (1 Cor. 2:10). What we achieve spiritually can be done only in the power of the Holy Spirit. But we cannot reverse this statement: not everything the Holy Spirit can do can be done in and through us. The fact that he searches the depths of God does not necessarily imply that, one day, we will be able to do the same.

A related point is whether believers will ever see God other than in the face of Jesus Christ, as seems to be suggested by John 14:9 ("Whoever has seen me has seen the Father") and 2 Corinthians 4:6 (". . . the light of the knowledge of the glory of God in the face of Jesus Christ").[34] Roman Catholic theologian Hans Urs von Balthasar said, "Nowhere for one moment is the glory of God severed from the Lamb, the Trinitarian light separated from the light of Christ, who became Man."[35] How true this is! Contemplating God is contemplating the Triune God: Father, Son, and Holy Spirit—and the glory of the Son can never be severed from the resurrection glory of his humanity. Whether contemplating God will be *limited* to seeing Christ is a difficult question—but at any rate, contemplating God can never again be *severed* from contemplating the glorified Son of Man. Stated more strongly, there will be no beholding the deity without beholding the humanity, because God, in the Son, has forever associated himself with the human.

12.3   Activities

12.3.1 Reclining and Eating

The Father's house will be the place of the great banquet that God will organize for his people, and that he will enjoy with his people, a banquet that the righteous will enjoy among themselves. God's feasts are usually described in terms of eating and drinking (cf. §§12.2.4 and 12.3.2). When the Bible speaks of the "only One, who is God, who is in the bosom of the Father" (John 1:18 ESV notes),

---

34. Cf. Hulsbosch (1963), 179.
35. Von Balthasar (1961), 206.

this too seems to portray a banquet: the Son was reclining from eternity at table with the Father, as his beloved Son lying in his bosom. Similarly, we find Lazarus reclining at table, lying "in the bosom of Abraham" (Luke 16:22–23). Both descriptions contain metaphorical language, but this does not make these scenes any less real.

If taken literally, the latter picture is that of the disembodied Lazarus lying in the bosom of the disembodied Abraham. As argued before, this picture makes sense only if we view it as something that continues and blossoms in the resurrection state, when the risen Lazarus will be lying in the bosom of the risen Abraham (see §5.1). All the other pictures of the eschatological banquet are post-Parousia and post-resurrection, such as: "Blessed are those servants whom the master finds awake when he comes. Truly, I say to you, he will dress himself for service and have them recline at table, and he will come and serve them" (Luke 12:37).

In connection with eternal bliss, several times we find the picture of eating and drinking, which is not only a picture of fellowship, but also of eternal enjoyment: "To the one who conquers I will grant to eat of the tree of life, which is in the paradise of God" (Rev. 2:7). "Blessed are those who are invited to the marriage supper of the Lamb" (19:9; cf. related pictures in 2:17, "the hidden manna"; 7:17 KJV, "feed"). Jesus himself said to his disciples: "I tell you I will not drink again of this fruit of the vine until that day when I drink it new with you in my Father's kingdom" (Matt. 26:29). And in a parable: "Enter into the joy of your master" (25:21, 23; VOICE: "[C]ome join my great feast and celebration").

It borders on the superfluous to observe yet once again that these verses have been applied by expositors to the intermediate state, although some of the older expositors have connected them with the resurrection state, or with the new heavens and the new earth. Others speak of "heaven" in an unspecified way, which usually seems to blur the distinction between the intermediate state and the resurrection state.[36]

Concerning the Messianic kingdom, we have this precious Old Testament description:

> On this mountain the LORD of hosts will make for all peoples a feast of rich food, a feast of well-aged wine, of rich food full of marrow, of aged wine well refined. And he will swallow up on this mountain the covering that is cast over all peoples, the veil that is spread over all nations. He will swallow up death forever; and the Lord GOD will wipe away tears from all faces, and the reproach of his people he will take away from all the earth, for the LORD has spoken (Isa. 25:6–8).

This does not (necessarily) refer to the post-resurrection state; yet, the passage definitely evokes some of the ambience of the eternal state of the believers.

12.3.2 Fellowship

The Father's house is the place where "eternal life" finds its natural home (see extensively chapter 9). In the person of the God-Man Jesus Christ, this life has descended to humanity (1 John 1:1–2; 5:20), and has been imparted to those who believe in him. However, only in the Father's house will they be able to know and to enjoy this life to the full.[37] There, they will experience what is entailed for them in this eternal life: fellowship with the Father, and with his Son Jesus Christ (1 John 1:3; cf. John 17:3), and we may add: all this in the power of the Holy Spirit (cf. 2 Cor. 5:14).

The other word for fellowship is communion. Two people have communion with each other when they have important things "in common."[38] If we have communion with the Father (1 John 1:2), what do we have in common with him? The answer can be only the Son. More specifically, fellowship with, and joy in, the Son. He

---

36. See, e.g., https://www.biblehub.com/commentaries/matthew/26-29.htm.
37. Cf. Matt. 25:46; John 4:36; 12:25; Rom. 6:22; Gal. 6:8; Jude 1:21.
38. This is not simply an English wordplay: the Gk. word *koinonia* (Lat. *communio*) means "communion," and the Gk. word *koinos* means "in common" (Acts 2:44; 4:32).

who is the Son of the love of his Father (Col. 1:13 DRA) has become our very life (1 John 5:12). If we have communion with the Son, what do we have in common with him? The answer can be only the Father. More specifically, fellowship with, and joy in, the Father. He who could be called by the Son "my Father," has now become "our Father" as well (cf. John 20:17). Not in the sense of Creator—the way every orthodox Jew can address God as "Father" (cf. Ps. 103:13; Isa. 63:16; 64:8; Mal. 1:6; 2:10)—but in the unique Johannine sense: if the Son has become our life, his Father is necessarily our Father. The person who has received the eternal Son as the life that is in him, and will eternally be in him, can call the eternal Father of this Son their own Father.

Fellowship with divine persons is a lofty matter that approaches the Eastern Orthodox notion of *theōsis*. Literally, this Greek word means "deification," a term going back to a famous statement by Athanasius that might be easily misunderstood: "He [i.e., God the Son] became human [Greek *enēnthrōpēsen*, in which we recognize *anthrōpos*, "a human"], in order that we might be made divine [Greek *theopoiēthōmen*, in which we recognize *theos*, "God," and *poieō*, "to make"]."[39] In somewhat more palatable biblical language, this can be stated as follows: Christ became a partaker of the human nature (cf. Phil. 2:6–8; Heb. 2:14), in order that humans would become "partakers of the divine nature" (2 Pet. 1:4).

Please notice that such "partaking" does not annul the ontic distance that exists between the Creator and the creature, but it does mean sharing God's glory[40] as well as the most intimate fellowship with God. From this also flows the fellowship with other believers, as indicated in 1 John 1:1–4 (". . . so that you too may have fellowship with us; and indeed our fellowship is with the Father and with his Son Jesus Christ"). "God is faithful, by whom you were called into the fellowship of his Son, Jesus Christ our Lord" (1

---

39. *De incarnatione* 54; see extensively, Ouweneel (2009b), chapter 14.
40. Cf. John 17:22; Rom. 8:30; Col. 3:4; Rev. 21:10–11.

Cor. 1:9). "The grace of the Lord Jesus Christ and the love of God and the fellowship of the Holy Spirit be with you all" (2 Cor. 13:14).

12.3.3 Rule

No disembodied believers dwelling in the intermediate state are now reigning with Christ. The righteous who have been raised from the dead will not reign with Christ before the arrival of the Messianic kingdom during the "thousand years" (Rev. 20:4–6). However, this rule will not be limited to this period: God's servants "will reign forever and ever" (22:5; cf. 2:26–27, "The one who conquers and who keeps my works until the end, to him I will give authority over the nations, and he will rule them with a rod of iron, as when earthen pots are broken in pieces, even as I myself have received authority from my Father").

The faithful servants will receive authority over five or ten cities (Luke 19:17, 19; cf. Matt. 25:21) (given whatever figurative sense one prefers to take this). In the eternal state, too, when God will be all in all (1 Cor. 15:28), believers will share in the rule over all God's creation, which will then be a new creation. We must carefully distinguish between the two positions that believers hold here. Toward God, the human creational position is that of a servant (see the following sections). But toward (the rest of) creation, from Genesis 1:26–28 onward, the human creational position is that of a ruler because this is part of having been created "in the image and after the likeness of God" (although humans are, since the Fall, fallen rulers). In the eternal state, this rulership will become full reality. On the one hand, the righteous will eternally remain "servants" (Rev. 22:3, literally even "slaves"); on the other hand, they will eternally remain rulers, "kings."

It makes little sense to ask *over what subjects* the righteous will exercise their kingship because we know so little about the eternal resurrection state. In any case, the righteous will receive authority over all God's works of creation, but even apart from this we can speak of their royal *dignity*. The Lord has "made us unto our God kings [literally a "kingdom," here: a totality of kings] and priests: and we shall reign [literally "reign[41] as kings"] on the earth" (Rev. 5:10 KJV; cf. 1:6). Forever slaves of the Master—forever kings under the King of kings.

12.3.4 Service

The verb "to serve"[42] expresses in the most general sense of the word the task of the righteous in the eternal state. On the one hand, they share in the rule *over* all God's creation; on the other hand, they will be *subject to* the Triune God, and will serve him: "And there shall be no more curse, but the throne of God and of the Lamb shall be in it [i.e., in the New Jerusalem], and His servants shall serve Him" (Rev. 22:3 NKJV). The Greek word for "to serve" that is used here is *latreuō*, which is rendered by the ESV and others as "to worship" (see the next section), but in other passages the latter translations also render it as "to serve" (e.g., Rom. 9:3; 2 Tim. 1:3).

Indeed, the service intended here is specifically the service consisting of worship. But it is broader than that; see, for instance, the use of the related Greek noun *latreia* in Romans 12:1, "I beseech you therefore, brethren, by the mercies of God, that you present your bodies a living sacrifice, holy, acceptable to God, [which is] your reasonable service [other translations, worship]" (cf. this wider meaning in John 16:2; Heb. 9:6, "service"; ESB: "ritual duties").

As a (very unrefined) portrait of these servants, I like to think of the "seven princes of Persia and Media, who saw the king's face, and sat first in the kingdom" (Est. 1:14). They were "princes," yet still servants. They saw the face of the king, as the angels see the face of God in heaven (Matt. 18:10), indicating their attitude of humble service.

In §6.4 we examined the notion of the Father's house men-

---

41. Actually, the English word "reign" implies kingship, since it comes from Lat. *regere*, i.e., "to rule as a *rex* [king]."

42. Bavinck (*RD*, 4:727) used four verbs; he spoke of "knowing" (§12.2.5), "serving" (§12.3.4), "glorifying" and "praising" God (§12.3.5).

tioned in John 14:1–3; it can hardly be separated from the notion of the Father's house in John 2:16, an expression referring to the earthly temple in Jerusalem. If this is correct, the "many rooms" are the priestly chambers in both the earthly and the heavenly temples; see especially Ezekiel 41:6–7. In the house of the Father there are "many rooms" for many heavenly priests; these are believers (cf. Heb. 10:19–22; 13:15). They are both a "holy" and a "royal priesthood" (1 Pet. 2:5, 9; cf. Rev. 1:6; 5:10). Forever and ever they will perform their heavenly "temple service" for the Lord. Revelation 7:15 speaks of those who "are before the throne of God, and serve [Gk. *latreuō*] him day and night in his temple."[43]

12.3.5 Worship

Especially in Revelation, the eternal worship rendered in heaven by angels as well as by saints, to God as well as to the Lamb, is mentioned many times:[44]

> And when he [i.e., the Lamb] had taken the scroll [out of God's hand], the four living creatures and the twenty-four elders fell down before the Lamb, each holding a harp, and golden bowls full of incense, which are the prayers of the saints. And they sang a new song, saying, "Worthy are you to take the scroll / and to open its seals, / for you were slain, and by your blood you / ransomed people for God / from every tribe and language and people and / nation, / and you have made them a kingdom and priests to our God, / and they shall reign on the earth." Then I looked, and I heard around the throne and the living creatures and the elders the voice of many angels, numbering myriads of myriads and thousands of thousands, saying with a loud voice, "Worthy is the Lamb who was slain, / to receive power and wealth and wisdom and might / and honor and glory and blessing!" And I heard every creature in heaven and on earth and under the

---

43. Regarding the heavenly "temple," see Rev. 11:19; 14:15, 17; 15:5–6, 8; 16:1, 17.
44. Astonishingly, Hendriksen (1959), 60, thought here especially of a passive "listening" to the heavenly music.

earth and in the sea, and all that is in them, saying, "To him who sits on the throne and to the Lamb / be blessing and honor and glory and might forever and ever!" And the four living creatures said, "Amen!" and the elders fell down and worshiped (Rev. 5:8–14).[45]

It is amazing that Barnes' Notes on the Bible applies all of this to the intermediate state: "The idea here [in Rev. 5] is, therefore, that the representatives of the church in heaven—the elders—spoken of as 'priests' [v. 10] are described as officiating *in the temple above in behalf of the church still below,* and as offering incense while the church is engaged in prayer" (ital. added).[46] This interpretation relies on the traditional notion of the church militant, which is the church on earth, as distinct from the church triumphant, which consists of the saints who are already "in heaven," that is, *in the intermediate state* (see §§3.2.2 and 12.2.5). In opposition to this, this book has emphasized repeatedly that Interim Theology—the common view of the intermediate state—is mistaken. There will indeed be a *triumphant church*—but not before the Parousia and the resurrection, that is, at the very moment when there is no longer a *militant church* on earth.

> *He who testifies to these things says,*
> *"Surely I am coming soon."*
> *Amen.*
> *Come, Lord Jesus!*
>
> Revelation 22:20

---

45. Rev. 5:8–14; cf. 4:10–11; 7:9–12; 11:16–18; 19:1–8.
46. https://biblehub.com/commentaries/revelation/5-8.htm.

APPENDIX 1

Debated Bible Passages

Psalm 73:24   This verse does *not* refer to the "heavenly glory" of the intermediate state (see §4.2.2).

Ecclesiastes 12:5–7   This passage does *not* refer to an intermediate state (see §4.2.1).

Matthew 3:2   The "kingdom of heaven" does *not* refer to the intermediate state but to the Parousia and the Messianic kingdom (see §1.4.1).

Matthew 10:28 This verse does *not* imply that human beings are a dualism (or dualistic combination) of an immortal soul substance and a mortal body substance (see §§2.1.2, 8.3.2, 10.3.1).

Matthew 19:16 "Eternal life" does *not* refer to the intermediate state but to (a) the believer's present life; (b) the Messianic kingdom; and (c) the life of the Father's house (see chapter 9).

Luke 8:52–55 Believers being "asleep" (i.e., dead) does *not* imply that they are in a kind of coma (see §5.5).

Luke 23:43   The word "paradise" does *not* imply that "paradise" is the specific name of the abode of deceased believers (see §5.2).

John 14:2-3   The "house of the Father" does *not* refer to the intermediate state but to the Parousia and the resurrection state (see §6.4).

Romans 7:24   "Deliver from this body of death" does *not* imply that a supposed immortal soul must be set free from the prison of the body (see §1.2.3).

1 Corinthians 3:15   This "fire" does *not* point to the existence of purgatory (see §6.3).

2 Corinthians 5:1   The "eternal house in the heavens" is *not* "heaven" (in the sense of the intermediate state), but the resurrection body (see §5.3).

Hebrews 4:9   The "Sabbath rest" is *not* the rest of believers during the intermediate state, but the rest belonging to the Messianic kingdom culminating in the new heavens and earth (see §12.2.3).

Hebrews 11:16 The "better, heavenly country" is *not* "heaven" (in the sense of the intermediate state), but the Messianic kingdom, as the glorified believers will experience it ("from above") (see §12.2.2)

Hebrews 12:23 The "spirits of the righteous made perfect" are dwelling *not* in the intermediate state but in the resurrection state (see §§1.2.2, 1.2.3 and 1.3.3).

James 2:26   The distinction between "body" and "spirit" does *not* imply that human beings are a [dualism dualistic combination?] of an immortal spirit substance and a mortal body substance (see §§2.1.2).

1 Peter 1:4   An inheritance "kept in heaven" is something very different from heaven *itself* supposedly being the believer's inheritance (see §12.2.2).

1 Peter 3:19   The preaching to spirits in "prison" does *not* imply a descent of Jesus into Hades (or even hell) between his death and his resurrection (§§6.1.2 and 6.2.1).

Revelation 20:4–6   The "first resurrection" does *not* refer to a spiritual resurrection; it is just as physical and momentaneous as the "second resurrection" (see §11.3).

Revelation 20:14   This verse proves that Hades and hell (*gehenna*) are very different things (see §§4.3 and 4.4).

APPENDIX 2

Key Terms

aevum (Lat.)   intermedium of time and eternity (§3.4.3)

aiōn (Gk.)   world, age (§1.2.1)

"asleep (falling)"   passing away (§5.5)

death   four meanings (§§2.4.1, 10.3.1)

eternal life   three basic meanings (chapter 9)

Hades (Gk.)   grave, realm of the dead (§§4.3 and 4.4)

heaven   sky, cosmos (§3.5.2), God's abode (§§3.5.3, 4.1.1)

ᶜolam (Heb.)   world, age, eternity (§1.2.1)

paradise   garden of God (§5.2)

Sheol (Heb. *sh'ol*)   see Hades

skēnē (Gk.)   tent, tabernacle, booth (§ 10.1)

sōma (Gk.)   body (§8.2.3)

soul   many meanings (§§2.1.2, 6.1.1, 8.1.2, 8.1.3, 8.4.1)

spirit   many meanings (§§3.4.3, 6.1.2, 8.1.3, 8.4.1)

"third heaven" see heaven (§3.5) and §5.3.

APPENDIX 3

Rejected Doctrines

amillennialism   see §§9.4.1, 12.1.2, 12.1.3

asceticism   see §§8.2.3, 10.4.2

body-soul dualism   throughout the book (especially chapter 8)

evolutionism   see §2.3.1

existentialism   see §8.4.2

functionalism   see §8.1.2

individualism   see §§1.3.1, 2.2.3

Interim Theology   throughout the book

logicism   see §8.5.2 (see also rationalism)

materialism   see §§2.1.1, 8.1.2, 8.4.2, 8.5.3

mysticism   see §§8.2.3, 10.4.2

Neo-Platonism   see §§8.1.1, 8.2.2, 8.3.2

BIBLIOGRAPHY[1]

Aalders, G. C. 1936. *Het boek Genesis*. Vol. 3: *Hoofdstuk 31:1–50:26*. KV. Kampen: Kok.

———. 1948. *Het boek de Prediker*. COT. Kampen: Kok.

Adeyemo, T., ed. 2006. *Africa Bible Commentary: A One-Volume Commentary*. Grand Rapids, MI: Zondervan.

Alcorn, R. 2004. *Heaven*. Carol Stream, IL: Tyndale House Publishers.

Alford, H. 1884. *The Revelation*. London: Rivingtons.

Allen, R. B. 1990. *Numbers*. EBC 2. Grand Rapids, MI: Zondervan.

Armstrong, H. A., ed. 1967. *The Cambridge History of Later Greek and Early Medieval Philosophy*. Cambridge: Cambridge University Press.

Ashley, T. R. 1993. *The Book of Numbers*. NICOT. Grand Rapids, MI: Eerdmans.

Augustine. n.d.-1. *The City of God*. Available at https://www.newadvent.org/fathers/ 120120.htm.

———. n.d.-2. *Of the Morals of the Catholic Church*. Available at http://www.gnosis.org/ library/democ.htm.

Badham, P. 1976. *Christian Beliefs about Life after Death*. London: Macmillan.

---

1. Bibliographies tend to become shorter nowadays because of references in footnotes to websites; for instance, I have made use of biblehub.com for older expositors such as Albert Barnes, Joseph Benson, John Gill, Matthew Henry, Jamieson-Fausset-Brown, and Matthew Poole.

Balke, W. 1999. *Calvin and the Anabaptist Radicals.* Eugene, OR: Wipf & Stock.

——, J. C. Klok, and W. van 't Spijker. 2009. *Johannes Calvijn: zijn leven, zijn werk.* 2nd ed. Kampen: Kok.

Balthasar, H. U. von. 1983. *The Glory of the Lord: A Theological Aesthetics.* Vol. 1: *Seeing the Form.* Edited by J. Fessio and J. Riches. Translated by E. Leiva-Merikakis. New York: Crossroads Publications. 1961. *Herrlichkeit: Eine theologische Ästhetik.* Vol. 1: *Schau der Gestalt.* Einsiedeln: Johannes Verlag.

Barnett, P. 1997. *The Second Epistle to the Corinthians.* NICNT. Grand Rapids, MI: Eerdmans.

Barth, K. 1956. *Church Dogmatics.* Translated by T. H. L. Parker et al. Vols. 1/1–4/4. Louisville, KY: Westminster John Knox.

Bauer, Walter, Frederick W. Danker, William F. Arndt, and F. Wilbur Gingrich. 2000. *A Greek-English Lexicon of the New Testament and Other Early Christian Literature.* 3rd ed., revised and edited by Frederick W. Danker. Chicago: University of Chicago Press.

Bavinck, H. 1920. *Bijbelsche en religieuze psychologie.* Kampen: Kok.

——. 2002–2008. *Reformed Dogmatics.* Edited by J. Bolt. Translated by J. Vriend. 4 vols. Grand Rapids, MI: Baker Academic.

Berdyaev, N. A. 1960. *The Destiny of Man.* 4th ed. Translated by N. Duddington. New York: Harper & Brothers.

Berkhof, H. 1966. *Christ the Meaning of History.* Translated by L. Buurman. Richmond, VA: John Knox Press. 1958.

——. 1986. *Christian Faith: An Introduction to the Study of the Faith.* Translated by S. Woudstra. Rev. ed. Grand Rapids, MI: Wm. B. Eerdmans.

Berkhof, L. 1981. *Systematic Theology.* 4th rev. and enlarged ed. Grand Rapids, MI: Eerdmans.

Berkouwer, G. C. 1962. *Man: The Image of God.* Translated by D. W. Jellema. Studies in Dogmatics. Grand Rapids, MI: Eerdmans.

———. 1972. *The Return of Christ.* Translated by J. Van Oosterom. Studies in Dogmatics. Grand Rapids, MI: Eerdmans.

Bernard, J. H. 1979. *The Second Epistle to the Corinthians.* EGT 3. Grand Rapids, MI: Eerdmans.

Beuken, W. A. M. 1978. "1 Samuel 28: The Prophet as 'Hammer of Witches'." *Journal for the Study of the Old Testament* 3, no. 6: 3–17.

Blum, E. A. 1981. *1, 2 Peter, Jude.* EBC 12. Grand Rapids, MI: Zondervan.

Böhl, E. 2004 (repr. 1887). *Dogmatik.* Amsterdam: Scheffer.

Bouma, C. 1927. *Het evangelie naar Johannes.* KV. Kampen: Kok.

Brakel, Wilhelmus à. 1992 (repr.1700). *The Christian's Reasonable Service.* Translated by B. Elshout. Edited by J. Beeke. 4 vols. Grand Rapids, MI: Reformation Heritage Books.

Brower, K. E. and M. W. Elliott, eds. 1997. *Eschatology in Bible and Theology: Evangelical Essays at the Dawn of a New Millennium.* Downers Grove, IL: InterVarsity Press.

Brown, C., ed. 1992. *The New International Dictionary of New Testament Theology.* 4 vols. Carlisle: Paternoster.

Bruce, A. B. 1979. *The Synoptic Gospels.* EGT 1. Grand Rapids, MI: Eerdmans.

Bruce, F. F. 1971. "Paul on Immortality." *Scottish Journal of Theology* 24, no. 4: 457–72.

———. 1984. *The Epistles to the Colossians, to Philemon, and to the Ephesians.* NICNT. Grand Rapids, MI: Eerdmans.

Bunyan, John. 1853. *The Pilgrim's Progress.* Buffalo, NY: G. H. Derby & Co. Available at https://ccel.org/ccel/bunyan/pilgrim/pilgrim.i.html.

Calvin, J. 1534. *Contre les Anabaptistes*. In: *Ioannis Calvini Opera quae supersunt omnia* (*Corpus Reformatorum* Series II). Vol. 7. Halle (Germ.): C.A. Schwetschke.

_____. 1849. *Commentaries on the Second Epistle of Paul the Apostle to the Corinthians*. Translated by J. Pringle. Grand Rapids, MI: Christian Classics Ethereal Library. Available at https://ccel.org/ccel/calvin/calcom40/calcom40.iii.html.

_____. 1960 (1559). *Institutes of the Christian Religion*. Translated by F. L. Battles. The Library of Christian Classics. 2 vols. Louisville, KY: Westminster John Knox Press.

_____. 1965. *The Epistles of Paul the Apostle to the Galatians, Ephesians, Philippians, and Colossians*. Grand Rapids, MI: Eerdmans.

Carson, D. A. 1984. *Matthew*. EBC 8. Grand Rapids, MI: Zondervan.

Carey, G. 1977. *I Believe in Man*. London: Hodder & Stoughton.

Chafer, L. S. 1983. *Systematic Theology*. 8 vols. 15th ed. Dallas: Dallas Seminary Press.

Clinton, S. M. 1998. *Peter, Paul, and the Anonymous Christian: A Response to the Mission Theology of Rahner and Vatican II*. Available at http://www.toi.edu/Resources/ Anonomous2.pdf.

Cohen, A. 1983. *The Soncino Chumash*. SBB. London: Soncino.

_____. 1985. *The Psalms*. SBB. London: Soncino.

_____ and A. J. Rosenberg. 1985. *Proverbs*. SBB. London: Soncino.

Cullmann, O. 1962. *Christ and Time: The Primitive Christian Conception of Time and History*. 3rd ed. London: SCM.

Dahood, M. 1966–70. *Psalms*. 3 vols. AB. Garden City, NY: Doubleday.

Darby, J. N. n.d. *Synopsis of the Books of the Bible* (https://www.sacred-texts.com/bib/cmt/ darby/).

Davidson, F., ed. 1954. *The New Bible Commentary*. 2nd ed. London: Inter-Varsity Fellowship.

Davies, W. D. 1980. *Paul and Rabbinic Judaism*. 2nd ed. London: SPCK.

D'Costa, G. 1985. "Karl Rahner's Anonymous Christian: A Reappraisal." *Modern Theology* 1.2:131–48.

De Bondt, A. 1938. *Wat leert het Oude Testament aangaande het leven na dit leven?* Kampen: Kok.

Defares, J. G. 2009. *Sporen van God: Feiten en fictie over God, Jezus en Hiernamaals*. Naarden: Strengholt United Media.

Dennison, J. T., Jr., ed. 2008–14. *Reformed Confessions of the 16th and 17th Centuries in English Translation*. 4 vols. Grand Rapids, MI: Reformation Heritage Books.

Denziger, H. and A. Schönmetzer. 1997 (1854). *Enchiridion symbolorum definitionum et declarationum de rebus et morum*. Freiburg: Herder.

De Vuippens, I. 1925. *Le Paradis terrestre au troisième ciel:Exposé historique d'une conception chrétienne des premiers siècles*. Paris: Librairie Saint-François-d'Assise.

Dijk, K. 1955. *Over de laatste dingen: Tussen sterven en opstanding*. 2nd ed. Kampen: Kok.

Dods, M. 1979. *The Gospel of John*. EGT 1. Grand Rapids, MI: Eerdmans.

Dooyeweerd, H. 1939. "Het tijdsprobleem en zijn antinomieën op het immanentiestandpunt, 2." *Philosophia Reformata* 4:1–28.

_____. 1984 (repr. 1953). *A New Critique of Theoretical Thought*. 4 vols. Jordan Station, ON: Paideia Press.

Douma, J. 2004. *Genesis: Gaan in het spoor van de Bijbel*. Kampen: Kok.

D'Souza, D. 2009. *Life after Death: The Evidence*. Washington, DC: Regnery Press.

Duffield, G. P. and N. M. Van Cleave. 1996. *Woord en Geest: Hoofdlijnen van de theologie van de Pinksterbeweging.* Kampen: Kok/ Rafaël Nederland. English edition: *Foundations of Pentecostal Theology.* Lake Mary, FL: Creation House, 2008.

Erickson, M. J. 1982. "Biblical Inerrancy: The Last Twenty-Five Years." *Journal of the Evangelical Theological Society* 25, no. 4: 387–94.

_____. 1998. *Christian Theology.* Rev. ed. Grand Rapids, MI: Baker Book House.

Fahner, C. 1997. "Vizier op het einde van de tijd: Bijbelse-theologische waardering van eigentijdse ontwikkelingen in het licht van de eindtijd." In *Meer dan mensenkennis! Over kennis in de maatschappij van morgen.* Edited by W. Büdgen et al., 204–218. Heerenveen: Groen.

Fitzpatrick, E. 2016. *Home: How Heaven and the New Earth Satisfy Our Deepest Longings.* Ada, MI: Bethany House Publishers.

Fontana, D. 2005. *Is There an Afterlife? A Comprehensive Overview of the Evidence.* Ropley: O Books.

Foster, J. 1991. *The Immaterial Self.* London: Routledge.

Fowler, S. 1981. *On Being Human: Toward a Biblical Understanding.* Potchefstroom: PU vir CHO.

France, R. T. 2007. *The Gospel of Matthew.* NICNT. Grand Rapids, MI: Eerdmans.

Froom, L. E. 1950. *The Prophetic Faith of Our Fathers.* Vol. 1. Washington, DC: Review and Herald.

Gaebelein, A. R. 2012 (repr. 1913–22). *The Annotated Bible: The Holy Scriptures Analyzed and Annotated: John.* London: Forgotten Books.

Geesink, W. 1925. *Van 's Heeren ordinantiën.* 2nd ed. Kampen: Kok.

Gehlen, A. 1950. *Der Mensch: Seine Natur und seine Stellung in der Welt.* 4th ed. Berlin: Junker & Dünnhauptverlag.

Geldenhuys, N. 1983. *Commentary on the Gospel of Luke*. NICNT. Grand Rapids, MI: Eerdmans.

Gispen, W. H. 1952. *De Spreuken van Salomo*. Vol. 1: *Hoofdstuk 1:1–15:33*. KV. Kampen: Kok.

Godet, F. 1879. *Commentary on the Gospel of John*. Edinburgh: T. & T. Clark.

Goslinga, C. J. 1968. *Het eerste boek Samuël*. COT. Kampen: Kok.

Grant, F. W. 1889. *Facts and Theories As to a Future State: The Scripture Doctrine Considered with Reference to Current Denials of Eternal Punishment*. 2nd ed. New York: Loizeaux Brothers.

———. 1897. *The Numerical Bible: The Gospels*. New York: Loizeaux Brothers.

———. 1902. *The Numerical Bible: Hebrews to Revelation*. New York: Loizeaux Green.

Greijdanus, S. 1925. *De brief van den apostel Paulus aan de Epheziërs*. KV. Kampen: Kok.

———. 1931. *De eerste/tweede brief van den apostel Petrus*. KV. Kampen: Kok.

———. 1955. *Het evangelie naar Lucas*. 2 vols. 2nd ed. KV. Kampen: Kok.

Grosheide, F. W. 1954. *Het heilige evangelie volgens Mattheüs*. CNT. Kampen: Kok.

———. 1959. *De tweede brief aan de kerk te Korinthe*. CNT. Kampen: Kok.

Grudem, W. 1988. *The First Epistle of Peter*. TNTC. Leicester: InterVarsity.

Haak, T. 1918 (repr. 1657). *The Dutch Annotationsupon the Whole Bible*. London: Henry Hills.

Hamilton, V. P. 1995. *The Book of Genesis Chapters 18–50*. NICOT. Grand Rapids, MI: Eerdmans.

Harless, A. G. C. 1834. *Commentar über den Brief Pauli an die Epheser.* Stuttgart: Liesching.

Harris, M. J. 1976. *2 Corinthians.* EBC 10. Grand Rapids, MI: Zondervan.

———. 1983. *Raised Immortal: Resurrection and Immortality in the New Testament.* Grand Rapids, MI: Eerdmans.

Harris, R. L., G. L. Archer, and B. K. Waltke. 1980. *Theological Wordbook of the Old Testament.* 2 vols. Chicago: Moody Press.

Hart, J. H. A. 1979. *The First Epistle General of Peter.* EGT 5. Grand Rapids, MI: Eerdmans.

Hartley, J. E. 1988. *The Book of Job.* NICOT. Grand Rapids, MI: Eerdmans.

Helm, P. 1989. *The Last Things: Death, Judgment, Heaven, Hell.* Edinburgh: The Banner of Truth Trust.

Hepp, V. 1937. *Dreigende deformatie II: Symptomen: Het voortbestaan, de onsterfelijkheid en de substantialiteit van de ziel.* Kampen: Kok.

Heyns, J. A. 1988. *Dogmatiek.* Pretoria: NG Kerkboekhandel.

Hendriksen, W. 1959. *The Bible on the Life Hereafter.* Grand Rapids, MI: Baker.

Henry, C. F. H., ed. 1962. *Basic Christian Doctrines.* New York: Holt, Rinehart & Winston.

Hodge, C. 1994 (repr. 1859). *Commentary on the Second Epistle to the Corinthians.* Grand Rapids, MI: Eerdmans.

Hoek, J. 2004. *Hoop op God: Eschatologische verwachting.* 2nd ed. Zoetermeer: Boekencentrum.

Hoekema, A. A. 1979. *The Bible and the Future.* Grand Rapids, MI: Eerdmans.

———. 1986. *Created in God's Image.* Grand Rapids, MI: Eerdmans.

Hommes, N. J., J. L. Koole, P. G. Kunst, H. N. Ridderbos, and R. Schippers. 1946. *Het Nieuwe Testament van verklarende aanteekeningen voorzien.* Kampen: J.H. Kok.

Hough, R. E. 2000. *De christen na het sterven*. Doorn: Zoeklicht.

Howe, Q., Jr. 1987. *Reincarnation for the Christian*. Adyar: Theosophical Publishing House.

Hughes, P. E. 1962. *Paul's Second Epistle to the Corinthians*. NICNT. Grand Rapids, MI: Eerdmans.

Hulsbosch, A. 1963. *De schepping Gods: Schepping, zonde en verlossing in het evolutionistische wereldbeeld*. Roermond/Maaseik: J.J. Romen & Zonen.

Jager, O. 1984. *De dood in zijn ware gedaante*. Baarn: Ten Have.

Jamieson, R., A. R. Fausset, and D. Brown. 1934 (repr. 1871). *Commentary Critical and Explanatory on the Whole Bible*. Grand Rapids, MI: Zondervan.

Johnson, A. F. 1981. *Revelation*. EBC 12. Grand Rapids, MI: Zondervan.

Joyce, J. 1992 (repr. 1916). *A Portrait of the Artist as a Young Man*. Mineola, NY: Dover Publications.

Keil, C. F. and F. Delitzsch. 1976–77. *Commentary on the Old Testament*. 10 vols. Grand Rapids, MI: Eerdmans.

Kelly, W. 1923. *The Epistles of Peter*. London: C.A. Hammond.

Kickel, W. 1967. *Vernunft und Offenbarung bei Theodor Beza*. Neukirchen-Vluyn: Neukirchener Knox.

König, E. 1927. *Die Psalmen eingeleitet, übersetzt und erklärt*. Gütersloh: Bertelsmann.

Küng, H. 1984. *Eternal Life? Life after Death as a Medical, Philosophical, and Theological Problem*. Garden City, NY: Doubleday.

Kuyper, A. 1892. *E Voto Dordraceno*. Vols. 1 and 2. Amsterdam: J.A. Wormser.

_____. 1929. *Asleep in Jesus: Meditations*. Grand Rapids, MI: Eerdmans.

375

_____. 2019. *Common Grace: God's Gifts for a Fallen World*. Vol. 2: *The Doctrinal Section*. Edited by J. J. Ballor and J. D. Charles. Translated by N. D. Kloosterman and E. M. van der Maas. Bellingham, WA: Lexham Press.

_____. n.d. *Dictaten Dogmatiek*. 5 vols. Kampen: Kok.

Ladd, G. E. 1974. *A Theology of the New Testament*. Grand Rapids, MI: Eerdmans.

Lapide, P. 2002. *The Resurrection of Jesus: A Jewish Perspective*. Eugene, OR: Wipf & Stock.

Leupold, H. C. 1942. *Exposition of Genesis*. London: Evangelical Press.

Lewis, C. S. 2002 (repr. 1945). *The Great Divorce*. London: HarperCollins.

_____. 2003. *A Mind Awake: An Anthology of C. S. Lewis*. Edited by C. S. Kilby. Donaldsonville, LA: Harvest Books.

Lewis, G. R. and B. A. Demarest. 1996. *Integrative Theology: Historical, Biblical, Systematic, Apologetic, Practical*. 3 vols. Grand Rapids, MI: Zondervan.

Liefeld, W. L. 1984. *Luke*. EBC 8. Grand Rapids, MI: Zondervan.

Longman, T., III. 1998. *The Book of Ecclesiastes*. NICOT. Grand Rapids, MI: Eerdmans.

Luce, H. K. 1933. *The Gospel According to St. Luke*. Cambridge: Cambridge University Press.

McCarter, P. K., Jr. 1980. *I Samuel: A New Translation with Introduction, Notes and Commentary*. Anchor Bible Commentary. Vol. 8. Garden City, NY: Doubleday.

MacCullough, J. A. 1930. *The Harrowing of Hell: A Comparative Study of an Early Christian Doctrine*. London: T. & T. Clark.

McGrath, A. E. 2017. *Christian Theology: An Introduction*. 6th ed. West Sussex, UK: John Wiley & Sons, Ltd.

MacGregor, G. 1989. *Reincarnation in Christianity: A New Vision of Rebirth in Christian Thought.* Adyar: Quest Books.

McNeile, A. H. 1915. *The Gospel According to St. Matthew: The Greek Text with Introduction, Notes, and Indices.* London: Macmillan.

Marshall, I. H. 1978. *The Gospel of Luke: A Commentary on the Greek Text.* Grand Rapids, MI: Eerdmans.

Matter, H. M. 1965. *De brief aan de Philippenzen en de brief aan Philémon.* CNT. Kampen: Kok.

Metzger, B. M. 1975. *A Textual Commentary on the Greek New Testament.* 2nd ed. London/New York: United Bible Societies.

Moody, R. 2001. *Life After Life: The Investigation of a Phenomenon–Survival of Bodily Death.* San Francisco: HarperOne.

Moreland, J. P. and D. M. Ciocchi, eds. 1993. *Christian Perspectives on Being Human.* Grand Rapids, MI: Baker Books.

Morris, L. 1971. *The Gospel According to John.* NICNT. Grand Rapids, MI: Eerdmans.

Mounce, R. H. 1977. *The Book of Revelation.* NICNT. Grand Rapids, MI: Eerdmans.

Müller, J. J. 1984 (repr. 1955). *The Epistle of Paul to the Philippians.* NICNT. Grand Rapids, MI: Eerdmans.

Murray, A. 1984. *The Spirit of Christ.* Bloomington, MN: Bethany House Publishers.

A New English Translation of the Septuagint. 2014 (repr. 2009). Including corrections and emendations made in the second printing (2009) and corrections and emendations made in June 2014. Oxford: Oxford University Press. Available at http://ccat.sas.upenn.edu/nets/ edition/.

Noordegraaf, A. 1990. *Leven voor Gods aangezicht: Gedachten over het mens-zijn.* Kampen: Kok.

Noordtzij, A. 1934–1935. *Het boek der Psalmen.* 2 vols. KV. Kampen: Kok.

Noordtzij, A. 1983. *Numbers*. Translated by E. van der Maas. Bible Student's Commentary. Grand Rapids, MI: Zondervan.

Oosterhoff, B. J. 1972. *Hoe lezen wij Genesis 2 en 3? Een hermeneutische studie*. Kampen: Kok.

Osei-Bonsu, J. 1991. "The Intermediate State in the New Testament." *Scottish Journal of Theology* 44:169–94.

Oswalt, J. N. 1998. *The Book of Isaiah*. Vol. 1: *Chapters 1–39*. Vol. 2: *Chapters 40–66*. NICOT. Grand Rapids, MI: Eerdmans.

Ouweneel, W. J. 1976. *What Is Eternal Life?* Sunbury, PA: Believers Bookshelf.

———. 1978. *Het domein van de slang: Christelijk handboek over occultisme en mysticisme*. Amsterdam: Buijten & Schipperheijn.

———. 1982. *"Wij zien Jezus": Bijbelstudies over de brief aan de Hebreeën*. 2 vols. Vaassen: Medema.

———. 1984. *Psychologie: Een christelijke kijk op het mentale leven*. Amsterdam: Buijten & Schipperheijn.

———. 1986. *De leer van de mens: Proeve van een christelijk-wijsgerige*. Amsterdam: Buijten & Schipperheijn.

———. 1988–90. *De Openbaring van Jezus Christus: Bijbelstudies over het boek Openbaring*. 2 vols. Vaassen: Medema.

———. 2007a. *De Geest van God: Ontwerp van een pneumatologie*. Vaassen: Medema.

———. 2007b. *De Christus van God: Ontwerp van een christologie*. Vaassen: Medema.

———. 2008. *De schepping van God: Ontwerp van een scheppings-, mens- en zondeleer*. Vaassen: Medema.

———. 2009a. *Het zoenoffer van God: Ontwerp van een verzoeningsleer*. Vaassen: Medema.

———. 2009b. *Het heil van God: Ontwerp van een soteriologie*. Heerenveen: Medema.

_____. 2011. *Het verbond en het koninkrijk van God: Ontwerp van een foederologie en basileologie*. Heerenveen: Medema.

_____. 2012. *De toekomst van God: Ontwerp van een eschatologie*. Heerenveen: Medema.

_____. 2014. *Wisdom for Thinkers: An Introduction to Christian Philosophy*. St. Catharine, ON: Paideia Press.

_____. 2015. *Searching the Soul: An Introduction to Christian Psychology*. St. Catharines, ON: Paideia Press.

_____. 2017. *The World Is Christ's: A Critique of Two Kingdoms Theology*. Toronto: Ezra Press.

_____. 2019. *Het Israël van God: Ontwerp van een Israëltheologie*. Hoornaar: Gideon.

_____. 2020. *The Eden Story: A History of Paradise, from Its Demise to Its New Rise*. St. Catharines, ON: Paideia Press.

_____. Forthcoming-a. *The Eternal Kingdom*. Toronto: Ezra Press.

_____. Forthcoming-b. *The Eternal Word*. Toronto: Ezra Press.

_____ and G. de Korte. 2010. *Rome en Reformatie: Overeenkomsten en verschillen na vijfhonderd jaar Hervorming*. Heerenveen: Medema.

Pannenberg, W. 1992–1994. *Systematic Theology*. Translated by G. W. Bromiley. 3 vols. New York: T&T Clark International.

Patterson, R. D. and H. J. Austel. 1988. *1, 2 Kings*. EBC 4. Grand Rapids, MI: Zondervan.

Paul, M. J., G. van den Brink, and J. C. van den Bette. 2004. *Bijbelcommentaar Genesis / Exodus*. Studiebijbel OT 1. Veenendaal: Centrum voor Bijbelonderzoek.

Pawson, D. 2007. *De weg naar de hel: Eeuwige kwelling of verdelging?* Putten: Opwekkingslectuur. English edition: *The Road to Hell*. Travelers Rest, SC: True Potential Publishing, Inc.

Pember, G. A. 1975. *Earth's Earliest Ages*. Grand Rapids, MI: Kregel Academic & Professional.

Pickering, H., ed. n.d. *Heaven: The Home of the Redeemed*. London: Pickering & Inglis.

Pittenger, W. N. 1980. *After Death/Life in God*. New York: Seabury Press.

Plessner, H. 1928. *Die Stufen des Organischen und der Mensch: Einleitung in die philosophische Anthropologie*, Berlin/Leipzig: De Gruyter.

Plummer, A. 1922. *The Gospel According to Saint Luke*. 5th ed. ICC. Edinburgh: T. & T. Clark.

Polman, A. D. R. 1956. "Antropologie II." *Christelijke Encyclopedie*. Vol. 1. 246–48. Kampen: Kok.

Popma, K. J. 1958–1965. *Levensbeschouwing: Opmerkingen naar aanleiding van de Heidelbergse Catechismus*. 8 vols. Amsterdam: Buijten & Schipperheijn.

———. 1961. *Heersende te Jeruzalem*. Goes: Oosterbaan & Le Cointre.

Prenter, R. 1967. *Creation and Redemption*. Philadelphia, PA: Fortress.

Prince, D. 2006. *De pijlers van het christelijk geloof*. Beverwijk: Derek Prince Ministries Nederland. English edition: *Foundational Truths for Christian Living*. Lake Mary, FL: Charisma House.

Prod'hom, S. 1924. *Simples entretiens sur les évangiles: Jean*. Vevey: H. Guignard.

Quistorp, H. 1941. *Die letzten Dinge im Zeugnis Calvins*. Gütersloh: Bertelsmann.

Rahner, K. 1978. *Foundations of Christian Faith: An Introduction to the Idea of Christianity*. Translated by W. V. Dych. New York: Seabury Press.

Ratzinger, J. 2007. *Jesus of Nazareth: From the Baptism in the Jordan to the Transfiguration*. Translated by A. J. Walker. New York, NY: Doubleday.

————. 2011. *Jesus of Nazareth*. Part Two: *Holy Week. From the Entrance into Jerusalem to the Resurrection*. San Francisco: Ignatius Press.

Rice, J. R. 1975. *"In the Beginning": A Verse-by-Verse Commentary on the Book of Genesis*. Murfreesboro, TN: Sword of the Lord Publishers.

Ridderbos, H. N. 1975. *Paul: An Outline of His Theology*. Translated by J. R. DeWitt. Grand Rapids, MI: Eerdmans.

Ridderbos, J. 1955/1958. *De Psalmen*. 2 vols. COT. Kampen: Kok.

Ross, A. P. 1991. *Proverbs*. EBC 5. Grand Rapids, MI: Zondervan.

Sailhamer, J. H. 1990. *Genesis*. EBC 2. Grand Rapids, MI: Zondervan.

Salmond, S. D. F. 1979. *The Epistle to the Ephesians*. EGT 3. Grand Rapids, MI: Eerdmans.

————. 2006 (repr. 1901). *The Christian Doctrine of Immortality*. Whitefish, MT: Kessinger.

Sanders, J. 1992. *No Other Name: An Investigation into the Destiny of the Unevangelized*. Grand Rapids, MI: Eerdmans.

Schilder, K. 1932. *Wat is de hel?* 2nd ed. Kampen: Kok.

————. 1935. *Wat is de hemel?* Kampen: Kok.

Schlatter, A. 1987. *Die Korintherbriefe*. Stuttgart: Calwer Verlag.

Senior, D. 1976. "The Death of Jesus and the Resurrection of the Holy Ones." *Catholic Biblical Quarterly* 38:312–29.

Sevenster, J. N. 1955. "2 Cor. 5:8: Einige Bemerkungen über den 'Zwischenzustand' bei Paulus." *New Testament Studies* 1:291–96.

Shushan, G. 2009. *Conceptions of the Afterlife in Early Civilizations: Universalism, Constructivism and Near-Death Experience*. New York/London: Continuum.

Sikkel, J. C. 1923. *Het boek der geboorten: Verklaring van het boek Genesis*. 2nd ed. Amsterdam: H.A. van Bottenburg.

Slotki, I. W. and J. Rosenberg. 1983. *Isaiah*. SBB. London: Soncino.

Smythies, J. R. and J. Beloffs, eds. 1989. *The Case for Dualism*. Charlottesville, VA: University Press of Virginia.

Spitta, F. 1890. *Christi Predigt an die Geister (1. Petr. 3:19ff): Ein Beitrag zur neutestamentlichen Theologie*. Göttingen: Vandenhoeck & Ruprecht.

Spykman, G. J. 1992. *Reformational Theology: A New Paradigm for Doing Dogmatics*. Grand Rapids, MI: Eerdmans.

Stanley, A. P. 2008 (repr. 1855, 1882). *The Epistles of St. Paul to the Corinthians*. Whitefish, MT: Kessinger.

Strachan, R. H. 1979. *The Second Epistle General of Peter*. EGT 5. Grand Rapids, MI: Eerdmans.

Strack, H. L. and P. Billerbeck. 1922–1928 (repr. 1986–97). *Kommentar zum Neuen Testament aus Talmud und Midrasch*. 6 vols. München: Beck.

Summers, R. 1972. *Commentary on Luke*. Waco, TX: Word.

Swaab, D. F. 2014. *We Are Our Brains: From the Womb to Alzheimer's*. New York: Random House.

Tasker, R. V. G. 1958. *The Second Epistle of Paul to the Corinthians*. TNTC. London: Tyndale.

Telder, B. 1960. *Sterven . . . en dan?* Kampen: Kok.

_____. 1963. *Sterven . . . waarom? Over sterfelijkheid en onsterfelijkheid in Bijbels licht*. Kampen: Kok.

Tenney, M. C. 1981. *The Gospel of John*. EBC 9. Grand Rapids, MI: Zondervan.

Thornton, L. S. 1956. *Christ and the Church*. London: Dacre Press.

Thrall, M. E. 1965. *The First and Second Letters of Paul to the Corinthians*. CBC. Cambridge: Cambridge University Press.

Toon, P. 1986. *Heaven and Hell: A Biblical and Theological Overview*. Nashville, TN: Thomas Nelson.

Towner, P. H. 2006. *The Letters to Timothy and Titus*. NICNT. Grand Rapids, MI: Eerdmans.

Tsumura, D. T. 2007. *The First Book of Samuel*. NICOT. Grand Rapids, MI: Eerdmans.

Van Deursen, F. 1988. *De voorzeide leer*. Vol. I^N: *Prediker – Hooglied*. Amsterdam: Buijten & Schipperheijn.

Van Doornik, N. G. M., S. Jelsma, and A. van de Lisdonk. 1956. *A Handbook of the Catholic Faith*. New York: Doubleday.

Van Gelderen, C. and W. H. Gispen. 1953. *Het boek Hosea*. COT. Kampen: Kok.

Van Gemeren, W. A. 1991. *Psalms*. EBC 5. Grand Rapids, MI: Zondervan.

_____, ed. 1996. *The New International Dictionary of Old Testament Theology and Exegesis*. 4 vols. Carlisle: Paternoster.

Van Genderen, J. 1998. *De Bijbel en de toekomst: Een blij vooruitzicht voor wie gelooft*. Heerenveen: Groen.

_____ and W. H. Velema. 2008. *Concise Reformed Dogmatics*. Translated by G. Bilkes and E. M. van der Maas. Phillipsburg, NJ: Presbyterian and Reformed Publishing Company.

Van Hille, C. 1913. "Ziekentroost, welke eene onderwijzing is in het geloof en den weg der zaligheid, om gewillig te sterven." In *De berijmde Psalmen met eenige Gezangen, in gebruik bij de Gereformeerde Kerken in Nederland*. Edited by F. L. Rutgers, in cooperation with H. Bavinck and A. Kuyper, 93-100. Maassluis: Uitgevers-Genootschap "Biblia." Available at https://archive.org/details/deberijmdepsal00gere/page/92/mode/2up.

Van Leeuwen, J. A. C. 1928. *Het evangelie naar Markus*. KV. Kampen: Kok.

Van Leeuwen, P. J. 1955. *Het christelijk onsterfelijkheidsgeloof: Een bijbels-dogmatische studie*. 's-Gravenhage: Boekencentrum.

Van Lommel, P. 2011. *Consciousness Beyond Life: The Science of the Near-Death Experience*. London: HarperOne.

Van Niftrik, G. C. 1970. *Waar zijn onze doden?* Den Haag: Voorhoeve.

Verkuyl, J. 1992. *De kern van het christelijk geloof.* Kampen: Kok.

Visscher, H. 1937. *De oorsprong der ziel in het licht der Gereformeerde levensbeschouwing*. Zeist: Van Lonkhuyzen.

Vogel, H. 1949/50. "Ecce Homo: Die Anthropologie Karl Barths." *Verkündigung und Forschung* 1949/50:102–128.

Vollenhoven, D. H. Th. 1933. *Het calvinisme en de reformatie van de wijsbegeerte*. Amsterdam: H.J. Paris.

Vonk, C. 1969. *De doden weten niets*. Franeker: T. Wever.

Vos, G. 1979. *The Pauline Eschatology*. Phillipsburg, NJ: P&R Publishing.

Waltke, B. K. 2004. *The Book of Proverbs*. Vol. 1: *Chapters 1–15*. NICOT. Grand Rapids, MI: Eerdmans.

Walvoord, J. F. 1966. *The Revelation of Jesus Christ*. Chicago: Moody Press.

Wendland, H. D. 1954. *Die Briefe an die Korinther*. Göttingen: Vandenhoeck & Ruprecht.

Wenham, D. 1973. "The Resurrection Narratives in Matthew's Gospel." *Tyndale Bulletin* 24:21–54.

Wenham, J. W. 1981. "When Were the Saints Raised? A Note on the Punctuation of Matthew xxvii.51–53." *Journal of Theological Studies* 32, no. 1: 150–52.

Westcott, B. F. 1950 (repr. 1902). *The Epistle to the Hebrews*. Grand Rapids, MI: Eerdmans.

Wood, L. J. 1985. *Hosea*. EBC 7. Grand Rapids, MI: Zondervan.

Wright, J. S. 1991. *Ecclesiastes*. EBC 5. Grand Rapids, MI: Zondervan.

_____. 2007 (repr. 1956). *Man in the Process of Time: A Christian Assessment of the Powers and Functions of Human Personality.* Whitefish, MT: Kessinger.

Wright, N. T. 2003. *The Resurrection of the Son of God.* London: SPCK.

_____. 2016. *The Day the Revolution Began: Reconsidering the Meaning of Jesus's Crucifixion.* London: HarperOne.

Wuest, K. S. 1977 (repr. 1942). *First Peter in the Greek New Testament.* Grand Rapids, MI: Eerdmans.

Youngblood, R. F. 1992. *1 & Samuel.* EBC 3. Grand Rapids, MI: Zondervan.

Zahn, T. 1913. *Das Evangelium des Lucas.* Leipzig: Deichert.

SCRIPTURE INDEX

40:35	281

Leviticus

4:7—34	158
12:1—4	69
16:14—15	186
17:10	158
17:10—14	219n.11
17:14	158
18:5	60
19:31	204, 205n.32
20:6	204, 205n.32
20:24	204
20:27	205n.32
23:34	279
23:43	280
26:11	279n.10
26:19	92

Numbers

2	279
5:3	279n.10
6:24—26	350n.31
12:5—8	350n.31
12:6—8	100
16:30	108, 109n.54
16:32—33	112
16:33	108
20:25—28	128
23:10	99
23:21	43n.13
35:34	279n.10

Deuteronomy

4:19	97n.6
4:24	293n.30
5:16	60
10:14	91, 93, 140, 140n.38
11:11	92
12:11	279n.10
12:15	220
12:20—21	220
12:23	219n.11
14:23	279n.10
16:2	279n.10
16:6	279n.10
16:11	279n.10
18:10—12	204
18:11	205n.32
23:16	279n.10
23:17—18	290n.27
24:16	180n.63
26:2	279n.10
26:15	138
28:23	92
29:23	322n.31
31:16	107
31:26	278
32:11	113
32:22	109
32:40	97n.6
32:50	107
33:27	252
34:5—6	117
34:6	203

CPSIA information can be obtained
at www.ICGtesting.com
Printed in the USA
BVHW041934200123
656741BV00003B/18